051355

**Advertising and
Consumer
Psychology**

Advertising and Consumer Psychology

Edited by
Larry Percy
CREAMER INC
Arch G. Woodside
University of South Carolina

LexingtonBooks
D.C. Heath and Company
Lexington, Massachusetts
Toronto

Library of Congress Cataloging in Publication Data

Percy, Larry.
    Advertising and consumer psychology.

    Includes index.
    1. Advertising—Psychological aspects—Addresses, essays, lectures.
I. Woodside, Arch G. II. Title.
HF5822.P42   1983   659.1′01′9   82-48006
ISBN 0-669-05766-5

Second printing, October 1984

Published simultaneously in Canada

Printed in the United States of America on acid-free paper

International Standard Book Number: 0-669-05766-5

Library of Congress Catalog Card Number: 82-48006

Contents

Contents

Figures

Tables

Preface

This book contains the eighteen papers presented at a workshop on advertising and consumer psychology, held in the spring of 1982. The workshop was sponsored by CREAMER INC and the Division of Consumer Psychology of the American Psychological Association.

These are particularly exciting times for students of advertising. Many traditional questions about advertising are being addressed from new perspectives. New theories, methodologies, models and analytic procedures are being applied to this area and are starting to yield valuable and, sometimes, confusing insights.

Among the most promising approaches are from cognitive psychology, neurophysiological psychology and the application of new multivariate techniques. These areas and many others are well covered in this book by some of the preeminent people in the field.

The workshop chairmen and editors of this book, Larry Percy and Arch Woodside, are to be commended for recognizing the need for this workshop and for diligently assembling this distinguished group of scholars. Similarly, we owe a debt to each of the authors for sharing some of their most recent work with us.

Leon B. Kaplan

Introduction

Larry Percy and
Arch G. Woodside

The link between psychology and communication has been forged in the crucible of social psychology over the last half-century. Yet while this link is the subject of an almost limitless literature, not until quite recently has the more-specific link between advertising as a form of communication and consumer psychology been developed. Nevertheless, by implication, much of the early work that has helped us better to understand effective communication has also formed the foundation for understanding how to stimulate effectively a desired response to advertising.

Perhaps the strongest association with today's notion of consumer psychology and its application to advertising that finds a historical foundation in the early development of social psychology is the study of attitude. During the 1920s and early 1930s, as social psychology began to make its presence felt, a strong interest became evident for attitude research. For the most part, this early activity was concerned with attitude-measurement issues. This was the era of descriptive advances in measurement and scaling procedures within the limits of inferential statistics. At the same time, definitions of attitude abounded until Allport (1935), in reviewing the massive outpouring of work in the area, boiled the definitions down to attitude as a learned predisposition to respond to an object or class of objects in a systematic and consistent manner.

During the period from the mid-1930s until the mid-1950s, little creative effort was applied to the study of attitude. This did not mean, however, that important work that was to have a significant influence upon future advertising research also was wanting. One of the most significant movements in learning theory was flourishing at Yale around 1940, with Hull and his stimulus-response learning theorists. This notion was expanded upon in the late 1940s by Lasswell (1948), a political scientist, as he added to what, in advertising terms, could be thought of as the message, the receiver, and its effect subsumed by the learning theorists. His now-famous dictum for describing communication, "Who says what to whom, with what effect?" significantly added the source to the communication process. All that remained was how, a representation of the medium or delivery system.

As the 1940s drew to an end, another series of research destined to have an important impact upon future advertising research was underway at Yale. Hovland and his colleagues were engaged in the Yale Communication Research Program, seeking to understand better human psychological processes by studying the effects that various communication stimuli have upon attitudes and behavior. Broad investigations of this influence process were reported by Hovland, Janis, and Kelley (1953), followed by a series of monographs evaluating the mediating processes involved in attitude change.

The work set the stage for a resurgence in interest in the study of attitude not in terms of static relationships but more as a dynamic process of attitude changes and the factors that produced them. While there was no shortage of attitude-change theory resulting from this renewed study (for an excellent review, see Insko 1967), as once again attitudes became the major interest of social psychologists, it was perhaps not until McGuire's (1968a) seminal work on the nature of attitude change that a model for communication-induced attitude change began to emerge.

This model, if we may think about it as such, McGuire called an "information-processing paradigm," and with it the integration of response effects with processing effects became apparent. His original matrix of persuasive communication divided the communication process into a set of five independent variables, serving as row headings, analogous to Lasswell's understanding of the communication process: (1) source (who?), (2) message (says what?), (3) receiver (to whom?), (4) channel (how?), and (5) destination (with what effect?). The dependent variable of communication-induced attitude change then was refined from Doob's (1961) analysis as a stochastic process involving at least five behavioral steps: (1) attention, (2) comprehension, (3) yielding, (4) retention, and (5) action. McGuire's subsequent analysis examined the relationship between the independent communication variables and their impact upon each of the dependent attitude-change variables. He later applied this thinking specifically to advertising, taking an information-processing approach to understanding the development and evaluation of effective advertising (McGuire 1978).

Borrowing heavily from McGuire, Wyer (1974) built upon his two-factor model of persuadability, especially in the reception and integration of new information (McGuire 1968b), in looking at people as information processors. He provides a review of most of the theoretical and empirical issues involved up to that point in attitude-change theory and research. In this review, Wyer explores the manner in which beliefs and attitudes are developed and modified from the perspective of cognitive psychology. Taking this information-processing model and applying it to advertising, one looks at the receiver as capable of receiving information (attending to the message), operating upon it according to certain rules (processing the message), and then storing the results of this processing in long-term memory (response to the communication), altering the content of the receiver's cognitive structure where necessary (an attitude or belief change), and ultimately acting upon the results (a buyer response in the market).

Within this context, we go beyond the set of social-psychology principles with which McGuire dealt, adding primarily the areas of structure and organization in memory. Wyer (1974) felt that an information-processing orientation to communication required the consideration of the effects of differences in the amount of information a receiver must process at any given time, plus the complexity of the cognitive rules required to process new information adequately. A receiver obviously is limited in the amount of information he or she can assimilate and process at one time. When the informational demands upon the receiver exceed these limits, he or she may attend only to that subset of information presented that seems relevant to his or her objectives, and frequently these will not necessarily be those of the advertiser. In addition, if the receiver does perceive an information overload, he or she may use different, simpler rules for integrating the message content than would be the case if there were more time available to decode and process it, or if there were less information to process. The implication here for modality in presentation is quite obvious: More complex messages should be avoided in broadcast.

With such a rich tradition upon which to draw, the late 1970s saw the emergence of a new body of literature and research that attempted to apply these relevant psychological principles to specific marketing and advertising questions. As mentioned, McGuire (1978) looked specifically at the consequences of psychological principles mediating advertising effectiveness. Lipstein and McGuire (1978) compiled an impressive bibliography of the communication process for the Advertising Research Foundation that relied heavily upon the literature of psychology—a bibliography of 7,000 entries classified in terms of input and output factors involved in advertising research.

Also in 1978, Britt provided a practical example of how 188 psychological principles are involved intimately in understanding marketing and consumer behavior. In his book Britt posits a new psychological model of marketing, one that revolves around individual rather than group behavior. He identified six stages in communicating, not unlike many other models presented in a variety of marketing texts: (1) exposing, (2) attending, (3) perceiving, (4) learning (and remembering), (5) motivating, and (6) persuading. His contribution, however, is in the application of the model and the psychological principles involved to marketing problems. In addition, Britt described five sets of mediating variables that affect the marketing communication process: (1) needs and wants, (2) sociocultural factors, (3) mental set, (4) personality factors, and (5) other internal and external stimuli. Unlike McGuire's independent variables (source, message, channel, receiver, and destination) that serve as a set of effects, these variables are outside the communicator's control. Because of this, understanding the likely impact of each upon the communication process is critical to more-effective marketing communication.

Where Britt covered the broad spectrum of marketing communication and the influence of consumer psychology, Percy and Rossiter (1980) looked specifically at advertising, discussing it in terms of the mediating influence of consumer psychology upon strategic advertising decisions. They outlined the importance of message-processing effects and their impact upon communication responses, which usually are defined as cognitive in nature: awareness, beliefs, attitudes (affect), and intention.

The importance of understanding consumer psychology in making advertising decisions is underscored by the connection between the obvious need to process an advertisement's message (if only at a subcognitive level) and the various psychological principles that mediate the subsequent response. Processing usually is thought to occur in short-term memory, with appropriate processing responses established as traces in long-term memory. In most cases it is necessary to preserve these resulting communication effects over time before they mediate a buyer response; hence, the importance to advertising of understanding how processing leads to the desired communication effect.

Following Osgood, Suci, and Tannenbaum (1957), Percy and Rossiter (1980) have suggested that the successful processing of an advertising message (as with almost any form of communication) requires three steps: (1) attention, (2) decoding, and (3) encoding. This assumes, of course, that the receiver has been exposed in some fashion to the advertising—for example, by reading through a magazine in which an advertisement appears or watching a television show within which a commercial appears. Typically, this initial decision by the receiver as to whether or not to expose himself or herself is a decision about the medium, not about the message or even about the individual vehicle (Berelson 1949; McLuhan 1964; Ehrenberg 1968; Wells 1969). The receiver may choose to subscribe to a particular magazine or not; he or she may develop a viewing habit or not. It then follows that once the media habit is established, the likelihood of the receiver's exposing himself or herself to a particular message increases. Unfortunately, as Pool (1973) points out, no easy measure of exposure exists. Usually the only way to know whether or not a receiver has been exposed is to ask him. If this is done on the spot, it may distort the situation; if it is done later, exposure becomes confounded with recall.

Assuming exposure has taken place, attention to advertising may be either reflexive or selective, and a great deal has been written in the psychology literature on both subjects. In the case of reflexive attention, there is little more than physiological reaction to a change in external stimuli within a receiver's immediate environment, such as a switch from editorial to pictorial content in a magazine or story line to commercial on television. Selective attention requires some prior thought that actively seeks information toward a relevant goal, an extreme example being the use of the *Yellow Pages*.

Following attention, decoding is an awareness that what the receiver is attending to is advertising. It reflects a denotative or literal understanding of the substance of the message, but it does not imply an attitude formation. As Rossiter and Percy (forthcoming) point out, this requires successful encoding—that is, a transmission of connotative or evaluative meaning. Historically, the encoding process has been called "acceptance" by Hovland and his colleagues and "yielding" by McGuire. More recently, however, encoding has been embraced by cognitive-response theory (compare Perloff and Brock 1980; Wright 1974) and in this form has enjoyed a great deal of success in explaining persuasion based upon attitudes. While it is normally necessary for attention, decoding, and encoding to occur prior to successful communication, this is not always the case. As Rossiter and Percy have discussed, in certain instances when only role learning is involved, attention and decoding may be sufficient. Zajonc (1980) has speculated that affect and cognition are under the control of separate and partially independent systems that can influence each other in a variety of ways and that both constitute independent sources of effects in information processing. This idea suggests that decoding may not be necessary or that decoding may not always occur before encoding prior to successful communication. Attitude formation (encoding) could be made in the total absence of recognition memory (a measure of decoding).

As mentioned earlier, Percy and Rossiter (1980) have suggested that response to advertising can be classified into four effects: awareness, beliefs, attitudes, and intention. This is a logical extension of McGuire's information-processing paradigm, and while it implies a hierarchy of effects, such a model is not necessary to the effective application of those goals. In fact, any number of buyer response models such as Ehrenberg's (1974), Krugman's (1967), or even Festinger's (1957) theory of dissonance/attribution tend to be compatible with this notion of objectives for the response to advertising. This is an important distinction and one that positions the psychology of the receiver for advertising independent of any psychological mediation of buyer response in the market (much of which has been detailed by Britt).

Percy and Rossiter (1980) also build upon McGuire's matrix of communication by discussing in depth the psychological principles important to the strategic development of advertising. Specifically, they detail source (who?), message (says what?), receiver (to whom?), media (how?), and postcommunication effects (to what effect?)—again, consistent with Lasswell. While these principles are very similar to the independent variables of McGuire, they are related specifically to advertising effects. In fact, these five variables are perhaps the most critical concerns for advertising not simply because they are so fully involved in the process of developing strategy but because they are in fact those variables the advertiser controls. He decides upon the target audience (receivers), how to position the brand (source), what to say in a particular advertisement or commercial (message), where to place the advertising (media), and what response is desired (post-communication effect). The importance of understanding the relationship among these variables and the appropriate psychological principles involved cannot be minimized.

In the early 1970s, McGuire (1973) suggested that the then-current flourishing of research in persuasive communication probably had reached its zenith. He expected that sometime around 1985 another resurgence would occur when exciting leads would develop out of the undercurrent of residual work in the area, providing insight that would attract a new generation of enthusiastic researchers. The evidence from this book suggests that we are perhaps enjoying that new flourishing now, as we break away from recall-based measures of advertising response, explore more deeply cognitive response to advertising, attempt to correlate physiological measures like brain waves with more-traditional psychological measures, explore more deeply the psychology of the words and pictures in advertising, and look for new and more-effective measuring instruments.

Part I
In Search of How
Advertising Works

Part I presents perspectives for searching out how advertising works. In chapter 1, Petty and Cacioppo describe two psychological routes mediating advertising messages and consumer behavior. The central route is thinking about the true merits of information and advocacy in the advertising message. Message comprehension, learning, and retention are integral on the central route to arriving at an enduring positive or negative attitude change. The secondary, or peripheral, route is associating positive or negative cues with an attitude object—for example, a product. In the peripheral route, attitude change is the result of affective cues in the message environment or the results of very simple decision rules that allow a consumer to evaluate a message without engaging in any extensive issue or product-relevant thoughts. Petty and Cacioppo provide empirical evidence to support the existence of these two psychological routes to persuasion. They present an example of how to design the same ad to allow for both routes to be taken by different consumers.

How advertising works has been a topic in the behavioral sciences from 1900 to today. Scholars and practitioners in advertising can learn the intellectual and empirical roots in the resulting literature. In chapter 2, Nicosia examines this literature. Reading chapter 2 is particularly satisfying for learning both where advertising consumer psychology has come from and where it is going.

An advertising campaign is the totality of advertising with a common look and appeal that is used for a period of time. Understanding how advertising-campaign changes occur may be basic to learning how advertising works. In chapter 3, the results of a content analysis of 116 ad campaigns in two product categories are presented by Krum and Culley. The length of the campaigns ranged from twenty-one years for the Jack Daniel's bourbon to a little over a year for Winston cigarettes (15 campaigns in twenty-one years). Krum and Culley conclude that a continuing advertising-campaign strategy can lead to outstanding results for heavily advertised consumer products such as cigarettes and liquor.

1 Central and Peripheral Routes to Persuasion: Application to Advertising

Richard E. Petty and
John T. Cacioppo

The goal of advertising is to influence people's behavior. This may involve convincing a person to purchase a particular product, but it may involve also convincing a person to vote for a particular candidate or to change a very important personal behavior (for example, a public-service message against smoking). In many important respects, then, we may view the psychology of advertising as the psychology of influence or persuasion. Given the strong parallels between the psychology of persuasion and the psychology of advertising, it is not surprising that the theories that have been proposed by researchers working within each domain are quite similar. Nevertheless, within each field a large number of theoretical approaches are vying for attention. For example, it is not uncommon for textbooks on the psychology of persuasion to describe from ten to twenty unique theories of attitude change (Insko 1967; Kiesler, Collins, and Miller 1969; Petty and Cacioppo 1981a; Smith 1982). Most of these theoretical approaches have been used to account for a variety of advertising phenomena as well (Engel and Blackwell 1982; Kassarjian 1982; Sandage, Fryburger, and Rotzoll 1979).

In a review of the many approaches to attitude change, we suggested that even though the different theories of persuasion have different terminology, postulates, underlying motives, and particular effects that they specialize in explaining, the various approaches to persuasion can be thought of as emphasizing one of two distinct routes to attitude change (Petty and Cacioppo 1981a). One, called the *central route*, views attitude change as resulting from a diligent consideration of information that is central to what people feel are the true merits of the advocacy. The theoretical approaches that fall under this route have emphasized factors such as the comprehension, learning, and retention of issue-relevant information (Eagly 1974; McGuire 1969; Miller and Campbell 1959); the nature of a person's idiosyncratic cognitive responses to issue-relevant information (Brock 1967; Greenwald 1968; Petty, Ostrom, and Brock 1981; Wright 1980); and the manner in which a person combines and integrates issue-relevant information into an overall evaluative reaction (Anderson 1971; Fishbein and Ajzen 1975; Wyer 1974).

3

In contrast to this focus on the information that is central to an evaluation of the merits of an advocacy, a second group of theoretical approaches
to persuasion has developed that emphasizes a more-*peripheral route* to attitude change. Under this second view, attitudes change because the attitude
object has been associated with either positive or negative cues or the person
uses a simple decision rule to evaluate a communication (for example, the
more arguments the better). These cues and decision rules may shape attitudes or allow a person to decide what attitudinal position to adopt
without the need for engaging in any extensive issue-relevant thinking. The
approaches that fall under the peripheral route have emphasized factors
such as whether or not the advocacy falls within a person's latitude of acceptance or rejection (Sherif, Sherif, and Nebergall 1965), whether or not
some transient situational utility is associated with adopting a particular attitude (Schlenker 1980), and whether or not the advocacy is associated with
basic cues such as food (for example, Janis, Kaye, and Kirschner 1965) and
pain (for example, Zanna, Kiesler, and Pilkonis 1970) or more-secondary
cues such as credible (for example, Kelman and Hovland 1953), attractive
(for example, Mills and Harvey 1972), and powerful (for example, Kelman
1961) sources. These variables can influence attitudes whether or not any information relevant to the merits of the issue are presented or considered
(Maddux and Rogers 1980; Norman 1976; Staats and Staats 1958).[1]

Unfortunately, none of the unique theories of persuasion yet has provided a comprehensive view of attitude change. For example, cognitive-
response theory, an exemplar of the central-route approach, makes the
assumption that people usually are interested in thinking about and
elaborating incoming information or self-generating issue-relevant thoughts
on a topic (compare chapter 5). Yet, as Miller and his colleagues (1976) have
noted, "It may be irrational to scrutinize the plethora of counterattitudinal
messages received daily. To the extent that one possesses only a limited
amount of information-processing time and capacity, such scrutiny would
disengage the thought processes from the exigencies of daily life" (p. 623).
Clearly, a general framework for understanding attitude change must consider that attitudes do not always change in a thoughtful manner. A general
framework for persuasion should specify the variables that increase as well
as reduce the likelihood that extensive cognitive activity will accompany attitude change. A framework also should specify the consequences of
thoughtful and nonthoughtful attitude changes.

Our goal in this chapter is to describe briefly our elaboration likelihood
model (ELM) of attitude change (Petty and Cacioppo 1981a) and to note its
applications to advertising communications. The basic tenet of the ELM is
that different methods of inducing persuasion may work best, depending
upon whether the elaboration likelihood of the communication situation
(that is, the probability of message or issue-relevant thought occurring) is

high or low. When the elaboration likelihood is high, the central route to persuasion should be particularly effective, but when the elaboration likelihood is low, the peripheral route should be better. In the first part of this chapter, we discuss the antecedents of the two routes to persuasion and present some recent empirical support for the distinction between the two routes. In the remainder of the chapter, we address the consequences of the two routes to persuasion, and we consider the direct implications of the two routes for advertising communications.

Description of the Two Routes to Persuasion

Motivation and Ability to Think

Figure 1-1 presents an abbreviated diagram of the ELM, specifying the two routes to persuasion [see Petty and Cacioppo in press (a), for further details]. The model begins by posing the question of whether or not a person is motivated to think about the communication to which he or she is exposed. As we noted earlier, it does not make sense for a person to think about every communication that is received. Several variables have been shown to affect a person's motivation to think about a message. For example, we have found that messages on personally relevant issues elicit more scrutiny than messages with few personal implications (Petty and Cacioppo 1979b). As an issue becomes more personally involving, it becomes more important to form a reasoned and veridical opinion. The greater motivation to think about a message when personal relevance is high results in people being better able to distinguish cogent from specious arguments for high- than low-involvement messages.

Just as some messages typically may evoke more thought than others, we also have found that some people usually are more motivated to think about messages than are other people. In a series of studies on the need for cognition (Cacioppo and Petty 1982), we have found that consistent individual differences exist in the propensity of people to engage in and enjoy effortful thinking. Some people tend to find tasks requiring extensive cognitive activity to be fun, whereas others prefer to avoid them. We have found that people who are high in their need for cognition are motivated to scrutinize persuasive messages more carefully than people who are low in their need for cognition, and they therefore show greater differentiation of strong from weak message arguments (Cacioppo and Petty in press). Other variables that have been shown to affect a person's motivation to think about a persuasive message include the use of rhetorical questions in the framing of the message arguments (Petty, Cacioppo, and Heesacker 1981), the number of people presenting the message arguments (Harkins and Petty

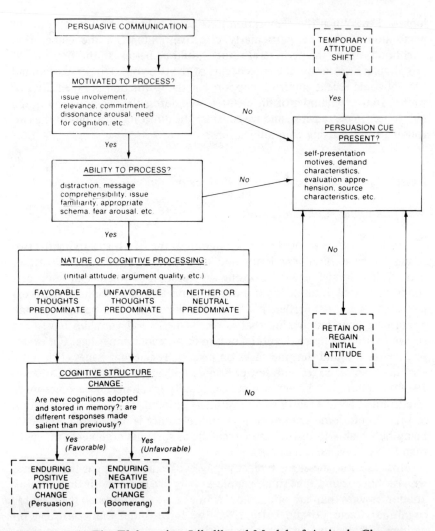

Figure 1-1. The Elaboration Likelihood Model of Attitude Change

1981), the number of people responsible for evaluating the message (Petty, Harkins, and Williams 1980), whether the advocated position is pro or counterattitudinal (Cacioppo and Petty 1979), and others.

Having the motivation to think about a persuasive message is not sufficient to insure that the central route will be followed, however. A person must also have the ability to think about the issue-relevant information presented. A number of variables can affect a person's ability to think about a message. For example, on the one hand, to the extent that a message is accompanied by distracting stimuli, the ability to think about a message is decreased and people are less able to differentiate strong from weak arguments (Petty, Wells, and Brock 1976). On the other hand, as a message is repeated a moderate number of times, people have a greater opportunity to think about the arguments presented and to show a greater differentiation of cogent from specious arguments (Cacioppo and Petty 1979; 1980a). Other variables that affect a person's general ability to think about a message include factors such as the medium of message presentation (Chaiken and Eagly 1976), the complexity of the message (Regan and Cheng 1973), the amount of prior information and experience with the issue (Cacioppo and Petty 1980b; Wood 1982), and others.

Determinants of Favorable and Unfavorable Thoughts

When a person is both motivated and able to think about a persuasive communication, it becomes important to understand the nature of the cognitive responses generated. Most research has focused on two kinds of cognitive responses: favorable, or positive, thoughts (pro-arguments) and unfavorable, or negative, thoughts (counterarguments) (see Cacioppo, Harkins, and Petty 1981). Knowing that a person has the motivation and ability to think about a message does not allow a determination of what kind of cognitive responses will be elicited. The variables affecting motivation and ability to think that we have mentioned already, like the personal relevance of the issue, tend to do so in a fairly objective manner. Under these conditions, the most important determinant of the nature of the cognitive responses elicited resides in the quality of the arguments presented in the communication. Arguments that point to desirable consequences for the message recipient or significant others tend to elicit primarily favorable thoughts, whereas arguments that point to undesirable consequences for the message recipient or significant others (even though the arguments are worded to favor the advocacy) tend to elicit primarily unfavorable thoughts. The more the desirable consequences are elaborated upon (as motivated, for example, by high personal relevance or enabled by message repetition), the more favorable connections the person may make to his or her own life (Krugman 1965) and the more persuasion that will result. Similarly, the more undesirable consequences are elaborated upon, the more negative connections the person may make to his or her life, and the less persuasive the message will be. People may even make so many negative connections to their own lives that they shift in a direction opposite to that advocated in the message (boomerang).

Sometimes the arguments contained in a message may be quite ambiguous, or the message may contain no arguments that can be elaborated upon. When this occurs, and the person is highly motivated and able to think about the advocacy, it is unlikely that a person's cognitive responses will be guided by argument quality. Instead, a person's thoughts may be guided by an initial attitude on the topic (for example, Judd and Johnson 1981). If the communication advocates a position that is pro-attitudinal, further thought about the issue may lead the person to retrieve from memory a variety of favorable thoughts or to generate new positive implications of the advocacy, but if the communication advocates a position that is counterattitudinal, further thought about the issue may lead the person to retrieve from memory a variety of unfavorable thoughts or to generate new negative implications of the advocacy. In an impressive program of research on the effects of "mere thought" (thinking about a stimulus or issue when no new information is presented about it), Abraham Tesser (1978) and his colleagues have demonstrated that the content of thought may be guided by an initial attitude. Thus, in the absence of any new information with increased thought, stimuli or issues about which a person initially feels positive become even more favorably evaluated, but stimuli or issues about which a person initially feels negative become even more unfavorably evaluated. Consistent with figure 1-1, however, these effects only occur when motivation and ability to think about the issue are high (Tesser and Leone 1977).

Although the quality of the arguments presented in a message and the person's initial attitude may be the two most important determinants of whether favorable or unfavorable cognitive responses are elicited by a communication, a number of other variables also may influence the nature of a person's thoughts by either motivating or enabling a particular bias to the thought content. For example, Wells and Petty (1980) had subjects listen to a personally relevant pro-attitudinal or counterattitudinal message while they were instructed to nod their heads in either a vertical or a horizontal direction. The two researchers hypothesized that because of the strong association between vertical head movements and agreement responses and between horizontal movements and disagreement responses (Eibl-Eibesfeldt 1972) that the head-movement manipulation would bias the nature of the thoughts elicited by the message. Specifically, they proposed that vertical movements would be compatible with and would facilitate the production of favorable thoughts but would be incompatible with and would inhibit the production of unfavorable thoughts. Conversely, horizontal movements should produce the reverse pattern. Although measures of thought production were not taken in the study, the attitude results were consistent with the hypothesis. For both the pro- and counterattitudinal messages, subjects who engaged in vertical movements expressed more agreement with the message than subjects who engaged in horizontal head movements.

The head-movement manipulation in the preceding study was thought to bias the nature of thoughts by making it easier or more difficult for people to generate a particular kind of cognitive response, an ability manipulation (compare Laird et al. 1982). Other factors have been shown to elicit particular kinds of cognitive responses primarily by affecting motivation. For example, we have found that a forewarning of persuasive intent motivates counterarguing during the presentation of an involving counterattitudinal message and results in greater rejection of the advocacy than if no forewarning is provided (Petty and Cacioppo 1979a). To ensure that the forewarning of persuasive intent did not simply increase message-relevant thinking in general, we employed a communication composed of strong arguments (that is, in the absence of the forewarning, the message elicited primarily favorable thoughts). Thus, a manipulation that increased scrutiny in an objective manner should have led to more favorable thoughts rather than counterarguments and more rather than less persuasion.

In another study, we found that a salient self-schema may render people particularly susceptible to arguments that are relevant to their self-conception (Cacioppo, Petty, and Sidera 1982). In this study, employing a procedure adapted from Markus (1977), we identified two groups of students who were attending a major Catholic university. Some of the students tended to think of themselves as more religious than legalistic in moral orientation, whereas others viewed themselves as more legalistic than religious. Subjects received a pro-attitudinal message that employed either a religious or a legalistic perspective on an issue (for example, the abolition of capital punishment). In evaluating the arguments, the students rated the arguments that were consistent with their self-schemata as more persuasive than the arguments that were inconsistent. This result was especially intriguing because all of the arguments employed in the messages were selected to be weak (that is, they elicited primarily unfavorable thoughts from aschematic subjects). Thus, when the weak arguments matched the subjects' self-conceptions, rather than objectively recognizing the flaws in the arguments, they selectively elaborated upon them in a favorable manner.

It is important to note that all of the research on variables that bias the nature of cognitive responses has been conducted holding the argument quality employed in the messages constant. Thus, this research does not necessarily indicate that biasing factors such as forewarnings or self-schemata render argument quality unimportant but that biasing factors operate in addition to argument quality in determining cognitive responses to persuasive messages. In order to determine the relative importance of argument quality versus some biasing variable, it would be necessary to manipulate both in the same experiment and to determine the percentage of variance for which each accounted. We doubt that this would be a particularly informative line of research, however, because depending upon the strength of the specific operationalizations employed, we suspect that either argument quality or biasing factors could be shown to be prepotent.

Evidence for the Two Routes to Persuasion

Our discussion of the central and peripheral routes to persuasion suggests that under certain circumstances, attitudes will be formed and changed depending primarily upon the manner in which a person evaluates the issue-relevant information presented but that at other times, attitudes will be formed and changed without any extensive cognitive work. Before proceeding to our discussion of the consequences of the two routes to persuasion and the implications of each for advertising communications, it is important to document the proposition that the two kinds of persuasions exist. In order to provide an appropriate test of the two routes, it is important to construct two kinds of persuasion contexts: one in which the elaboration likelihood is high (that is, a person is both highly motivated and able to engage in issue-relevant thought) and one in which the elaboration likelihood is low (that is, either motivation or ability to think is absent or substantially reduced). In the experiments we describe next, the ability to think was held constant at a high level across the experimental conditions (for example, the messages and issues employed were easy to understand, no extraneous distractions were present, and so on). Motivation to think was manipulated by varying the personal relevance of the opinion issue. Following the procedure of Apsler and Sears (1968), subjects in the high- and low-relevance conditions were exposed to the same experimental stimuli, but subjects in the high-relevance conditions were led to believe that the issue under consideration would likely have direct personal consequences for them, whereas subjects in the low-relevance conditions were led to believe that the issue had few personal consequences. Given that all subjects have the ability to think about the attitude issue and message, subjects in the high-relevance conditions should follow the central route to persuasion, and subjects in the low-relevance conditions should follow the peripheral route.

Source Cues versus Message Processing

In one test of the central/peripheral framework, we asked college students to listen to a message on headphones that advocated that seniors be required to pass a comprehensive exam in their major area as a prerequisite to graduation (see Petty, Cacioppo, and Goldman 1981). Three variables were manipulated in the study: (1) personal relevance—the speaker advocated that for half of the subjects the policy should begin in the next year, thereby affecting all of the students personally, and for the other half, that the policy should take effect in ten years, thereby affecting no current students; (2) message arguments—for half of the subjects the message contained eight arguments that were pretested in order to ensure that they were cogent and compelling (strong arguments), and for the other half the message contained eight arguments that were pretested to insure that if thought about, college students would find them specious (weak arguments); and (3) source expertise—for half of the subjects the source was described as a professor of education at Princeton University (expert source), and for the other half the source was described as a junior at a local high school (nonexpert source). Following exposure to the communication, the students reported their attitudes on the senior comprehensive-exam proposal.

The results of this study are graphed in figure 1-2. On the one hand, when the students thought that the exam proposal had little relevance to them, their postcommunication attitudes were influenced significantly only by the expertise of the message source; the quality of the issue-relevant information presented had no effect. On the other hand, when the students thought that the exam proposal had direct consequences for them, their attitudes were affected significantly only by the quality of the issue-relevant information presented; the source-expertise manipulation had no effect. In sum, under high-relevance conditions, subjects exerted the cognitive effort required to evaluate the issue-relevant arguments presented, and their attitudes were a function of this information processing (central route). Under low-relevance conditions, attitudes were determined by the salient source-expertise cue but were unaffected by argument quality (peripheral route).

Message Cues versus Message Processing

In the preceding study, attitudes in response to a high-relevance communication were affected primarily by message factors, and attitudes in response to a low-relevance communication were affected primarily by source factors. It is important to note, however, that the central/peripheral distinction is not between message and source factors. As we noted earlier, the central/peripheral distinction has to do with the extent to which issue-relevant thought determines attitudes rather than reliance on salient positive and negative cues or simple decision rules. Thus, according to the ELM, some message factors like the quality of the message arguments should have a greater impact on persuasion when motivation and ability to think are high, but other message factors like the mere number of message arguments presented could have a greater impact on persuasion when motivation and/or ability to think are low. In order for the quality of message arguments to have an impact on persuasion, the arguments must be thought about, but the mere number of message arguments can have an impact on persuasion without any extensive issue-relevant thinking if people employ the simple but reasonable decision rule: The more arguments in favor of something, the better it must be.

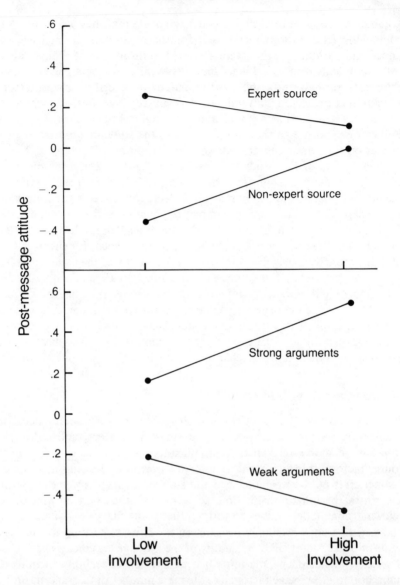

Data from R.E. Petty, J.T. Cacioppo, & R. Goldman, "Personal Involvement as a Determinant of Argument-Based Persuasion *Journal of Personality and Social Psychology*, 40 (1981),
pp. 847-855.

Note: Top panel: Persuasion as a function of the interaction of recipient involvement and the
expertise of the message source. Bottom panel: Persuasion as a function of the interaction of
recipient involvement and the quality of message arguments.

Figure 1-2. Persuasion as a Function of Recipient Involvement and Expertise of Message Source

In an attempt to compare the effects of message cues versus message processing under high- and low-involvement conditions, we again exposed college students to a message advocating that seniors be required to pass a comprehensive exam in their major as a requirement for graduation. Personal relevance was manipulated in this study by telling half of the students that the proposal was scheduled to take effect at their university the following year, and the other half were told that the proposal was scheduled to take effect at a distant university the following year. Two aspects of the message that the students read were manipulated. First, half of the subjects read a message containing nine arguments in favor of the proposal, and half read a message containing three such arguments. In addition, for half of the subjects the arguments were cogent and compelling, whereas for half the arguments were weak and specious. Three arguments were printed on each page of the written communication that the students received, and each argument was elaborated in a distinct paragraph. Subjects in the nine-arguments conditions therefore read three pages of material, whereas subjects in the three-arguments conditions read one page that contained three arguments randomly selected from the nine arguments possible. After reading the message, the students were asked to provide their own attitudes on the comprehensive-exam proposal.

The data are graphed in figure 1-3. As expected, on the one hand, when the issue had high relevance, subjects' attitudes were affected by the quality of the message arguments only; the number of arguments presented had no effect (central route). On the other hand, when the issue was of low relevance, attitudes were affected by the mere number of arguments presented but not by their quality (peripheral route). Thus, under low involvement, the effect of increasing the number of arguments presented from three to nine was to increase persuasion whether the arguments added were strong or weak. Under high involvement, however, increasing the number of arguments increased agreement when the arguments were strong but reduced agreement when the arguments were weak.

Consequences of the Two Routes to Persuasion

The research we have reviewed clearly indicates that different factors have an impact on persuasion under high- and low-personal-involvement conditions and suggests that the distinction between the central and peripheral routes to persuasion has some validity. In addition, other research suggests two very important consequences of the two routes to persuasion. (1) Attitude changes that occur via the central route may persist longer than attitude changes that occur via the peripheral route, and (2) attitudes formed via the central route may predict subsequent behavior better than attitudes formed via the peripheral route.

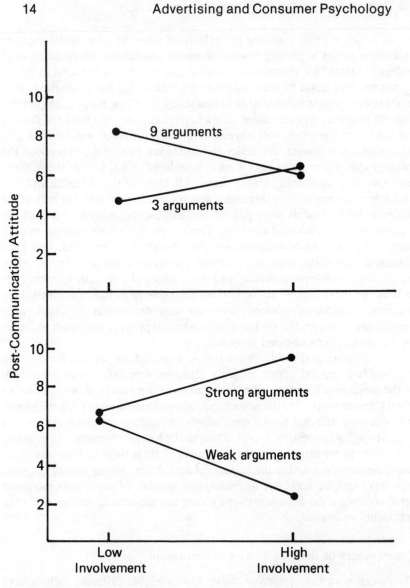

Data from Petty & Cacioppo, 1982.

Note: Top panel: Persuasion as a function of the interaction of recipient involvement and the number of message arguments used. Bottom panel: Persuasion as a function of the interaction of recipient involvement and the quality of message arguments.

Figure 1-3. Persuasion as a Function of Recipient Involvement and Number of Message Arguments

Evidence that the two routes differ in the temporal stability of the attitude changes they produce comes from a study of anticipatory attitude shifts by Cialdini et al. (1976). In the relevant conditions of this study, college students were led to believe that soon they were going to discuss either a personally involving or uninvolving issue with another student who took a position opposite to their own. The major result of this study was that students who were about to engage in a discussion with an opponent on a high-involvement issue showed attitude polarization in anticipation of the discussion, but students who were about to discuss a low-involvement issue showed anticipatory moderation. In addition, the high-involvement group showed significantly more issue-relevant cognitive activity (as assessed by thought listing) in preparation for the discussion.

An interesting feature of this study was that after the subjects' initial anticipatory attitude shifts were monitored, all of the subjects were told that they would not be engaging in a discussion on the issue after all. They were told that all they would have to do was to fill out a final attitude scale. On this second measure of attitudes, taken after the expectation of discussion was canceled, the researchers obtained an intriguing result. The subjects who initially had polarized remained polarized relative to controls, but the subjects who initially had moderated were no longer any more moderate than controls. Thus, the subjects who had not engaged in any extensive issue-relevant thought in connection with their attitude shifts returned to their original attitude positions, but the subjects who did think about the issue prior to the anticipated discussion retained their new attitudes. These data suggest that to the extent that attitude changes are bolstered by issue-relevant cognitive activity, the changes produced are longer lasting than if such activity is absent. When an attitude change is based on an extensive foundation of issue-relevant beliefs, and when these beliefs are rehearsed, the attitude change is likely to persist because the issue-relevant beliefs are likely to remain salient (especially if they are self-generated) (see Slamecka and Graf 1978). Furthermore, even if a few of the favorable thoughts elicited at the time of message exposure are forgotten, others are likely to remain. Conversely, attitude changes that result from one prominent cue (for example, an attractive source) or one simple inference (for example, if there are so many arguments it must be good) are much more vulnerable to forgetting. These changes are likely to endure only if the person has been exposed to the persuasive message many times, rendering the cue or inference relatively permanent. Even then, however, such attitude changes likely would be highly susceptible to counterpropaganda because the person has so little on which to base a positive or negative opinion. Thus, the new attitude would be difficult to defend if severely challenged (see also Chaiken 1980; Cook and Flay 1978; McGuire 1964).

As we noted earlier, research also suggests that attitudes formed or changed via the central route may be more predictive of behavior than attitudes formed or changed via the peripheral route. In one study, for example, Sivacek and Crano (1982) explored the relationship between attitudes and behavior for two groups of people. The attitudes of interest in their study concerned an impending Michigan statewide referendum to raise the legal drinking age from nineteen to twenty-one. The two groups of people studied were those who would be affected personally by the proposal (that is, they would not be twenty-one by the time the new law went into effect if passed) and those who would not be affected personally. Even though both groups expressed equally strong attitudes against the proposal to raise the drinking age, more people who would be affected personally by the proposal agreed to engage in behaviors consistent with their negative attitudes than people who would not be affected personally. If we can assume that the attitudes of people who would be affected personally by the proposal were formed via the central route (extensive issue-relevant thought), whereas the attitudes of those who would not be affected were formed via the peripheral route (identifying with the opinions of their friends), then the results of Sivacek and Crano are consistent with the view that the central route produces attitudes that are more consistent with behaviors than those produced by the peripheral route. This may be because attitudes formed via the central route are more salient in memory and thus people are more able to act upon them, or it may be that people hold these attitudes with more confidence and thus are more willing to act on them (see also Fazio and Zanna 1981).

Implications of the Two Routes to Persuasion for Advertising Communications

Empirical Evidence

In order to provide an initial test of the applicability of the two routes to persuasion for advertising communications, we sought to replicate our basic research using mock magazine advertisements as stimuli. In our first experiment (Petty and Cacioppo 1981b), we presented college students with a booklet containing six magazine advertisements. Five of the ads were for real but relatively unfamiliar products (for example, Lux cigarettes), and one of the ads was for a fictitious product (Vilance shampoo). Three variables were manipulated with respect to the bogus product. First, preceding each ad in the booklet was a brief description of the purpose of the advertisement. All subjects read the same descriptions for the real ads, but the description for the bogus shampoo ad was varied to create two different personal-relevance conditions. In the low-involvement condition, the description stated that the company intended to market the shampoo in European countries only but that it had distributed its materials to universities throughout the United States in order to have them evaluated. In the high-involvement condition, the description stated that the students' university had been chosen for research purposes because the shampoo would be test marketed soon in their local community. Thus, low-involvement subjects were led to believe that it was unlikely that they would ever be able to purchase the product, whereas high-involvement subjects were led to believe that they would be able to purchase the product soon.

Four different versions of the Vilance shampoo ad were prepared. Each ad looked similar in that it pictured a man and woman in their early twenties giving the reasons why they liked Vilance shampoo. The two variables manipulated in the ad were the attractiveness of the couple featured in the ad and the cogency of their reasons for liking the shampoo. In the high-attractive ads, a photograph of a couple that had been rated previously as extremely attractive was used, and in the low-attractive ads a photograph of a couple that had been rated previously as somewhat unattractive was employed. An extremely unattractive stimulus was not used since these typically do not appear in advertisements. In the strong-arguments version of the ad, the text that accompanied the photograph presented arguments for the shampoo that had been rated previously as compelling and persuasive (for example, Vilance contains minerals that strengthen each hair shaft so it helps to prevent split ends). The weak-arguments text presented reasons that had been rated previously as unpersuasive (for example, Vilance has a down-to-earth brown color that makes us feel natural).

Following exposure to the entire advertising booklet, the subjects responded to a variety of questions about the ads. The crucial measure of attitude consisted of the average of subjects' ratings of Vilance shampoo on a series of semantic differential scales. It is not surprising that an analysis of this measure revealed that the subjects liked the product significantly more when the ads contained strong rather than weak arguments and that they liked the product significantly more when the ads depicted an attractive rather than an unattractive couple. Of greater interest, however, was a significant argument-quality-by-involvement interaction. This interaction revealed that the quality or cogency of the arguments presented in the ad had a much greater impact on attitudes toward the advertised product when the ad was of high rather than low personal relevance (central route). The source-attractiveness-by-involvement interaction was not significant, however, indicating that contrary to expectations, the source cue was not more important for the low- than the high-relevance ad.

We can find a variety of possible explanations for the failure to find evidence for the peripheral route to persuasion in this study (for example, the involvement and attractiveness manipulations may have been too weak), but in retrospect we have found one explanation to be the most compelling. Specifically, we suspect that in addition to serving as a peripheral cue, the physical appearance of the models in the ad may have been viewed as important product-relevant information. For example, for the particular product employed (shampoo), the attractiveness of the models (especially their hair) may have served as persuasive visual testimony for the product's effectiveness. Alternatively, it may have been that for the particular consumer segment tested (college students), the physical appearance of product users is a particularly salient dimension for product evaluation. To the extent that either explanation is correct, it serves as an important reminder that just as features of a persuasive message (for example, the number of arguments) may serve as powerful peripheral cues under low-personal-relevance conditions, features of the message source (for example, attractiveness) may serve as cogent purchase-relevant arguments for certain kinds of products or people.

In order to provide a more-sensitive test of the two routes to persuasion with advertising communications, we conducted a conceptual replication of our initial study, making several important changes (Petty, Cacioppo, and Schumann 1982). University undergraduates again were asked to examine a booklet containing a variety of advertisements. This time, twelve ads were in the booklets, and one was for a fictitious new product, Adze disposable razors. Before beginning to look through the ad booklet, we informed subjects that at the end of the study we would ask them to select a modest gift. Subjects in the high-involvement group were told that they would be able to select from a variety of disposable-razor products, rendering our bogus razor ad highly involving. Subjects in the low-involvement group were told that they would be able to select from a variety of toothpaste brands (one ad for toothpaste was included in the ad booklet).

We constructed four different versions of the ad for Adze disposable razors. Each ad presented an artist's design of the product, the pictures of a man and woman who endorsed the product, and six statements about the product. In the famous-endorser ads, the headline of the ad read "Professional athletes agree: Until you try new Adze disposable razors you'll never know what a really close shave is." In addition, the ad featured the pictures of two well-known and -liked golf and tennis celebrities (see figure 1-4). In the non-famous-endorser ads, the headline read "Bakersfield, California, agrees . . ." This ad featured pictures of ordinary citizens. It is important to note that unlike our initial study in which the physical appearance of the endorsers might have served as important product-relevant information, it is likely that for most people, the celebrity status of the endorsers would be irrelevant to an evaluation of the merits of a disposable razor. Yet, celebrity status still could serve as a positive peripheral cue. Similar to the

PROFESSIONAL ATHLETES AGREE

*Until you try new
ADZE disposable
razors you'll never
know what a
"really close shave"
is.*

- **Scientifically Designed**
- New advanced honing method creates unsurpassed sharpness.
- Special chemically formulated coating eliminates nicks and cuts and prevents rusting.
- Handle is tapered and ribbed to prevent slipping.
- In direct comparison tests the ADZE blade gave twice as many close shaves as its nearest competitor.
- Unique angle placement of the blade provides the smoothest shave possible.

GET THE ADZE DIFFERENCE!

Note: Celebrity photos are blacked out for proprietary reasons.

Figure 1-4. Mock Advertisement for ADZE Disposable Razors

shampoo study, the strong-arguments version of the Adze ad contained statements that had been rated previously as compelling (for example, "handle is tapered and ribbed to prevent slipping"), whereas the weak-arguments version of the ad contained statements that had been rated as unpersuasive (for example, "designed with the bathroom in mind").

After perusing the entire ad booklet, the subjects responded to a variety of questions about the advertised products. Attitudes toward Adze razors were assessed by having subjects respond to three semantic differential

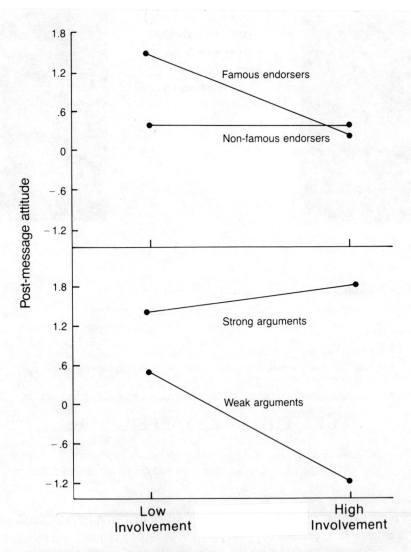

Data from Petty, Cacioppo, & Schumann, 1982.

Note: Top panel: Product attitudes as a function of the interaction of recipient involvement and celebrity status of the product endorser. Bottom panel: Product attitudes as a function of the interaction of recipient involvement and the quality of message arguments.

Product Attitudes as a Function of Recipient Involvement and Celebrity Endorser

sion about the product class (high involvement), the quality of the product-relevant information provided in the ad had a stronger impact on attitudes than when no decision was imminent (low involvement). Under low involvement, the nature of the endorsers (famous or not) had a significant effect on attitudes toward the product, but this manipulation had no impact under high involvement. Thus, different kinds of information-processing activities occurred under high and low involvement as expected by the ELM (see figure 1-1). In addition to the attitude measures, we asked subjects to rate the likelihood of their purchasing Adze disposable razors the next time they needed a product of this nature. Attitudes toward Adze razors proved to be a better predictor of behavioral (purchase) intentions under high ($r = .59$) than under low-involvement conditions ($r = .36$). Thus, as expected by the ELM, attitudes change via the central route were more predictive of behavior than attitudes changed via the peripheral route.

Summary and Conclusions

This chapter outlined two distinct routes to persuasion. The central route occurs when a person is both motivated and able to think about the merits of the advocacy presented. Depending upon whether the advocacy elicits primarily favorable or unfavorable thoughts, either persuasion, resistance, or boomerang may occur. Attitude changes induced via this route tend to be relatively permanent and predictive of subsequent behavior. When a person is either not motivated or able to evaluate the merits of an advocacy, then he or she may follow a second route to persuasion. Under this peripheral route, it is not assumed that the message recipient will undertake the considerable cognitive effort required to evaluate the merits of the advocated position. Instead, people's attitudes may be affected by positive and negative cues or simple decision rules or heuristics that allow them to evaluate the advocacy quickly. As we noted earlier, the accumulated research on persuasion has identified a large number of such cues and heuristics that can influence attitude change (see McGuire 1969; Cialdini, Petty, and Cacioppo 1981). These peripheral changes, however, tend to be relatively temporary and not highly predictive of subsequent behavior.

How can the central/peripheral framework be applied in a particular advertising situation? Consider an advertisement for cigarettes that depicts a man and a woman on horseback, riding through majestic mountain terrain. At the bottom of the ad is the headline, "20 REASONS WHY CALBOROS ARE BEST," along with a list of twenty statements. Will attitude changes induced because of this ad occur via the central or the peripheral route? Our framework suggests that in evaluating or designing an ad for a particular product, it is extremely important to know what information dimensions are crucial for people who desire to evaluate the true merits or implications of the product (in this case, cigarettes). On the one hand, to smokers over fifty, the most important information may relate to the health aspects of the brand (for example, tar content). For this group, an effective ad would likely have to present considerable information about the medical consequences of the brand if it were to be effective in inducing influence via the central route. If the twenty statements listed in the ad presented cogent information about the health aspects of Calboros over competing brands, favorable thoughts may be rehearsed, and a relatively permanent change in attitude that had behavioral (that is, purchase) implications might result. On the other hand, for teenage smokers, who may be more concerned with impressing their peers than with their health, the major reason why they smoke may relate to the image of the particular brand (for example, tough man, independent woman) (see Chassin et al. 1981). For this group, the presentation of the rugged outdoor images might provide important product-relevant information that would elicit numerous favorable thoughts and enduring attitude changes with behavioral consequences. It is interesting that for the nonsmokers over fifty, the majestic scenery might serve as a peripheral cue inducing momentary liking for the brand and that for the teenage nonsmokers, the twenty statements might lead to momentary positive evaluations of the brand because of the simple belief that there are many arguments in favor of it. In neither case would these favorable attitudes have behavioral implications.

Although we have focused on the role of personal involvement with an issue or product in this chapter, as we noted earlier, there are a variety of determinants of the route to persuasion. The central route is the more difficult to produce because the message recipient first must be motivated and able to think about the issue or product-relevant information provided. An advertisment can be constructed so as to maximize the likelihood of thinking [for example, emphasizing personal relevance, increasing the number of message sources; see Petty and Cacioppo, in press (b)], but some uncontrollable factors in the persuasion environment (for example, distraction) may render one's efforts useless by reducing the elaboration likelihood. In addition, even if a message recipient is motivated and able to think about the merits of the issue or product, the message must elicit primarily favorable thoughts rather than neutral thoughts or counterarguments. Thus, the message should contain cogent arguments or should employ some technique to bias thinking in the favorable direction (for example, using arguments consistent with a person's self-schema; see Cacioppo et al. 1982). If a change can be produced via the central route, the benefits are clear—the attitude change will tend to persist and will be predictive of subsequent behavior.

Since the central route to persuasion is rather difficult, the peripheral route sometimes may be an effective advertising strategy. Since the peripheral route induces only a temporary change, however, it will be necessary to remind the recipient constantly of the cue or decision rule upon which he or she based the new attitude. Lutz (1979) provides the example of a person who drives Hertz rental cars not because the person has thought about the attributes of the company but only because he has been reminded constantly that a sports star endorses the company. If the favorable attitude about Hertz had been based on a full consideration of the positive features of the company, the favorable attitude likely would persist on its own. Since the favorable attitude is based on a positive peripheral cue, however, the favorable attitude persists only so long as the cue remains memorable (accomplished through advertising repitition). Such continually repeated positive cues may give a person sufficient confidence to act on the basis of the attitude and to try the advertised product. It is interesting that once the person has tried the product, it may become more personally involving and may make the person more likely to think about the content of future advertisements about the product. In this manner, a peripheral change can lead to a central one.

Note

1. It is important to note that the various theoretical approaches to attitude change and the variables whose effects they try to explain may not fall clearly under one or the other route in all circumstances. For example, the theoretical process of self-perception (Bem 1967) might lead to a simple inference (peripheral route) under some conditions or to extended issue-relevant thinking in others (compare Petty and Cacioppo 1983). In addition, we note that the distinction we have made between the central and the peripheral routes to attitude change has much in common with the recent psychological distinctions between ''deep'' versus ''shallow'' processing (Craik and Lockhart 1972), ''controlled'' versus ''automatic'' processing (Schneider and Shiffrin 1977), ''systematic'' versus ''heuristic'' processing (Chaiken 1980), ''thoughtful'' versus ''scripted'' or ''mindless'' processing (Abelson 1976; Langer et al. 1978), and earlier formulations on different kinds of persuasion (for example, Kelman 1961).

2

Advertising Management and Its Search for Useful Images of Consumers

Franco M. Nicosia

One of the challenges set forth by this book is to identify the ways psychology and advertising have interacted in the past and to develop suggestions about improving this interaction in the future. In this chapter, we focus on only the contributions of the behavioral sciences to advertising. We take stock of various images that may be related to advertising strategies and tactics, identify some directions of future research, develop a realistic appreciation of the management question So what?, and delineate some bases for further dialogue between action and research.

The chapter begins with a workable definition of the terms *advertising, images* of humankind, and *contributions* of the latter to the former. Then we posit a general paradigm to guide our review and discussion of past and future images that may contribute to advertising. Both the review and the discussion are only a beginning step toward a systematic understanding of the opportunities for future work.

Advertising, Images, and Contributions

Advertising, images, and contributions have different connotations and even private denotations. The tasks of this chapter require an agreement on the meaning of these three words.

Advertising

Advertising may mean a specific ad, a specific campaign, a specific sponsor, an entire industry, a profession, the entire mass-communication institution, or only one of its components (for example, advertisers, agencies, media, regulatory/legislative bodies, and so forth). For our purposes, advertising means the specific management problems faced by officers in the private and public sectors. To illustrate:

My colleague, James Coyne, has been an invaluable chaperon in assuring that I do not misuse central psychological constructs.

At the brand-management level, which attributes should be the content of the brand's advertising plan for the next six months, given a market segment?

At the product-management level, should Volkswagen cars (Rabbit, Scirocco, Dasher, Jetta, and so on) be advertised as U.S.-made cars?

At the corporate level, would it be too risky to advertise a new soap (for example, Dial) as made by a well-known meat packer (Armour)? Or should one advertise the diversification of Mobil Oil into retailing, and if yes, how?

At the federal level, how can advertising help to recruit the appropriate persons for the air force? Or, can advertising help the National Highway Traffic Safety Administration to persuade people to wear seat belts?

At the state level, can advertising help the California Energy Commission instill/create/increase conservation ethics (values) in the people of California?

At the advertising-agency level, what should one say (strategy), how can it be said (creative), through which media (buying)?

In approaching any advertising problem, we make a number of possible assumptions about human behavior, ranging from the assumptions that a group of people prefers white-looking teeth for health reasons or for social/self reasons, that social institutions (for example, the family or the place of work) affect behavior differently, or that an entire culture perceives saving in terms of the rainy days or in terms of *carpe diem* (circa 100 A.C.), *après de mois le deluge* (circa 1750 A.C.), narcissism (do my own thing), and commitment either to oneself or to others.

The contributions of psychology to advertising can be identified only with respect to specific management problems and related goals (for example, from the creation of awareness and comprehension to short-term objectives such as sales, market share, and profit to basic and ecological long-term goals like return on investments). In addition, the nature, relevance, and perception of these contributions depend upon the level and locus of the organization where the communication problem is experienced and the type of organization experiencing the need to advertise—for example, private or public, for profit or not for profit, and regulatory agency or legislative body.

Images

There are many answers to the question of what makes humans act, think, and feel. Political and monotheistic religions have posited a number of all-encompassing views either describing, and/or prescribing, the functioning of humankind. The humanities and the arts have elaborated other visions. A variety of philosophies—from the postulation of pure randomness to strict teleological perspectives—have tried to encode different visions into different logics (that is, different ad hoc systems of internal consistency).

These all-encompassing visions are not concrete enough to assess their possible contributions to advertising. We shall only consider those visions, or images, that specify what is relevant for a specific problem. A useful image of humankind (1) suggests some clear constructs/variables as uniquely associated with what people do, think, and feel and, one hopes, (2) indicates how the suggested constructs/variables interact among themselves over time so as to yield some types of actions, thoughts, and feelings rather than other types.[1]

This definition of image should not astound us because an advertising professional, Donald Kanter (1957), made it explicit for all. To paraphrase his words, if we adopt a Freudian image of the intended audience, then we shall choose to observe certain variables rather than others and shall use a certain methodology, whereas if we believe that the functioning of the audience is captured by a Veblen's image, that is, conspicuous consumption, then we shall choose other variables and another methodology.

This definition has been echoed in the marketing literature (without a reference), but as in the case of frequent uses of Maslov's vision, the word *image* has acquired quasi-philosophical universalities; has been deprived of its operational content, and has been enveloped by imposing words such as *theory*, *model*, and so forth. Our examination of which image may contribute to which advertising problem(s), however, relies on Kanter's practical definition.

Contributions

Have images of humankind contributed to advertising management in the past, and for which types of problems, in which kinds of organizations, and so on? As we review known and less-known images, we shall ask these and other questions.

Images of consumers can be an input into management thinking but cannot replace it. We do not imply that, for instance, an account executive may say: I attended a seminar in consumer psychology and learned that a substantial number of men and women need to feel assertive, self-reliant, and rugged. I also learned that visually, the color red and a sailor's tattoo may relate to such a need; acoustically, the sound "r" pronounced in the Shakespearean theater's fashion also relates to such a need; and the tactile sense of a hard box is related to such a need. Thus, on the basis of this image, I have recommended the production of the new cigarette Marlboro.

This meaning of contribution is too specific, impractical, and theoretical. We only mean that various fields of psychology and related disciplines can inform the choice of those variables and of their relationships that are relevant to a specific advertising problem. By and large, then, we begin the modest and long-term task of filing in the following matrix.

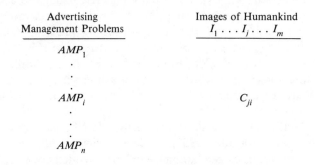

The list of advertising management problems (AMP) may include questions concerning the possible effects of advertising dollars on returns on investment, the possible content(s) of an ad, and so on. The list of potentially useful images of consumers (I) may include images ranging from stimulus-response (S-R) postulations to very complex information-processing descriptions. In each cell of the matrix, we would record whether an image—for example, a response-reinforcement image (I_{rr})—may contribute to the formation of brand loyalty (AMP_{bl}). Any given row in the matrix would indicate how many images, if any, may contribute to a given advertising problem, and any column would record the kinds of advertising problems to which a given image may offer some contributions.

A Reference Paradigm

A simple accounting scheme or paradigm is used to organize our discussion of useful images of human nature. This paradigm states: The behavior (B) of an individual or group can be accounted for by interactions over time (F) among some of the variables inherent to the individual or group (I) and some of the variables external to it (E).

Behavior (B) means not only the act of purchase (or repurchase) but also any other observable act such as storing and disposing of beer cans, repairing the lawn mower, using the insurance policy that is assumed to take care of flood damages, or transferring the chore of maintaining home appliances to the original manufacturer. I means any of the variables and processes that have been posited to operate within the skin of an individual or within the social boundaries, formal and informal, of a group. Similarly,

E includes all variables and processes in the environment surrounding I as posited by many disciplines. This paradigm is familiar to most of us. We use it as a point of reference for the identification and evaluation of the images discussed here.

To set the stage for our inquiry, we assert that the variety of advertising-management problems cannot be answered by one image of humankind. In the private sector, brand managers' needs—for example, to conceptualize and monitor how the current users and nonusers function—vary according to changes in the corporate-marketing and product-portfolio strategy, the behavior of competitors, and the stage of the brand's life cycle. In addition, the needs of a brand manager may differ from those of a person in charge of corporate-communications programs. Similarly, in directing the functioning of the entire advertising institution (for example, Should advertising be taxed?, a question answered affirmatively in the United Kingdom two hundred years ago), legislators may find it useful to adopt imges of humankind that differ from those useful to a specific regulatory commission. Also, the dialogue between advertisers and regulators, or between advertisers and agencies, could be improved if the parties at least were aware that their differences often are caused by altogether different images of what makes people tick—their actions, feelings, and thoughts (Nicosia 1974; 1977).

1900-1935: The Discovery of Useful Images

Many of the images informing our work today, and many of the current debates about their usefulness, found clear roots and growth during 1900-1935. There seems to be a belief that, during these early decades, advertising strategies and tactics were based only on a strict (Watsonian) S-R image of human nature. From this point of view, knowledge of mental processes mediating the stimulus with the response is not necessary for advertising decisions because simple conditioning, associative processes deliver the objectives assigned to advertising. This belief is incorrect.

The avoidance by users of the S-R image of anything that resembles a mental construct must be interpreted in the historical context of these early decades. S-R researchers were aware that words such as *arousal* and *drive* are also mental constructs. The real concern, instead, was on the measuring of any construct and the hope that measures at the skin of a human were at least reliable. Then, as now (see chapters 12 and 13), the issue is whether measures of events occurring at the skin or inside the skin somehow are associated with observable behavior as well as events occurring outside a subject's skin (for example, changes in the story unfolding through the ad).

From the end of last century, an established trade and academic advertising literature extensively uses terms such as *reasons why, appeals,* and *needs*. By the 1910s a number of images other than S-R are used, even in down-to-earth how-to manuals.[2] By the 1920s, the several images of human nature that are still used today are treated in standard chapters of textbooks (for example, see Poffenberger 1925[3]; Starch 1923; and the abridged edition 1927). Similarly, most of today's debates about the usefulness of psychological images to advertising are already well defined (for example, most incisive and modern statements about images other than S-R are in Link 1932, especially chapter 4).

In using such images for management problems, our grandfathers were also familiar with the problems of (1) measuring constructs, (2) measuring the possible relationships among two or more constructs, and (3) the pros and cons of laboratory versus field approaches to the conceptual and empirical operations in (1) and (2). (See Starch 1927; Poffenberger 1925; White 1927.) Among the surprises in discovering the quantitative awareness of our grandfathers, a most revealing one is the description of the tachistoscopic method. Poffenberger (1925, pp. 185-187) was more aware of the distinction between measuring a construct and measuring the construct's relationship to another than many of the present grandchildren, for perhaps the latter are still coping with multivariate statistical inference rather than using scientific-method procedures to apply the appropriate image of humankind to the appropriate advertising problem.

For our purposes, it is even more important to see that we also can identify a number of advertising-management problems where these images were employed.

Applications of a Strict S-R Image

The S-R image is used when advertising is to contribute to sales. The conceptual and empirical content of Link's book (1927), and of Watson's introduction to it, are a complete elaboration of *Sales = f(Advertising)*.

Both independent (stimulus) and dependent (response) variables are measured in dollars. The relationship *f* may be a mathematically stated and empirically measured association or simply estimated empirically. Above all, *f* has no psychological or social meaning(s). Most past and current applications of operations research and statistical inference are, explicitly or otherwise, informed by this image. In these applications, the meaning of *f* ranges from the term of "response function" (see, for example, Ackoff and Emshoff 1975) to some notion of "randomness" (see, for example, Bass 1974).

Modern uses of the S-R image have made progress in employing developments in statistical inference and in computational abilities. There has been little progress, however, in using this image for assessing its contributions to short-term goals (for example, profit) and, more important, long-term goals (for example, returns on investments).[4] A puzzling lack of progress has been in the determination of the optimal advertising budget. Applications of some form of mathematical programming appeared at the beginning of the 1960s to help management to determine both the optimal budget and its optimal allocation of media.[5] Several agencies and clients explored the new possibilities, and by the second half of the 1960s, a reasonable perspective had been gained (for example, Zangwill 1965; Gensch 1968). Since then, however, academic literature seems to have concentrated only on finding the optimal allocation to media of a given budget. Although this question is relevant to the agencies' media buyers, it ignores the more-crucial corporate question: How much to spend? The literature seems to ignore that the power of mathematical programming is to determine simultaneously the optimal budget (a corporate question) and the optimal allocation to media of the optimal budget (a media buyer's question).

In summary, uses of a strict S-R view of human nature appear to be justified when information about how consumers function at the skin or inside the skin is not essential for a given problem. In this sense, probably most of the questions raised at the corporate level concerning sales, optimal budget, profit, and returns may be answered by the use of this image. Further, a strict S-R image may or may not be a useful image, depending upon a number of factors. For example, given the unique marketing mix of Coca Cola during these early years—especially an intensive/extensive distribution strategy—the blanketing of each store outside and inside with the omnipresent red disc and an elegant lettering in white, "Coca-Cola," with the same lettering on the glass bottle and in print ads, is an appropriate use of a S-R image.

The Discovery of the Organism

From the end of the last century on, the functioning of a human becomes the focus of many disciplines, some with very applied purposes—for example, medicine. For our purposes, two images of the human organism (O) that produces certain behaviors emerge. In one, the organism is a process of physical events; in the other, it is a process of psychological events. There is a great deal of give-and-take between these two images of the organism. A most notorious case is the birth of clinical psychology (Freud was an M.D. well before he became concerned with a class of behaviors other than physical disease). Today, a psychiatrist still must understand the organism first in terms of physical events; only after gaining an M.D. can one then move on to the understanding of psychological events. The distinction between a physical and a psychological view of the organism of an individual is becoming blurred. Nevertheless, it can help us to identify which image is useful to which advertising problem.

Applications of the Physical Organism's S-R Image

S-R researchers were involved quite actively in the study of the physical processes in the organism. They knew a great deal about motor skills, the nervous system, and the major operations of the five senses. They were skillful in measuring events occurring at the skin of a human. By the mid-1920s, advertising research has adopted and adapted measuring procedures ranging from GSR to the tachistoscopic method. When management is concerned with the content of the stimulus, measures of physical events were seen, then as now, as means to answer two questions: what to say (a strategic question) and how to say it (an execution question that might be relevant to the artist). Since the 1930s, new procedures in evaluating the content of an ad have been refinements on the previous ones (for example, the parametrization of a pupil's dilation proposed in the late 1960s).

These uses of a physical image were limited to the measuring of events occurring at the skin and to the labeling of these measures as if they were indicators of internal states such as affective or readiness-to-act states. Only in the last few years have we seen an approach to measuring what is happening within the skin and to establishing the psychological meaning or equivalent of what is physically happening. We return to this topic later.

Applications of the Psychological
Organism's S-R Image

A number of advertising problems may be approached usefully by adopting an image of the human organism as consisting of psychological processes. The various lists of motives in the literature signal a concern with one psychological process: motivation. Although the lists were sequences of imaginative words, empty of operational meaning to anyone facing advertising problems, they signify at least a teleological image of human behavior— an image that re-emerged forcefully in the 1950s as the second era of motivation.

This image gives direction to management efforts to communicate; that is, a necessary condition for communication to occur is for the sender to relate to the seeker of information in terms of the seeker's motives (or, we may add, needs, drives, dreams, wants, aspirations, and so forth). This lesson is still useful today. But how does one appeal to motives? By the mid-1920s, this problem had already decomposed into its main components, each corresponding to a different psychological stage and process that may improve or dampen efforts to communicate. If we believed that the contribution of psychology to understanding the processes through which a stimulus may be internalized begins, for example, with Lazarsfeld's founding of the Office of Radio Research in the mid 1930s and with Hovland's work at Yale in the late 1940s, then our reading of advertising literature of the 1920s is a lesson in modesty.

The processes studied during these early years are those on which we still work today: physical perception, psychological perception (giving meaning to a physically perceived stimulus), attention, selective/motivated perception and attention, memory as affected by previous purchase and previous exposure, memory as affecting perception and attention, feelings as a main cause of perception/attention/memory, and so on, including the issue of primacy versus recency effects.

The methodological controversies of today were already clearly delineated, too. For instance:

> Strong and Franken measured attention value in terms of recognition, while Starch measured it primarily in terms of recall. These two memory methods do not measure the memory value of an advertisement in which the advertiser should be most interested. [Poffenberger 1925, p. 197]

We can raise several questions. When we study the processes through which a stimulus may be internalized, are we rediscovering or are we improving on what we already knew fifty years ago? If we are improving, are we doing so with a clear reference to a specific advertising problem?; that is, paraphrasing the quote, which psychological events are of most interest to the advertiser for which specific problem?

Some Unmet Challenges

From 1900 to 1935, basic images of human nature were identified and used for a number of advertising problems, ranging from those of concern to corporate management (the creating of revenues) to those concerning the content of an ad, either for strategic or for execution purposes. These images share something basic. They are all concerned with the one-way flow from the sender of information to the seeker's internalization of it. Today, much of our work is still focused on this one-way flow.[6] However, these images give us no suggestions of what will occur after a response.

This creates a challenge to consumer psychology for at least one reason: For the last thirty years, one image has suggested that a stimulus can be used to reinforce a desired response. Does this image contain useful contributions? We are aware of only one professional (Moran 1972) who has outlined explicitly the opportunities to use advertising to reinforce past purchases. This response-reinforcement image makes for a broader challenge. An aspect of this broader challenge was explored by the early work of Kuehn (1962), who applied learning stochastic models to brand-switching data, and by the later work of Massy, Montgomery, and Morrison (1970) and their students, who used Markov chain methods. From the point of view of a response-reinforcement image, the previous purchase(s) is the stimulus that may increase the probability of repurchasing the same brand. Some researchers have suggested that one can look at such probability (or transition rate) as the response to appropriate advertising stimuli (for example, Nicosia 1967). We are not aware of professional and academic work that has examined systematically how advertising can be used to strengthen brand loyalty.

The challenge of positioning advertising so as to have useful roles after the fugitive instant of a purchase might be met by a recent interest in consumer satisfaction. For some, satisfaction is conceptualized as a state (often, as the ultimate state of blissful and eternal happiness), and here we do not expect useful contributions to the management of advertising by brand managers, corporate managers, and public policymakers. In other work, satisfaction is visualized as a process. This process has been made operational only as a before-after research design, and accordingly, we have not learned much about the process itself.

Not much is known about satisfaction as a process (for example, Lazarsfeld 1959; Nicosia 1966), but exploring its nature may contribute to advertising. We could begin to observe postpurchase activities and the associated changes in the physical/psychological organism—for example, along the lines indicated by Wilton and his doctoral student Tse in chapter 17. The applications of cognitive dissonance in the early 1960s by Engle, Kollat and Blackwell (1968) can be seen as efforts in mapping out the feedback processes that underlie satisfaction and brand loyalty.

A major difficulty for studying these feedback processes is the identification of relevant classes of postpurchase activities. Work has begun to identify activities crucial for gaining insights into corporate and public-policy problems—for example, can advertising help consumers to become more concerned with safety (that is, seat belts) or with energy consumption? Over the years, the following classes of postpurchase activities have emerged as the most promising (for example, see Nicosia and Glock 1968; Nicosia and Witkowsky 1975; Nicosia and Mayer 1976; Nicosia and Wind 1978): storage, use, maintenance, repair, and disposal.

Advertising could expect additional contributions from psychology if it were willing to realize that consumers do not die after the performance of prepurchase and purchase activities. After all, the verb *to purchase* is not equal to the verb *to consume*. The observation of postpurchase activities and associated social-psychological changes may yield images of modern consumers that suggest how to reposition some advertising as a powerful postpurchase stimulus.

The period under review suggests other opportunities. One emerges by observing that we usually focus on only one element of the environment—the advertisement. The interdependence of this environmental variable with others such as the package/product design, the kind of store handling the brand, and other marketing variables is much overlooked. We still have not made much progress in this direction (see, for example, Bogart 1982).

Another opportunity becomes evident when we observe that the images reviewed so far assume that the stimulus goes through a medium and then, in a fashion analogous to an intravenous syringe, the medium directly injects the message into the consumer's skin. No other environmental elements are considered explicitly. In what follows, we shall see new images mapping out the ways a stimulus may reach a consumer.

From 1935 to the Present: The Continuing Search for Useful Images

Around the mid-1930s, a major cross fertilization of visions, eventually creating new images, occurred in the country. Much of it coincided with the exodus from Europe of Fromm, Katona, Lazarsfeld, Lewin, and others. Many of them shared ties with the research milieu in Vienna and other continental European cities, especially with research ranging from pre-Gestalt to Gestalt. In a few years, the emerging images got their first test of "relevance to management problems" (fully reported in Stouffer et al. 1949) with the World War II efforts and soon found new relevance tests in other problem areas including communication research and, eventually, advertising.

In this section, we focus only on several major new and old images that may have contributed to advertising problems since the mid-1930s. The discussion is organized into the same headings used for the previous time period: images concerning the variables operating within the individual I and images concerning the E (those in the environment of the individual).

Psychological Images of the Organism

Some of the old images merge into new images, and other images emerge from extant images. Three main contributions, almost in chronological order, are of interest to advertising management.

The Second Era of Motivation. From the late 1940s through the 1950s, professionals and academicians returned to the considerations of what motivates consumers to do the things they do. What psychological processes energize human efforts into buying or not buying, for example, instant coffee (Haire 1950), ready mixes, or TV dinners (see Ferber and Wales 1958)?

The label of *motivation research* given to this period is misleading because it stresses the use of measuring instruments and methodologies ranging from the TAT and Rorschach to sentence completion, and so on. What is relevant to management, however, is not methodology but whether the notion of motivation is a key to the functioning of consumers. In this rediscovery of motives, a key improvement is the moving from words empty of operational content to the search for specific forces operating in the individual as she or he transacts with the environment. One of the founders of motivation research, Earnest Dichter, argues that the best way to define which image underlies his work in terms of compartmentalization of humans into academic disciplines in the term *culture personality*—that is, a blending of the *I* and *E* classes of variables that is appropriate to a managerial problem (personal conversations).

There is another improvement in this second era of motivation: Consumers are assumed to manage the conflict among different and often contradictory motivations. For example, advertising had positioned instant coffee so as to relate it to the desire of household makers to be efficient. It had ignored the possibility that consumers may prepare and serve coffee so as to satisfy also another motivation, that of caring for one's family, and thus, brewing of coffee is a way to satisfy this need. By catering to only one of the motivations, advertising failed to present instant coffee as a solution to the conflict between being efficient and caring (brewing coffee).

The image's stress on conflict was of interest to other areas of psychology. The most obvious case is the work of one of the founders of social psychology and attitude theory—Lewin. The cases not so obvious in the advertising literature are for example, the semantic differential,[7] cognitive dissonance, balance, congruence, and so on. In these images, the focus is on tension among opposing forces and how an individual may go about managing tensions by some change either in mental states and/or behavior.[8]

The motivation image certainly did inform advertising decisions concerning the identification of appeals and the solution of conflicting tendencies in the psychological organism. Its popularity, however, began to decrease, and accordingly, we turn to one image that sprang up in the early 1960s and that gradually went through such a series of metamorphoses as to become almost unrecognizable, if not lost altogether, by the end of the 1970s.

Attitude Theories. Social psychology became established by the 1950s, and one of its key constructs is that of attitude. Several definitions of attitude already had emerged, and attempts were made to reconcile the rather substantial differences (Lazarsfeld 1959). The definitions of attitude having an impact on the advertising profession were those proposed, for example, by Krech and Crutchfield (1948) and by the Hovland group (1953).

The contributions of psychology to advertising were rather direct up to the 1950s. However, a social/academic event—the birth of a consumer-behavior discipline in the applied milieu of business school—created a new, perhaps only mediating and perhaps filtering, source of possible contributions. Consumer behavior was for many decades a synonym of consumer economics (not to be confused with the neoclassical demand theory of Hicks and others). By the mid-1950s, the term had acquired a new meaning in a couple of readers (Clark 1955; 1958). Newman (1957) alludes to consumer behavior in his publication.

Then, two distinct orientations within the emerging discipline of consumer behavior appeared in the years 1958-1963. On the quantitative side, with an emphasis on economics of the industrial-organization type, operation research, or statistical inference, we see the early work by, among others, Kuehn (Carnegie Tech), Massy (Massachusetts Institute of Technology), and Frank (Chicago). This research was informed by an S-R image and began to find applications for prediction of advertising effects on sales through the 1960s and the 1970s (for example, the decision-calculus school, and some of Bass' group work). Also on the quantitative side, but with an emphasis on the behavioral sciences, another orientation emerged. Among the earlier contributors, one can mention Perloff (Purdue), Engle (Michigan), Nicosia (U.C. Berkeley) and D. Cox (Harvard). The two orientations may stem from a need for specialization: in the early years it looked almost impossible to pursue concurrent work on all the variables and possible processes identified in the thorough list prepared by Morgan in 1958. Although it would seem useful to reunite these two orientations—an S-R image with a psychological-organism S-R image (Nicosia 1978)—their contributions of consumer behavior to advertising management remain still divided.

The contributions by the behavioral orientation are a bit difficult to identify uniquely. The early grandfathers shared the notion that an attitude is a mental representation of an entity (a consumer good or a company) consisting of three dimensions: (1) cognitive (the elements of which are called percepts, or knowledges, information bits, and so on about the entity); (2) affective; (3) conative (a tendency to move toward or away from the entity). By the mid-1960s, the new discipline had become aware of a number of issues, some of them still today relevant to our purposes. For instance, the discipline's reliance on attitude as mediating between an ad and a purchase makes its contributions virtually identical to those from communication research. In addition, both disciplines seem to imply that attitude is a process rather than a mental state. However, although much writing is under the label of attitude formation and change, then and to a large extent today the empirical work in both disciplines is based on a simple comparative static design—the before-after design (Nicosia and Rosenberg 1972).[9]

Two other issues were also of concern during the mid-1960s. (Much of this concern, unfortunately, has not been recorded in so-called scholarly publications.) The first issue was whether or not there were conceptual and empirical bases to distinguish between the affective and the conative dimensions of attitude.[10] The second issue was in some ways an answer to the first; namely, the affective and conative dimensions may only attempt to capture the notion of motivation as proposed not only during the second era of motivation but also in early work by Lewin (that is, the notion of valence). Still today, as we hear of thinking versus feeling ads, we have assessed neither the usefulness of the distinction affective-conative nor even the distinction between cognition and motivation (Nicosia 1979; Tetlock and Levi 1982).

The mid-1960s saw some efforts to deal with these issues in ways relevant to advertising management. Engle's work on cognitive dissonance was a strong signal that consumer behavior is more than communication research. Similarly, Nicosia outlined the possible feedbacks from consumption activities into some mental processes associated with these activities and underlying the formation of brand loyalty (or relative satisfaction; see 1966, pp. 109-112, 185-188; Lipstein 1965).

Amstutz (1967) and Nicosia (1966) handle the distinction cognition versus motivation in much detail. To illustrate, Nicosia begins by defining a mental representation of a consumer good or service as a cognitive structure having a number of dimensions (pp. 163-164). To the extent that an ad is internalized, the internal organization of this cognitive structure may evolve into a weak disequilibrium (an attitude), and if additional ads or other stimuli about the advertiser's brand are also internalized, the disequilibrium may be intensified further with a corresponding sharper focus on the advertiser's brand. Nicosia works out the dynamic process of attitude formation and its development into a motivational strong drive (chapter 7, especially pp. 215-219), including references to well-known empirical work in the advertising profession.

Although relying on different professional data, Amstutz (1967) gives an independent but remarkably equivalent description. Further, the "attitudinal/motivational" drive is generalized to the case of many brands by Lipstein (1965) by means first of mathematically stated dynamic psychological processes and then by the appropriate estimation procedures (see also Nicosia 1968; Nicosia and Rosenberg 1972).

The work of these and other authors shares a stress on relevance to management problems—for example, the subtitle of Nicosia's book (1966) is *Marketing and Advertising Implications*. In addition, their work is the beginning of continuing efforts toward constructing comprehensive views of decision processes. For instance, the next effort is the eclectic text by Engle, Kollat, and Blackwell (1968); then, in his effort to contruct a comprehensive paradigm beyond his dissertation, Sheth joins Howard in proposing a new paradigm of consumer behavior (Howard and Sheth 1969). Later on, among others we see the paradigms by Hansen (1972) and then Markin (1974).

During this evolution of comrehensive paradigms, an increasing focus on psychological mechanisms gradually led to the emergence of at least two different conceptualizations. In one, the challenge is to clarify as well as to debate the cognitive-motivational distinction within the construct of attitude. In the other, either the attitude construct changes its original content or loses its central importance. These two conceptualizations have different impacts on the potential applications to advertising. Accordingly, we discuss the two separately.

The Cognitive-Motivational Aspects of Attitude. In the comprehensive paradigms by Amstutz (1967) and Nicosia (1956), there is an attempt to give an equal role to cognitive and noncognitive mental activities. The relevance to advertising of understanding how an individual comes both to know and to feel about a brand can be illustrated as follows.

The content of an ad may change appropriately depending upon the answers to the questions: Is a market segment in the process of acquiring knowledges (information bits) about a brand? Is this segment in the process of developing some cathectic/conative qualities in the information about the brand? Are these cathectic/conative qualities becoming stronger and more sharply focused on one rather than another brand? Are these qualities about a brand more permanently reinforced by the feedbacks originating from both consumption activities such as storing, using, maintaining, repairing, and disposing and environmental stimuli such as word of mouth, group norms, and the brand's advertising?

The potential usefulness of finding answers to these questions can be illustrated by a brief reference to two orientations. In one of them (Nicosia 1969; 1978), an ad is seen as information that attempts to change some qualities of a consumer's mental representation of a brand. The mental representation is an organization of information bits about the brand. This organization can be described by using different (mathematical) languages—for example, from systems of differential equations to set or fuzzy-sets languages or directed-graphs theory.

After sharing the pros and cons of these different languages to describe how a stimulus structure may change the organization of the mental representation of a brand, both in 1969 and 1978 Nicosia settles on directed-graphs theory. A mental representation of a brand consists of the information bits about a brand, each bit being a node in a graph, and the relationships among these nodes are a set (or a set of sets) of arcs. As usual, the number and kinds of information bits represent the cognitive aspect of the brand's mental representation. But the cathectic/conative aspects—that is, the motivation quality signifying the driving force toward or away from a brand—are captured by the kind of organization among the percepts. Different specific configurations of arcs among the perceived attributes (that is, differences among types of attributes' organizations) may or may not energize or motivate an individual selectively to acquire and process information and to behave.

In this view, the conative and affective aspects are not orthogonal to the cognitive aspect of a mental representation; they are the resultant of specific types of percepts' organizations. Accordingly, it is not useful, and it may even be misleading, to measure things such as the liking of perceived brand attributes, the beliefs about such attributes, and so on.

Several properties discriminate among different nodes/arcs organizations. For empirical purposes, Nicosia constructs a weak measure of how percepts about a brand can be organized, which he calls the relative "centrality/peripherality" of each perceived attribute within a graph, and then presents two different empirical studies. The managerial purpose of both studies is exactly the same: Choose the advertising stimulus that changes the mental representation of a brand the most. In each study, the advertising effect on the brand's mental representation is analyzed first in the traditional way; namely, find which attribute indicates a better response to the ad. Then, the ad's effect is reanalyzed with the focus on the organization of the perceived attributes; that is, find which attribute is more or less central to the brand's mental representation.

In each study, the findings of the two analyses point to opposite recommendations to management. The findings of the traditional analysis suggest that the content of the ad should be addressed to the attributes that change the most. In the organizational analysis, however, the attributes that change the most contribute the least to the change of the entire mental representation, and the attributes that change the least are those that contribute the most to change of the entire mental representation; accordingly, the ad's content should be addressed not to the attributes that changed the most but to those that changed the least.[11] (These published findings do not discuss cost considerations.)

This emphasis on the internal structure of a brand's mental representation is also evident in the second orientation. Reynolds systematically makes operational Kelly's (1969) notion of "linkages" (working with a number of colleagues from Gutman (1975) to chapter 4 with Olson in this book). This operationalization, briefly illustrated in chapter 4, will probably become a major aid to advertising questions concerning strategy (the choice of the what-to-say so as to relate to consumers' deeply rooted perceptual organizations) and, perhaps more marginally, through copy pretesting, to questions of implementation (the choice of the copy line, or the how-to-say-it).

At present, a trade-off exists between the orientation of Olson and Reynolds and associates and that of Nicosia. Olson and Reynolds can capture empirically a broader and deeper domain of perceptual organizations than Nicosia, but these organizations are static in the sense that they do not give insights into the questions concerning Nicosia—namely, the motivational, or energizing, potential in a perceptual organization and the process by which a perceptual organization may interact with the information in an ad.

For our purpose of identifying images useful to advertising management, these two orientations are attempts to answer the questions (Nicosia 1979): What is the difference between cognition and motivation? If there is a difference, is it relevant to advertising and marketing management? And, ultimately, why do consumers cognize and process information if they are not motivated to do so? The orientations by Reynolds, Nicosia, and others now unfolding in the area of advertising also may be in timely tune with the very recent rethinking in basic psychology by, among others, Zajonc (1980) and Lazarus (1982). In both applied and basic psychology, there is a realization that notions such as motivation, emotion, and feeling have been overlooked for at least a decade.

The Cognitive Era. From the late 1950s to the 1970s, an increasing amount of research in social psychology was informed by a cognitive image of human nature. The psychological mechanisms in the organism are assumed to attend to the computations necessary to define a problem, to gather information about possible solutions, and by linear or nonlinear functional operations, to compute a good-enough solution. This emphasis probably was amplified by the birth of computer languages, their initial uses for the simulation of checkers and chess players' thinking, and by the eventual establishment of the artificial-intelligence field. Two other approaches to problem solving—given the problem, though—also contribute to the acceptance of an image of humankind as a cognitive, problem-solving mechanism: statistical decision theory and, relatively less, some game theoretic solutions to given problems.

From the mid-1960s on, work in advertising and marketing also began to adopt a cognitive image of a consumer's functioning with the move by Sheth from MIT to the University of Illinois, at Urbana, the academic residence of Fishbein. Now working with Howard, Sheth proposed a definition of attitude that places the conative aspect on the left side of a definitional sign of equality and the cognitive plus/times the affective aspects on the right side of the equal sign (Howard and Sheth 1969). Sheth's co-workers and his early doctoral students are among the opinion leaders in the diffusion and adoption of a Fishbein-like idea of attitude. A few years later, Wilkie and Pessemier (1973) count several scores of Fishbein-like definitions in the work by academicians and professionals.

One key feature of these emerging definitions of attitude is an increasing tendency to say that attitude is an intention and, then, that intention is some arithmetic composite of what a consumer knows—that is, the brand's attributes, the liking of such attributes, the beliefs about these attributes, and so forth. Thus, impressive efforts are invested either to assess which arithmetic operations may satisfy the as-if criterion (the test par excellence in artificial-intelligence programs) or which cognitive and related percepts satisfy the definitional equality with, or predict the measure of, intention. Accordingly, there is a gradual turning of attention away from the dynamic, energizing notions of motivation, emotion, and feeling. By some cognitive mental activities of acquiring and combining information bits—that is, by processing information—a consumer may develop the intention to buy a brand. By the mid-1970s, not only the process of attitude formation and change but also many other psychological processes became only cases of information processing. A new image is born: the consumer is an information-processing entity (McGuire 1978; Bettman 1979; Harris 1982).

Work inspired by this image ignores the question: Why does a consumer process information to begin with? The only answer we can find is that provided in the 1930s by economics: the neoclassical formulation of demand theory. The economist's answer is as usual parsimonious: The (motivational) assumption that a consumer attempts to satisfy his or her preferences as much as possible.

The disappearance of the notion of attitude and its attendant motivational implications for advertising and consumer research and the focus on computational-cognitive activities is stressed further by the comprehensvie paradigms of consumer decision processes formulated in the 1970s. Hansen's approach is entitled *Consumer Choice Behavior: A Cognitive Theory* (1972), and Markin describes his efforts with the title *Consumer Behavior, a Cognitive Orientation* (1974). This stress on the cognitive functioning of a consumer is related in many ways to the dominance of cognitive images in social psychology. Despite strong warnings by some of the early cognitive theorists (Kelley 1969; Neisser 1980; Zajonc 1980), the human organism is deliberate, computational, and even rational.

The usefulness to advertising of a cognitive image may be increased if we could spell out some criteria to assess the organism's computational abilities. Possibly, a cognitive consumer is doing a good job if she or he is rational in the sense of, for example, computing/processing information with precision, accuracy, reliability, and so forth. It is doubtful, however, that such definition of rationality would be relevant to a brand manager, to the air force, or to the Environmental Protection Agency. We may use another definition of rationality, that of economic theory. In economics, a subject is rational only in the sense of striving for some consistency between his or her preferences and the stream of acts preceding and following the fugitive instant of purchase.

There is a risk of misinterpreting economics. During the last thirty years, much consumer work has assumed mistakenly that economic rationality means prescribing what a consumer should, ought to, prefer. Economics is an amoral science, and it does not prescribe to humans what their preferences ought to be. The misuse of economics has created a noneconomic image of a rational consumer; if it were to prevail, we would expect to see further contributions of confusion into advertising decisions by private and public managers.

The distinction of thinking-versus-feeling ads raises an issue related to computational rationality. For example, for which kinds of products/ brands, and which kinds of audiences, is an image of a consumer as a computational, problem-solver human more useful than an image of a feeling motivational consumer? Ultimately, as Kanter (1957) told us so aptly a long time ago, there is more to measurement methodologies than we are sometimes willing to recognize. The method we choose (recall or recognition) depends upon the image we adopt to begin with.

The Personality Traits. Personality theories have proposed an image of the organism where the notion of traits is very central. A number of traits' configurations (personality inventories) have been developed, measured, and applied over decades in child development, education, occupational choice, personnel management, group behavior, and political choice. A first advertising application of personality theory was that by Koponen (1960) with the help of an advertising agency, J. Walter Thompson. After lively debates, a researcher working for an advertising agency wrote an assertive postmortem to advertising uses of personality traits (Wells, 1966). Later on, however, Jacoby (1969) showed how the previous research was actually an example of how not to find relationships between traits and choice (see also Brody and Cunningham 1968). The renaissance led to the systematic review by Kassarjian (1971) and then to an elaboration of Jacoby's theme—why previous research has failed and how an understanding of the organism's functioning and an appropriate research methodology may uncover relationships between traits and choice of interest to advertising management (Nicosia 1978, pp. 29-33). This past optimism, however, has not led to the volume of research one would expect.

We postpone the examination of physical images of the organism to the next section, which is devoted to the future. As some of the chapters in this book strongly suggest, the potential contributions of physical images may be one of the main future challenges to our work. In what follows, we turn our attention to the *E* of the consumer and the related images.

Social Images of the Organism

The environment of a human is eminently social. At birth, we are equivalent in terms of genetic potential, and our physical organisms evolve through the cycles of life in similar ways. The psychological organism, however, evolves in different ways across and within cultures. The social environment becomes the main source of the content (variables and processes) of the psychological organism.

Social institutions are the principal sources of information and influence; they range from the family, the school, the church, and the place of work to organized passive/active sports (for example, spectators' tennis or private tennis clubs) to types of retailers and to mass media. These specific social institutions and their changes must be accounted for in advertising management—from the corporate to the brand-manager levels. Rena Bartos of J. Walter Thompson (1982) and Leo Bogart of the Newspaper Advertising Bureau (1982)—both examples of scholar/academic qualities—have restated the importance of the consumers' social context. Advertising professionals have been aware of the social images of consumers emerging during the 1950s and 1960s. The role of reference groups—from face-to-face to anticipatory groups—was examined systematically by Zaltman (1965), and the effects of the social visibility of certain goods were illustrated by Charles Glock and others (see findings in Bourne 1957).

Social Institutions as Mediators. A traditional image implied that mass media impart information to a consumer directly, in a way equivalent to a syringe administering a medicine. Social-psychological research on people's political choice, farmers' choices of management practices and equipment, physicians' choice of prescription drugs, and consumers' choice showed this image to be incorrect. In addition, information and influence did not trickle down from, say, Her Majesty the Queen but were mediated by different institutions, their norms, and the individual's willingness to apply such norms to his or her behavior.

Social-psychological research also found that some of the mediating institutions are formal but that others are informal. The discovery of the power of word of mouth is now augmented by the discovery of the power of the informal group, and somewhat associated with these discoveries, the notions of the taste maker and innovator are enriched by the notion of the informal (horizontal) opinion leader. It eventually becomes clear that information and influence flow through combinations of channels: word of mouth at the face-to-face and group levels, commercial sources (salesperson), and mass media in the case of both the individual consumer and the organizational buyer (see, for example, Robertson 1971; Zaltman, Duncan, and Holbek 1973).

These enriched images of the organism's social environment are associated with changes in advertising choices at the strategic and tactical levels. The usual well-dressed young woman illustrating the new cleanser is replaced increasingly by a realistic representation of a woman coping with cleaning tasks. This woman often appears together with a peer, and the natural conversation between the two communicates the superior qualities of the new cleanser. Some of the more-imaginative and powerful uses of a social image appear in the use of famous black athletes. The famous black football player or boxer is a meaningful symbol to a ghetto child. This physical meaningfulness is transferred to broader social aspirations for the child by the athlete's showing the importance of reading or of proper nutrition.

During the 1950s and 1960s, there was an intense give and take between the intuitive vision of the creative advertising person and psychological work elaborating the discovery of new social images of humankind more in tune with the developments of a postindustrial and affluent United States. During the 1970s, however, this interplay seemed to dry out, at least in terms of published debate and research.

Social Institutions as Sources of Motivation. By the end of the 1970s, there was a rekindling of interest in the roles of social institutions. Mayer and Foote (1975) derived from an extensive literature review the notion that different institutions guide the ways people allocate their time to different activities, which in turn imply the purchase/use of different products. In this image, consumers' needs are not satisfied by the attributes intrinsic to a product/brand; on the contrary, the relevant attributes are those that lead to the allocation of an increasing amount of discretionary time (and income) to activities (or needs) like return to nature. Accordingly, the attributes of a battery for a pocket flashlight are not its long hours of service but its ability to satisfy the need to camp outside or to hunt at night in the African jungle. In a word, the content of an ad is addressed to the activities/situations that specific norms of certain social institutions find permissible or desirable.

That norms administered by institutions affect the motivational directions and content of consumption activities (not only purchase) is debated in Nicosia and Witkowsky (1975) and then, with a number of illustrations, in Mayer and Nicosia (1981). Those ads that focus on the situation as a way to convey the psychological meaning of a product are addressed to the norms of institutions that make certain activities and the related use of time permissible/desirable.

In looking at advertising strategies, changes in institutions and in their norms affect the quantity and content of advertising by other institutions. Bogart (1982) shows that changes in the mass-media institutions brought about by the explosion of telecommunications may enable consumers to become even more selective in their active seeking for specific ads than they are today. This may affect newspaper advertising by retailers. The so-called deflection hypothesis advanced by Nicosia and Mayer (1976) is another example of changes in social institutions impacting the entire spectrum of consumers' activities.

The potential usefulness of considering social institutions as sources of, and constraints upon, consumer motivation is illustrated by an empirically dramatic example. By the end of 1973, public policymakers became aware of the energy crisis and undertook programs to send information to consumers. As in the sad story of seat belts during the 1960s, these programs adopted a cognitive image of consumers: All one needs to do is to give consumers information because they will internalize it, process it, and derive the computational rational decision to start saving energy. No available evidence suggests that these informational programs have worked. At best, surveys by the Environmental Protection Agency suggest a period of low awareness, followed by some increase in awareness but explained away by assumed conspiracies by big business, and/or by big government, and by the end of the 1970s, by a reasonable increase in verbal awareness that there is an energy crisis.[12] Also, there is no evidence of success by private organizations who either joined these informational programs on their own (for example, oil companies) or were convinced to join by regulation (for example, public utilities). Even the president of the United States gave it a try by wearing a sweater in front of a warm fire burning in the fireplace (that is, the old trickle-down image of humankind at work again). In these and other cases, advertising relied on images of consumers that ignored the filtering and motivational roles of social institutions.

Some evidence, however, shows that specific institutions did have an effect in leading to some energy saving by consumers. Consider the use of gasoline for transportation and other sources of energy for heating/cooling space. For years the purchase of smaller and more-fuel-efficient cars has increased to the recent level of 25 percent or more (in California, the proportion has been around 50 percent for several years). Some computations indicate that, although consumers have been driving more, some overall reduction in gasoline use has occurred. We neither know whether or not advertising might have been a factor nor know of changes in major institutional norms that may be associated with the decrease. But there are major changes in two social institutions. One is the formation of the OPEC organization; the other is the explicit choice not to create the institution of rationing but to use the institution of the market to let price become the measure of value of gasoline as perceived by both sellers and buyers.

Consider now the use of energy for heating/cooling households, and observe the use of advertising separately from changes in institutions and/or their norms. We observe only the following. Federal and several state governments use the tax institution to provide incentives. In addition, some state public-utility commissions change their norms to affect rate-making criteria. Further, the California Public Utility Commission orders the private and municipal utilities to offer zero-interest loans for the purchase and use of insulation devices; that is, the commission has transformed production organizations into lending organizations. These utilities in turn use advertising to encourage the applications for zero-interest loans.

So far, advertising is not used for changing institutions and their norms. This is wise because advertising cannot alter basic changes in the family that deeply affect energy consumption. For example, more and more families consist of one head of household, and perhaps a few children; in more and more families both spouses are out and return home at different times and, accordingly, may cook meals and heat/cool space at different times. Advertising also cannot change the location of two major social institutions: the place of sleep and the place of work. From the point of view of the emerging social images of human nature, advertising can be used efficiently only to interpret institutional norms because these norms, together with cultural values, are the forces that operate within and around the psychological mechanisms of the organism.

Cultural Values. The term *cultural value* is popular. Cultural values are presumed to be somewhere in the social environment of the consumer and either to direct and/or constrain a consumer's feelings, thoughts, and actions. In this section, we approach the question of how values may contribute to identify and to solve advertising problems along two lines of thought. First, we inquire into the nature of, and process(es) related to, the term *cultural values* and second, into what is done today with the term.

As in the case of the term *motives*, we find very long and different lists of cultural values. In marketing, the proposed lists seem to be the result of different writers having read different novels by Faulkner. In the social sciences, there have been attempts to make operational the notion of cultural value (for example, the achieving society by McClelland and the instrumental-terminal notions by Rokeach). Even if these operationalizations were reliable and valid, the questions remain: Are they useful to aid advertising decisions by private and public managers? Where are cultural values to be found? How do they affect consumers' behavior? From the social-psychological point of view we have adopted, cultural values must be internalized deeply into the psychological organism (see, for example, Nicosia 1966, chapters 4 and 5) and must have a very strong impact on people's feelings, thoughts, and acts. In addition, it is doubtful that any cultural value can affect consumers directly.

A general imperative like "achieve" must be interpreted for each specific class of daily activity, each class performed in specific institutions— for example, at home, at school, at work, on the tennis court. Nicosia and Mayer (1976) thus suggest that each social institution interprets cultural values by formulating norms that apply to the activities performed within it. Their deflection hypothesis illustrates how achieving no longer can operate in the traditional sense of being productive in the factory, and given changes in the norms governing consumption, achieving now can operate only onto consumption activities. If this new image of the social environment is correct, advertising cannot change cultural values. Advertising may at best amplify or dampen the effects of cultural values; furthermore, it can do so only by working on the norms administered by social institutions. An illustration of current experience is appropriate.

The legislative charge to the California Energy Commission, created in the mid-1970s, is to give new life to the traditional values of thriftiness, parsimony, frugality, and concern with the distant tomorrow and to create the new overall value of conservation ethics. After endless soul searching and public debates, public-policy decisions have been focused on modifying the behavior of institutions such as utilities (for example, a zero-interest program) and housing industries (for example, construction standards) and on relying on the institutions of government (for example, tax deductions for purchases of insulation) and the market (for example, prices, rebates, and rates). Advertising has been used only to create awareness of the energy crisis and to inform consumers of the available fiscal inducements.

As for what is done today, the challenge posed to the private sector by Yankelovich's list and measures of cultural values in the early 1970s (the eleven-year-old Yankelovich *Monitor* 1981 survey) has been successful enough to open the door to another successful initiative by Stanford Research International Values and Lifestyle (the VALS survey). Altogether, the continuing sales of these two surveys of cultural values would indicate their usefulness to advertisers. As cited earlier, Bartos finds the surveys useful at J.W. Thompson; other agencies also use these surveys in their strategic-planning and media choices (audience targeting) and in their advice to clients. In our experience, these constructs and measures of cultural values give further information about the nature and changes of consumers' social environment and thus a sense of the directions governing those mental activities we have called feeling, thinking, and doing (Nicosia 1977).

Today and Tomorrow

There has been a pervasive give and take between the images proposed by psychology and related disciplines and the practice of advertising management in the private and public sectors. We have identified a few of the major images and have discussed their past and future contributions to different types of advertising problems. This section begins with a summary of our findings and concludes with a sketch of the potential contributions of emerging images of consumers as physical organisms.

The S-R Image

Throughout this century, a class of advertising problems has been approached from the point of view of the S-R image. The typical use is when there is a need to know the contribution of advertising to sales—that is, to assess the relationship *Sales = f(Advertising)*. In the future, the relationship posited by the S-R image can be used for much more essential problems than finding the optimal allocation of a given advertising budget to media, for the corporate question is How much should be the ad budget? The worth of advertising depends on the relative worth of the other elements in the marketing mix in creating not only sales but also, more basically, in reaching an optimal use of scarce resources—that is, return on investment.

Other advertising problems could rely profitably on this image. At the level of the entire economy, for instance, a detailed review by Jacobson and Nicosia (1981) on the possible relationships between gross national product (GNP) or personal-consumption expenditures and all advertising expenditures revealed a paucity of sustained efforts, pointed out crucial limitations of past research in the method and/or data used, proposed an ideal research design for those concerned with the future of the advertising institution, and presented initial empirical results that cast doubts on key assumptions made by economists and public policymakers about the roles of advertising in the economy.

Response-Reinforcement Image

Most of us are aware that, depending upon the product category and specific brand, many consumers who recall/recognize an ad bought the advertised brand before being exposed to the ad. Professionals are also aware of the need for advertising not only to remind consumers of a brand but also to reinforce the experience of past purchases. However, researchers inspired by psychology and related disciplines have ignored the potential contributions of this image to the formation and maintenance of brand loyalty.

In the future, one would expect less concern with the overresearched prepurchase and purchase activities. Pioneering efforts in using this image can contribute to the broader problem of studying the specific ways consumers experience a product after its purchase. Chapter 17 by Wilton and Tse is a promising signal that once satisfaction is conceptualized as a process, it may be possible to understand how advertising can interact fruitfully with postpurchase activities and related psychological experiences. Set in this broader context, the response-reinforcement image can help management also in the area of managing a portfolio of brands and products through stages more responsive to consumers' changing needs, wants, aspirations, and other forces driving their social and psychological behavior. This image also could guide efforts by corporations to be good citizens and efforts by public agencies to identify legitimate complaints.

Social Images

Both the S-R and response-reinforcement images are useful to those advertising problems where information about what is inside the skin of a consumer is relatively less important than in other problems. Some social images have yielded useful information about how ads may reach a consumer. These images have diminished the importance of the trickle-down view and have given a realistic understanding of the working of different channels of information, their interactions over time, and in several product categories, the relative impact of different channels on the act of purchase.

Some other social images, beginning with the early studies of the role of reference figures and reference groups, have posited that information in the environment is relevant to a consumer decision process only if it has been internalized psychologically. Recent extensions of this position capture the meaning of those creative persons who, in constructing the ads' contents, portray the product within a social context and meaning. New social images go a step further. They postulate that institutional norms do more than regulate consumer activities—from prepurchase to, above all, postpurchase. These norms in fact may be major sources for social motivation. Finally, to the extent that institutions concretely interpret the broad principles embedded in a society's cultural values, the functioning and changes of a society's institutions (from the family to the place of worship) may be the most relevant market factors for planning advertising strategies (Bartos 1982; Bogart 1982). To be successful, advertising must understand and relate to changes in the institutional fabric of a society. Equally important, advertising cannot change postpurchase activities that are locked into deeply entrenched institutions. Informational campaigns by the private and public sectors concerning pollution, energy conservation, safety, and so on cannot contribute directly to changes in behaviors; these campaigns can be called on only to support efforts to change the nature and the norms of social institutions.

Images of the Psychological Organism

By the end of the 1930s, the profession of advertising and psychology already had identified most of the key stages and processes that preside at the internalization of a stimulus. (The notion of low involvement had not been postulated for the radio, perhaps because people had not yet become blasé). In addition, the substantive sophistication in those thirty years was supported by high quantitative awareness and skill. The internalization of a stimulus has remained a deep concern but, for some reasons, has been studied only in relation to prepurchase activities. If both professionals and academicians recognize that modern consumers spend most of their scarce time and efforts in postpurchase consuming activities—that is, experiencing the product or service[13]—then both may discover profitable opportunities in addressing advertising to postpurchase activities.

Within the current concern with a limited number of consumer activities, past and current contributions are, in the main, directed to three advertising problems: (1) choice of media so as to communicate to a consumer target, (2) strategic choice of the end line, and (3) choice of the copy line. During the last several decades, these three choices have relied on different images concerning the psychological mechanisms of the organism.

There has been a striking pendulum cycle in the use of one or another image of human nature. During the first three decades of this century, a substantial effort was made to understand the force(s) driving different consumers to do, think, and feel as they do. This first motivation era was followed by a second in the 1950s. Although mislabeling it as the motivation-research era, professionals and researchers had begun to face a new consumer during the 1950s, one who was experiencing the first flood of affluence and who was motivated by forces that were becoming different from those driving the consumer who experienced the Depression. Staple material goods such as bread and butter become inferior goods; symbols such as motor- and sailboats and trips to Europe are among the early signals of a consumer striving to find new meanings, functional in a social-psychological rather than material sense.

As affluence spread during the 1960s and 1970s, more and more citizens were enabled to search for symbols relevant to their selves. Calling this striving and experimenting society the do-my-own-thing society does not have to be derogatory. It could mean, instead, the story of humans searching in the area of consumption (not purchase) activities for new norms to replace those prevailing in a society that had been production oriented; it could mean searching for the concrete meaning of the proverb that man does not live by bread alone. Advertising strategies and tactics tried to be in tune with this search—from the micromini skirt through the failure of the maxi, to Charlie—but researchers did not.

Some psychologists have tried to give equal relevance to the motivational and cognitive content of the psychological organism, but the majority gradually turned their efforts to a cognitive aspect of human nature. Motivation became encoded into neatly arranged hierarchies, gradually losing its

intrinsic energizing and dynamic qualities and acquiring a resemblance to
Plato's ideal and perennial structure of things in the universe. Academic
research began to buy the idea that a consumer first cognizes the attributes
of a brand and that only after this psychological operation a consumer computes whether she or he likes which attributes. Then, through other arithmetic operations, the consumer computes an intention to buy that, in turn,
is mediated by computations of probabilities—that is, expectancies and the
like—that might lead to an act of purchase.[14]

Perhaps this is an overcharacterization of the current cognitive image of
a consumer. Yet, several of us feel that the pendulum has swung too far,
and we have asked, What happened to motivation? (for example, Nicosia
1979). Even some of the social psychologists who gave the original impetus
to a cognitive orientation have voiced their concerns (Kelley 1969; Zajonc
1980). One of them believes that cognitive-oriented research is no longer interested in human reality. In reviewing a symposium on social knowing,
Neisser writes, "[Research of this type] would reveal that the author's primary
interest was not in the phenomena themselves but in the theoretical issues
and concepts of social psychology. . . . The thing to study, I suppose, is not
'social knowing' but social reality," (1980, pp. 603 and 604).

Professionals also have expressed concern about the extreme position
taken by a cognitive image of consumers. Light (1980), of Ted Bates advertising agency, sees the birth of another motivation era. Plummer and
Holman (1981), of Young and Rubicam, underscore the need to relate to
noncognitive forces energizing consumers; ask for a return to the consideration of motivation, emotions, and feelings; and argue for a balanced image
of consumers. Finally, although explicitly based only on a question of
measurement methods (recall versus recognition), the release in 1980 of the
FC&B advertising agency study of thinking versus feeling ads reinforces the
professional call for a motivational-cognitive image of consumers.

There is another reason for reintroducing the constructs of motivation,
emotions, and feelings in our images of consumers. Most researchers have
come to believe that cognitive activities do/must precede the formation of
cathectic and conative orientations toward an entity. However, Zajonc
(1980) has argued that either both processes may be on concurrently or that
feeling types of mental activities precede and in some ways direct/focus
cognizing activities. In advertising, and using a literature vastly different
from that of Zajonc, Plummer and Holman (1981) also argue for the new
temporal sequence in the internalization of a stimulus from feeling activities
to cognizing activities. Some of us now disagree with Goethe's belief that
"we see only what we know," for we are ready to say that we see only what
we want to know.

All in all, future efforts should be toward finding an image that at least
balances cognitive-motivational activities in ways relevant to advertising

problems. Among these problems, we can list those concerning the content of an ad with respect to the what to say and how to say it and those concerning the targeting of the ad toward appropriate audiences through appropriate media.

Another direction for our future efforts is to explore whether or not the distinction cognition-motivation is tenable, on what grounds, and for which applied purposes. Although arguing that Zajonc (1981) uses cognition in the narrow sense of computational activities, Lazarus also doubts that the distinction is tenable (1982). The same doubt underlies chapter 10 by Mitchell. Maybe the distinction is one of those Aristotelian-given dichotomies that still pervade Western culture. Perhaps we have been wearing such a distinction as our glasses and, true to Goethe's saying, we have seen plenty of cases fitting the discriminating power of our glasses.

How do we know that some mental activities are cognitive and others motivational? We may want to doubt that the cognitive-affective-conative aspects of an attitude are orthogonal to each other and to consider the possibility that organizations of knowledges (cognitive aspect) like a mental picture of a brand may differ on some (graph-theoretic) properties. Each set of properties is inherent to each organization of cognitions; accordingly, such properties are not other dimensions of the mental representation. A set of properties may signify that the organization is in a state of disequilibrium and in the process of resolving that state by moving toward or away from that brand. Nicosia defines this tendency as the motivational quality—intrinsic in the organization of cognitions (1969; 1978). The findings of two empirical studies reported earlier are a weak evidence (weak in the sense that they were based only on statistical inference) that the avoidance of the motivation-cognition distinction produces novel recommendations to management. Some other bases for avoiding the motivation-cognition distinction may be provided by the progress in the understanding of the physical organism.

Images of the Physical Organism

Our grandfathers were well versed in the observation and measurement of a number of physical activities occurring at or within the skin. A number of basic disciplines have provided more fine-grain descriptions of the physical content of the organism along the following main lines of inquiry: the anatomy and, more broadly, the morphology of the human body; chemical activities; and biochemical activities, especially in the volitive/brain system. A somewhat separate and extremely complex line of inquiry traces the interactions among several of these activities in the hope of eventually reaching a picture of the overall functioning—physiology—of the human body. If progress is measured in terms of useful applications of the results of such inquiries, then we must be impressed. Useful applications have occurred increasingly—that is, in medicine, psychiatry, sports medicine, and in the management of astronauts' work (Gatty 1981).

This research and its applications were bound to be noticed by some of us. For instance, Kroeber-Riel (1979) brought to our attention the role of a hormone, adrenaline, in the internalization of a stimulus. Krugman (1981) and Weinstein (1980) began to explore brainwave activities as possible indicators of how humans internalize a stimulus. Some of us discovered that the forebrain is divided into two halves (a non-Aristotelian dichotomy) and have been tempted to use this as a basis for reifying dichotomies entertained in psychology. And some of us have begun to think about using another dichotomy—the forebrain and the midbrain—as a possible basis for supporting the suspicious dichotomy of thinking versus feeling.

We may be constructing the foundations for years of research to come. The following list, however, indicates that we may be caught again by a number of suspicious dichotomies.

Dimensions	*Taxonomy (partial)*	
1. Activities (only mental)	1.1 Thinking	1.2 Feeling
2. Language Corresponding psychological state	2.1 Verbal Awareness	2.2 Nonverbal Nonawareness
3. Locus of activity (brainwaves)	3.1 Forebrain, Left hemisphere	3.2 Forebrain, Right hemisphere
4. Locus of activity (anatomy)	4.1 Forebrain	4.2 Midbrain
5. Measuring method	5.1 Recall	5.2 Recognition

Are they based on generally accepted views in the basic disciplines? Among those who work on the physiology (the functioning) of a human body, the answer is no (for example, Pribram 1980; Timiras 1982). At best, one can think of tendencies, often not statistically significant. The current picture of the physical organism is that of a complex set of homeostatic processes, of redundant weakly nested sets of loops and feedback controls, with an incredible ability for plasticity, for substitutability.

We are very far from applying this developing knowledge to stimuli such as advertising or a teacher's lecture, but the opportunities may be here. If we were producing robots, drugs, bubble memory devices, fiber optics, or returnable containers, then corporate management and public policymakers would certainly give us R&D funds; that is, they would be willing to risk support for systematic research, hoping that something useful would result in the long run.

However, we are not in production and related work; we are in marketing and advertising. Management in the private and public sectors asks us to know what the result will be, by tomorrow. If we cannot prove that a couple of surveys or a month of experiments will yield some usable result by tomorrow, then our proposals will not be accepted.

Our work is not yet perceived as fundamental. Acquiring knowledge about human behavior is not perceived as the long, systematic, modest process of inquiry so well described by chapters 12 and 13. These scholars find themselves at the same stages that Brache, Kepler, and Galileo were—working alone, making do, and writing to each other. We have to prove ourselves. At present, we can only help each other and hope that our great grandchildren will move away from statistical inference and join us in observations of reality, of consumers. One day, they will be welcomed in the laboratories that are still the exclusive preserve of inquiries about matter rather than feelings.

Notes

1. In the context of scientific method, the specification in (1) corresponds to the notion of anatomy, and the specification in (2) corresponds to the notion of physiology; see, for example, a number of works by mathematical economists since the 1930s. For consumer behavior, see, for example, Nicosia (1966, chapters 1 and 7).

2. *The Advertiser's Handbook*, 2d ed. (Scranton, Pa.: International Textbook Co., 1921), p. 10.

3. Poffenberger's table of contents lists chapter titles such as "Attention to Advertising"; "Attention and Magnitude"; "Attention and Repetition"; "Perception and Discrimination"; "The Comprehension of Advertising"; "The Feelings and Their Influence"; "The Feeling-Tone of Types . . . , of Colors and Color Combinations, . . . of Language"; "Memory and Association"; "Belief and Conviction" (*sic*); and "Individual and Group Differences."

4. Research aimed at assessing whether advertising may have an effect on sales with longer or shorter lags would be an exception. However, much of this research has relied on SIC industry data. The same basic reservations to the use of SIC data for assessing the roles of advertising in creating excess profits and so forth apply here, too (see, for example, Nicosia 1974, especially chapter 12; Jacobson and Nicosia 1981, "Introduction"). Research that

may lead to insights on advertising contributions to profit and returns on investment is that based on the data set originally known as PIMS.

5. Breaking established norms among agencies in the early 1960s, BBD&O advertised, "Linear programming showed one BBD&O advertising agency client how to get $1.67 worth of effective advertising for every dollar in his budget."

6. For a most recent and comprehensive article relying only on this unidirectional flow in advertising, see Preston (1982).

7. For some unknown reasons, the very specific adjectives and their underlying dimensions of the semantic differential were never noticed in advertising and marketing work, and for some other unknown reasons, this work came to name semantic differential as any set of any assortment of adjectives presented in a bipolar layout, with n intervals.

8. Be that as it may, by the end of the 1950s these images reappear as if they were cognitive problem-solving images of consumers.

9. The methodology described by Macoby and Roberts (1972) puts them among the few social psychologists who have dealt explicitly with the fact that a before-after design cannot capture any process of formation and change.

10. Recent outputs from applications of Lisrel software package(s) suggest a statistially based distinction and even pass a number of validity tests. In our opinion, these a posteriori interpretations should be reflected in at least a priori distinctions in the measuring procedures. If we do not satisfy this minimum requirement, then we can interpret Lisrel outputs in terms of constructs available in economics.

11. For a different structural approach to examine how a stimulus may have different impact on the desired change in the mental representation of a brand, corporation, or political candidate, see, for example, Coleman (1964).

12. For research on consumers and energy conservation using a cognitive and/or Fishbein-like image of human nature, see the special issue of the *Journal of Consumer Research*, December 1981.

13. A haircut or hairdo is experienced and reacted to as a consumer re-enters his or her environment. An insurance policy is stored like any other physical product and may not be found with the necessary speed in an emergency; it is maintained during its life (and advertising is often used to encourage this activity at times of renewal) and so on.

14. Research guided by this image of a consumer (that is, a consumer that goes through all the operations summarized in this discussion) most usually stops its observations with the act of purchase. It would seem reasonable to stop here rather than continuing with the study of the following consumption activities, for the enormous number of prepurchase computations must have drained all the motivational energies available to this type of consumer.

3 Advertising-Campaign Change: Lessons from Leading Cigarette and Liquor Brands

James R. Krum and
James D. Culley

Most researchers and textbook authors writing about advertising strategies have focused on individual ads or commercials. Advertisements and commercials are more than individual entities, however; they play a role in a systematic effort aimed at accomplishing a set of objectives—they are part of an ad campaign. Unlike an individual printed ad or radio or TV commercial that can be grasped and analyzed easily, an ad campaign is an intangible item of advertising effort. To the outsider, not privy to the advertising plans and objectives for a particular brand, the study of advertising campaigns is particularly difficult.

While the importance of individual ads and advertising campaigns varies from product category to product category and with the level (retailer, wholesaler, and manufacturer) and type (direct action versus indirect action) of advertising being done, the advertising campaign is probably critical to the success of products that sell on the basis of a brand personality or image such as leading cigarette and liquor brands. In the words of Jugenheimer and White, "The [advertising] campaign is perhaps the crucial concept in the entire advertising, marketing and selling process" (1980, p. 295).

Methodology

This chapter reports on a content analysis of twenty-one years (1960-1980) of magazine advertising for eighteen leading brands in two cigarette- and seven liquor-product categories as follows:

Filter cigarettes	Marlboro King Size (Red) and Winston King Size (Red)
Menthol cigarettes	Salem King Size and Kool Filter Kings
American blended whiskey[1]	Seagram's 7 and Calvert Extra[2]
Bourbon whiskey	Jim Beam (White Label) and Jack Daniel's (Black Label)[3]

Canadian whiskey	Seagram's V.O. and Canadian Club
Gin	Gordon's Distilled London Dry and Seagram's Extra Dry
Rum	Bacardi Light-Dry and Ronrico Extra Dry-White
Scotch whiskey	Dewar's White Label and J & B Rare
Vodka	Smirnoff 80 Proof and Gordon's 80 Proof[4]

With two exceptions, the brands listed here were the two top brands in sales in 1980; the leading brand is listed first.

The study was designed to describe and measure variations in advertising-campaign continuity and to examine differences and similarities in advertising appeals for leading cigarette and liquor brands. Cigarettes and liquor were chosen because:

The products in a given cigarette- or liquor-product category (rum or gin, for example) are relatively homogeneous;

The brand personality created by advertising for these products is very important to the success of these brands;

A large percentage of advertising for these product categories is readily available in magazines;

For these products, there is little or no product change over time.

With one exception, we restricted our analysis to ads for brands that were in existence in 1960, the beginning of the period studied. In product categories where more than one product carried the same brand name—for example, Barcardi and Jim Beam—we limited our observations to ads for the most popular product carrying the brand name. The number of ads examined varied from brand to brand. We sought more ads when there were frequent campaign or executional changes. With three exceptions—Kools, Gordon's Vodka, and Calvert Extra—we were able to find magazine ads for the entire twenty-one-year period. [These exceptions resulted from the brand being withdrawn periodically from magazines (Kools, 1960-1964), the introduction of the brand (Calvert Extra, 1963), or the lack of magazine advertising for the brand (Gordon's Vodka, pre-1964)].

What Is an Advertising Campaign?

An advertising campaign is not a single ad, no matter how explosive. A campaign is a series or sequence of advertisements, carefully planned, coordinated, and executed over a period of time. Weilbacher (1979) defines an ad campaign as "the totality of advertising with a common look and appeal that a particular product, service, or company uses for a period of time" (pp. 184-185).

The reasoning behind one advertising campaign has its roots in one of the most basic influences on human behavior—repetition. Advertisers typically agree that repetition is one of the keys to successful advertising. However, two questions arise: How much repetition is necessary to increase retention to some desirable level? At what level does repetition begin to decline in value? To neither of these questions does a set answer exist. The amount of repetition needed in a campaign depends upon the nature of the product, the quality of the advertising message, the medium being used, the complexity of the message to be learned, the strength of need for the product, and a host of other variables.

Several rules regarding repetition in a campaign exist. For example, advertising messages for established products should be spaced over a period of time. This tactic serves to remind consumers of the product without causing the boredom and perhaps the negative response of massive (concentrated) advertising (DeLozier 1976). Repetition of a central theme with some variation usually is considered superior to repetition of identical messages (Robertson 1970).

Campaign Appeals

To describe an advertising campaign, we must talk in terms of the target market for the ad and the appeal underlying the ad campaign. The campaign appeal reflects the principal idea behind a campaign. Ad-campaign appeals can be broken down into a number of categories, but most heavily advertised consumer goods use either product-related or consumer-related appeals. Product- and consumer-related appeals can be divided further into many categories, but because of the nature of major cigarette and liquor brands (little product change, price relatively insignificant, frequently purchased, high market awareness, and so on, only six types of appeals typically are used.

Product-Related Appeals

Product appeals do not emphasize a human need but allude to one. The burden falls upon the prospect to interpret the need the brand satisfies. Because advertisers understand the influence of needs upon selective perception, they often leave some ambiguity in the message and allow the consumer to interpret the message in line with his or her perception of what the advertiser is appealing to.

Our analysis of product-related appeals for the leading cigarette and liquor brands found four major product appeals being used:

Product pure and simple,

Product heritage,

Superior product leadership,

Product and its uses.

Consumer-Related Appeals

Unlike product-related appeals, consumer-related appeals clearly communicate a given need. For the cigarette and liquor brands studied, consumer-related appeals fall primarily into two major classifications and several subclassifications:

Problem solution;

Self-improvement:

Emphasizing people:

Recognizable people,

Nonrecognizable people:

single individuals,

couples,

groups;

Emphasizing places;

Emphasizing sex.

Slogans

One important element in the execution of most cigarette and liquor ads is the slogan used to emphasize the campaign appeal. The slogan always says the same thing in exactly the same way. Sometimes the slogan is secondary to the overall appeal of the ad and may, in fact, appear unrelated to the rest of the ad. Thus, a common slogan, in and of itself, does not define an advertising campaign.

The unchanging nature of an ad slogan or an ad execution offers an advantage in its own right. Constant repetition in an unaltered form tends to bring the slogan or execution into such close association with a product and a company that the slogan or execution almost substitutes for the product or company name. Table 3-1 lists the six longest running slogans that are still in use by major cigarette and liquor brands. These slogans appear in practically every ad for the brand and are an indication of advertising continuity.

The position and importance of the slogan in ad campaigns vary. On the one hand, Marlboro ads present the entire slogan or a part of it in headline form. On the other hand, "Leaves You Breathless" has always been secondary to other themes in Smirnoff advertising. A number of variations of the Kool slogan have been used, including the recent "C'mon up." Other slogans that have been used for an extended period of time include "Winston Tastes Good Like a Cigarette Should"; "Say Seagram's and Be Sure"; and "Best in the House in 87 Lands." The first two were abandoned in the mid-1970s. The Canadian Club slogan continues to be used periodically (for example, it appeared in the headline of a new campaign that began in 1981). This slogan was not included in table 3-1 because it was not used continuously.

Slogans seem to come about in one of two ways: (1) as a special effort to emphasize a particular product or company attribute or consumer benefit or (2) as an evolution from the appeal behind a particularly successful advertising campaign. Using a slogan based on a successful campaign appeal seems to be a practical tactic for several reasons. As a reminder of a past appeal, such a slogan can contribute to a feeling of continuity between the two campaigns. Also, the advertising investment in a particular campaign is extended by carrying over a slogan into subsequent campaigns.

Table 3-1
Longest Running Cigarette and Liquor Slogans in Current Use

Brand	Slogan	Years
Dewar's	"Dewar's Never Varies"	21
Smirnoff	"Leaves You Breathless"	21
Jack Daniel's	"Charcoal Mellowed Drop by Drop"	20
Marlboro	"Come to Where the Flavor Is, Come to Marlboro Country"	17
Kool	"Come Up to Kool" (or variations)	16
Bacardi	"The Mixable One"	13

Continuity in Advertising Campaigns

We know that advertisers change campaigns from time to time. Are campaigns changed abruptly or gradually? How frequently do advertisers run multiple campaigns at the same time? Do advertisers copy an obviously successful competitive ad campaign? Are ad-agency changes always accompanied by campaign changes?

To help answer such questions, we devised a scoring system to measure advertising-campaign changes. We differentiated between two types of campaign changes. A major change in campaign appeal received two points. A significant tactical change that continued the same appeal received one point. Any campaign change implies a change in execution. Each change in execution received one point. For this reason, the totals in the tables that follow include three points for a major campaign change and two points for a minor campaign change. Thus, if there was more than one execution of a campaign, there was no point designation for the initial execution. The campaign in effect at the beginning of our study (1960) received three points in all cases. We made no attempt to determine whether this initial campaign continued an appeal begun earlier. The minimum number of points (3) implied that a campaign in effect in 1960 continued through 1980.

Two problems arose in implementing the classification system. In the early 1960s, the campaigns of a few brands (Jim Beam, Seagram's 7 Crown) showed considerable variety in both appeal and execution and almost defied classification. The second problem was discriminating between a minor campaign change and a change in execution. This was especially difficult for Winston advertising during the extended period of "Winston Tastes Good Like a Cigarette Should." Because of major shifts in the execution of this theme every year or two, we called them tactical campaign changes. This decision was based upon a test of resemblance: If executions do not resemble each other, they represent a tactical campaign change. These problems, while noteworthy, only affected a small percentage of the designations in tables 3-3 through 3-6.

Table 3-2 shows the amount of variation in campaign continuity for the eighteen brands studied. Total points have been divided by number of years (twenty-one in most cases) to rank the brands. The number of campaigns in the twenty-one years ranged from one for Jack Daniel's to fifteen for Winston. Detailed analysis of campaigns for the product categories represented by the first four brands in table 3-2 can be found in tables 3-3 to 3-6. For example, tables 3-3 and 3-4 show the campaigns (numbered lines) and executions (lines beginning with letters) for the leading brands of filter cigarettes and bourbon whiskey, categories that account for the extreme cases of campaign continuity.

Table 3-2
Ranking of Leading Cigarette and Liquor Brands, by Advertising Changes, 1960-1980

Rank	Brand	Number of Campaigns	Total Points	Points per year	Sales from 1975-1980
1	Jack Daniel's	1	3	0.14	Rapid Growth
2	Marlboro	2	7	0.33	Growth
3	Grodon's Vodka[a]	3	7	0.41	Stable
4	Dewar's	3	12	0.57	Growth
5	Salem	5	12	0.57	Growth
6	Bacardi	5	12	0.57	Rapid Growth
7	Smirnoff	5	14	0.67	Growth
8	Canadian Club	5	15	0.71	Stable
9	Gordon's Gin	6	16	0.76	Decline
10	Kool[b]	5	14	0.88	Decline
11	Calvert Extra[c]	5	14	0.88	Decline
12	Ronrico	7	20	0.95	Growth
13	Seagram's Gin	8	21	1	Growth
14	Seagram's V.O.	9	21	1	Stable
15	Seagram's 7 Crown	10	23	1.1	Decline
16	J & B	10	28	1.33	Decline
17	Jim Beam	12	29	1.38	Growth
18	Winston	15	33	1.57	Decline

[a]Seventeen years (no magazine advertising, 1960-1963).
[b]Sixteen years (no magazine advertising, 1960-1964).
[c]Sixteen years (brand was introduced in 1963; no magazine advertising, 1973-1974).

Continuity versus Discontinuity in Advertising Campaigns

Table 3-7 shows the length in years of the ad campaigns studied. For the eighteen brands, the average length of the 116 campaigns we identified was 4.2 years. Because of the open-ended nature of our data, this figure would be higher if we had included data about the campaigns in progress at the beginning and end of the study. A separate compilation was made of the 78 campaigns contained entirely within the twenty-one years of the study. The average length was 3.2 years. This understates the average campaign length

Table 3-3
Campaigns for Filter Cigarettes

Year	Marlboro (Philip Morris Inc.)			Winston (R.J. Reynolds Industries)		
	Agency	Campaigns and Executions	Sales[a]	Campaigns and Executions	Agency	Sales[a]
1960	Leo Burnett	1. Relaxing man with or without tattoo [3]	22	1. "It's what's up front that counts" [3]	Wm. Esty	50
1961			24			55
1962		2. Marlboro Country [3]	26	2. Still life, focus on pack [2]		60
1963		a. Selectrate Filter (1962-1964)	26			67
1964		b. "Come to where the flavor is" (1964-1980) [1]	25	3. Couples at play, sequenced drawings [2]		69
1965			27	4. Couples at play, trite slogans [2]		71
1966			31	5. Corrected billboards: "like your cigarette should" [2]		75
1967			34			84
1968			39			83
1969			44	6. Cutouts of sporting equipment picturing couples [2] 7. Pop art [2] 8. "Me and my Winston" [2] 9. Grammar lesson: "as" [2]		80
1970			51			82
1971			59			82
1972			69	10. "Winston's Down Home Taste" [2]		84
1973			79	11. Picture frames: "How good it is" [2]		88
1974			86	12. Silhouettes of people by the sea [2]	Daneer-Fitzgerald Sample	90
1975			91	13. Look America in the eye: "I smoke for taste" [3]		91
1976			94			90
1977			97			88
1978			101			85
1979			104	14. Lumberjack: "When your taste grows up" [3]		82
1980			110	15. Working men wearing hats: "Nobody does it better" [2]	Wm. Esty	82
Total	2 campaigns	7 points		15 campaigns 33 points		

Note: Numbers in brackets indicate number of points for campaign.
[a] Billions of cigarettes from annual cigarette surveys published by *Business Week*.

Table 3-4
Campaigns for Bourbon Whiskey

Year	Jim Beam (American Brands) Campaigns and Executions	Agency	Sales[a]	Jack Daniel's (Brown Foreman) Campaigns and Executions	Agency	Sales[a]
1960	1. Beam family tree [3]	Edw. H. Weiss & Co.	1,700	1. Jack Daniel's Hollow [3]	Gardner Advertising	< 500
1961	2. "Worthy of your trust" [2]		1,800			< 500
1962			1,875			< 500
1963	3. "Yes, there was a Jim Beam" [2]		1,925			< 500
1964	4. "Since when do you drink bourbon?" [3]		1,975			< 500
1965			2,100			< 500
1966	5. Sean Connery [2]	Campbell Ewald	2,275			< 500
1967	6. Still life, emphasis on bottle [2]		2,375			< 500
1968			2,525			< 500
1969	7. 175th anniversary [2]		2,650			< 500
1970			2,650			650
1971	8. Generation gap [3]	Edw. H. Weiss & Co.	2,650			800
1972			2,650			850
1973	9. You can't improve on the original [2]	Lee King & Partners	2,600			950
1974			2,600			1,050
1975			2,600			1,175
1976	10. Ripley's Believe It or Not [3]		2,625			1,400
1977			2,675			1,525
1978	11. "Since when do you drink Jim Beam?" [2]		2,750			1,875
1979	12. "Switch to Jim Beam" [3] a. Couples (1979-1980)		2,825			2,200
1980	b. Drink (1979-1980) [1]		2,950			2,625
Total	12 campaigns 29 points			1 campaign 3 points		

Note: Numbers in brackets indicate number of points for campaign.
[a]Thousands of cases.

Table 3-5
Campaigns for Scotch Whiskey

Year	Dewar's [Rapid American (Schenley)] Campaigns and Executions	Agency	Sales[a]	J & B (Grand Metropolitan/Liggett Group/Paddington) Campaigns and Executions	Agency	Sales[a]
1960	1. Highlander [3] a. Various clans (1960) b. Dewar's Highlander (1960) [1]	Kleppner	< 500	1. Pennies more in cost, featuring Dickens [3] a. Less than half page (1960-1961) b. Full page (1962-1965)	E.T. Howard	525
1961	c. "Welcome Scotch the World		550			600
1962	Over (1961-1968) [1]		550			950
1963			575			1,125
1964			625			1,225
1965			700			1,400
1966			750	2. "Pours more pleasure" [3] a. Focus on people (1966-1970)		1,650
1967	2. Profiles [3]		900	b. Focus on bottle (1967-1970) [1] 3. "I don't know who he is . . ."		1,775
1968			1,050	(1967-1968) [3]		2,075
1969	3. Authentic [2] a. Pure authentic, bottle of	Leo Burnett	1,375			2,175
1970	highlander(1969-1979 periodically)		1,700	4. Pleasure principle [2] a. Woman (1971)		2,400
1971			2,125	b. Bottle and glass (1971-1972) [1]		2,650
1972			2,200	5. Experiments in pleasure, mixed drinks [2]		2,750
1973			2,325	6. Scotch and the single girl [2] 7. Rare pleasure [2]		2,725
1974			2,375			2,775
1975	b. "In a constantly changing world, we don't" (1975-1978) [1]		2,175	8. Rare taste, man or woman [2] 9. Still life [2]		2,550
1976			2,100	a. Rare taste (1975-1979)		2,550
1977			2,150	b. Rare scotch (1977-1979) [1]		2,525
1978			2,200			2,650
1979			2,300			2,600
1980	c. "The good things in life stay that way" (1980) [1]		2,350	10. "It whispers" [3]	Backer & Spielvogel	2,325
Total	3 campaigns 12 points			10 campaigns 28 points		

Note: Numbers in brackets indicate number of points for campaign.
[a]Thousands of cases.

Table 3-6
Campaigns for Vodka

	Smirnoff (Heublein, Inc.)			Gordon's Vodka (Renfield Importers Limited)		
Year	Campaigns and Executions	Agency	Sales[a]	Campaigns and Executions	Agency	Sales[a]
1960	1. Celebrity series [3]	L.E. Gumbiner	1,950			< 500
1961	2. Avant-garde [2]		1,975			
1962			2,050			∨ 500
1963			2,150			∨ 500
1964		Gumbiner-North	2,250	1. Patent on smoothness [3]	Grey Advertising	∨ 500
1965			2,450			∨ 500
1966			2,750			∨ 500
1967			2,950			600
1968		Dodge & Delano	3,200			725
1969			3,375			975
1970	3. Life-styles [2]		3,600			1,225
1971	a. Relaxing (1970)		3,875	2. Happy vodka [2]		1,275
1972	b. Recipe in corner (1971-1977) [1]	Tinker, Dodge & Delano	4,350			1,375
1973			4,700			1,550
1974			5,325			1,725
1975			5,500			1,775
1976			5,800	3. Smoothest, happiest vodka [2]		1,675
1977	4. Fantasy [2]	Tinker, Campbell-Ewald	5,875			1,625
	a. Sexually provocative (1977-1979)					
1978	b. Food (1978-1979) [1]		6,150			1,650
1979	5. Smirnoff style [2]		6,300			1,650
	a. Fun with friends (1979-1980)					
	b. Seduction (1980) [1]					
1980			6,100			1,850
Total	5 campaigns 14 points			3 campaigns 7 points		

Note: Numbers in brackets indicate number of points for campaign.
[a] Thousands of cases.

Table 3-7
Length of Advertising Campaigns for Leading Cigarette and Liquor Brands

Number of Years	Number of Campaigns	Percent of Total
10-21	10	8.6
5-9	25	21.6
4	18	15.6
3	9	7.8
2	31	26.7
1	23	19.8
Total	116	100

because campaigns still running are not included. In all probability, the average campaign length for leading brands of cigarettes and liquor is between 4 and 4.5 years.

Frequent campaign changes were made for most of the eighteen brands studied—47 percent of the 116 campaigns analyzed had run for two years or less. Notable examples of brands with frequent campaign changes are Jim Beam, Seagram's VO, Seagram's Gin, Winston, J & B, and Seagram's 7 Crown.

Jack Daniel's, Marlboro, and Bacardi are the best examples of success through continuous advertising (see table 3-8). In addition to these brands, Dewar's and Canadian Club have had long-running campaigns. Both brands have done well in the highly competitive, low-growth scotch and Canadian whisky markets. Also worthy of mention is Smirnoff, the number-seven brand in table 3-2. Consistently creative, trend-setting advertising graphics and a steady diet of drink recipes permitted Smirnoff to hold the comfortable position of the second largest selling liquor product for practically every year during the past decade.

The five Seagram's brands occupy consecutive positions (11-15) on table 3-2. This shows a corporate commitment to campaign change even

Table 3-8
Longest Currently Running Cigarette and Liquor Campaigns

Brand	Campaign	Number of Years
Jack Daniel's	Jack Daniel's Hollow	21
Canadian Club	World Adventure Series	21
Marlboro	Marlboro Country	19
Bacardi	Mixable	13
Dewar's	Profiles	12
Dewar's	Authentic	12

though four of the brands have remained with the same agency. The R.J. Reynolds brands present a marked contrast. While Winston campaigns have changed every year or two, Salem shows below-average change. In another comparison, Gordon's follows a philosophy of below-average change for its brands. Leo Burnett, the only agency with a leading cigarette and liquor brand, also shows a commitment to advertising-campaign continuity. In addition to the high rank for the Marlboro campaign, there have been no major changes in Dewar's advertising since Burnett originated dual campaigns in 1969.

Sales of paired brands in a product category provide another indication of the results of campaign continuity. The success that Marlboro and Barcardi have experienced with consistent advertising over Winston and Ronrico with frequently changing advertising bolsters the argument in favor of a campaign-continuity strategy. However, further analysis shows that five of the nine category leaders fall into the second half of table 3-2. For example, Jim Beam, the leading bourbon since 1969 with consistent sales gains each year, ranks next to the bottom of the list. Beam's current growth rate, of course, is small in comparison to its rival, Jack Daniel's.

In another comparison, five of the nine brands in the second half of table 3-2 have experienced sales declines between 1975 and 1980, while only one brand in the top nine shows a comparable decline. This comparison, which includes the outstanding success of Jack Daniel's and Barcardi, presents an apparent positive relationship between campaign continuity and sales. However, an alternative hypothesis must be considered also. In some cases, campaign changes may result from declining sales. Our data, of course, do not provide definitive proof for either hypothesis.

Current or Simultaneous Campaigns

Except for holiday or minority-targeted campaigns, most of the brands studied ran one campaign at a time. There were notable exceptions, however.

A good example is the use of concurrent campaigns for Dewar's. In 1969, Leo Burnett originated the "profiles" and "authentic" campaigns for Dewar's—each directed to a different market segment. Another example is J & B that periodically has run a general-audience campaign and a separate campaign designed for women (for example, Scotch and the Single Girl). This use of segmented advertising is one reason why J & B ranks so high in terms of advertising changes. Canadian Club, another user of simultaneous campaigns, also has tended to run longer campaigns. On a number of occasions there have been three different Canadian Club campaigns running in the same year, not including holiday and minority-group campaigns.

Smooth versus Abrupt Campaign Changes

Some campaign changes for the eighteen brands studied were abrupt rather than smooth. The three Ronrico campaigns from 1966 to 1973 are a good example of abrupt changes. Their mid-1960s campaign featuring women that suggested, "Tonight offer her a daiquiri made from Ronrico, . . . then watch her sip into something light and comfortable," was replaced abruptly in 1967 by "Ron Rico. Didn't he introduce the Panther Tango at the Palace in 1928?" In 1979, hoping that the identity crisis was solved by the 1967 campaign, Ronrico replaced humor by a still-life campaign that was a carbon copy of the Bacardi advertising of the period. We have tagged this third campaign, the "No rum reflects Puerto Rico like Ronrico" campaign. All three abrupt campaign changes were accompanied by ad-agency changes.

J & B Scotch campaigns between 1966 and 1973 provide an example of a smooth campaign-change strategy. The "pours more pleasure" campaign (1966-1970) gave way to the "pleasure principle" (1971), "experiments in pleasure" (1972), and "rare pleasure" (1973).

Similarity in Ad Campaigns

We found several examples of one brand copying the creative strategies of a competing brand. In some cases, the campaigns were so similar that we wonder whether the reader could really tell them apart. For example, V.O. advertising in the 1970s seemed to be reacting to Canadian Club advertising. V.O.'s "couples relaxing at sports" campaign followed by two years the "turn to couples" in the Canadian Club adventure campaign. Likewise, "Only the Ritz is the Ritz" and "Only Tahiti is Tahiti" campaign of V.O. seems to copy creative approaches pioneered by Canadian Club.

In no other cigarette or liquor category was the close resemblance between advertising campaigns more evident than in Salem and Kool ads. Until very recently, both made heavy use of couples in green settings. Coolness in Kool advertising competes with Salem's freshness appeal. Both campaigns at different times responded to problems faced by smokers. In 1973, Salem listed "naturally grown menthol" as an ingredient while Kool used the phrase "Only Kool with pure menthol . . . ." It is interesting that, while lakes and streams are used by both brands, the waterfall, a Kool creative element for a decade, did not appear in Salem ads.

Advertising Agencies and Campaign Changes

Table 3-9 lists the advertising agencies employed in 1980 to promote the eighteen brands discussed in this chapter and the number of agencies per

Table 3-9
Number of Major Cigarette and Liquor Brands per Advertising Agency, 1980

	Number of Brands	
Agency	Liquor	Cigarettes
Backer & Spielvogel	1	
Leo Burnett	1	1
Cunningham & Walsh		1
Doyle Dane Bernbach	2	
William Esty		2
Gardner Advertising	1	
Grey Advertising	2	
Lee King & Partners	1	
McCaffery & McCall	1	
Ross Roy-Compton	1	
Tinker, Campbell-Ewald	1	
Warwick, Welsh & Miller	3	

Number of Agencies per Brand, 1960-1980

	Number of Brands	Percent of Brands
One agency	12	67
Two agencies	5	28
Five agencies	1	6

brand during the twenty-one-year period covered by the study. We should note that agencies frequently merge or change names; thus, the brand tables present what appears to be a more-diverse picture. For example, Canadian Club has had one agency with three different names. The extreme case is Ronrico, a Seagram's brand, which has used five different agencies to battle the success of Barcardi. It is interesting that the four other Seagram's brands have had but one agency. Leo Burnett is the only agency with both a leading cigarette (Marlboro) and liquor (Dewar's) brand, both of which lead their respective product categories. The cases of multiple liquor brands with one agency, of course, indicate brands of the same manufacturer. As one would expect, in almost every case, an ad-agency change was accompanied by a major campaign change.

Summary and Conclusion

This chapter reported the results of a content analysis of hundreds of magazine advertisements for eighteen leading cigarette and liquor brands for the period of 1960-1980. The study identified a total of 116 advertising campaigns that varied in length from one to twenty-one years.

Ad-campaign appeals can be broken down into a number of categories, but virtually all of the 116 campaigns studied used one of four possible product-related appeals or one of two consumer-related appeals.

The position and importance of the slogans in ad campaigns varied. Sometimes the slogan was secondary in importance to the overall ad, so much so that some slogans appeared unrelated to the rest of the ad in which they appeared. Slogans seem to come about in one of two ways: They are a special effort to communicate about a particular product or company attribute (for example, Dewar's "never varies," Jack Daniel's "is charcoal mellowed drop by drop"), or they evolve from an appeal used in a past ad campaign (for example, Bacardi is "the mixable one"; "Say Seagram's and Be Sure").

The average length of the 116 campaigns studied was between four and four and a half years. The length of the individual campaigns ranged from twenty-one years for Jack Daniel's (only one campaign for the entire period studied) to a little over a year for Winston (fifteen campaigns in twenty-one years). With nearly half the campaigns studied running two years or less, campaign continuity seems to be the exception rather than the rule.

While most advertising campaigns ran consecutively, there were a number of examples of concurrent campaigns for the same brand. In some cases—for example, Dewar's—concurrent campaigns were designed to influence different market segments. In other cases—for example, Canadian Club—different themes of interest to the same market were run simultaneously. Almost every brand studied ran a holiday campaign concurrently with the ongoing campaign.

J & B is a good example on the one hand of a campaign-change strategy that used a smooth transition from one campaign to the next. The Ronrico campaigns from 1966 to 1973, on the other hand, illustrate the use of abrupt campaign-change strategies.

Most leading liquor and cigarette brands change advertising agencies infrequently. For example, twelve of the eighteen brands stayed with the same ad agency for the entire twenty-one-year period. At the opposite extreme is Ronrico, a Seagram's brand, which used five different agencies to battle the success of Bacardi.

Our conclusion is that advertising-campaign continuity strategy can lead to outstanding results for heavily advertised consumer products such as cigarettes and liquor. Creating a campaign with long-run appeal and sticking with it is the essence of great advertising. However, an agency and advertiser must be willing also to change or to abandon a campaign that is not working. However, there seems to be little justification for change for the sake of change.

Notes

1. Whiskey is spelled two different ways in this chapter. Scotch whisky and Canadian whisky are usually spelled without an *e*.

2. This is the number-three brand behind Kessler, a brand with limited sales and advertising in the northeast.

3. Jack Daniel's technically is not a bourbon whiskey.

4. This is the number-three brand behind Popov, a lower-priced brand with limited advertising.

Part II
Cognitive Responses
to Advertising

Decoding advertising messages is how consumers process messages to answer the question What is it? Decoding occurs at several processing levels. These levels do not necessarily occur in one particular sequence and are as follows:

Is it an ad or editorial material?

If an ad, what is the product category?

What brand is being advertised?

What features/benefits are being associated with the brand in the ad?

Are the associations presented in the ad believable?

Consumers may not necessarily decode an advertising message at all of these levels. The decision may be made that additional decoding is not worth the effort, or consumers may jump mentally to a second type of message-processing form—message encoding.

Encoding is how consumers answer the question Is it for me? In Zajonc's terms, encoding can be identified to be feeling while decoding is thinking related to a message. Similar to decoding, encoding may occur at several levels:

Does the situation depicted in the ad relate to me?

Have I ever been in the situation in the ad?

Are the actions depicted in the ad rewarding to me?

Would I find rewarding what is suggested by the ad message?

Should I act now to buy the product advertised?

Encoding and decoding may be separate and partially independent systems, independent in that either may occur first and that either may end without the other being activated. More likely, both may occur almost simultaneously. Results from left/right-brain research indicate that consumers may jump back and forth from thinking versus feeling while attending to ad messages.

How consumers cognitively process advertising messages is the topic of part II. How do consumers go about developing decoding and encoding thoughts related to advertising messages?

The structures of cognitive processes from advertising messages are the topics of chapter 4. Olson and Reynolds develop ''a rudimentary taxonomic scheme [of message-produced cognition] of attributes, consequences, and values based on levels of abstraction.'' The authors use a free-elicitation approach to measure cognitive structures—that is, consumers respond freely, in their own words, following simple tasks. The authors propose summary cognitive maps as a method of depicting how consumers relate message elements to their own values. Values are desired end states of existence. The importance of communicating product features to benefits to appropriate values is the strategic implication of chapter 4.

In chapter 5, Brock and Shavitt advocate producing commercials that attain stipulated cognitive-response criteria. Such an approach requires experimental variations of commercial content. Before reaching these conclusions, Brock and Shavitt compare cognitive responses and learning formulations of communication. They conclude that it is possible to specify conditions in which incomprehensible messages will be more persuasive than comprehensible counterparts. A detailed literature review on cognitive-response analysis is included in chapter 5.

The focus on the consumer as an active information processor in contrast to traditional learning theories is broadened by Saegert and Young in chapter 6. Similar to Brock and Shavitt in chapter 5, these authors describe message elaboration by the consumer as a substantial mediating cause for achieving advertising impact.

Details of a specific experiment on cognitive response as a mediating variable affecting purchase intentions are presented in chapter 7. Woodside offers ten recommendations on how to do research on cognitive responses to advertising messages. The results of the one study reported in chapter 7 support previous findings that ad recall is not affected by the level of consumer involvement with the ad. The author suggests that the question of whether or not consumers generate one or more thoughts while being exposed to an ad is a useful measure of the ad's effectiveness.

The six studies reviewed in chapter 8 lead Shanteau and Ptacek to conclude that the quality of information used to describe a product is more important than the quantity of information. The consumer-perceived importance of the information presented in an ad is an important issue for advertising strategy. Since weights of product attributes vary widely across different usage situations, consumer-preference orderings for brands will vary by usage situations.

Evidence is presented by Shanteau and Ptacek that consumers may average rather than add information to form an overall evaluation about a brand. Averaging is analogous to combining two liquids of different temperature that then reach an intermediate temperature. The implication is that presenting more information on different product features may produce lower evaluations than producing information on one product feature.

4
Understanding Consumers' Cognitive Structures: Implications for Advertising Strategy

Jerry C. Olson and
Thomas J. Reynolds

What do advertising managers need to know to develop efficient, successful strategies and tactics? A broad but somewhat trite answer is that they need to understand their consumers. Certainly, an understanding of consumers—in particular, an understanding of the reasons for their behavior—is extremely useful for developing effective advertising strategies.

Consider some of the basic questions about consumers that advertisers often ask but seldom answer satisfactorily: What do consumers know about my product/brand or those of my competitors? What do people think about when they consider buying a brand in my product category? What motivates people to buy my product? How do people respond to this advertisement, this promotion, this package design, this new brand, and so forth? Why do they respond like that? If advertisers knew the answers to questions like these, they would be well on their way to understanding the consumer. Such an understanding also would aid greatly in dealing with the difficult issues of advertising practice. However, advertisers have not produced satisfactory answers to such questions, perhaps because they have not developed the conceptual tools and measurement procedures that are necessary to determine such answers.

We believe that a key factor in developing a useful understanding of consumer behavior, perhaps the most important aspect, is consumers' cognitive structures of knowledge in memory. Researchers have widely recognized that such memory structures exert a major influence on behavior—both overt motor behaviors and internal mental behaviors; that is, cognitive structures are essential in explaining information-processing behavior and, in turn, the overt behaviors like purchase choice that are a function of those cognitive processes.

Some of the ideas discussed here were derived from research supported by grant no. 5901-0410-8-0151-1 to Olson from the Competitive Grants Office, Science and Education Administration, U.S. Department of Agriculture. We also acknowledge support from the Marketing Science Institute where Olson spent 1981-1982 as a visiting research professor, during which time he prepared this chapter.

It is important to recognize that knowledge structures or cognitive structures are not totally new concepts. Marketers and advertisers have been talking about consumer knowledge and cognitive structures for a long time, although usually not in those terms. For instance, familiar terms such as *product perceptions, brand-attribute beliefs, brand attitudes, brand images, brand personalities*, and so on refer to kinds of knowledge about products and brands. As this knowledge becomes organized, interrelated, or associated, it can be considered to form a structure of knowledge or cognitive structure.

Note that, at least conceptually, we do not restrict our consideration of the contents of a brand cognitive structure only to beliefs about product attributes. Almost any kind of mental representation can be considered as a component or element in cognitive structure, including beliefs, attitudes, and intentions as well as emotions and feelings, values, images and moods and representations of tastes, smells, and motor actions. Each of these representations can be considered to encode part of the meaning of an object such as a brand. Although these mental representations obviously differ along several dimensions and controversies exist as to the psychological reality of some of them, we suggest that all of these elements potentially can be represented in memory and, thus, are possible components of cognitive structure. Further, we believe it is important to develop theoretical schemes— really taxonomies of mental representations—to distinguish among these cognitive elements in interesting, useful ways.

In this chapter we present the rudimentary features of one such taxonomy of consumers' cognitive structures. We also describe the basic characteristics of a set of measurement procedures that have been used to identify these elements of cognitive structure. Finally, we discuss some of the implications for advertising research and strategy offered by such a perspective.

Conceptualizing Cognitive Structures

How should we conceptualize cognitive structures? Perhaps the most general perspective is to model cognitive structures as an associative network (compare Wickelgre 1981). Here, each mental representation or cognitive element—that is, each thing one knows about—is considered as a node in a network. Each node is linked to other nodes via associations or arcs. A network of associated representations might then be considered a cognitive structure.

Much work in cognitive psychology has focused on postulating and testing rather formal models of memory structure (for example, alternative hierarchical models). In contrast, relatively little consideration has been given to conceptualizing the content of memory. However, the content of memory is at least as interesting and important as its structure, especially to the advertising practitioner. For instance, many of the questions posed earlier seem to require more attention to the content of memory than to its organization. *What* do people think about when they think about my product, or company, or advertising campaign? *What* motivates behavior? *What* do people know about my brand?

We must emphasize, however, that we are also interested in aspects of structure. We certainly need to understand the basis for the linkages or associations between specific concepts—for example, the types of associations that people make between a specific attribute of a product and its subsequent benefits. In fact, these connections are key elements of content in that the associations encode the meaning of any particular node. Any single cognitive representation has little or no meaning; its meaning is defined by the concepts with which it is associated. This close relationship between memory content and structure implies that they cannot be examined independently. Content is revealed only through structure and vice versa. In sum, we are interested in the structure (though at a less-abstract level than that usually examined in cognitive psychology) as well as the content of cognitive structures in memory.

A few marketing researchers have developed conceptual schemes to describe the content and organization of consumers' cognitive structures, though not at the typical level of analysis used in cognitive psychology. For instance, Young and Feigin (1975) described the Grey benefit chain in which a product is linked to a concept termed the *emotional payoff* through a chain of benefits:

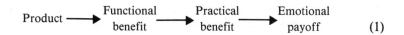

$$\text{Product} \longrightarrow \begin{array}{c}\text{Functional}\\\text{benefit}\end{array} \longrightarrow \begin{array}{c}\text{Practical}\\\text{benefit}\end{array} \longrightarrow \begin{array}{c}\text{Emotional}\\\text{payoff}\end{array} \qquad (1)$$

Gutman (1977; 1982) and Gutman and Reynolds (1977; 1979) have presented a means-end model (compare Howard 1977; Tolman 1932) of associated concepts beginning with product attributes and ending with terminal values (Rokeach 1973):

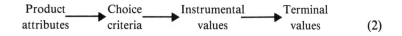

$$\begin{array}{c}\text{Product}\\\text{attributes}\end{array} \longrightarrow \begin{array}{c}\text{Choice}\\\text{criteria}\end{array} \longrightarrow \begin{array}{c}\text{Instrumental}\\\text{values}\end{array} \longrightarrow \begin{array}{c}\text{Terminal}\\\text{values}\end{array} \qquad (2)$$

Myers and Shocker (1980) described a similar set of linked concepts:

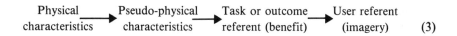

$$\begin{array}{c}\text{Physical}\\\text{characteristics}\end{array} \longrightarrow \begin{array}{c}\text{Pseudo-physical}\\\text{characteristics}\end{array} \longrightarrow \begin{array}{c}\text{Task or outcome}\\\text{referent (benefit)}\end{array} \longrightarrow \begin{array}{c}\text{User referent}\\\text{(imagery)}\end{array} \qquad (3)$$

Other researchers have discussed conceptual distinctions among types or levels of product attributes. Geistfeld, Sproles, and Badenhop (1977) identified three levels: an A level that includes abstract, multidimensional, difficult-to-measure attributes; a B level of less-abstract, still multidimensional, but measurable attributes; and a C level that denotes concrete, unidimensional, and measurable attributes. In similar fashion, Cohen (1979) discussed three levels of product attributes—namely, defining attributes or descriptive characteristics, instrumental attributes that include what the product does for the user, and valued outcome states.

We can see this work as attempts to develop taxonomies of the content and linkages in consumers' cognitive structures of product-related knowledge. Marketing researchers are beginning to conceptualize the important kinds of mental representations about products that people have acquired and the way in which these representations are organized or structured in memory.

Next, we present our taxonomy, which is similar to these earlier schemes. First, it is necessary to select the general basis for a taxonomy of cognitive representations in order to discover how cognitive representations differ? A potentially useful distinction among cognitive elements involves their level of abstraction. One basis for deciding on the level of abstraction of a particular mental representation might be in terms of its relationship to self (Gutman and Reynolds 1979); that is, as the linkages between representations and one's self-concept becomes stronger and more direct, the level of abstraction could be said to be higher.

Abstraction also can be thought of in much the same way as Geistfeld, Sproles, and Badenhop (1977) and Cohen (1979) did. Representations that are relatively direct reflections of physical features of the product (for example, color) may be considered concrete, or low in abstraction. Representations that are recodings of several concrete attributes (for example, style) involve higher-order meanings and are more abstract. Product characteristics at even higher levels of abstraction might be represented by functional consequences of product use (called benefits in the case of positive outcomes). Here we can see the closer linkages to self referred to by Gutman and Reynolds (1979) coming into the analysis. At the highest levels of abstraction, we can represent a product in terms of the values that may be achieved by its purchase and use. Obviously, such values are tied closely to our ideas of self (essentially by definition), and they are very abstract—that is, they are several levels away from any physical referent.

In summary, we have developed a rudimentary taxonomic scheme of attributes, consequences, and values based on levels of abstraction. These representations are ordered hierarchically from lower to higher levels of abstraction to form a kind of cognitive structure—a means-end structure (Howard 1977; Tolman 1932):

$$\text{Attributes} \longrightarrow \text{Consequences} \longrightarrow \text{Values} \qquad (4)$$

In our working model of consumer cognitive structures, we have made even finer distinctions in terms of abstraction by dichotomizing each of the three levels in model 4:

$$\underset{\text{attributes}}{\text{Concrete}} \longrightarrow \underset{\text{attributes}}{\text{Abstract}} \longrightarrow \underset{\text{consequences}}{\text{Functional}} \longrightarrow \underset{\text{consequences}}{\text{Psychosocial}} \longrightarrow \underset{\text{values}}{\text{Instrumental}} \longrightarrow \underset{\text{values}}{\text{Terminal}}$$

$$(5)$$

These categories permit a rather fine-grained analysis of the types of mental representations that a person may have stored about a product, the levels of abstraction reflected by those representations, and the extent to which those representations are linked together to form an overall means-end structure.

We should emphasize that all of these links are not present in every case. In certain instances, a consumer may know a brand has a particular product characteristic yet know little about the performance consequences of that attribute or of the valued end states the attribute can help to achieve. Thus, that person possesses little abstract meaning for this product attribute. In the next section we discuss the procedures we use to identify these concepts and linkages.

Identifying the Content and Organization of Cognitive Structure

We take a free-elicitation approach to measuring cognitive structure (compare Olson and Muderrisoglu 1979); that is, most of our techniques are characterized by the fact that subjects are given simple tasks to which they can respond freely, in their own words. It is as if the task elicits the responses from the subject without much thinking or cognitive effort. We design directed elicitation tasks that we hope will force subjects to verbalize, first, the salient concepts or distinctions they use to differentiate between products or brands (or whatever stimuli are of interest) and, second, the linkages, if any, among those concepts and outcomes/benefits and basic values; that is, we interpret subjects' verbal responses as reflecting the content and organization of their memory structures. Some of our directed elicitation tasks are intended to force consumers to reveal their means-end structures (see model 5) for a particular domain such as a product category. Then we apply a set of analytic procedures to these complex sets of individual-level responses that combines them into an aggregate, or group-level, map of cognitive structure.

The following discussion offers a simplified, bare-bones description of our approach for identifying the content and structure of consumers' cognitive structures. We should note that in an actual study we would not necessarily use these techniques exactly as specified here. We might make extensive modifications to these methods, and we probably would use additional procedures as well. Later in the chapter we discuss a general example of how this information can be used in the process of developing advertising strategy. There are, however, many other applications to which this kind of data regarding consumers' cognitive structures can be put, including copy testing, market segmentation, campaign monitoring or tracking, identifying new business opportunities, and product positioning. Space restrictions preclude a discussion of each application.

Triad Sorts

Usually we begin with a directed elicitation procedure derived from the basic repertory grid methodology, called the triadic sort task (see Kelly 1955). First, we select several examples from the domain of interest (for example, brands in a product category) and divide these into sets of three called triads. Then we present subjects with one triad at a time and ask them to "Tell me how two of these are alike and different from the third." The subjects state as many distinctions as they can and then are presented with the next triad, and so on.

This procedure is intended to elicit the salient distinctions a person uses to discriminate among stimuli in that domain (compare Gutman and Reynolds 1979; Kelly 1955). Although these distinctions may be at any level of abstraction, we usually find that most consumers make distinctions at the relatively concrete level of product attributes. However, some may discriminate products or brands at the more-abstract level of consequences. Occasionally, we find a consumer whose initial discriminations among products are at a value level, but this is rare. In sum, the triad task reveals the salient concepts used to discriminate (think about) the stimulus domain, but it does not reveal the entire means-end cognitive structure.

Laddering

To identify the full set of linkages proposed in model 5 (if they exist), consumers are given a laddering task. The purpose of laddering is to force the consumer up the ladder of abstraction—that is, to uncover the structural aspects of consumer knowledge as modeled by the means-end chain (for example, Gutman 1982; Gutman and Reynolds 1979). The laddering task begins by asking consumers to rate the concepts they elicited in the triad sort, often in terms of their importance in a purchase decision. Then the interviewer says something like, "You mentioned that (*a concept*) was important (or unimportant) to you. Why is it important (or unimportant)?" After the consumer answers, the interviewer asks the same basic question again but in terms of the subject's answer: "Why is that important to you?" The why questions are repeated for each answer until the respondent stops. It is usually clear when respondents reach the end because they will say something like "just because," or "it just is," or they will shrug their shoulders and say, "I don't know."

Not every laddering reaches the values level, although many do. The factors that determine the specific content and elaborateness of the means-end structure are not well specified as yet, but it is certain they are numerous and complex. They probably include the importance of the domain (its centrality), the type of initial distinctions that begin the ladder, and personalitylike traits of the consumer, among many other influences. Laddering data stimulate a variety of interesting questions about consumers' cognitive structures. For instance, at what level of the means-end structure do consumers normally make distinctions among brands in a product category? Do product categories (or consumers) vary in this respect? How complete is the means-end chain from the initial distinctions to basic values? Is there a small set of basic values to which all (or most) of the lower-level distinctions are linked? Next we describe the analytic procedures by which we aggregate the cognitive structures of different consumers and develop group-level, normative maps of cognitive structure.

Data Analysis

As the readers can well imagine, a variety of analyses can be performed on the large number of verbal responses produced by the triad and laddering tasks. The possibilities range from individual-level analyses like detailed descriptions (from different theoretical perspectives) of each respondent's idiosyncratic cognitive structure to quantitative analyses of the combined responses from many subjects. This section presents a description of one type of aggregate analysis that we have used with some success. Other analytic approaches are possible, of course. This set of analyses focuses on the verbal responses to the laddering task. Our objective is to produce an aggregate cognitive map that is normatively descriptive of the key features of the means-end structures of most subjects in a sample.

Content Analysis

The first step in analyzing the large number of laddering responses is to conduct a thorough content analysis of all the elicited concepts. We try to develop categories, or concept codes, that capture the essential aspects of most of the thoughts expressed by subjects in response to the laddering tasks. Then each thought/response from each subject is assigned a category code. This procedure removes the idiosyncratic expressions of similar basic thoughts. Thus, all laddering responses are now expressed in a set of standard concepts.

Some limitations to these procedures deserve mention. First, we recognize that different responses that are assigned the same cognitive code really may reflect somewhat different meanings. These meanings may be evident from the elicitation contexts provided by the different subjects. Identifying such subtle differences in the meaning of concepts requires a strictly individual-level analysis. We have sacrificed this level of precision in our content analysis in order to develop an aggregate cognitive structure that is reasonably faithful to the structures of most individuals. Second, our usual sample size of 40 to 50 consumers may seem too small to provide a representative set of concepts. However, we have found that relatively few new concepts are generated when the sample size is increased, even up to as many as 250 subjects. Moreover, each subject produces three to five ladders that greatly increases the number of means-end chains available for analysis. Finally, it seems that people have a similar and rather limited set of concepts in their cognitive structures, at least for the fairly mundane products we have examined so far. Even so, the resulting set of concepts should be considered a sample of the total population of concepts that people have in their cognitive structures for a domain, not a complete set.

Structural Analysis

By these procedures we identify the concepts of cognitive structure, the nodes, if you will, of an associative network theory of memory. It remains to identify the linkages among the concepts, the arcs of the network model. We begin by constructing a square matrix in which the rows and columns are denoted by the concept codes developed in the content analysis. The unit of analysis here is an adjacent pair of concepts—a linked pair of responses from the laddering task. Each pair of concepts is entered into the matrix by the following procedure. An entry is recorded in a particular row/column cell of the matrix each time the row concept preceded the column concept in the ladder responses; that is, whenever the row concept was the probe stimulus that elicited the column concept, an entry is made into that cell. Thus, the total entries in any cell of the matrix corresponds to the number of times (across all subjects) that particular concept (row) directly elicited the other concept (column).

This scoring procedure produces an asymmetrical dominance matrix. One can think of this matrix as a symbolic structure representing the aggregated cognitive structure for the group of subjects. We admit that certain features of cognitive structure are not captured in this analysis. For instance, we do not have direct information about the relative strength of the associations; we know only the frequency with which direct links were elicited. However, if desired, procedures could be developed to provide direct indications of strength (for example, subjects could rate the strength of each of their associations).

Then, all the cell entries are converted to binary form in order to simplify subsequent analyses and to eliminate associations that are mentioned infrequently. We select a somewhat arbitrary cut-off, usually four or five mentions, and assign a 1 to all cells that have that many entries or more and a 0 to the other cells. By this procedure, we have determined which linkages or associations among concepts will be considered as significant connections in subsequent analyses. We justify this procedure of ignoring connections that are mentioned seldom by our objective of developing a normative structure that reflects the key features of most individuals' structures. Here, we are not interested in studying differences among idiosyncratic structures.

Value-Structure Map

The resulting binary matrix is then treated as a directed graph that provides the basis for diagrammatically representing the normative cognitive structure as a complex tree diagram. A hypothetical example of such a diagram is presented in figure 4-1. The value-level concepts are positioned at the top because they are the abstract end concepts that are linked through a series of associations to the less-abstract concepts. The more-concrete attribute concepts tend to be positioned toward the bottom of the map since they are most often the probes that begin (or occur early in) the laddering process. Because of its focus on the value end states, we call this aggregate cognitive structure a value-structure map.

Note that the revealed structure in figure 4-1 is quite consistent with the network model of memory discussed earlier. The value-structure map identifies not only the concepts that are normatively salient across most subjects but also the major (most frequent) interconnections among those concepts. Both the content and structural characteristics are conceptualized from the means-end theoretical perspective discussed earlier; that is, the concepts usually are ordered in a hierarchical fashion such that relatively concrete concepts like product attributes lead to more-abstract concepts like consequences of use that in turn point to highly abstract end states like terminal

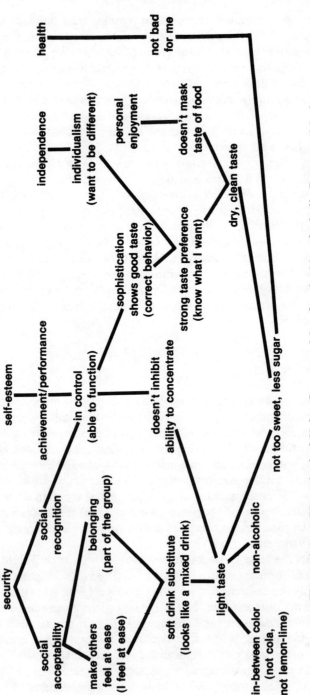

Figure 4-1. A Hypothetical Value-Structure Map for the Nonalcoholic-Beverage Market

values. Because such a structure is presumed to exert a powerful influence on behavior including choice behavior, information-processing behavior, and perceptual behavior, it can be called a perceptual map. Essentially, it describes how a particular group of subjects tends to perceive or think about a specific subdomain of the world. Note, however, that the amount, type, and depth of information provided by our approach is quite different from the perceptual maps generated by multidimensional scaling procedures. We believe our approach provides much richer data that has significantly greater practical usefulness.

Implications for Developing Advertising Strategy

In preceding sections we briefly described some of our procedures for identifying the content and organization of consumers' cognitive structures. We also presented an example of the fascinating kinds of data they provide. These data have many implications for a variety of problems facing advertisers, from copy testing to campaign evaluation to developing an advertising strategy. Strategy decisions, of course, pervade all the other issues and, thus, are of critical importance. Therefore, we conclude this chapter with some brief comments about advertising strategy and a description of how our procedures can be useful in developing effective advertising strategy.

What is Advertising Strategy?

First, what does advertising strategy mean? What are its key features? At what level and with what factors is strategy concerned? From our means-end perspective, the higher-order levels in cognitive structure—that is, the instrumental and terminal values of model 5—are a key aspect of advertising strategy. Strategists must select the values (or end states, goals, or benefits) that they will emphasize in the advertising. In addition, they must determine how the advertising will connect the product to these key end states. Finally, the specific characteristics of advertising—the product attributes mentioned, the models, the camera angles, the scenes presented, the plot, and so forth—must be selected and put together in such a way as to communicate effectively the connection between purchase and use of the product and achievement of the valued goal state.

The preceding discussion implies that multiple decisions at different levels are involved in developing advertising strategy. To distinguish these multiple features of advertising strategy a bit more clearly, we have identified five broad characteristics of advertising strategy. In a sense, these features identify different levels of analysis or different types of decisions involved in strategy formation. To be effective, each level or characteristic of the strategy must be appropriate for the audience; that is, each level of the strategy must fit with the cognitive structures of the target consumers. Moreover, the five levels of strategy must fit together in a consistent, mutually reinforcing way. The five levels of our advertising strategy model are listed from the broadest, most general level to the most concrete:

1. *Driving force:* the value orientation of the strategy; the end level on which to focus in the advertising;
2. *Leverage point:* the manner by which the advertisement will tap into, reach, or activate the value or end level of focus; the specific key way in which the value is linked to the specific features in the advertisement;
3. *Executional framework:* the overall scenario or action plot, plus the details of the advertising execution. The executional framework provides the vehicle by which the value orientation is to be communicated—especially, the gestalt of the advertisement; its overall tone and style;
4. *Consumer benefit:* the major positive consequences for the consumer that are to be communicated explicitly, verbally or visually, in the advertising;
5. *Message elements:* the specific attributes, consequences, or features about the product that are to be communicated, verbally or visually.

An Example

Making these five levels of decisions in developing an advertising strategy is a difficult task. We believe that all five types of decisions can be aided by appropriate information about consumers' cognitive structures. The following example shows how the value-structure map that we derive from the means-end responses elicited during laddering tasks can help the advertising strategist. First, consider again the hypothetical cognitive-structure map for the nonalcoholic-beverage market illustrated in figure 4-1. Note that each distinct branch or pathway of connected concepts represents a means-end ministructure within the overall cognitive structure. Figure 4-2 presents one of those means-end chains and shows how each level could be translated into one of the five decision levels involved in strategy formulation.

We believe that the levels-of-abstraction means-end conceptualization of cognitive structure provides a useful framework for thinking about advertising strategy. Also, we believe that the data we have developed regarding these cognitive structures are useful aids for developing and evaluating advertising strategies. Higher levels of abstraction—the concepts

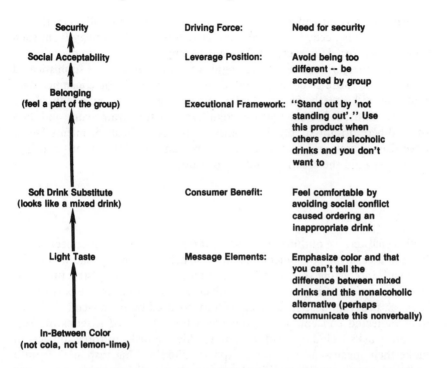

Security	Driving Force:	Need for security
Social Acceptability	Leverage Position:	Avoid being too different -- be accepted by group
Belonging (feel a part of the group)	Executional Framework:	"Stand out by 'not standing out'." Use this product when others order alcoholic drinks and you don't want to
Soft Drink Substitute (looks like a mixed drink)	Consumer Benefit:	Feel comfortable by avoiding social conflict caused ordering an inappropriate drink
Light Taste	Message Elements:	Emphasize color and that you can't tell the difference between mixed drinks and this nonalcoholic alternative (perhaps communicate this nonverbally)
In-Between Color (not cola, not lemon-lime)		

Figure 4-2. Relationships between Components of Advertising Strategy and Specific Elements in a Means-End Cognitive Structure

closely related to self such as feelings, expressive values, and psychological consequences—indicate possible end states that an advertiser might select as the driving force in an advertising strategy. Concepts at lower levels of abstraction, such as product attributes and functional outcomes, can provide clues as to possible means to those ends that could be communicated in the advertising. Finally, the strategist must develop a story, or overall plot (the executional framework), by which he or she can tie together all of these features and communicate them in an interesting, effective manner. Taken together, the choice of the ends and means and the particular ways in which their connection is communicated (benefit, executional framework, and leverage point) constitute an advertising strategy. In summary, this conceptualization of strategy is consistent with our means-end cognitive-structure model, and thus, our approach should prove useful for the analysis and development of advertising strategies.

We hasten to point out that we do not believe that it is easy to develop effective advertising strategy, even with data about consumers' means-end cognitive structures. Not every branch in a value structure necessarily is translated easily into an advertising strategy. In fact, substantial creative effort and skill is needed to develop effective advertising strategy from such value structures. However, we do want to emphasize that the overall conceptual framework of means-end cognitive structures and the sophisticated measures of those structures produce an organized set of consumer data that can aid greatly in developing creative and impactive advertising strategy. Thus, it is clear that the cognitive-structure framework and data offered here do not supply direct answers to the difficult problems facing advertising creators. Rather, they are an efficient tool—heuristic devices—to aid the creative-thinking process.

Summary

In this chapter, we outlined a program of research directed at conceptualizing and measuring consumers' cognitive structures in ways that are consistent with interesting theoretical perspectives about memory structures and that have practical implications for advertising practice. In the part of our research program described here, we have focused on means-end chains of interconnected concepts in cognitive structure. We used a series of free-response tasks including triad sorts and laddering tasks to force subjects to make their means-end structures explicit. The resulting responses from a group of people can be combined to form a normative cognitive structure. Because our focus is on the more-abstract levels, or end states (usually values), in the structure, we term these value-structure maps. This theoretical approach and the resulting value-structure data can be put to several practical uses including copy testing, campaign evaluation, and new-product development. In this chapter, however, we have chosen to illustrate their usefulness as aids in developing effective advertising strategy.

Cognitive-Response
Analysis in Advertising

Timothy C. Brock
and *Sharon Shavitt*

Improved application of the cognitive-response approach to advertising requires control over the design and execution of in-the-market commercial messages. This chapter develops this thesis by reviewing core principles of cognitive-response theory, by addressing methodological issues surrounding applications of the appoaoch to advertisement wear out, and by suggesting new insights into the persuasion process that could flow from a new type of research. Such research would be distinctive in its employment of commercials that satisfied predetermined psychological criteria.

Before taking up the potential of cognitive-response analysis for advertising, we offer a selective reprise of the theory; the basic tenets have been published elsewhere (for example, Perloff and Brock 1980; Petty, Ostrom, and Brock 1981), and excellent discussions of thought-listing technology are also available (Cacioppo and Petty 1981; Wright 1980).

Cognitive responses are the thoughts and ideas evoked by persuasive communications. Researchers postulate that these thoughts determine both immediate and long-term acceptance of the persuasive communication. In effect, individuals persuade themselves to adopt the position advocated by the communication. The advocated position may be consistent with persons' initial attitudes, in which case their thoughts may reinforce and strengthen their initial evaluation. Or the communication may be sufficiently compelling so as to change individuals' beliefs and ideas about the topic.

Cognitive-response theory may be contrasted with theories of persuasion that emphasize how learning of message facts and arguments is affected by variables external to the recipient, such as message content, source credibility, and type of communication channel. Indeed, learning of message content has been assigned a central role in traditional formulations of the persuasion process (Eagly 1974; Hovland, Janis, and Kelley 1953; Hovland and Weiss 1951; McGuire 1968; 1969). In contrast to this traditional view that acceptance is heavily dependent upon comprehension of the persuasive message, the cognitive-response approach contends that the impact of situational and individual-difference variables on persuasion depends upon the extent to which individuals articulate and rehearse their own idosyncratic thoughts.

Cognitive Response versus Learning Formulations: Illustration of Conflicting Predictions

In the social-psychology laboratory at Ohio State University, the distinction between learning theories of persuasion, with their emphasis on learning and recall of message elements, and cognitive-response theory, with its emphasis upon articulation of own thoughts, was pushed to new limits in a doctoral dissertation (Padgett 1982) that provided extreme conditions of message comprehension. Undergraduate subjects listened to taped three-minute advocacies of nuclear disarmament. In one form, the message was spoken entirely in Greek, a language unintelligible to the subjects. In another form, the English version of the message was scrambled by a band-pass filter so that, while retaining the overtones and sonorities of ordinary speech, the message was entirely gibberish. Subjects were simply told that they would be hearing speeches about nuclear disarmament delivered at the United Nations and that, in some cases, either a simultaneous translation was lacking or there was channel interference. Subjects were not told what position the speech advocated. Next, subjects filled out standard thought listings (for example, Cacioppo and Petty 1979) and attitudinal ratings (for example, Petty, Cacioppo, and Golden 1981). It is not surprising that many subjects, slightly more than half, refused to fill out the dependent measures or did so in a rigid fashion because they complained they could not understand the message. However, 45 percent of the subjects checked different values on semantic differential and Likert scales and listed more than one thought, more than one cognitive elaboration of the message. What Padgett (1982) found, therefore, was a substantial number of subjects who provided attitudinal ratings and cognitive elaborations of unintelligible messages. This outcome is not readily predictable from any theories of persuasion that require comprehension and recall of message elements. The outcome is consistent with the cognitive-response-theory emphasis on idiosyncratic-thought production and self-persuasion.

Our purpose in mentioning Padgett's research was to underscore one important area of disagreement between cognitive-response theory and traditional emphases on message-content learning. Part of the continuing excitement of cognitive-response theory is its ability to generate counterintuitive predictions like assigning persuasive value to unintelligible messages. Given that the ratio of own thoughts to message-element thoughts certainly will be higher in response to incomprehensible than to comprehensible messages, it is possible to specify conditions under which an incomprehensible message will be more persuasive than its comprehensible counterpart.

Cognitive-Response Analysis: A Brief Recapitulation

The first use of thought elicitation in conjunction with an attitude-change paradigm was an early dissonance experiment in which non-Catholic subjects listed implications of becoming a Catholic (Brock 1962). Many of these written implications were, of course, counterarguments to the discrepant behavior, becoming a Catholic. The obtained cognitive responses were analyzed to show how cognitive restructuring can be instigated by attitude-change pressure. In 1967, Brock showed that undergraduate recipients who anticipated a discrepant communication (for example, increase tuition) listed counterarguments in proportion to the magnitude of discrepancy of the forthcoming persuasive message. A year later, McGuire (1968), Greenwald (1968), and Weiss (1968) called attention to the importance of cognitive responses in the attitude-change process. Over the next decade, cognitive-response measures were employed increasingly in accounting for the effects of a variety of independent variables including message discrepancy (Brock 1967), source credibility (Cook 1969), distraction (Osterhouse and Brock 1970), anticipated discussion (Cialdini et al. 1976), issue involvement (Petty and Cacioppo 1979), personal involvement (Petty, Cacioppo, and Goldman 1981), and message repetition (Cacioppo and Petty 1979; 1980).

It is instructive to look closely at an important advance in cognitive-response theory—two experiments by Petty (1977). In the first experiment, subjects were asked to read several arguments about a social dilemma and to list their thoughts on the issue. The experimenter then assessed subjects' ability to recall their own thoughts and the message arguments, as well as their opinions on the two choice-dilemma questions, both immediately and a week later. On the one hand, the results showed that students recalled a greater proportion of their throughts than the arguments contained in the message. Moreover, ability to recall message arguments was not correlated with the delayed-opinion items, even when the arguments were weighted as to judge-rated and subject-rated persuasiveness. On the other hand, a significant relationship appeared between the ability to remember one's own thoughts and the delayed measures of opinion.

In another experiment, subjects read five highly or low persuasive arguments on the topic of raising the driving age to twenty-one. Subjects listed five thoughts on the subject and were instructed to memorize either their five thoughts or the five arguments. Attitude change was assessed both immediately and a week later by comparing the two experimental groups and a control group that read five neutral statements on the driving issue. The results revealed that regardless of whether they memorized thoughts or arguments, subjects who read the highly persuasive arguments were most favorable to increasing the driving age to twenty-one when attitudes were measured immediately. Only subjects in the highly persuasive message condition who memorized their thoughts continued to favor increasing the driving age to twenty-one when attitudes were assessed a week later. The results support the cognitive-response prediction that rehearsal of one's thoughts is a more-important determinant of persistence of persuasion than one's rehearsal of message arguments.

Petty's (1977) results are consistent with the rest of the cognitive-response literature (Petty, Ostrom, and Brock 1981) in showing a virtual

absence of relationship between recall of message arguments and acceptance of the message. The most noteworthy outcome, however, is his suggestion that own-thought rehearsal is the key determinant of long-term persistent attitude change.

Do Persuasion-Elicited Thoughts Cause Attitude Change?

Cogent analyses of this question were published by Wright in the *Journal of
Consumer Research* (1980) in an article, "Message-Evoked Thoughts: Persuasion Research Using Thought Verbalizations," and by Cacioppo,
Harkins, and Petty (1981) in a chapter, "The Nature of Attitudes and
Cognitive Responses and Their Relationships to Behavior." These authors
reviewed a variety of experimental studies that favored the thoughts-cause-
attitudes chain. According to Cacioppo, Harkins, and Petty:

> Implementation of statistical procedures to assess causal ordering of
> cognitive responses and persuasion has indicated that cognitive responses
> may have mediated yielding to persuasion (e.g., Osterhouse & Brock, 1970)
> but that the reverse causal ordering was not operating (e.g., Petty &
> Cacioppo, 1977). The most parsimonious account of these findings is that
> cognitive responding can mediate yielding to persuasion. This does not
> mean that a third variable is not mediating both cognitive responses and
> yielding to persuasion in some contexts. It means only that the simplest ac-
> count of a wide body of literature is that cognitive responding influences
> the final attitude. [p. 49]

When cognitive responding is manipulated directly, the causal pathway
is especially clear. For example, Cacioppo and Sandman (1981) report
physiological interventions aimed at increasing counterarguments.
"Operantly conditioned and pace-maker induced accelerated heart-rate led
to the generation of more counterarguments and greater resistance to persuasion compared to basal or decelerated heart rate" (p. 103).

In sum, there is good evidence that cognitive responses in persuasion are
one important causal determinant of attitude change.

Potential of Cognitive-Response Analysis for Advertising

In the late 1960s, before the explanatory promise of cognitive-response
analysis had spread beyond the invisible college of experimental social
psychologists to students of persuasion in marketing and other applied
disciplines, Leavitt, Waddell, and Wells (1970) elicited thoughts about commercials. As part of a standard day-after recall test, respondents were asked

"What did the commercial make you think of? That is, what thoughts came to your mind as you watched it?" Leavitt and co-workers used the designation personal-product response to code thoughts that referred clearly to an advertised product, that involved a personal experience, and that used the first-person singular or plural. Good intercoder agreement was obtained, 95 percent, as well as very high test-retest reliability for four cereal commercials, .93. More important, the researchers obtained two kinds of evidence for the validity of the elicited thoughts. The first was a significant association between extent of personal-product responses and a subsequently obtained report, from the same respondents, of intent to purchase. The second evidence came from a follow-up experiment in which Chicago housewives agreed to refrain from eating during the morning of their research appointments. The hungry housewives gave more personal-product reponses to food commercials than a control group of housewives who ate just before viewing the same commercials. Thus, Leavitt and associates provided an early demonstration of the fruitfulness of measuring idiosyncratic cognitive responding.

Leavitt, Waddell, and Wells were sensitive to the problem of reactivity of the thought-elicitation question: "Perhaps the respondent felt committed to buying the product after telling the interviewer about her personal response. This problem would be avoided by using as the experimental variable *commercials with different levels of response* instead of respondents with different levels of response" (1970, p. 15). Their suggestion to use commercials that met predetermined response levels is important because it adumbrates the main theme of this chapter—namely, produce commercials that attain stipulated cognitive-response criteria.

Since adequate reviews of cognitive-response-theory implications for commercial messages have been published (for example, Wright 1980; 1981; Cacioppo and Petty 1980; Petty and Cacioppo 1983), we focus on two studies (Cacioppo and Petty 1980, experiment 2; Calder and Sternthal 1980) because they dealt with a central issue in advertising—namely, the effect of advertisement repetition on persistent attitude change—and because they illustrated our methodological concerns. In these experiments, analysis of cognitive responses was used to account for factors that might determine advertisement wear out. By wear out we mean "the reduction, with repetition, of the commercial's power to persuade, or to engender favorable attitudes toward the product [that is, brand preference, in conrast to brand awareness]" (Cacioppo and Petty 1980, p. 98).

Effects of Massed Repetitions on Advertisement Wear Out

Cacioppo and Petty posited the following two-factor cognitive-response formulation for message repetition:

Repeated exposure to the same message through moderate levels should act primarily to provide additional opportunities for attending to, thinking about, and elaborating upon the message arguments. At high levels of message repetition, however, reactance and/or tedium should begin guiding *and biasing* message elaborations and thereby alter persuasion—in other words, motivational factors may directly affect cognitive response processes, which then modulate persisting attitude change. Hence, we expected that the relationship between message repetition and persisting attitude change would be curvilinear (increasing then decreasing) across exposure frequencies when very convincing message arguments were used. [1980, p. 102]

Preliminary Study. In a preliminary study, experiment 1, introductory psychology students listened to messages on headphones, and message repetitions were massed—that is, heard all at once, not spaced apart by other programming. Attitude scores, corrected to partial out effects other than repetition of content, supported the two-factor formulation. Figure 5-1 from Cacioppo and Petty (1980, p. 106) shows that long-term attitude change (measured a week after the communication) increased and then decreased with repeated exposures to the message. At the same time, there was a tendency for counterargumentation to decrease and then increase (see the bottom panel of figure 5-1). Hence, the conclusion that the attitudinal effects of repeated presentations were attributable, at least in part, to the elicited cognitive responses appeared to have high internal validity.

Method of Experiment 2. In the follow-up experiment, community volunteers participated in a study of the sound quality of commercials (Cacioppo and Petty 1980). The individuals were assigned randomly to the cells of a three (exposure frequency: one, three or five presentations)-by-three (argument type: strong, weak, or novel) between-subjects factorial design. The messages advocated an unpopular action—namely, increasing the subscription price of the local newspaper. These commercials consisted of question-and-answer pairings that allowed a listing of arguments in favor of the newspaper price increase. The arguments were strong (for example, the paper plans to use the money to increase news coverage), weak (for example, the paper plans to use the money in ways similar to those used when it last increased the price), or novel and weak (for example, the paper plans to use the money to increase advertising space and cut down on excess news coverage). As in the preliminary experiment, the messages were massed, heard all at once, and followed by thought listing. Finally, a week to two weeks later, the principal attitude-dependent measure was administered in disguised fashion, as part of an unrelated survey.

Results of Experiment 2. The attitudinal results shown in figure 5-2 indicated that the strong message was more effective than the weak or novel

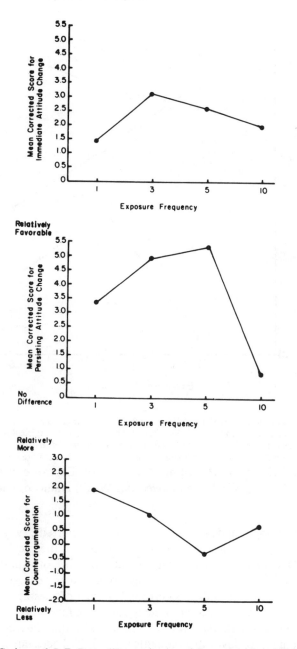

Source: J.T. Cacioppo & R.E. Petty, "Persuasiveness of Communications is Affected by Exposure Frequency and Communication Cogency: A Theoretical and Empirical Analysis of Persisting Attitude Change," in *Current Issues and Research in Advertising*, J. Leigh & C. Martin, eds. (Ann Arbor: University of Michigan, 1980), p. 106. Reprinted with permission.

Figure 5-1. Effects of Exposure Frequency on Mean Corrected Scores for Cognitive and Attitudinal Response

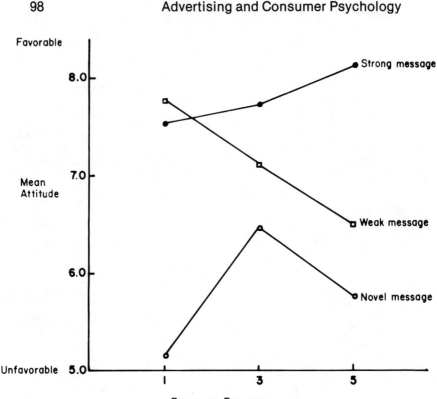

Source: J.T. Cacioppo & R.E. Petty, "Persuasiveness of Communications is Affected by Exposure Frequency and Communication Cogency: A Theoretical and Empirical Analysis of Persisting Attitude Change," in *Current Issues and Research in Advertising*, J. Leigh & C. Martin, eds. (Ann Arbor: University of Michigan, 1980), p. 112. Reprinted with permission.

Figure 5-2. Effects on Persisting Attitudes of Exposure Frequency to Strong, Weak, and Novel (but Weak) Audiocommercials

message (Cacioppo and Petty 1980). More important, wear out was demonstrated by the declining attitude scores for the weak and novel messages. One could speculate that a greater number of exposures would have led to wear out in the strong message condition as well. Analysis of the cognitive-response data indicated effects for type of message: The strong message elicited fewer counterarguments and more favorable thoughts than the weak or novel messages. The authors concluded that the extent to which counterarguments or favorable thoughts were elicited determined the extent to which message arguments were accepted or believed.

Comment. Experiment 2 is noteworthy in that it constitutes one of the few studies in which analysis of listed thoughts could account for attitudinal differences between messages and in which the messages were constructed to mimic real commercials with varying strengths. Independent manipulation of commercial attributes was a valuable advance, a point to which we return later in this chapter. The results were also noteworthy in that they implicated cognitive responses to commercials as a determinant of persistent attitude change.

The experiment left some loose ends, however. The authors proposed that "when message repetition becomes excessive, and as unbiased analyses cease, motivational factors operate upon these message elaborations, and recipients focus their cognitive energies on counterarguing the now obnoxious appeal" (Cacioppo and Petty 1980, p. 117). This interpretation implied increase in counterarguing with increase in exposure frequency as in experiment 1 and as in previous laboratory research (Cacioppo and Petty 1979, p. 103). However, such an increase in counterarguing was not obtained in the present experiment. Clearly, naturalistic study of higher-exposure frequencies may be needed to allow increased counterarguing to reveal itself. In real life, wear-out-instigating counterarguing may not occur until after ten or more exposures (we return to this issue in the next section).

A second problem concerns overall external validity. Massed presentation of taped interviews about newspaper price increases, while outfitted here with an adequate cover story, is remote from typical commercial fare and the ordinary regimen of commercial presentations. Commercials usually do not focus upon justification of price increases and usually are spaced apart with interstitial programming. Unfortunately, the literature appears to be completely devoid of appropriate research: for example, within-subjects designs with massed versus naturalistically spaced repetitions of alternate forms of the same commercial. This design not only would afford an experimental assessment of the differences in types of spacing but also would do so with much more power. A within-subjects design uses each subject as his own basis for comparison so that differences in behavior across experimental conditions are detected more easily.

Effects of Spaced Repetitions on Wear Out

Method. Calder and Sternthal (1980) used real commercials with naturalistic spacing. Although details about the ingredients of the commercials were omitted from their report, they tell the reader that commercials were for two nationally distributed products, one that is purchased in supermarkets and that is unfamiliar to subjects and another that is a nonsupermarket product that is well known. The subjects, Northwestern University students, were paid to watch TV programs over a three-week period and were run in groups of about twenty; their average age was about twenty-one. Table 5-1 shows how the materials were distributed, and table 5-2 gives the overall design for the experiment. Figure 5-3 indicates the flow of events

Table 5-1
Stimulus Materials

			Flight Length		
			1	*3*	*6*
Week	*Session*	*Program*	*Session*	*Sessions*	*Sessions*
1	1	Cannon			X
	2	Blue Knight			X
2	3	Hawaii 5-0			X
	4	Cannon		X	X
3	5	Barnaby Jones		X	X
	6	Bronk	X	X	X

Source: B.J. Calder and B. Sternthal, "Television Commercial Wearout: An Information Processing View," *Journal 1 Marketing Research* 17 (1980):173-186. Reprinted with permission.
Note: The X's denote programs viewed.

during a program. The pool-size factor refers to the number of different commercials that were shown for a particular brand. In terms of subjects' reactions to product A, the number of different commercials for product A constitutes the pool size, whereas the number of commercials for product B is the environmental pool size. After the last session, subjects listed their thoughts. Finally, the subjects were shown commercials for products again and rated the semantic differential items. The authors argued that this procedure insured that all subjects were reacting to the same stimulus and thus minimized the effects of previous viewings.

Results. The semantic differential ratings were factor analyzed to produce derived scores for evaluation of the commercials and of the two products. The rationale for this approach to multiple dependent variables was that there was no a priori way of knowing what a given adjective pair—for example, not useful/useful—meant to subjects. It might reflect an attitudinal position or possibly some other judgmental dimension. The use of factor-analytic-derived scores meant that the items comprising commercial evaluation were the same for products A and B but that the items comprising product evaluation were different: A included bad/good, harmful/beneficial, and foolish/wise; and B included bad/good, nonuseful/useful, and undesirable/desirable.

The main results for evaluation, as shown in figure 5-4, indicated wear out for judgments of both products and both commercials as a function of flight length. In advertising jargon, *flight length* refers to the number of sessions for which a group of subjects was exposed to a given combination of pool size and environmental pool size. Thus, with eighteen exposures of real commercials, embedded naturalistically in real programming, decay in attitude was demonstrated strikingly. With the exception of the commercial

Table 5-2
Summary of the Experimental Design

		One Session			Three Sessions			Six Sessions		
Pool Size	Environmental Pool Size	Exposures	Pool-Size Redundancy	Environmental Redundancy	Exposures	Pool-Size Redundancy	Environmental Redundancy	Exposures	Pool-Size Redundancy	Environmental Redundancy
1	1	Low	High	High	Moderate	High	High	High	High	High
	3	Low	High	Low	Moderate	High	Low	High	High	Low
	1	Low	Low	High	Moderate	Low	High	High	Low	High
3	3	Low	Low	Low	Moderate	Low	Low	High	Low	Low

Flight Length spans the three session groups.

Source: B.J. Calder and B. Sternthal, "Television Commercial Wearout: An Information Processing View," *Journal of Marketing Research* 17 (1980):173-186. Reprinted with permission.

Note: Subjects saw either 3 (low exposure), 9 (moderate exposure), or 18 (high exposure) commercials for product A and product B. For a given product (A or B), either the same commercial was seen each time (high pool-size redundancy) or each commercial was seen only a third of the time (low redundancy). For the environmental product (A for B and B for A), either the same commercial was seen each time (high environmental redundancy) or each commercial was seen only a third of the time (low environmental redundancy). A particular configuration of these three values identifies a cell in the design.

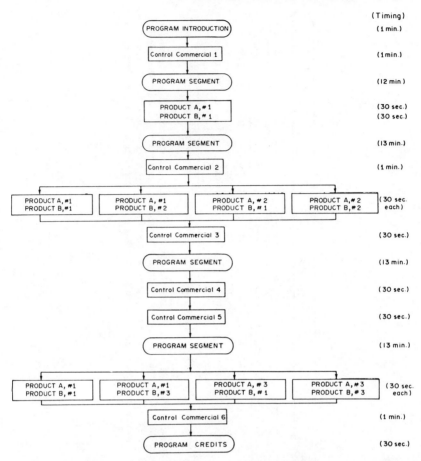

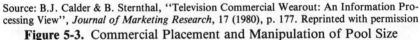

Source: B.J. Calder & B. Sternthal, "Television Commercial Wearout: An Information Processing View", *Journal of Marketing Research*, 17 (1980), p. 177. Reprinted with permission
Figure 5-3. Commercial Placement and Manipulation of Pool Size

for product B, this wear out was not affected by the number of executions for the product (pool size) or the product's dominance in executions (environmental pool size).

The results for the cognitive-response data were mixed. Product A elicited more total thoughts as a function of flight length, but there were no parallel effects on measures of positive and negative thoughts. For product B the results showed, in line with the theoretical formulation, that cognitive processing became more negative at extreme flight lengths. Specifically, an index score (positive-negative thoughts) increased from low to moderate exposures and decreased from moderate to high exposures. Of course, this inverted-U function was akin to that obtained for favorable thoughts in laboratory studies of message-repetition effects (for example, Cacioppo and Petty 1979, p. 103).

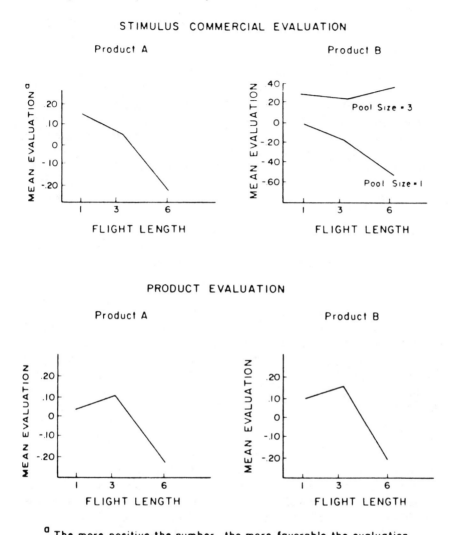

STIMULUS COMMERCIAL EVALUATION

Product A   Product B

PRODUCT EVALUATION

Product A   Product B

[a] The more positive the number, the more favorable the evaluation

Source: B.J. Calder and B. Sternthal, "Television Commercial Wearout: An Information Processing View", *Journal of Marketing Research*, 17 (1980), p. 185. Reprinted with permission.

Figure 5-4. Effects of Flight Length (Repetitions) on Evaluations of Commercials and Products

Comment. We agree with the authors' speculation that the absence of more-robust support for the mediational role of cognitive responses stems from the huge time gaps between viewings of the commercials and the one-time listing of thoughts that came at the end of the last session. While we wish that listings had been collected in greater temporal proximity to the viewings of the commercials, we appreciate how such collection might have interfered with the naturalism of meeting as a group in multiple sessions, ostensibly to rate TV programs.

Finally, Calder and Sternthal (1980) speculated as follows: "It is likely that many of the cognitive responses subjects generated were not closely related to the stimulus commercials" and, further, that "cognitive responses may not take the form of positive or negative stimulus reactions" (p. 186). We agree with Calder and Sternthal that cognitive responses need not take the form of positive and negative stimulus reactions and that cognitive responses unrelated to communication stimuli might occur. However, what is puzzling in their treatment is their apparent neglect to scrutinize the responses they did collect to ascertain whether and to what extent responses "not closely related to the stimulus commercials" were in fact occurring. According to cognitive-response theory, such idiosyncratic and derivative responses may influence long-term acceptance of commercials perhaps because they are the original constructions of the recipients and not merely rote parrotings of elements from the commercial message (Perloff and Brock 1980).

We have described the studies of Cacioppo and Petty (1980) and Calder and Sternthal (1980) in some detail because they attempted to elucidate the mediational role of cognitive responses in advertisement acceptance. Although a number of methodological weaknesses were noted, all of the shortcomings, with one exception, appeared readily remediable in subsequent replications. The one exception that may take advertising researchers greater effort to correct is the current lack of control over the principal independent treatment, the commercials. Recall that for proprietary reasons, Calder and Sternthal (1980) could provide no inkling to the reader concerning the substance of their focal commercials.

Such chains have to be cast off. The main practical agenda of this chapter is to induce directors of advertising, and other managers (brand managers) who are responsible for requisitioning commercials, to break the hegemony of the creative departments. Commercials should be designed, from the beginning to meet predetermined psychological criteria, just as Clark Leavitt suggested more than a decade ago (Leavitt, Waddell, and Wells 1970, p. 15). For example, commercials could be designed to meet the following standard: a decline or no increase in counterarguing with fifteen exposures. Art, wit, and theme consistency are rubrics for sets of criteria that should be subordinated to psychological effectiveness, defined, we suggest, in cognitive-response terms.

The student of cognitive-response analysis (for example, Petty and Brock 1981) readily understands why the laboratory investigator needs to concoct experimental persuasive communications and why he cannot be constrained to use preexisting editorials or other rhetorical messages. In

Cacioppo and Petty (1980) we have just seen the utility of their construction from scratch of commercials that varied in strength and novelty. In order to capitalize upon the potential of cognitive-response analysis for advertising, it is essential to have the cooperation of creative departments. Cooperation by ad creators with researchers not only will lead to commercials that are resistant to the corrosion of wear out but also will facilitate new insights into the persuasion process. These insights could constitute a basis for more-effective advertising.

In the concluding sections of this chapter, we speculate about the shape and texture of these crucial insights. Clear exposition of our hunches led us to think in terms of research plans and designs. In most of these designs, experimental variation of commercial content is an essential feature.

**Impact of Rehearsal of Message Arguments
and of Own Thoughts on Acceptance
and Recall of a Commercial Message**

Cognitive-response theory emphasizes the role of own thoughts in determining the immediate and persisting acceptance of a persuasive message. Can commercial messages be designed that instigate cognitive responding with own thoughts to a greater extent than cognitive responding with message elements? If so, recipient-generated responses should lead to more-persuasive impact than message-originated or message-modifying responses.

Another question concerns the extent to which the recipient of an advertisement perceives his responses as uniquely his own in contrast to perceiving his responses as similar to those of other recipients of the message. Cognitive-response theory suggests that unique, idiosyncratic responding will increase persistence of message acceptance. The proposed study, therefore, includes a manipulation of perceived response uniqueness.

Three separate experiments should be performed to assess the impact of thought rehearsal on persuasion. In all three experiments the subjects will view a TV commercial for a lotion. In the story-board experiment, subjects will rehearse thoughts about the message by filling in missing printed statements below the pictures that comprise the story board. This technique is akin to reproducing the script for the commercial when presented with ordered snapshots of the commercial. In the playback-sans-audio experiment, the commercial will be played several times without sound, thus omitting any voices or voice-overs. Recipients may rehearse message elements or their own responses or both. In the third experiment, product use, subjects will be given standard instructions for sampling the lotion so that the time spent in trying out lotion is equivalent to the writing time for story board and for watching playback sans audio.

The purpose of these treatments is to study rehearsal under varying conditions of product vividness and message distractibility. We assume that product vividness will be greater under product use than story board or playback sans audio. We assume that distraction will be maximum under playback sans audio. In each of the three experiments there would be three basic conditions: A = message arguments, B = own thoughts, and C = control. An overview of the design is given in figure 5-5. In condition A, subjects will be induced to rehearse and retain the arguments contained in the television commercial. In condition B, the rehearsal and retention emphasis will be on their own throughts (cognitive response). Condition C (control) subjects will not be induced to retain any information.

Three different versions of a television commercial will be produced for these three conditions. These same commercials will be used in all three experiments. The design is essentially the same in each study, with the major difference being the type of rehearsal-inducing task employed.

Cognitive Uniqueness

Following the rehearsal phase, subjects in condition B of all three experiments will undergo a uniqueness manipulation. They will be told by the experimenter that he has looked over the thoughts they listed immediately after seeing the ad. Half of the subjects will be assigned randomly to the low-uniqueness subgroup and will be informed that their thoughts were representative of the majority of respondents. The experimenter may say, "A lot of people shared your ideas. Those are important considerations for many people, and you expressed them well." The other half of the subjects, in the high-uniqueness subgroup, will be told that their responses were quite unique, that no else had thought of those answers: "Very few people thought of what you thought of. Those are important considerations and you expressed them well."

Hypotheses

The prediction is that, in all three experiments, subjects in the own-thought-rehearsal condition (condition B) will show greater recall of their own thoughts and will be more persuaded by the ad and will show greater preference for the advertised brand than subjects in the other two conditions.

Stage 1 (Message)	*Condition A*	*Condition B*	*Condition C*
Ad viewing	Ad emphasis is on recall of message.	Emphasis is on production and retention of own thoughts.	No emphasis is on any type of recall.
Stage 2	*Condition A*	*Condition B*	*Condition C*
Thought listing	All subjects are asked to list their own thoughts (cognitive responses) about the commercial. Experimenter then goes to search for cards.		
Stage 3 (Rehearsal)	*Condition A*	*Condition B*	*Condition C*
Story boards (experiment 1)	Fill-in captions with parts of message.	Fill-in with own ideas of what could be said.	Story board is for another ad. Fill-in with own ideas.
or Playback sans audio (experiment 2)	Same ad (without audio) is played back to subjects.		Different ad is played to subjects (without audio).
or Product use (experiment 3)	Subjects are given a sample of the product to try in the lab.		Subjects are given another (irrelevant) product to try in the lab.
	Experimenter returns, saying he will mail cards.		
Stage 4 (Uniqueness)		*Condition B*	
		Low uniqueness: Subjects are told their responses were very similar to those of many other respondents. *High uniqueness*: Subjects are told their responses were very unique, relative to other respondents.	
Stage 5 Dependent measures	Measure of belief about product (attitude scale), recall of message points, recall of own thoughts listed, behavioroid measure (rank order of preference for brands), and behavioral measure (choice of one).		

Figure 5-5. Experimental Design: Rehearsal of Message Arguments and Own Thoughts

The rehearsal techniques of the three experiments are being tried in our laboratory for the first time. We know of no previous experimental advertisement research that varied message content to instigate differential cognitive responding, that provided different postmessage thought-rehearsal conditions, and that yoked message to rehearsal condition so as to maximize idiosyncratic positive responding and corresponding persistent acceptance of the message.

Test of Three Theories of Cognitive-Response Effectiveness: Ownness Bias, Self-Schematic Processing, and Personal Involvement

A number of investigators have shown that self-originated rather than message-paraphrasing or message-modifying responses are better recalled and more determinative of persistent persuasion. Why is this so? There are at least three conceptually distinct accounts. Perloff and Brock (1980) propose an ownness bias, according to which persons place a high value on products associated with the self, including their own responses to a persuasive message. Individuals may prize especially their own thoughts because of territorial motivation; coveting personal space may extend to cognitive components of that space. From another perspective, an ownness bias may stem from uniqueness motivation, individuals' need to see themselves as different from other people. Thus, own thoughts are viewed as more unique, original, creditable, and hence, of greater value than arguments contained in someone else's persuasive message. Higher valuation of own thoughts is expected to occur especially in propaganda situations—that is, those in which intent to persuade is perceived. Three other motivational determinants may contribute to the ownness bias: (1) instinctual libidinal investment in extensions of the self (psychoanalytic school), (2) innate tendency to value like-self objects (Kohlberg's stages), and (3) suspicion of external communicators and ascription to them of hidden motives.

Self-schematic-processing theory (Markus 1977) states that people possess a better-developed cognitive schema for self-related information than for other types of information. Thus, information about the self or associated with the self (like one's thoughts) can be processed more extensively than information from other sources. Deeper and more-extensive processing of own thoughts should lead to more-persistent acceptance of a persuasive message if the elicited thoughts are primarily favorable to the message's advocacy. Closely related to self-schematic processing are demonstrations that self-generated material is better remembered than information produced externally (for example, verbatim points from the message). Finally, it is possible to ask subjects to encode information for its meaning to them versus to others, not the subjects. The meaning of the information is likely to be more salient in the former condition and to lead to more-persuasive impact.

The third theoretical perspective stems originally from marketing-literature notions such as personal involvement, needs connections, bridging experiences, and the like (for example, Greenwald, Leavitt, and Obermiller 1980; Krugman 1967). According to these accounts, establishing and/or strengthening links between one's needs and a particular product should increase involvement and the self-generation of cognitions that contribute to greater persuasive impact.

We envisage a crucial experiment in which we pit the three theoretical accounts—ownness bias, self-schematic processing, and personal involvement—against one another. As in the previous rehearsal-impact study, we would use the format of the thought-elicitation procedure to make one or the other of the three processes salient. The outcome of the experiment will help to clarify what is going on in self-persuasion and thereby will guide construction of commercial messages that capitalize on the most likely internal mental process.

Context of Cognitive Responses: Advertisement versus In Store

The relationship between the advertisement context, in which cognitive responses are first elicited, and the context in which those responses must be accessed to influence purchasing behavior has not been studied. Often, of course, there is no match between the advertisement context and the in-store context (Bettman 1979). Recent psychological research on state-dependent learning indicates that what is learned in a particular state—for example, a happy mood—may be better recalled when that same state is aroused again rather than a competing state—for example, a depressed mood. It is possible, at least by analogy, that cognitive responses to advertisements are more readily accessed when an individual is in the original ad-reception environment—for example, watching TV—than when he or she is shopping at his or her favorite supermarket. This is because watching TV induces feelings that are more similar to the feelings engendered during the original production of those cognitive responses.

How can cognitive responses be elicited so that transfer occurs from the ad-reception context to the purchase context—for example, from the watch-TV-at-home context to the shop-in-store context? The importance of own thoughts (as opposed to message elements) is especially apparent in answering this question. Message responses that are stimulus bound (for example, reproduction of message points) rather than recipient bound are less likely to get transferred to the in-store context.

We propose testing commercials that heighten the link between store thoughts and favorable thoughts about the product. The objective here is not traditional in-store recognition but in-store reproduction or in-store accessibility of self-generated favorable responses to the product. Ostrom and Brock (1968) reported a technique whereby subjects are led to make direct bonds between a belief and a value. In their study, they paired statements from a persuasive message that subjects had just read with general ideas or values, which supposedly were relevant in some way. The subjects were to circle one key word in the message excerpt and one key word in the general idea and then draw a link between them. The centrality of the general values was manipulated through differential selection of the ideas, based on results of a previous scaling study. The purpose of the task was to facilitate the linking of newly acquired (message-advocated) attitudes to values. This same technique can be applied to making direct bonds between the consumer's notion of his or her store and favorable responses to an advertisement. In fact, the piped-in programming in certain stores and supermarkets already may be having a bonding effect. Several stores play their advertisements and jingles over their public-address system, thus reminding shoppers of advertised specials while they are in a position to make a purchase.

Effects of Program Context, Signal for Commercial, and Competitive-Ad Proximity on Cognitive Responses

The environment for a commercial ad may be dangerous to its health. The metaphor implies that ad effectiveness may be impaired by a number of exogenous factors. The most obvious is the context for the ad, the prior and posterior programming. Regarding prior programming, implications for cognitive responding are unclear because contrasting predictions are plausible. On the one hand, if a viewer's orientation toward prior programming is negative, then the ensuing commercial may gain favorable responses by being contrasted with the negative-thought-eliciting prior programming. On the other hand, negative feelings toward the prior programming could carry over and contaminate the ensuing commercial. Ambiguity similarly surrounds possible effects of posterior programming. Thus, the effect of the positivity/negativity of a program environment on an ad appears to be an open empirical question.

Program intensity may affect cognitive responses in more-predictable ways. By program intensity, we mean the extent to which the typical viewer or reader becomes preoccupied and involved with the program material. The hypothesis is that more-favorable cognitive responses will be elicited by ads that are presented in a context of low rather than high intensity of adjacent programming. If preceding programming is very intense, attentive cognitive processing of the ensuing ad will be impaired. Similarly, if the ad is followed by intense programming, cognitive-response processes will be impeded by processing of the program itself. Postadvertisement programming that was unengaging and reminiscent in some ways of the preceding advertisement would present an ideal environment for favorable cognitive responding. Our hunch is that favorable cognitive responding will succumb more readily than counterarguing to high-intensity postadvertisement programming. Of course, we recognize that while high-intensity programming can impair cognitive processing of an ad, it may help in other ways by preventing channel switching. How frequently does a trade-off arise between viewer retention and cognitive-response instigation?

In addition to program positivity and program intensity, the signal that a commercial is imminent may affect cognitive responding. To signal a commercial by saying, in effect, "Here's a message you ought to think about because other thoughtful viewers have found it helpful" might work better (elicit fewer counterarguments) than typical lead-ins such as "don't go away," and so forth. Lead-ins to commercials influence cognitive responding by affecting the likelihood that the viewer is open and ready to elaborate upon the points in the message. Most lead-ins appear to fail in this respect because they appear to constitute forewarning that stimulates counterarguing (Brock 1967).

Another environmental variable is the temporal proximity of competing advertisements. In this discussion it is helpful to distinguish between an original, or focal, ad or product and a second, or competing, ad or product. Our hunch is that spacing of more than ten minutes may be necessary to permit adequate processing of cognitive responses to the focal advertisement. However, this rule of thumb could be liable to many exceptions. For example, if the focal ad includes comparison with a competing product, encountering the competitor soon after the focal ad might reinforce a superiority claim that had been made in the focal ad.

The temporal interval between the focal and a competing ad can be varied. An interesting hypothesis is that a focal-competing ad sequence that allows the viewer to refute the competitor would redound to the effectiveness of the focal ad. For such refutation to occur, a short time interval may be more advantageous than a long one. Thus, in cluttered communication environments, ads can be designed to capitalize on close temporal proximity of competing ads. The advent of a competitor can be made an occasion for the viewer to rehearse cognitive responses that extol the superiority of the original product.

Role of Rhetorical Questions in Commercial Speech

Many commercial messages deal with products that have low personal relevance for a large segment of the audience. Does the cognitive-response approach offer some device for instigating favorable cognitive responding even when the audience is not interested? One such device may be rhetorical questions such as, for example, "Isn't Duz wonderful for . . ."; "Don't you agree that . . ."; "Doesn't this show how . . ."; "Isn't it clear that . . ."; and "Don't you now think that . . ."

Recent cognitive-response research findings indicated that when a message was of low personal relevance and when recipients were not naturally processing the ordinary form of the message diligently, the use of rhetoricals increased cognitive responding (Petty, Cacioppo, and Keesacker 1981). By rhetorical rephrasing, a message with strong arguments became more persuasive while a message with weak arguments became less persuasive. These researchers did not obtain these results when the message was of high personal relevance; here, where recipients already were motivated to process the message, the use of rhetoricals only disrupted thinking.

Since a common marketing objective is to induce favorable thinking about low-relevance products, the task here is to rewrite copy for ads in order to vary the number of rhetorical questions. The effects of rhetoricals will be examined on cognitive processing of ads promoting products that are initially low versus high in personal relevance. A shopper who is a nonlaunderer might experience favorable attitude change toward Duz if the commercial is couched rhetorically. Conversely, frequent users of detergent, who naturally would engage in considerable cognitive elaboration of a Duz commercial, might experience reduced liking for Duz because their free flow of favorable cognitive elaborations was disrupted by the rhetoricals.

Effects of Number of Sources in a Commercial Message: More Is Better if They Are Independent

The cognitive-response approach has been applied to a hitherto overlooked variable in marketing research—namely, the sheer number of communicators who are promoting a product. The findings indicated that each time a new speaker appears, the recipient gears up to process the speaker's message (Harkins and Petty 1981). Variations of a strong message presented by many speakers were more effective than variations presented by one speaker or the same message presented by different speakers. Increasing the number of sources of a message increases thinking about the message content, and this increased thinking can result in increased persuasion if the message arguments are cogent.

An important factor that should influence the effect of multiple sources is the extent to which the sources of influence are perceived as independent. The greater the independence, the greater the effect of many sources. Full control over the content of commercial messages will enable the investigator to vary systematically the number of spokespersons and their perceived independence from one another. Often, when commercial advertisements employ multiple spokespersons, the persuasive impact of many sources is attenuated because the independence of the sources is left ambiguous for the viewer. Unless independence is established explicitly in the ad scenario, audiences undoubtedly perceive speakers within an ad as linked, as if they were members of the same committee.

Oral Report of Cognitive Responses to Test
Causal Mediation of Attitude Change

Most cognitive-response research has employed written rather than oral (verbal) listing of thoughts. The written listing procedure can be administered easily in group settings; it is relatively private and nonthreatening; and it requires only pencil and paper. However, oral listing may have advantages: for example, it can be obtained quickly (it is easier to speak than to write), thus minimizing forgetting one's responses to a stimulus, and it does not evoke any apprehension about written exposition skills (spelling, grammar, and so on).

Experience so far with oral collection of responses is sparse. Some researchers have found vast differences in subjects' willingness and ability to record consistently and accurately. These researchers suggested, therefore, that the greatest potential of the oral technique consists in its power to generate hypotheses by helping to identify important dimensions of a person's reportable subjective reactions (Cacioppo and Petty 1981, p. 314). Whether or not oral collection could be useful also in testing hypotheses remained an interesting but unanswered question.

Uses of oral collection in persuasion experimentation (for example, Janis and Terwillinger 1962) suggest that with brief training and appropriate technology, subjects can emit thoughts in unitized fashion so that counterarguments, support arguments, and so forth can be counted reliably. Continuing to explore the feasibility of oral collection has a strong theoretical justification. Oral collection may permit experimentation aimed at determining the most likely causal sequence when a given treatment typically affects both cognitive responses and attitude ratings. It is possible that the attitude ratings caused the cognitive responses—that is, that cognitive responses are merely rationalizations of a prior change in attitude. However, as we noted earlier in this chapter, this possibility has been discredited repeatedly by covariance analyses that hold constant statistically the postulated mediator between an initial variable and a final criterion variable. Significant effects of persuasion manipulations on attitudes tend to disappear when counterarguments and favorable thoughts served as covariants. While this statistical approach is satisfying, the most compelling evidence favoring the causal priority of cognitive responses to attitude change would be an experiment in which it was possible to observe counterargument differences among experimental conditions prior to attitude-rating differences among the same experimental conditions. This hypothetical outcome is depicted in Figure 5-6.

After an appropriate warm-up (to familiarize subjects with the procedure and to confirm an appropriate cover story) subjects would be confronted with message-concomitant distractions (for example, Keating and Brock 1974). One high-distraction and one low-distraction group would have their attitude measured after 30 seconds into the message, another high and low group would be measured 60 seconds into the message, another at 90, at 120, and so on until the end of the three-minute message. The purpose of this study is to demonstrate experimentally, rather than statistically, that differential cognitive responding (counterarguing to a counterattitudinal message, favorable thoughts to a pro-attitudinal message) precedes attitude change. The oral collection of cognitive responses appears necessary to achieve this close-up view of mental processes during persuasion and to verify a crucial theoretical premise.

The oral-report approach has the potential for generating and testing important hypotheses. However, in the final analysis, the ability to pursue fully the research directions suggested here rests on obtaining creative control over the design of commercial messages. The resultant development of advertisements that meet predetermined psychological criteria would insure a valuable research payoff—namely, a wealth of new and strongly supported insights into the advertisement persuasion process.

Summary

The analysis of cognitive responses, thoughts, and ideas evoked by persuasive communications has wide applicability for advertising. These thoughts have been shown to determine both immediate and long-term acceptance of the persuasive communication. This chapter reviewed the core principles of cognitive-response theory, contrasted it with more-traditional learning formulations of persuasion, and demonstrated that the cognitive-response approach is more able to account for important counterintuitive findings. Studies reviewed demonstrated the ability of this approach to account for a wide variety of effects and the amenability of cognitive responses to reliable and sensitive scoring (like for counterarguments). However, further understanding and improved application of persuasion-mediating cognitive responses to advertising require control over the design and presentation of in-the-market commercial messages.

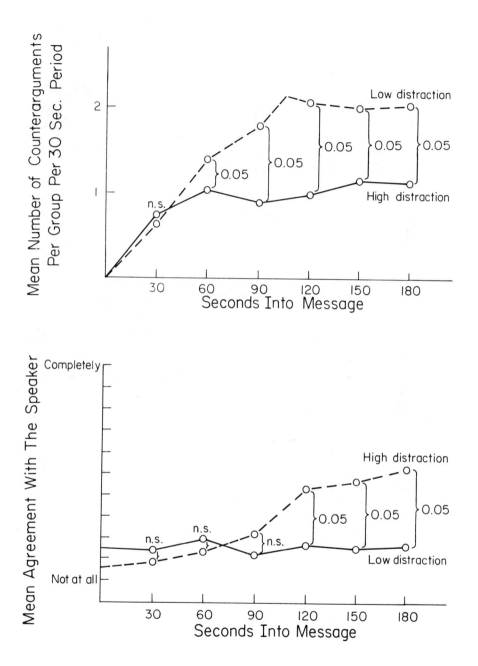

We are indebted to Gary Wells and Richard Petty for this depiction (personal communication).
Figure 5-6. How Counterargumentation Precedes Attitude Change

A central issue in advertising, the effect of advertisement repetition on persistent attitude change, was addressed by an examination of methodological issues surrounding the investigation of advertisement wear out. The results of such investigations have implicated cognitive responses to commercials as determinants of persistent attitude change. Further research is called for, and future experiments on cognitive responses to advertisements will have to begin to correct their most glaring weakness to date: the lack of control over the principal treatments (commercials) themselves. These experimental persuasive messages, from now on, should be constructed from scratch to meet predetermined psychological criteria.

Through experimental variation of commercial content, the study proposed will determine whether commercials can be designed to elicit cognitive responding with own thoughts to a greater extent than cognitive responding with message elements. It also will investigate the persuasive effects of thought rehearsal under varying conditions of product vividness and message distraction and the effects of perceived uniqueness of own thoughts on persuasion. The major prediction is that subjects who view an ad designed to instigate cognitive responding with own thoughts and who are given an opportunity to rehearse those responses will show greater recall of their own thoughts and will be more persuaded by the commercial than subjects in other conditions.

In the final sections of the chapter, the authors focused on the context in which cognitive responses are elicited and later accessed during purchasing decisions. They proposed that commercials be tested that heighten the link between thoughts in the shop-in-store context and favorable thoughts instigated in the message-reception context. The authors addressed the effects of cognitive tuning (expectancies to receive or to transmit information), the influence of the program in which a television commercial is embedded, and the effects of advertisements for competing products and proposed several appropriate research designs.

Levels of Processing and Memory for Advertisements

Joel Saegert and
Robert K. Young

There is broad interest in the psychology of memory by students of advertising effectiveness, especially since day-after recall is such a widely used method of copy testing ("Should 200 Viewers' Memories Decide?" 1980). The levels-of-processing theory has received a large share of this interest since it has been so popular as a topic of discussion by experimental psychologists during the past ten years. The primary contribution of the levels-of-processing theory to the field of advertising research is that it focuses attention on the viewer as an active information processor in contrast to traditional conditioning theories of learning that seem to focus more on variables such as the characteristics of the to-be-remembered stimulus and the number of stimulus presentations. This chapter describes briefly the levels-of-processing theory and some of its operational definitions, reports a series of experiments using brand-name memory as the dependent variable, and considers some implications of the theory for advertising strategy.

A Framework for Memory Research

The levels-of-processing theory was presented originally by Craik and Lockhart (1972) as a framework rather than a formal theory. Since that time, it has been the subject of dozens of experimental projects using a wide range of operational definitions and independent variables (see, for example, Cermark and Craik 1979). Even though it has been the target of some rather intense criticism on theoretical grounds, it still provides an interesting set of operational procedures that may have useful implications for both psychology and theories of advertising.

Craik and Lockhart's original proposal was a logical extension of a research paradigm used by Hyde and Jenkins (1973) to illustrate incidental learning effects. In an early experiment, Hyde and Jenkins asked subjects either to rate the pleasantness of words presented in a list or to count the number of *E*s appearing in each word. When later given a surprise recall task, subjects who had rated word pleasantness remembered nearly twice as many of the words as those who were engaged in the *E*-counting task.

117

Presumably, pleasantness rating requires attention to the semantic properties of the words to be recalled while letter counting does not. This semantic
processing is said to be responsible for improved recall.

Craik and Lockhart's view of this effect was that pleasantness rating requires that subjects subject stimuli to elaboration, a process that occurs at a
deeper level of cognition and that is said to facilitate acquisition, storage,
and/or retrieval of information. Such a process allows the active integration
of a word into previously existing networks of associated ideas that remain
available for subsequent retrieval. A study by Craik and Tulving (1975) used
an operational definition of varying levels of processing that since has been
the basis for numerous experiments. Subjects were asked questions about
words to which a yes or no response was to be made. Again, the orientation
of the subject was directed either to the semantic aspects of the words or to
some other, nonsemantic aspect. For example, when a subject was asked,
"Is the word a part of the body?," with presentation of the stimulus word
"waist," he or she would have to consult stored memory to see if ana-
tomical properties were characteristic of the word under consideration.
Thus, the word was related to other similar concepts stored in memory,
hence providing some deep processing of the word. Conversely, questions
such as "Is the word in lower-case letters?" or "Does the word have two
vowels?" would not require any attention to semantic properties and,
hence, would require only shallow processing. Moreover, Graik and Tulving proposed that a question like "Does the word rhyme with taste?" would
constitute an intermediate level of processing. They thus postulated that
depth of processing was a continuum from nonsemantic (physical, formal
properties at a shallow level) to semantic (meaningful properties at a deep
level) and that the deeper the processing, the greater the likelihood that the
subject would remember the word. A number of experiments reported by
Craik and Tulving have shown superior memory for deep processing and
have ruled out other interpretations of the effect.

Criticisms of the levels-of-processing theory were not long in coming.
Articles by Baddeley (1978) and Nelson (1977) suggested that the definition
of levels of processing proposed by Craik and Lockhart is circular: Items
are described as deeply processed if they are remembered better while better
memory is ascribed to deep processing of items. Moreover, these researchers showed empirically that what had been called maintenance processing
(presumably done at a shallow, nonsemantic level) did in fact result in effective retention under certain circumstances.

Subsequent experiments (for example, Seamon and Virostek, 1978) attempted to answer the criticisms by, for example, establishing independent
indexes of processing levels and showing that these did in fact predict varying levels of retention. However, Wickelgren (1981) has gone so far as to
proclaim that the theory has been disproved, in spite of the widespread use

of the levels-of-processing operational procedures, even in very recent studies. But even he conceded that levels of processing has "left a useful legacy of data and ideas generated in its disproof." One of these ideas has been that brand-name memory from advertisements will be improved to the degree that the viewer's attention can be drawn to the semantic properties of the brand being advertised. This has been demonstrated in a number of experiments with advertising stimuli using the Craik and Tulving (1975) research paradigm. Experiments by Saegert (1978), Reid and Soley (1980), and Saegert and Young (1981) have replicated the levels-of-processing effect under various conditions and have suggested some potentially useful strategies for advertising effectiveness. These studies are reviewed prior to presentation of some new experiments (Young and Saegert 1982) using variables of current interest in advertising.

Levels-of-Processing Experiments with Advertising Stimuli

For obvious reasons, much of the earlier consideration of memory factors in advertising has focused on the frequency of stimulus presentation (for example, Britt 1955; Sawyer 1974). The effects of repetition on acquisition and retention of brand information have important implications for media campaign scheduling, if for no other reason. However, a number of research ers have expressed interest in the levels-of-processing theory (Olson 1978; Bettman 1979) because it focuses attention on the consumer as an active information processor. The experimental research paradigm can be said to have some elements in common with the conditions of real advertising exposure. For example, the procedure can monitor the recall of real ads (as opposed to simulated ads or made-up brand names) through the use of an incidental rather than intentional learning task (as is done in day-after-recall tests). Also, the recall is assessed under conditions of high memory load that taxes the ability of the viewers; that is, since a large number of ads are presented, a condition like advertising clutter may be simulated.

However, researchers must recognize some limitations like the required focus of subject's attention on the ad. Another consideration is the theoretical criticism in the psychology literature that the Craik and Lockhart formulation is circular. In this chapter, we use the terms *semantic* versus *nonsemantic processing* instead of *deep* versus *shallow processing* to circumvent the problems of specifying the exact theoretical nature of levels-of-processing effects.

Demonstration of the Effect

An experiment by Saegert (1978) illustrated the basic semantic/nonsemantic effect with advertising stimuli. Thirty adult subjects were shown forty magazine ads at a rate of five seconds per ad. For each ad, the experimenter asked a question about the brand name shown, following the paradigm developed by Craik and Tulving (1975). These questions directed attention either to the semantic features of the brand name shown in the ad (for example, "Have you used this brand before?") or to nonsemantic features ("Is the brand name in blue letters?").

Following the presentation of all of the ads, the subjects were given surprise recall and recognition tasks. The results showed that about 13 percent of the brand names were recalled when a nonsemantic question was asked about the ads, while about 24 percent were recalled for those having a semantic question. Recognition performance was about 44 versus 67 percent for nonsemantic and semantic questions respectively. Thus, the experiment demonstrated superior memory for ads as a function of the processing given by the viewer, even though the presentation frequency was not varied.

Other Variables

Reid and Soley (1980) replicated the semantic/nonsemantic-processing experiment with television ads as stimuli. In this case, forty student subjects viewed the ads; questions asked pertained to the brand exposures throughout the course of the commercial rather than to a single print exposure. The results again showed the two-to-one superiority of recall for the semantic-processing condition although the overall amount of recall for the brand names was about double that of the Saegert (1978) experiment (perhaps because these were fewer ads to be recalled). Thus, the effect was replicated for ads that might actually be evaluated in day-after-recall copy testing.

A further study looked at twenty-four-hour recall as a function of semantic/nonsemantic-processing manipulations. Saegert and Young (1981) used a retention interval of twenty-four hours and again found that semantic-question ads were easier to recall (see figure 6-1). There was relatively greater forgetting of ads across the twenty-four-hour period under semantic-processing instructions (as compared to recall with an immediate retention interval), as we can see in figure 6-1. However, the absolute level of retention was still greater for the semantic-processing condition. One explanation for this result could be simply that there was more to forget in that condition. Another reason may be that although very few brand names were remembered in the nonsemantic-processing condition, those that were retained were remembered very well indeed. This would follow if those brand names had some otherwise especially memorable properties that promoted their retention in the first place and hence made them very resistant to forgetting across the twenty-four-hour retention interval. Of primary

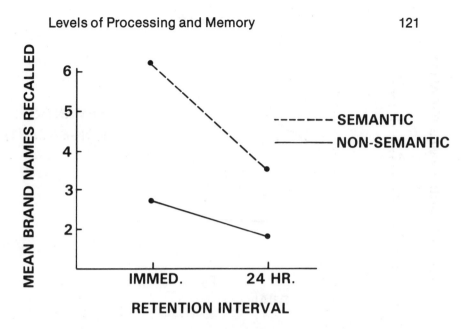

Source: J. Sargent & R.K. Young, "Comparison of Effects of Repetition and Levels of Process-ing in Memory for Advertisements," in *Advances for Consumer Research*, vol. 8 (1981), p. 432.

Figure 6-1. Mean Recall as a Function of Retention Interval and Type of
            Processing

importance, however, was the demonstration that the greatest memory per-formance, following twenty-four hours, was for the semantically processed ads. A further (unpublished) experiment by Young found the same relation-ship for a retention interval of one week.

These experiments have demonstrated that variability in memory can be a function of the observer's information processing rather than the frequency of stimulus presentation. An interesting question concerns the effect that variations in presentation frequency might have in combination with semantic processing. Young and Saegert (1982) varied the number of pres-entations in their experiment. Half of the subjects received the semantic/nonsemantic-processing procedure for a single exposure of each ad and half received a second exposure. Figure 6-2 shows the principal results. Both frequency of presentation and semantic/nonsemantic process-ing had effects on recall. However, of greater interest is the finding that the second-exposure trial interacted with the effects of the semantic-processing orientation; that is, while the second exposure increased recall of the nonsemantically processed ads by only 14 percent, the increase was 41 per-cent for the semantically processed ads. Thus, the two variables of presenta-tion frequency and semantic/nonsemantic processing seem to act in concert to produce a high level of recall of the ad brand names.

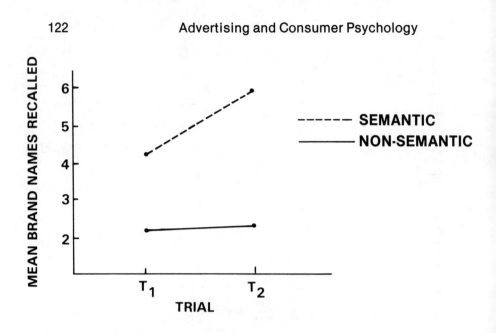

Source: J. Sargent & R.K. Young, "Comparison of Effects of Repetition and Levels of Processing in Memory for Advertisements," in *Advances for Consumer Research*, vol. 8 (1981), p. 433.
Figure 6-2. Mean Recall as a Function of Number of Presentation Trials and Type of Processing

Jacoby, Bartz, and Evans (1978) postulated a theoretical explanation for this interaction between processing type and exposure frequency. They hypothesized on the one hand that the effect of semantic/nonsemantic-processing differences occurs as a result of differential formation of organizational units containing the to-be-remembered material; on the other hand, they said repetition of the stimulus strengthens the associations within those organizational units. According to Jacoby and co-workers (1978, p. 337), "variables such as level of processing influence between-unit organizations, while repetition influences integration (within-unit organization). Between-unit organization determines the probability of accessing any particular unit, while integration determines recall of the contents of the unit given that it is accessed." In advertising terms, semantic processing could be said to increase the probability of accessing a given organizational unit containing the brand name to be remembered, while multiple-stimulus presentations determine the likelihood of recall of the brand name, once the unit is accessed. Thus, both frequency and type of processing variables appear to be important since they were shown to act in concert to improve recall performance.

Semantic/Nonsemantic Processing and
Some Current Advertising Issues

Two other issues concerning factors in advertising effectiveness are the effects of massed versus distributed (spaced) presentation and the level of involvement of viewers with the products being advertised. These were addressed in two new experiments using the semantic/nonsemantic-processing research paradigm with advertising stimuli.

Massed versus Spaced Presentation of Stimuli

The effects of massed versus spaced distribution of practice on the acquisition of advertising information has long been of interest to advertising theorists because of implications for media scheduling (for example, Britt 1978, p. 216). The issue is whether it is more useful to mass successive repetitions of ads close together in time or to spread them out over a longer period. One phenomenon in the psychological literature that may have some bearing on the issue is the so-called lag effect. Researchers have demonstrated consistently (for example, Hintzman 1976) that memory performance is superior when two successive presentations of the same item are interspersed with other list items. Moreover, the effect increases when even more intervening items are presented between the two repetitions. An example of the lag effect is that if the target word *apple* is to be recalled following two presentations, it will be more likely to be remembered if ten other target items are presented between the first and second exposures to *apple* than if only one other item separates them, and having twenty intervening items will result in even better recall.

In two reviews of the available experimental evidence, Hintzman (1976) has considered a number of hypothetical explanations for the lag effect. Wickelgren (1981) has summarized these as follows:

1. *Encoding variability:* Learning of an item improves the more disparate (spaced apart) the context in which its successive presentations are encountered and thus encoded.
2. *Deficient consolidation of the first presentation;* Time is needed between successive presentations to integrate an item, and this does not occur when a second exposure is massed.
3. *Deficient learning of the second presentation:* Recognition, or identification, responses to a word the first time it is presented are unnecessary if it recurs immediately, and this results in poorer encoding of massed items.

Wickelgren argues on the basis of experimental evidence that hypotheses 1 and 2 are unsupported but that hypothesis 3 is supported. He argues that encoding of the second presentation of a massed exposure can take place without all of the preliminary identification factors needed on a first (or spaced second) presentation and that this diminishes effective encoding operations.

An experiment was designed to replicate the lag effect with advertising stimuli and to consider the effect under semantic- and nonsemantic-processing conditions (Young and Saegert 1982). One hundred fifty-seven subjects were shown ad slides that were keyed to a tape recording programmed to play semantic and nonsemantic orienting questions. The ads were presented either once or twice, with lags of one, five, or twenty intervening items. The pool of advertisements used consisted of thirty-two ads for well-known brand names (for example, Exxon, Bayer, Dole, Singer).

The results of the experiment are summarized in figure 6-3. Disregarding the level-of-processing variable, the lag effect was replicated clearly with the ad stimuli. The one-presentation condition produced a mean recall

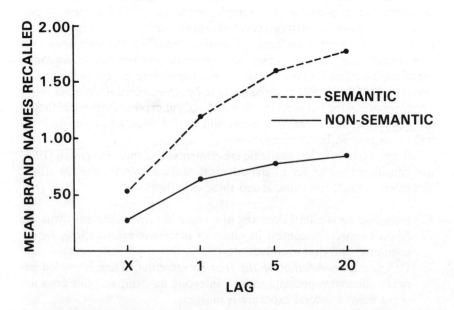

Source: R.K. Young & J. Sargent, "Further Experiments with Levels of Processing and Advertising Memory," Working Paper No. 18 (San Antonio: College of Business, University of Texas, 1982).

Figure 6-3. Mean Recall as a Function of Lag between First and Second Presentations

of only 0.80 item (out of 8 possible items, summing across levels of processing), while two presentations with lags of 1, 5, and 20 items intervening
resulted in recall of 1.80, 2.29, and 2.58 respectively. Thus, within this
relatively short presentation-interval situation, spaced presentation of ads
was clearly superior in maintaining ad memory.

As before, the overall difference was demonstrated between semantic
and nonsemantic processing: Recall was 5.08 for semantic processing but
only 2.39 for nonsemantic. Of greater interest, however, is the interaction
shown in figure 6-3 between type of processing and lag. The lag effect was
demonstrated much more dramatically in the semantic-processing condition. This seems to suggest that whatever the source of the lag effect, it
clearly occurs at a semantic level. If, for example, deficient identification
responses occur on a massed second presentation, as Wickelgren suggests
(1981), then these responses must be said to be semantic in nature; that is,
identification must be of a kind of "I know what that means" response,
rather than in terms of nonsemantic features. More can be said on this later
in the context of a discussion of Krugman's (1972) current theory of advertising effectiveness.

Level of Consumer Involvement

One of the most widely investigated topics in consumer research in the past
few years has been consumer product involvement. Although no universally
accepted definition of the construct has been forthcoming, researchers agree
that the idea pertains to the degree to which consumers behave actively
rather than passively with respect to products and their advertisements. For
example, Assael (1981), suggests that high-product-involvement consumers
are information seekers and processors who evaluate brands before purchasing and whose personal characteristics and reference-group beliefs are
related to consumption of the product; low-involvement consumers are said
to be the opposite (p. 83). Since variation in product involvement is said to
occur both within and among consumers and possibly across products, it is
necessary to specify very carefully what is meant by involvement for any
given use of the construct. For example, Lastovicka (1978) scaled involvement in terms of the degree to which consumers felt that they had knowledge about, engaged in information search for, and relied on past purchase
information about products prior to purchase.

Olson (1978) has suggested that there may be a relationship between the
level of involvement of a consumer and the degree to which semantic rather
than nonsemantic processing will be used in viewing advertisements. Young
and Saegert (1982) designed a study to investigate this possibility.
Specifically, they hypothesized that brand-name memory, as measured in

semantic/nonsemantic-processing experiments, would be greater for those products in which the subject had higher product involvement (knowledge, interest) and that semantically oriented processing questions would improve memory for high-involvement products compared to low-involvement products.

The experiment required an independent assessment of degress of involvement for product categories used in ad stimuli with the subject population at hand. In this study, as in most of the other studies reported here, college undergraduates were used as subjects. A procedure similar to that of Lastovicka (1978) was used to define operationally the involvement construct for the student population. A group of eighty-five students was given descriptions of two hypothetical consumers. Consumer A was described as being knowledgeable and experienced with a given product class (chewing gum was used as an example), while consumer B was described as knowing little about the product and needing to seek information from other sources prior to purchase (chalk was given as an example). Following this, the students were presented a list of fifty product categories such as soap, cars, and ballpoint pens and were asked to pick the fifteen products for which they were most like consumer A and the fifteen for which they were most like consumer B. The twelve most frequently named A or B product categories were identified for both male and female students (since the results indicated substantial differences across sex). These twelve were used as high-involvement and low-involvement product categories in an ad-memory experiment with semantic and nonsemantic orienting questions.

A number of variables such as retention interval, sex of subject, and presentation counterbalancing were manipulated or controlled in the experiment, but the variables of interest were the now-familiar semantic-versus-non-semantic-processing variable and the level-of-product-involvement variable described earlier. A total of 117 students (different than those in the involvement-assessment task) simultaneously were shown slides and played a tape asking either semantic or nonsemantic orienting questions.

The principal result is shown in figure 6-4. As we can see, the usual semantic/nonsemantic-processing effect was obtained, with semantic items recalled about twice as well as nonsemantic. The product-involvement variable also showed a considerable effect: Mean high-involvement-product brand-name recall was 2.36 (out of 12) compared to 1.76 for low product involvement.

The most interesting result of the experiment is again the interaction of type of processing with another independent variable—this time, level of product involvement. From figure 6-4, we can see that while semantic processing increased recall of both the high- and low-involvement items, the effect was substantially greater for the high-involvement ads. Apparently, the degree of product involvement makes little difference if the ad is not processed semantically.

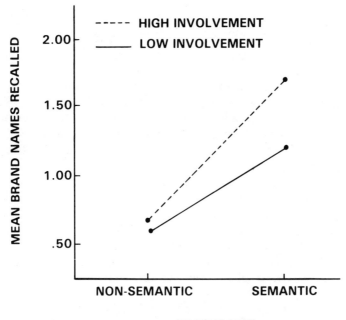

Source: R.K. Young and J. Sargent, "Further Experiments with Levels of Processing and Advertising Memory," Working Paper No. 18 (San Antonio: College of Business, University of Texas, 1982).

Figure 6-4. Mean Recall as a Function of Type of Processing and Level of Involvement

Implications of the Experiments

These experiments make a number of specific points about memory for brand-name stimuli. To the extent that memory factors are important in ad effectiveness (for example, as measured by day-after recall), the attention that viewers pay to the semantic aspects of the brand name seems critical in maintaining a memory trace. This has been shown in each case in which semantic processing was encouraged through the orienting question, as compared to nonsemantic orientation. The effect was found for print and television ads and was shown to hold over a twenty-four-hour retention interval.

Subsequent experiments illustrate subtler aspects of the semantic-processing phenomenon. For example, the effect was shown to interact with presentation frequency such that a second presentation trial provided another opportunity for semantic processing to occur, and this resulted in even greater retention of brands. This interaction has a basis in memory theory insofar as semantic processing is thought to improve formation of organizational structures around to-be-remembered items, while repetition is said to strengthen the associations within these structures (Jacoby, Bartz, and Evans 1978).

The constructs postulated in levels-of-processing theory may be related to Krugman's three-exposure theory (1972) of ad effects. Krugman's model postulates three stages of advertising effectiveness in which consumers are said to consider several different propositions on exposure to ads (see chapter 18). The first of these, the what-is-it? response, implies that a recognition or awareness process is occurring. The second proposition, the what's-in-it-for-me? response, seems to build on the awareness response and assigns an evaluation to the stimulus. These first two response stages seem to correspond to the semantic identification responses postulated to have occurred in the lag experiment with semantic processing. Krugman's third response implies a repetition effect, which according to the earlier discussion of the interactive effects of semantic processing and repetition, may strengthen bonds among elements of semantic structures formed in earlier stages.

Krugman (1972) proposes that ad memory will occur to the extent that a brand stimulus is recognized and identified as something familiar, is evaluated and assigned emotional connotations, and is reinforced through subsequent repetitions. Wickelgren (1981) has argued that the lag effect may result from deficient recognition responses on massed repetitions. In Krugman's terms, the viewer does not need to go through the phase of saying to him- or herself "What is it?" or "What's in it for me?" since he or she has just done so. Thus, the degree of processing required on first exposure is not needed if the second presentation is massed, leading to poorer encoding and, hence, less retention.

Finally, in the last experiment, the popular involvement variable resulted in better memory for high-involvement-product brand names; however, it appeared that even high-involvement products were retained poorly if nonsemantic processing was invoked. This implies that the semantic-processing procedure stimulates a kind of induced involvement that combines with prior product knowledge and interest (high product involvement) to maintain brand-name memory. We now can propose some suggestions for use of the induced-involvement idea in advertising design.

Suggested Applications of the Levels-of-Processing Theory

Controversy over the day-after-recall method of copy testing notwithstanding, it still seems reasonable to suppose that ad memory, both in terms of brand-name and product information, plays an important role in advertising effectiveness. If so, what strategic-planning suggestions for ad design can we add to the pool of ideas used by creative designers to improve ad memorability?

The levels-of-processing theory of memory research points the creative design of ads in the direction of the consumer as an active processor of information. Memorability of ads seems to be a function of the degree to which the viewer relates material to previously stored material in memory. Thus, any time an ad succeeds in involving the consumer in itself, the likelihood that it will be remembered increases.

An early example involving consumers in ads is Heller's (1956) demonstration that the performance of closure by a viewer, the filling in of missing elements in a brand name from which letters have been omitted intentionally, leads to improved memory performance. Other consumer researchers such as Krugman (1972); Leavitt, Waddell, and Wells (1970); and Wright (1974) have discussed the use of a personal mediator by which the viewer responds to an ad with a connection to a personal experience to improve memorability. Reid and Soley (1980) have suggested the improvement of ad memory by prompting audience members to relate information to personal experience and knowledge by, for example, asking viewers to image themselves in the context of the product or brand portrayed in the ad. We should point out, however, that Mowen (1980) was unsuccessful in an attempt to demonstrate this empirically.

While inducing semantic processing of ads typically might require a subtle request to imagine the consequences of brand adoption, more-dramatic examples of this invitation-to-participate procedure are possible. McDonald's recently asked, successfully it would seem, that consumers memorize the ingredients ("two all-beef patties, special sauce . . .") of their product. Salem cigarettes demanded that viewers complete their famous truncated jingle. And a Chivas Regal ad asked consumers, without providing any cues other than an hors d'oeuvre tray filled with caviar, to "guess what scotch is about to be served." Finally, a recent ad for a relatively unknown brand of French wine, Valbon, provided the ultimate in viewer participation in their ad (see figure 6-5). They carefully explained that French wine laws forbade their revealing the particular region from which their blended wine had originated. They suggested, however, that the zip code of the region did appear on the wine label and that consumers who were interested could write to the company to receive a complimentary French zip code directory to allow them to look up the region for themselves. It is highly likely that such semantic processing of this ad resulted, for those consumers who participated, in an extremely high level of memorability.

Reprinted with permission from *Gourmet* magazine and the Heublein Company.

Figure 6-5. An Extreme Example of Induced Involvement in an Advertisement

Conclusion

Advertising researchers face the task of positioning their work somewhere on continuum between the imponderable and the obvious. At one extreme, we face a phenomenon as complex as any in social science, one which may be destined to remain mysterious until we can chart neuronal responses to each specific advertising stimulus (see chapter 13). At the other extreme, advertising is so widely practiced and with such obvious success that it often seems that its effectiveness is limited by budgetary constraints alone. Somewhere in the middle, advertising researchers are left with the painful task of cataloging the relevant variables in advertising effectiveness and specifying their interrelationships.

Although it is unlikely that the kind of laboratory experiment exemplified by the levels-of-processing theory really includes the precise effects that occur in print or television advertising, the experiments performed with ad stimuli using the Craik and Tulving procedure at least point us to the viewer as information processor rather than as passive receptor. This attention should prove at least as useful in describing the role of memory factors in advertising as the discussions of classical and instrumental conditioning, stimulus generalization and discrimination, and reinforcement theory that currently make up the learning chapters of consumer-behavior texts. The important message of the levels-of-processing experiments is that recall of brand names is a function of the degree to which viewers pay attention to the semantic features of the brand names they encounter. Perhaps this principle will be useful to advertising strategists.

7

Message-Evoked Thoughts: Consumer Thought Processing as a Tool for Making Better Copy

Arch G. Woodside

Persuasion theories typically postulate cognitive activities as mediators between message transmission and message-caused changes in behavior (Wright 1980). Interest in learning thought processes stimulated by persuasions has increased due to Greenwald's (1968) argument that people store in memory personal reactions to a message, not the message. Earlier, Hovland (1951) emphasized that the best way to study the internal process of attitude change was to have subjects verbalize as completely as possible their thoughts as they responded to the communicator. Petty, Ostrom, and Brock (1981) view this cognitive-response approach as an attempt to bring the traditional approaches to the study of persuasion together by examining the thoughts elicited when a person anticipates, receives, or reflects on a communication.

In the most well-known research on message-evoked thought verbalization in advertising, Wright (1974; 1975) manipulated media presentation (audio versus print) and ad involvement (high versus low) of an advertisement for a soybean-based food innovation. The ad followed a lead-in message on an unrelated topic. The print ad produced 25 percent more total thoughts and twice as many support arguments or source derogations than the audio ad. Wright argued that the audio ad's pace discouraged extensive counterarguing since that was presumably a difficult activity given the unfamiliarity of the product being touted.

Wright and Rip (1980) measured high school students' thought verbalizations and utility functions after they had read messages promoting various colleges. The messages varied in degree of similarity in the attributes or in the comparison procedure discussed and in the use of imaginary instructions. Product-class advertising was found to influence how the subjects frame problems related to unfamiliar choices.

Little is known of the contents and how much thinking occurs by consumers while they receive or reflect on ad communications received in natural settings. In such settings consumers typically are confronted with message streams comprised of messages from different advocates touting competing options. This chapter reports on research to learn consumers' thought processes while they are receiving print message streams of ads and editorial materials. The study is a response to Chay's (1982) proposition that "we need to increase our efforts in understanding how advertising works, based on how the consumer works, if we are to know what can and cannot be measured in copy research" (p. 23).

In the study reported here, we took measures of total thoughts, editorial-related thoughts, brand-related thoughts, and the subjects' perceptions of the importance of their thoughts. We collected additional data on ad recall, comprehension, attitude, intention, and choice behavior following the collection of the thought verbalizations.

Wright (1974) has demonstrated that situational factors are likely to affect consumers' information handling of messages. He found that both content-processing involvement and message modality affected the influence of cognitive processes on acceptance of messages. Similar to Wright's study, our study includes two situational factors: (1) content-processing involvement and (2) mechanical features of the ads.

Hypotheses

Hypothesis 1: Increases in consumer involvement with the offers in advertisements produce increases in the number of ad-offer-related thoughts. Involvement is the amount of arousal or interest evoked by a particular communication (Mitchell 1979). Increases in ad involvement causes consumers to devote greater cognitive-processing capacity to either the offer in the ad or the style of the ad or both.

Mitchell, Russo, and Gardner (1981) proposed two general advertising-processing strategies:

> One strategy that might be used is to actively process the information from the ad with the goal of forming an overall evaluation of the advertised brand. We call this a brand evaluation strategy. Alternately, individuals may direct their processing toward some other goal, such as enjoying the ad for its entertainment value or making a stylistic evaluation of the ad. We call these nonbrand strategies. [p. 3]

The focus of the study reported here is on brand-evaluation strategies under low- and high-involvement conditions. Mitchell and co-workers (1981) have demonstrated that individuals' use of brand versus nonbrand strategies increases the amount of thought processing and accuracy of brand-related information in a high-attention-condition experiment.

Hypothesis 2: Increases in consumer involvement with offers in ads produce increases in consumer recall of the advertisements and of the central messages in the advertisements. Storage in memory of ad-related information is likely to occur when a consumer consciously produces ad-related thoughts—an activity likely to occur in a high- versus low-involvement condition.

Hypothesis 3: Increases in consumer involvement with offers in ads produce increases in consumer attitude toward buying the brands advertised, intention to buy the brands advertised, and choice of the brands advertised. The central rationale for this hypothesis is that involvement produces connections (Krugman 1967)—that is, thoughts linking the message content to one's personal experiences—and that connections produce positive attitudes, intentions to buy, and purchase of the brand advertised.

Hypothesis 4: The effects of consumer involvement with advertising offers occur for both black-and-white (b/w) and color-print ad-processing situations. If consumer involvement is a general mediating factor between message transmission and message recall, attitude, and intention changes, then the effect should be observed for different advertising situations.

Hypothesis 5: Consumer ad-related thought production affects consumer attitudes, intentions, and choice behavior toward the brand advertised. Hypothesis 5 is the crucial hypothesis in research on cognitive responses in persuasion. The production of thoughts during exposure to advertising has yet to be demonstrated to be related to intention and behavior to the choice advertised. Thought production demonstrates the impact of the ad message on the consumer's mind. If an ad message causes the consumer to produce connections, then the thoughts produced are likely to be used in prechoice deliberations. Thus, the focus of learning the effects of advertising on behavior should be on thought production, assuming that thought production and connections are related positively.

Research Design

Subjects

The subjects were sixty housewives who were known to be flower and/or vegetable gardeners and who lived in the suburbs of a southeastern U.S. city. The women were heterogeneous with respect to their education, occupation, and social class. Each housewife was compensated for her participation with a $10 choice in merchandise. Their choices were restricted to a list of ten products; most of the products were selected from the products advertised in the printed ads in the study.

Procedure

The city directory was used to identify potential subjects. Twenty residential areas from the suburbs were selected. Ten households were selected systematically from each residential area. The housewife in each household was sent a letter asking for cooperation in a communication study. Mention was made in the letter that a telephone call would be made for an appointment for an interview. The study was not identified as an advertising study.

A few days after the mailing, the subjects were contacted by telephone. Each was asked five questions: Have you visited the city zoo? Have you traveled on your vacation? Have you visited a state beach? Have you planted vegetable seeds in your yard? Have you planted flower seeds in your yard? If the subject answered positively to either or both of the last two questions, she was asked to meet with the interviewer. This procedure was used to select subjects who had an interest in gardening without forewarning them that they would be asked questions related to gardening ads. Over 80 percent of the subjects who qualified agreed to participate in the study.

All the interviews took place in the subjects' homes. Each subject was given one set of materials to read. Half of the subjects received three pages from *Southern Living* (January 1980, pp. 110-113) that contained an article, "Forcing Bulbs for Early Blooming," and nine b/w ads. Each b/w ad was approximately one-sixth of a page; the news story was one and two-thirds pages. Six of the b/w ads featured an offer for a free catalog on seeds or plants. Half of the subjects received five pages from the same issue of *Southern Living*; these pages contained six ads (two in four-color) and two articles, "Unlocking the Story of Midway Church" and "Fertilizing Trees and Shrubs." One color ad was a full page and the other was a half-page.

Instructions to the Subjects

For each set of subjects, half received instructions containing a high ad-processing treatment: "I will be asking you to evaluate the products and offers shown in the advertisements in the material. Please look over the ads and the editorial material." Subjects in the low-involvement ad-processing treatment did not receive these instructions.

To reduce the risk that subjects would edit some thoughts from their reports that intuition tells them, perhaps incorrectly, do not interest the researcher, priming instructions were given to all the subjects. A number of thought categories that should be reported were identified to the subjects. The intent was to reassure subjects that such thoughts are worth reporting without drawing great attention to them (Wright 1980, p. 156).

The following instructions were given verbally to all subjects:

Thank you for agreeing to participate in the study. The study is to learn about what is likely to be communicated by information in printed form. The first thing that I would ask you to do is to sit back, relax, and read a few pages of printed material. After reading the material I will ask you to tell me about the thoughts that occurred to you while reading. Please feel free to say your thoughts about any of the material that you see and read.

Please take your time while reading or looking at the material. Use your own regular pace when reading. There is no need to rush through the material.

You may say your thoughts aloud while you read or wait until after you read all the material. After you complete looking at and reading the material, I will ask you for the thoughts that occurred to you while you were reading the material.

The thoughts you have about any topic while reading the material are of interest. Please tell me about any thoughts or facts that you note to yourself while reading or looking at the pages.

Please say any thoughts that come to mind about how the material compares to your own life or to your family.

Please say any thoughts about if the material looks interesting or boring or if something or some action looks good or bad to you.

Please tell about any questions that you may ask yourself while reading, such as "I wonder what this means?" or "Is this true?"

Please say any opinions that you might have while reading, such as "I have always wanted to see this" or "Who cares about this?"

Following this general and priming instructions, the ad-involvement-manipulation instruction was administered randomly to half of the subjects. The interviewer tape recorded the subjects' thoughts and made notes of the thoughts and topics of the thoughts on a survey form.

Thus, no time limits were placed on the subjects for reading the materials. The subjects were free to decide whether or not to offer concurrent verbalizations or retrospective thoughts. Most (fifty-two) subjects provided concurrent verbalizations. Allowing such reporting reduces the threat to completeness due to memory losses. Other researchers suggest that retrospections about message-response thinking tend to overreport some types of thoughts and to underreport others (compare Wright 1980, p. 157).

Following the subjects' verbalizations of thoughts, the interviewer removed the printed material and placed it out of sight. He then asked the subjects to identify any additional thoughts about the material in general, the editorial material, and the advertisements.

Next the subjects were asked, "What products or services do you recall being advertised in the material?" This unaided-recall question was followed by an aided-recall question. Brands advertised and not advertised were shown in a list to the subjects. The subjects were asked to recall if the products were or were not advertised and to tell if they were not sure if the product was advertised.

Fill-in-the-blank message-comprehension questions then were given to each subject. The subject was asked to complete the second half of the central message (usually the headline or editorial story theme) for each ad and editorial story.

Then, attitude toward the behavior (A_b) was measured for the editorial story theme and ad offers. Eight-point disagree-agree scales were used. For example, "I would like to send for the free Park Seed flower and vegetable book."

Intentions toward the offer made in each ad were then requested of each subject, using zero- to nine-point scales.

The subjects next were requested to rate each of their thoughts for importance from extremely, moderately, or slightly important. (The discussion of the results for these important weights is not reported in this chapter.) The subjects' thoughts were read to them, and their thought weightings were requested for each thought.

Finally, the subjects were offered $10 in merchandise from one of ten products. Most of the products in the ads in the study were included in the $10 offer.

Two trained judges worked independently on identifying and classifying the contents of the thoughts for each subject. Agreement between the judges was reached in over 90 percent of the cases with respect to brand and positive/negative or neutral valences of the thoughts.

Results

The average number of total thoughts was about the same for the low- and high-involvement color treatments. The same result occurred for the low- and high-involvement treatments for the b/w-ad conditions. Nearly 13 thoughts per subject were produced in the color-ad treatments and 7.7 and 6.2 thoughts for the b/w-ad low- and high-involvement conditions respectively (see table 7-1 for details).

Table 7-1
Average Number of Thoughts on Editorial Material and Ads

| | Involvement | | Percent |
Content	Low	High	Change
Editorial Material			
Color	8.8	7.1	−19
b/w[a]	7	4.7	−33
Ads			
Color[a]	3.7	5.7	+54
b/w[a]	0.7	1.5	+114
Total			
Color	12.5	12.8	+2
b/w	7.7	6.2	−18

[a]Mean group difference significant at $p < .05$, t-test.

The results supported hypothesis 1. The number of ad-offer-related thoughts increased for the high- versus low-involvement conditions for both the color- and b/w-ad treatments. In general, the subjects devoted more processing capacity to the ads and less processing capacity to the editorial material in the high- versus low-involvement conditions. The percentage decline in the number of thoughts about the editorial material was less substantial than the increase in thoughts related to the ads.

Increases in the number of thoughts related to specific ads did occur between the high- versus low-involvement treatments (see table 7-2). The increases were more substantial for the b/w- versus color-ad treatments. The average number of thoughts related to the full-page color ad for Northrup King was lower in the high- versus low-involvement treatment; in the low-involvement color-ad condition, the Northrup King ad had the most ad-related thoughts compared to the Park Seed color ad and the b/w ads appearing in the material. Thus, the decline in the average number of thoughts related to the Northrup King ad in the high- versus low-involvement conditions provides additional evidence that individuals first are willing to devote just so much processing effort to receive information and, second, to shift processing capacity from one topic to another depending upon the message situation.

The percentage of subjects who had thoughts related to the Park Seed ad increased for high- versus low-involvement treatments for both the color- and b/w-ad conditions. These results are shown in table 7-3. Note in this table that only for the high-involvement color-ad condition did the majority of subjects have one or more thoughts related to Park Seed's ad offer. Evidently, consumers are not oriented to thinking about ad offers even when asked to do so.

Consumers who do express thoughts toward ad offers are prone to connect the ad messages to their personal experiences. Most thoughts expressed

Table 7-2
Average Number of Thoughts on Specific Ads in Low- and High-Involvement Ad Treatments

| | Involvement | | All |
Ad	Low	High	Subjects
b/w			
Park Seed	0.07	0.20	0.14
Alaska Cruise	0.47	0.87	0.67
Charleston Tourism	0.40	0.93	0.67
Color			
Park Seed	0.47	0.60	0.54
Northrup King	1.07	0.87	0.97

Table 7-3
Percentage of Persons who Mentioned Thoughts on Park Seed Ad and Ad Offer

| | Involvement | | |
Treatment	Low	High	Total
Color	27	53	40
b/w	7	20	13

included affective dimensions. For example, nearly all of the subjects expressed positive attitudes toward Park Seed's and Northrup King's ad offers among those who did express thoughts related to the ad offers (see tables 7-4 and 7-5).

Correct recall of the products advertised did increase for five of the b/w ads tested in the aided-recall test between the high- versus low-involvement conditions. Correct recall increased in all six cases for the color-ad high-versus low-involvement conditions. Tables 7-6 and 7-7 show these results.

Many subjects in the high-involvement b/w-ad condition could not recall the products advertised even with aided recall. Only 60 percent of the subjects could recall the Park Seed ad in the b/w-ad high-involvement condition (see table 7-6). Unaided recall was related positively to thought processing. Subjects who produced thoughts mentioning brands by name could recall the brands, while subjects who produced thoughts not related directly to brands could not recall the brands. This finding held for both low- and high-involvement conditions.

Table 7-4
Number and Kind of Thoughts on Park Seed While Reading

| | Color Ads | | b/w Ads | |
Factors	High Involvement	Low Involvement	High Involvement	Low Involvement
Attitude				
Positive	13	11	6	3
Negative	1	1	1	
Neutral		1	1	
Intentions to buy	5	3	1	0
n	14	13	8	3
Comments				
Color	2	3 (attractive)		
Familiar	3	4	3	2
Free offer	1			1

Table 7-5
Number and Kind of Thoughts on Northrup King while Reading (Color Ad Only)

Factors	High Involvement	Low Involvement
Attitude		
Positive	12	9
Negative	3	2
Neutral	2	7
Intentions to buy	2	1
n	17	18
Comments		
Appealing/attractive ad	5	4
Planting ideas	5	2
Familiar	1	1
Good ad	1	
Offer	1	1
Eggplant		4

Thus, hypothesis 2 is supported partially by the recall findings of the study. Consumer involvement with the ad offers produced increases in consumer recall of the ads. The second part of hypothesis 2 was not supported. Recall of the central message did not always increase with an increase in involvement with the ad offers for the b/w- and color-ad conditions. See tables 7-8 and 7-9. However, the central messages for the Garden Way Cart and Princess Cruise ads did remarkably well in being comprehended in both the low- and high-involvement conditions compared to the ads in the color-ad treatment, but neither of these two ads was in color. Thus, the results do not support the propositions that ad involvement and ad comprehension are related.

Table 7-6
Percentage of Persons Having Correct Recall of Ads in Aided Test for B/W Ads

Product	Advertised?	Involvement		Percent Change
		Low	High	
Weekend at Fripp	No	87	100	+ 13
Catalog for strawberries from Conners	Yes	40	60	+ 20
Herbst Seed Catalog	Yes	27	53	+ 26
Jackson & Perkins Catalog	No	87	73	− 14
Park Seed Catalog	Yes	40	60	+ 20
Burpee Seed Catalog	Yes	47	53	+ 7
Stark Brother's Seed Catalog	Yes	20	7	− 13
Subscription to *Southern Living*	Yes	27	53	+ 26

Table 7-7
Percentage of Persons Having Correct Recall of Ads in Aided Test for Color Ads

Product	Advertised?	Involvement Low	Involvement High	Percent Change
Travel to Florida	No	73	73	0
Cruise trip to Alaska and Canada	Yes	53	93	+40
Travel to Charleston	Yes	67	87	+20
Winston Cigarettes	No	93	93	0
Chevrolet	No	86	93	+7
Wood-furniture kit	Yes	73	93	+20
Work Cart	Yes	80	87	+7
Park Seed Catalog	Yes	80	87	+7
Jackson & Perkins Catalog	No	93	73	-20
Northrup King Catalog	Yes	53	67	+14
Burpee Seed Catalog	No	93	93	0
Thermo Solar Unit	No	93	93	0

The results did not support hypothesis 3. Increases in involvement with the offers in the ads did not produce increases in A_b, intentions, and choice of the brands advertised. See tables 7-10 and 7-11 for A_b results and tables 7-12 and 7-13 for average intention scores for the b/w- and color-ad conditions. The manipulation of ad involvement through verbal instructions did not affect A_b, intention, and choice behavior.

Table 7-8
Comprehension of Editorial and B/W Ads' Main Message

Statement	Response	Involvement High	Involvement Low	Total (n = 30)
For forcing bulbs, the most important factor for success is *top quality bulbs.*	None	1	0	1
	Incorrect	7	9	16
	Correct	7	6	13
Stark Brothers' Catalog shows how you can grow *an orchard in your backyard.*	None	9	11	20
	Incorrect	5	3	8
	Correct	1	1	2
With each catalog, Dave Wilson Nursery mails a *$4.00 Discount Certificate.*	None	13	15	28
	Incorrect	2	0	2
	Correct	0	0	0
Burpee Seed says its catalog is a *comprehensive planting and growing guide.*	None	13	11	24
	Incorrect	1	0	1
	Correct	1	4	5
Park Seed says its catalog is a *132-page book filled with the finest selection of flowers and vegetables.*	None	13	12	25
	Incorrect	1	1	2
	Correct	1	2	3

Table 7-9
Comprehension of Editorial and Color Ads' Main Message

Statement	Response	Involvement High	Involvement Low	Total (n = 30)
In 1778, a band of patriots	None	8	8	16
gathered at Midway Church to	Incorrect	5	5	10
blunt a British invasion.	Correct	2	2	4
No matter how far you travel	None	4	8	12
you will never see anything like	Incorrect	4	3	7
Charleston, S.C.	Correct	7	4	11
Princess Cruise wants you to	None	1	1	2
sail to *Alaska and Canada.*	Incorrect	2	4	6
	Correct	12	10	22
A solid wood investment is	None	5	6	11
Heirloom Kits.	Incorrect	3	5	8
	Correct	7	4	11
The work saver, the heart saver	None	3	4	7
is a *Garden Way Cart.*	Incorrect	0	0	0
	Correct	12	11	23
With Park Seed's Catalog, you	None	4	6	10
can *almost smell the fresh*	Incorrect	3	2	5
flowers and taste the luscious	Correct	8	7	15
vegetables.				
Northrup King offers *Basic*	None	6	5	11
Gardening Guides.	Incorrect	2	2	4
	Correct	7	8	15

The results supported hypothesis 4. The significant and nonsignificant relationships among ad involvement, thought processing, and A_b, intention, and choice measures were fairly consistent for the b/w and color conditions.

The results for Park Seed and other brands advertised supported hypothesis 5. Thought production increased positive attitudes, intentions to

Table 7-10
Number of Persons who Agree with Action Suggested in B/W Ads

Action	Involvement High	Involvement Low	t	p
Try forcing bulbs for early blooming	5.67	5.93	− 0.29	.78
Send for ticket information to Southern Living Show	4.27	6.07	− 1.78	.09
Send for free Herbst Catalog	4.33	4.47	− 0.12	.90
Send for free Park flower and vegetable book	5.87	6.07	− 0.22	.83
Send for free Burpee vegetable and flower catalog	4.80	4.80	0	1

Table 7-11
Number of Persons who Agree with Action Suggested in Color Ads

| | Involvement | | | |
Action	High	Low	t	p
Visit Midway Church	6.87	5.87	1.31	.10
Travel to Charleston, S.C.	7.93	7.47	1.77	.04
Take Princess Cruise to Alaska and Canada	5.80	4.40	1.46	.08
Send for Heirloom Kits catalog	4.67	2.40	2.33	.01
Send for Garden Way Cart's free information	4.20	4	0.19	.42
Send for Park Seed Catalog	6.40	5.07	1.31	.10
Send for Northrup King Basic Gardening Guide	5.47	4.93	0.53	.30
Send for a free Burpee Seed Catalog	3.87	4.40	−0.47	.32

buy, and gift choice of the products advertised. The results for Park Seed are reported in table 7-14. The findings were similar for both the color- and b/w-ad treatments except for the intention measure in the b/w-ad treatment.

Implications

Consumer involvement with ad messages is likely to affect thought generation of ad offers. Consumers are likely to connect ad-message-generated

Table 7-12
Number of Persons who Intend to Buy Products in B/W Ads
(n = 30)

| | Involvement | | | |
Type of Advertisement	High	Low	t	p
Park Seed	5.60	7.20	−1.17	.25
Dave Wilson Nursery	1.20	1	0.25	.80
Herbst Brothers Seedsmen	2.73	4.47	−1.29	.21
Conner Company	3	3.47	−0.32	.75
Burpee Seed	4.53	6.67	−1.42	.17
Thermo Solar Powered	0.73	3.40	−2.20	.04
Stark Brothers	3.47	3.73	−0.18	.86
Southern Living Show	4.40	7	−1.84	.08

Table 7-13
Number of Persons who Intend to Buy Products in Color Ads
(n = 30)

Type of Advertisement	Involvement		t	p
	High	*Low*		
Princess Cruise to Alaska and Canada	2.80	2.80	0	1
Travel to Charleston, S.C.	4.60	4.67	0.08	.94
Wood kit from Aeorogon Industries	4.27	3.53	0.51	.61
Garden Way Research Cart	2.73	2.67	0.05	.96
Park Seed Catalog	6.20	5.87	0.24	.81
Northrup King Basic Gardening Guide	4.60	5.13	−0.38	.71

thoughts to their personal experiences. If consumers generate such thoughts, their attitude toward purchase, intentions to purchase, and choice of the brand advertised are likely to increase. Persuasion research in thought verbalizations is likely to be useful for determining the relative impact of alternative copy approaches. Such research can be a practical pretest alternative to posttest recall measures of the impact of ads.

Additional research is needed on thought verbalizations of ad messages in natural print and broadcast settings. The results reported here are tentative findings. Readers should not draw conclusions until we can support these by further empirical work.

Table 7-14
Attitudes, Intentions, and Behavior of Persons with and without Thoughts on Park Seed

Type of Advertisement	Sample Size (n)	Attitudes		Intentions		Percent Accepting Gift from Park
		$\overline{X}$	s	$\overline{X}$	s	
Color						
Had thoughts on Park	12	7[a]	1.76	8.17[b]	1.59	83
No thoughts on Park	18	4.89	3.12	4.61	4.15	56
b/w						
Had thoughts on Park	4	7.25[c]	1.50	4.50[d]	4.36	75
No thoughts on Park	26	5.73	2.47	6.69	3.53	65

[a] $t = 2.11$, 28 d.f., $p < .05$.
[b] $t = 2.28$, 28 d.f., $p < .01$
[c] $t = 1.19$, 28 d.f., not significant.
[d] $t = -1.64$, 28 d.f., $p < .10$.

Recommendations for Thought-Processing Research

We recommend the following actions for practical research on consumer thought processing of advertising messages.

1. Include natural ad environments in testing; include editorial material and competing ads with exposures of your ads.

2. Do the research in natural viewing or reading environments; collect the data in the subjects' homes in order to try for the least possible disturbance to realism.

3. Use a tape recorder to collect data. Do not expect subjects to write their thoughts. Writing thoughts requires additional effort. Writing is a test of knowledge—spelling, thought construction, and grammar—and subjects may edit their thoughts if self-written reporting is required.

4. Provide detailed instructions to subjects. Use priming instructions to reduce subject self-editing of thoughts.

5. Do not identify the sponsor of the study. The subjects' knowledge of the firm sponsoring the study is likely to cause favorable thoughts, A_b, intentions, and choice behavior. This recommendation frequently is not followed in copy pretesting, especially when focus groups are used for ad pretesting.

6. Screen subjects to eliminate nonusers, loyal users, or those not identified in the target market. Select subjects by product behavior as well as geographic location.

7. Allow for pauses for subjects to process and verbalize their thoughts. Subjects may verbalize thoughts while their responses are being recorded by an experimenter using a paper and pencil. The data-collection procedure should be controlled in the study. Alternative data-collection procedures should be tested—for example, tape recordings only versus tape recordings and note taking by the experimenter.

8. Follow the order of data collection from thought processing to unaided recall to aided recall to comprehension to attitude toward the behavior to intention to choice behavior. In some tests only measure thought processing to A_b and intentions. Measures of recall and comprehension may produce unnatural effects on A_b and intentions.

9. Test multiple types of involvement manipulations. Low versus high versus very high involvement inducing ads should be created and tested. Inducing involvement by changing the instructions given to subjects needs to be followed by inducing involvement using more-realistic methods—that is, changing the involvement levels in the ads themselves (a thought produced by Terence Shimp, College of Business Administration, University of South Carolina, in a personal communication in January 1982).

10. Tests should be made using thought-processing research of b/w versus color ads, small- versus large-space ads, magazine versus Sunday news-

paper supplement ads, one positioning theme versus another, broadcast versus print media, and one product category versus another. A more-sophisticated understanding of how advertising works will result in a short period of time (two to three years) if advertisers are willing to do such research on consumer thought processing of ad messages.

8

Role and Implications of Averaging Processes in Advertising

James Shanteau and
Charles H. Ptacek

This chapter presents a cognitive framework for better understanding the communication effects of advertising. The framework is based on information-integration theory (Anderson 1971) that has been used to investigate the idea that consumer cognitive processes follow simple algebraic models (Bettman, Capon, and Lutz 1975; Troutman and Shanteau 1976; McElwee and Parsons 1977). Findings from a number of studies suggest that averaging is a very common psychological mechanism for consumer information processing (Shanteau, Troutman, and Ptacek 1977; Shanteau and Ptacek 1978). This chapter explores the evidence for and the implications of an averaging-processing structure in advertising.

The Cognitive Component in Advertising

Although a number of theories have been developed to describe the communication effects of advertising (see Smith and Swinyard 1982), most theories agree that the initial effect of advertising can be characterized as cognitive. For example, the traditional high-involvement hierarchy-of-effects model (Lavidge and Steiner 1961) characterizes an individual as going through a sequence of steps of increasing commitment to action: cognition→affect→conation. The low-involvement learning model (Krugman 1965) hypothesizes that affect is formed after purchasing and/or experiencing a product: cognition→conation→affect. In either case, the crucial first step involves the cognitive component.

In advertising, the cognitive process has received noticeably less attention than its affective and conative counterparts. For example, multi-attribute (Wilkie and Pessimier 1973) and expectancy-value (Fishbein and Ajzen 1975) attitude models traditionally are used to explain the affective component in advertising. Conation represents behavior directed toward action;

Preparation of this chapter was supported in part by Army Research Institute contract MDA 903-80-C-0029. The authors owe a special gratitude to C. Michael Troutman for his insightful comments on numerous phases of the research described here. The authors also wish to thank Norman Anderson, Gary Gaeth, James Gentry, Irwin Levin, Jordan Louviere, Ruth Phelps, and Paul Slovic for their comments on various aspects of the research.

in addition to forecasting models (Bass 1969), various market-mix models (Assmus 1975) and adoption/diffusion-process models (Mahajan and Muller 1979) have been developed for predicting consumer commitment, trials, and repeat purchasing.

Presently, no general cognitive models of information processing exist that advertisers can use to understand better the communication effects of advertising; affective and conative models tend to ignore the intervening states of information processing (McGuire 1976; Bettman 1979). Given this lack of understanding for consumer cognition, advertisers have relied on measurements of recall and recognition to evaluate the cognitive component. These measurements, however, provide little or no insight in regard to the underlying cognitive effects of advertising. Although the predictive validity of these memory-based measurements has been demonstrated to be relatively high (Haley and Case 1979), they cannot provide the neccessary diagnostics for explaining consumer cognitions.

Failure to understand how consumers cognitively process different pieces of information can lead to less-effective advertising. Many millions of dollars that could have been invested in productive advertising have failed to yield desired results because the message was not communicated effectively or because it was presented poorly (Colley 1961; Kotler 1980).

Information Processing and Averaging

To illustrate the importance of understanding consumer information processing, consider the different implications of an adding and an averaging processing rule. Suppose a consumer knows three good things about a product and then learns a fourth thing that is only moderately good. As described by McGuire (1976):

> If the person uses an additive rule of information integration, this new information of a moderately good product characterisic would increase the perceived attractiveness of the brand; but if the person is using an averaging rule of information integration, the new information of an only moderately good characteristic would decrease the brand's attractiveness. [p. 312)

Thus, the adding rule of information integration implies a cognitive system in which more is better. The adding rule, on the one hand, is analogous to combining two five-pound weights to form a ten-pound weight. Averaging, on the other hand, implies a cognitive balance analogous to combining two liquids of different temperature that then reach an intermediate temperature. Hence, the averaging rule implies a cognitive system where more may not be better.

The development of methods that can reveal the operation of integration rules like averaging constitutes a major contribution of information-integration theory (Anderson 1971; 1981). Two fundamental operations are associated with information-integration theory: valuation and integration. Valuation involves the measurement of weight and scale values. The integration function reflects the way in which consumers combine information.

The general model for averaging can be described as $J = \Sigma(w_i s_i)$, where $\Sigma w_i = 1$. The judgment (J) corresponds to the overall evaluation of the consumer. This is equal to the sum over all attributes of the weights (w_i) multiplied by the scale values (s_i). The weights, according to averaging, are constrained to sum to one.

The scale value represents the position of the information stimulus along the judgment dimension and is determined primarily by the content of the message (for example, "I like the advertised product characteristic"). Weight represents the importance of the information to the dimension of judgment and is influenced, at least partially, by the persuasive ability of the message (for example, "The advertised product characteristic is important to me"). Information relevance and salience, source reliability and believability, as well as quantity and quality of information are just a few of the factors that can influence how consumers weight different pieces of information. Because of its many determinants, the assessment of weights can yield considerable insight into a consumer's cognitive structure. Thus, weight values have been central in information-integration analyses of consumer judgment.[1]

Since weights must sum to one, any weight removed from one attribute must shift to another attribute. This implies an automatic trade-off process among the weight values. This trade-off process among weights characterizes the averaging process and distinguishes averaging from other models of consumer judgment. The next section demonstrates that averaging is a very common psychological mechanism for consumer information processing and that the weight parameter can provide a useful measure for understanding consumer judgment.

Empirical Results

In each of the six studies that we discuss in this section, consumers were asked to evaluate various products and/or services. In every case, the various brands were conceptualized in terms of component attributes. Averaging is then viewed as describing how overall evaluations are formed from the individual attributes. Due to space limitations, we can only summarize here; more-complete presentations can be found in the original papers. Also, where appropriate, we cite collateral evidence to provide additional support and elaboration.

Experiment 1

In the first study (described in Troutman and Shanteau 1976), expectant parents evaluated the quality of various baby products. Each product was described by levels along two relevant attributes. Disposable diapers, for instance, were presented in terms of absorbency (how much wetness could be soaked up) and durability (how well the diaper holds up while being worn). We explained to consumers that these attributes in fact were reported by *Consumer Reports* ("Disposal Diapers" 1968) to be important in evaluating the quality of these products.

Averaging was examined by comparing consumers' judgments for products described by two attributes with judgments for products described by only one attribute. Averaging implies that a diaper of high-absorbency and above-average durability should be evaluated less favorably than a high-absorbency diaper. In contrast, an adding model of the form used in most multi-attribute analyses makes the opposite prediction: High and above-average information should lead to a greater response than high information alone.

Consumers who were expecting a child within a month were asked to judge the overall quality of each brand alternative using an unmarked continuous scale. Consumers were to base their judgments solely on the information provided. Different products were described by using expert ratings of high, above average, below average, and low on each attribute. Consumers were told to think of these ratings as coming from *Consumer Reports* test results. The levels of the two attributes were combined by a four-by-four factorial design to yield sixteen different hypothetical brands. There were also eight additional brands described by each level of one attribute alone. These twenty-four brands were presented twice in random order.

The mean results for diapers are shown in figure 8-1. The solid lines correspond to the four-by-four factorial; for example, the upper-right point, with a mean judgment of slightly over 80, reflects a diaper with high absorbency and high durability. The dashed lines represent diapers described by only one attribute; for example, the right-most filled square, with a value of just under 80, reflects a high-absorbency diaper.

The most notable result in figure 8-1 involves the square values. In the upper right, the high-absorbency diaper (filled square) was judged to be of higher quality than the high-absorbency and above-average diaper (open square); that is, this result shows that additional moderately positive information lowered the evaluation of overall quality. This more-is-less outcome is predicted by averaging but not by adding; since the adding model predicts that more is better, the open square should have been higher than the filled square. Comparable, but inverted, results can be observed in the lower left for low and below-average information.

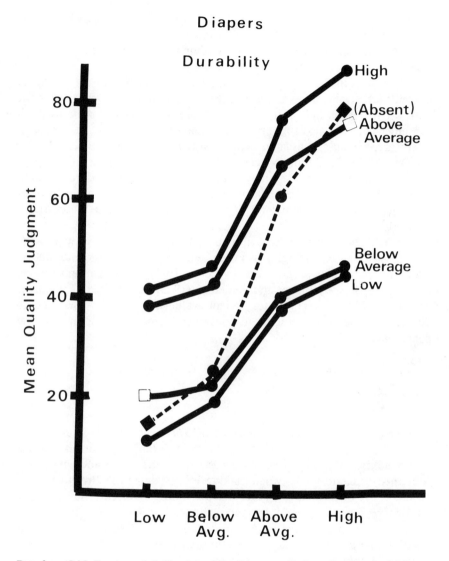

Diapers

Durability

Data from C.M. Troutman & J. Shanteau, "Do Consumers Evaluate Products by Adding or Averaging Attribute Information," *Journal of Consumer Research*, 3 (1976), pp. 101-106.

Notes: Solid lines connect products described using both attributes; dashed lines connect products described using only absorbency attribute. Averaging model predicts parallelism of solid lines and crossover of dashed line.

This (and the other plots) illustrate key role of graphical analyses in information-integration research. In contrast, actual data are seldom presented in analysis of other approaches to consumer modeling.

Figure 8-1. Mean Quality Judgments of Disposable Diapers Using Attributes of Durability and Absorbency.

We can extend this analysis to the slopes of the lines in figure 8-1. Averaging predicts that the one-attribute (dashed) line should be steeper than the two-attribute (solid) lines. In contrast, adding predicts that the one-attribute lines should be parallel to the two-attribute lines.[2]

The results in figure 8-1 clearly support the prediction of the averaging model. Statistical tests revealed that the one-attribute line was steeper for both attributes of the products used. Moreover, analysis of individual-consumer data revealed support for averaging in 97.5 percent of the cases. Therefore, averaging was supported consistently in these results.

One additional finding concerns the pattern of the two-attribute (solid line) judgments. These essentially parallel lines were observed both graphically and statistically. Parallelism leads to a particularly simple form of averaging called the constant-weight averaging model (see the "Discussion" section).

Comparable results to those in figure 8-1 have been observed widely. To cite some examples, averaging has been reported by Birnbaum and Mellers (1982) for judgments of used cars, by Levin (1974) for evaluation of prices in grocery stores, by Butzin and Anderson (1973) for children's judgments of toys, and by Brien (1979) for patient evaluation of medical services. In all, the evidence for averaging in consumer judgment is widespread and consistent.

Experiment 2

The second study (taken from Troutman 1977) dealt with an issue of continuing importance in the consumer literature—that of husband-wife decision making. The central question was How do husbands and wives combine their separate inputs when making joint judgments? Previous investigators have attempted to answer this question by concentrating on motivational or attitudinal variables (for example, Gottman 1979). In contrast, Troutman's approach was based on a cognitive analysis of husband-wife decision making. The research problem then was to describe how the decisions made jointly related to those made separately.

The strategy in this research was to use the averaging model to describe the joint decision-making process. In particular, the concern was for how weight values change in going from separate to joint judgments. To investigate this issue, expectant couples were asked to evaluate the quality of various medical services. The couples made judgments first separately and then jointly. When making joint judgments, both husband and wife had to agree mutually to the response.

The expermental procedure was similar to that described in experiment 1. Consumers were asked to evaluate pediatric medical services described by two attributes: doctor's ability and staff manners. Analyses similar to those in experiment 1 revealed that in almost all cases, the attributes were averaged to form the judgments.

The next, more-interesting, stage of analysis involved using the averaging model to derive the weight values for the various attributes. In each case, three weights were estimated (using a variation of the approach described by Norman 1976): (1) a weight for the ability attribute, (2) a weight for the staff attribute, and (3) a weight for the initial (or prior) opinion.

The resulting weight estimates were surprisingly similar for husbands and wives. The ability weight was .62 for wives and .58 for husbands, while the staff weight was .19 and .15 respectively. Moreover, the quality judgments also revealed a remarkably comparable pattern, especially given that husbands and wives were separated and not allowed to communicate during this initial phase of the research.

The joint judgments, however, were different from the separate judgments in three ways. First, the joint responses were 5 to 10 percent more extreme than the separate responses. Second, the joint judgments tended to be more unidimensional than the separate judgments—that is, the joint weight on ability is larger (.69) and the weight on staff is the same or smaller (.15) than the separate weights. Third, the initial weight for the joint judgments (.16) is less than for the separate judgments (.19 and .27 for wives and husbands respectively). Therefore, although there appeared to be little disagreement between the spouses initially, they nonetheless arrived at joint judgments that were different from the separate judgments.

These results suggest three conclusions. First, the weight parameter of the averaging model provides a useful basis for analysis of husband-wife decision making. Second, the decreased initial weight for the joint judgments may be explained by a mutual-reinforcement effect—that is, finding out that one's spouse agrees with you may remove any doubts that you may have had. Third, the increased unidimensionality of the joint judgments is reflective of a conflict-resolution strategy (concentrating on the most important attribute), even though the separate judgments suggest that there was little or no initial conflict to resolve. These results imply a lack of communication prior to the joint decision-making process so that husbands and wives apparently failed to realize their true degree of agreement.

Although there have been relatively few applications of averaging to small-group decision making, there are two notable exceptions. In a follow-up to the Troutman (1977) study, Brien (1979) conducted in-depth interviews with husbands and wives concerning their joint decision-making processes; the couples reported strategies that were compatible with the trends observed by Troutman for a variety of health-care domains. Also, Anderson and Graesser (1976) used an averaging approach to provide insights into the group-polarization (risky-shift) effect. Thus, averaging strategies are apparently descriptive of both individual and small-group judgments.

Experiment 3

The third study (taken from Brien 1979) involved an application of the averaging process to describe changes in consumer decision making. The research question was How would a major event, such as the birth of a child, influence the processes used in consumer decision making? Although numerous efforts have been made to describe the impact of various life events on consumers, most accounts have been based on attitudes and attitude change (for example, Fishbein and Ajzen 1975). In contrast, the approach used here was based on a cognitive analysis of changing consumer decision-making processes.

In this research, expectant couples were asked to estimate the likelihood of selecting alternative medical services involving obstetricians, pediatricians, and hospitals. Each of these services was described in terms of various attitudes (identified from pre-experimental interviews). The couples were asked to make joint likelihood judgments both before and after childbirth.

An additional purpose of this research was to compare consumers with different degrees of interest and experience in childbirth. Accordingly, there was one group of relatively naive first-time parents, a second group of prepared (through taking childbirth classes) first-time parents, and a third group of prepared second-time parents. By using the averaging model as a tool, the goal was to localize and to try to understand individual differences in the selection of medical services.

The results uniformly supported the predictions of averaging. Moreover, the differences both before and after childbirth and among groups could be summarized through weight estimates.[3] As an illustration, table 8-1 summarizes the weights in the three groups for the selection of obstetricians before and after childbirth. Three findings are evident. First, there are notable differences among the groups: the naïve-unprepared parents placed greatest weight on the physician's training and medical experience, whereas the experienced-prepared parents placed least weight on this attribute. Also, both prepared groups attached considerable weight to medical policies, while the unprepared group de-emphasized this attribute.

Second, there were some localized but interesting differences before and after childbirth. The naïve-unprepared and experienced-prepared groups were relatively unchanged by the childbirth experience. In contrast, the naïve-prepared group started out emphasizing training and experience (similar to the naive-unprepared group) but ended up emphasizing medical policies (similar to the experienced-prepared group). Thus, the impact of childbirth seems to have been most pronounced on the intermediate group.

Third, although not presented here to save space, comparable results were obtained for likelihood judgments of selecting pediatric services; that

Table 8-1
Weight Values for the Selection of Obstetricians for Three Groups of
Expectant Parents, before and after Childbirth

Group[a]	Attribute	Weight Before[b]	Weight After[b]
Naïve-unprepared	Medical policies	.27	.27
	Training and Experience	.40	.40
	Communication skills	.20	.25
Naïve-prepared	Medical policies	.33	.37
	Training and experience	.36	.28
	Communication skills	.20	.26
Experienced-prepared	Medical policies	.42	.43
	Training and experience	.16	.20
	Communication skills	.30	.27

Source: M. Brien, "Consumer Involvement in Health Care Evaluation and Decision Making" (Ph.D. dissertation, Kansas State University, 1979).
[a]Naive refers to first-time parents, and prepared refers to parents taking a childbirth class.
[b]The values do not sum to 1 because of some small interaction weights.

is, the unprepared group emphasized training and medical experience in selecting pediatricians, the experienced group emphasized medical policies, and the naive-prepared group changed the most following childbirth. For hospital services, the two prepared groups were similar in placing greatest weight on the attributes of hospital policies and hospital staff. In contrast, the unprepared group before childbirth placed greatest weight on the physical characteristics of the hospital; afterward, this group became more like the other two groups.

These findings demonstrate that the weight parameter in the averaging model can provide a useful description of how consumers make and change their decisions. Moreover, the weights were sensitive to some rather noteworthy patterns of group differences in consumer selection of medical services. Although the purpose of this chapter is not to pursue content-specific findings, the implications of these results for medical services are substantial.

While not directly concerned with analyses of consumer decisions, there have been several applications of averaging in studies of how experience influences the development of expert decision makers. For instance, Phelps (1977) found the model to be useful in describing the evolution of livestock judges' skills. Also, Ettenson (1981) used a similar analysis to compare the effects of educational versus professional experience in the development of auditors. Moreover, the averaging approach has been used as the basis for training experts in soil analysis and personnel selection to improve their decisions (for example, Gaeth and Shanteau, in press). Therefore, averaging has proved central in both the analysis and the introduction of changes into the decision process.

Experiment 4

The purpose of the fourth study (Shanteau and Ptacek 1978) was to analyze the effect of situational context and purchase motivation on consumer preferences. As before, the primarily analytic tool was the averaging model, along with the weight and scale values that go into the model.

Compared to the first three experiments, the stimuli and task setup were considerably more realistic. The choice alternatives were real products that were selected to exemplify various prespecified combinations of attributes. For instance, flashlight batteries that corresponded to different manufacturers (for example, Eveready) and type (for example, alkaline) were used. Consumers then were asked to estimate the likelihood of purchasing each battery in particular situations (for example, on a camping trip).

Consumers initially were allowed to inspect the products for any information normally available, including price. Various purchase situations (obtained from preliminary analyses) then were described. Consumers were asked to estimate the likelihood of purchase for every brand in each situation.

A plot of results for one representative consumer is shown in figure 8-2. The four panels provide the likelihood-of-purchase estimates for a set of nine batteries across four situations. Although there were some sizeable individual differences, the data shown are comparable to the types of differences found for other consumers.

While generally parallel, there were notable differences in the slope of the curves. These differences can be localized in the weights (see note 2). For camping-trip and home-flashlight situations, battery type was clearly the dominant attribute—for example, all standard batteries were preferred to all heavy-duty batteries regardless of manufacturer. Although the data are noisier, the opposite picture emerges for the on-hand situation; manufacturer was dominant, with all Eveready are preferred to all J.C. Penney, for example.

The pattern of changes across panels provides a particularly interesting form of support for averaging (Anderson and Lopes 1974). Averaging predicts that when weight shifts from one attribute to another (as in the first and second to the fourth panels), the lines both should decrease in slope and spread farther apart; that is, the trade-off of weights shows up as complementary changes in the slope (which reflects the weight of manufacturer) and the spread (which reflects the weight of battery type) of the curves. The results in this and in over 80 percent of the other cases support this prediction of the averaging model.

Even though changes in slope and spread had been anticipated, the complete reversal in preference ordering shown in the third panel was not. For the cassette-tape-recorder situation, Eveready alkaline was most preferred and K-Mart standard was least preferred. This is precisely the reverse

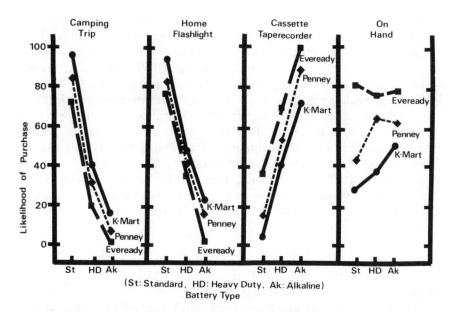

Data from J. Shanteau & C.H. Ptacek, "Situation Determinants of Consumer Decision Making," in Consumer Psychology Proceedings II, ed. L. Leavitt (Columbus: APA Division 23, 1978), pp. 19-20.

Each point corresponds to actual batteries selected according to attributes of Manufacturer and Battery Type. Different situations are summarized at top of each panel. Patterns of lines show both changes in slope due to weight shifts and changes in ordering due to scale value shifts.

Figure 8-2. Mean Likelihood-of-Purchase Judgments of Batteries for One Subject

ordering observed for the camping-trip and home-flashlight situations. In terms of averaging, these reversals in preference ordering are due to shifts in scale values; that is, what is good in one situation becomes bad in another. Similar shifts were observed for almost all consumers in making battery decisions.

Other studies have shown also that parameter values derived from an averaging analysis vary predictably as a function of the situational context. In a study by Norman (1977), for example, consumers evaluated alternative bus systems under two situations—work trips and leisure trips. Attribute weights varied as expected in the two situations: Bus fare had a greater weight for leisure trips, while walking distance carried greater weight for work trips.

Another aspect of the Shanteau and Ptacek (1978) study worth emphasizing is the use of individual-level analyses. Not only do such analyses provide a greater degree of precision than is usually obtained from aggregate analyses, but also they alleviate concerns about artifactual group results. As has been noted frequently, group analyses can be seriously misleading when trying to understand individual behavior. To cite one example, in an analysis of food preferences, Shanteau and Anderson (1969) found that group results seriously misrepresented individual decision strategies.

Besides avoiding erroneous conclusions, the ability to conduct individual consumer analyses also has important practical consequences. In Louviere and Kocur (1970), aggregate predictions about the use of public transportation were obtained by constructing individual models for 450 residents of Xenia, Ohio. These models then were used to make predictions about aggregate transportation-mode choice. These predictions were found to account for 80 to 90 percent of the variance in the residents' trip decisions. This is a notably higher value than obtained in typical group analyses.

Experiment 5

In the fifth study (Levin and Herring 1981), the researchers made an effort to determine the ability of an averaging-based analysis to predict actual consumer-choice behavior. Although the studies reviewed up to this point have demonstrated the descriptive ability of averaging, there has been little effort at independent validation of the results. The key question becomes whether averaging models can account for marketplace choices by consumers.

The research methodology used was based on having consumers first evaluate a set of vacation-trip alternatives. The attributes used to describe these alternatives were distance traveled, air costs, driving costs, number of travelers, and time of year. For each alternative vacation, consumers evaluated the relative economy, safety, and desirability of flying and driving. Independent information on the method of travel, cost, and so on then was gathered on each consumer's most recent vacation.

To determine the validity of the averaging-based analyses, various predictions were made about the trips. For instance, predictions were derived as to whether driving or flying would be a more desirable means of transportation. Similarly, the effects of time of year on the vacation trips was examined.

The results revealed that the averaging analyses were quite successful in discriminating consumers who traveled by plane and those who traveled by car. Furthermore, the averaging approach was able to predict some rather interesting choice pattens among economy, safety, and desirability that were observed in the vacation trips.

In addition, the results allowed insights into the effects of time of year on vacation trips. Based on the averaging analysis, it was clear that many consumers were concerned about the safety of driving during the winter. Those consumers who held such concerns were in fact most likely to have flown on their winter vacation trips. Thus, the averaging approach was capable of diagnosing some of the reasons behind the mode of transportation chosen.

Several other recent studies also have verified that the averaging analyses are capable of predicting choice behavior. For instance, Meyer, Levin, and Louviere (1978) found that a simple summary measure of the model was able to account for 70 percent of the variance in the selection of car versus bus transportation. Adding situationally defined constraints to the model improved the predictive ability to 95 percent. Moreover, the weight parameter was found to be particularly informative in distinguishing consumers who favored bus or car or who were neutral. Levin and Louviere (1982) extended these results to show that the weight values were related logically to changes in external conditions—for example, a raise in gasoline price.

Thus, it appears that averaging analyses, especially when combined with situational variables, are capable of making quite accurate choice predictions. Of course, the generalizability of any experimental finding depends on a variety of factors such as the quality of the research design, subject sampling procedures, and so forth. Nonetheless, averaging-based predictions apparently have the potential of high levels of accuracy.

Experiment 6

For the last example, a set of data is presented that originally was collected as part of a large-scale marketing-research project coordinated by Ptacek (1974). In the studies cited previously, the research was conducted by academic investigators whose primary interest was in evaluating the usefulness of the averaging model. With some exceptions, there was relatively little interest in these studies with the substantive outcome of the research results.

In contrast, the Ptacek (1974) project was a portion of a professional marketing-feasibility study. As such, the substantive results were of particular interest; indeed, there was no concern originally with examining psychological processes. However, a reanalysis of the data collected for this book illustrates some interesting extensions of the averaging approach.

A total of 526 homemakers participated in the study funded by a large midwestern food processor. The research, conducted in New Jersey and Minnesota, was designed to evaluate the feasibility of a new concept in frozen vegetables. This concept involved a combination of vegetables with a sauce packaged in a polybag. A total of twenty-four prototypes were prepared for evaluation by the homemakers. Each prototype vegetable combination was evaluated in two ways. First, consumers were asked for their reactions to a verbal description of a specific product before tasting it. Second, consumers were asked for their reactions after they had the opportunity to taste the product.

The consumers' responses to the products were measured using degree of liking as defined on a traditional nine-point hedonic scale. Each consumer evaluated four of the twenty-four prototypes. The products and the presentation order were rotated to control for any serial position bias and so forth.

For illustrative purposes, a subset of the vegetable/sauce combinations was selected to approximate a factorial design. As shown in figure 8-3, there were three base vegetables (green beans, corn, and peas) and three sauce types (cream, butter, and tomato). Although not listed for simplicity, the prototypes were constructed with slightly different ingredients to suit the particular characterisics of the vegetables involved.[4]

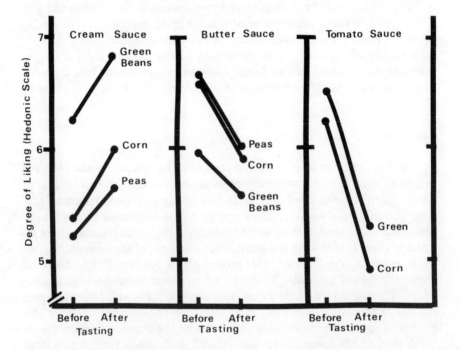

Responses measured on a nine-point hedonic scale. Base vegetables were green beans, corn, and peas; sauces were cream, butter, and tomato. Near-parallel lines support predictions of averaging.

Figure 8-3. Mean Degree of Liking for Vegetables in Sauce before and after Tasting

The results before and after testing appear remarkably similar to figures 8-1 and 8-2—that is, the lines are parallel. There are, however, three exceptions. First, although the points within each panel are close to parallel, there are notable differences among panels. In particular, vegetables in cream sauce are liked better after tasting, while vegetables in a butter or tomato sauce are liked less after tasting.

Second, the relative ordering of the vegetables in each panel appears to be a function of the sauces involved—for example, green beans are most preferred in a cream sauce but are least preferred in a butter sauce. This result, which is similar to the situation effects reported in experiment 4, shows that the scale values for the vegetables depend upon the level (or type) of sauce.

Third, the last panel (with tomato sauce) only has two lines. This is because no prototype was developed for peas in tomato sauce. In real product development, such omissions from a perfect design represent a common state of affairs.

Even with these exceptions, the results are remarkably orderly. This suggests that the same sorts of processes described for earlier studies apparently underlie these judgments as well. In particular, the weight and scale value mechanisms assumed by averaging also would seem to apply to figure 8-3.

Although it is not possible to test directly for averaging in this data set, relevant evidence has been reported in a laboratory study by Oden and Anderson (1971). They had consumers evaluate the favorability of meals formed by the combination of vegetables and a main course. When a neutral vegetable was added to a favorable dish, it decreased overall favorability; when added to an unfavorable dish, however, the vegetable increased the favorability. Thus, combinations appear to follow the predictions of averaging.

Other applications of the present approach to the analysis of food items by Anderson and Norman (1964) and Shanteau and Anderson (1969) also provide basic support for the averaging framework. For instance, Shanteau and Anderson found that lunches consisting of a sandwich and a drink are combined in a parallel manner. Therefore, the present results are compatible with previous laboratory-based investigations.

Modeling Consumer Cognitive Processes

The most frequently used approach for modeling consumer cognitive processes employs the expectancy-value framework (Fishbein and Ajzen 1975; Smith and Swinyard 1982). From the present perspective, the important aspect of expectancy-value models is their reliance on an adding rule of information combination. Mathematically, the difference between adding and averaging models is that adding models normally impose no constraints on the weight parameters, whereas averaging models require the weights to sum to unity. Because of the constraint on the weights, averaging implies the presence of a cognitive interaction; that is, the effect of any one piece of information is inherently dependent on the other information presented. Thus, as the weight on any single piece of information is varied, so must the other weights vary in a compensatory fashion.

The presence of this cognitive interaction differentiates averaging from adding models. We can see evidence of such a trade-off mechanism in both figures 8-1 and 8-2 and in numerous other analyses of averaging (Shanteau, Troutman, and Ptacek 1977). It is particularly noteworthy that weight trade-offs, and hence support for averaging, have been observed in a variety of consumer settings involving durable and nondurable goods (for example, Troutman and Shanteau 1976), products and services (for example, Brien 1979), and low- and high-involvement consumer choices (Shanteau and Ptacek 1978). Overall, the evidence of an averaging-type weight trade-off in consumer judgment is pervasive.

Accordingly, adding models that fail to incorporate explicitly a weight-trade-off mechanism may be called into serious question. In contrast, since averaging models incorporate weight trade-offs directly, they are capable of providing useful insights into the cognitive processes underlying consumer judgment. Therefore, the averaging approach is important because it does a better job of capturing the ongoing decision processes used by consumers (Shanteau 1983; Shanteau and Troutman 1975).

Forms of Averaging

Although the evidence reviewed to this point clearly supports an averaging rule, the exact form of this rule has not yet been specified. Such a specification is important for determining both the precise mathematical model and the corresponding functional relation between weights and scale values.

The concept of averaging entails the existence of separate weights for each piece of information. However, two variants of the averaging model given in the section "Information Processing and Averaging" exist:

1. The relative weights are constant across all levels of s_i. This model is referred to as the constant-weight model.[5]
2. The relative weights may vary across levels of s_i. This model is referred to as the differential-weight model.

The constant-weight model is a linear (or parallel) model. Experiments 1 (Troutman and Shanteau 1976) and 2 (Troutman 1977) represent instances of the constant-weight model. In comparison, experiments 4 (Shanteau and Ptacek 1978) and 6 (Ptacek 1974) are consistent with the differential-weight model. The latter model is characterized by nonlinear (or nonparallel) cognitive processes, which are quite likely to be found where situational variables are under investigation (Anderson 1971; Oden and Anderson 1971; Park 1976; Shanteau, Troutman, and Ptacek 1977).

One important difference between the two model forms concerns the relation between weights and scale values. On the one hand, under the constant-weight model, the weights and scale values are assumed to be independent of each other. Based on the present empirical evidence, this assumption seems most likely to apply in relatively simple consumer settings. According to the differential-weight model, on the other hand, the weight and scale value may influence one another. Empirically, this version appears most applicable when situational or other complex characteristics are involved. Thus, evidence for both forms of averaging have been found in research on consumer judgment.

Implications for Advertising Communication

Averaging has three important consequences for the communication of advertising information. The first and most significant is that the quality of information used to describe a product is more important than the quantity of information. Indeed, providing additional moderately positive information may decrease the overall consumer impression in some circumstances (see experiment 1). Since this point has been emphasized elsewhere (for example, Troutman and Shanteau 1976), we will not belabor it here. Nonetheless, the less-may-be-better finding has important consequences for selection of advertising strategy.

The second consequence associated with averaging is that it provides a theoretical basis for the concept of weight. In advertising, the weight parameter is often more important than scale value because of the manipulability of the weight-trade-off process. For example, although several factors may influence weight, the source of information is particularly important for advertising; that is, a given message will have a greater influence when attributed to a more-reliable or -believable source. As noted by Anderson (1981), source-reliability weight shifts can be viewed as involving the subjective probability that the source information is correct.

The third consequence concerns the versatility and applicability of the weight parameter. According to averaging, weight reflects the concept of contextual relevance; that is, an attribute may be important in one situation and relatively unimportant in another. Relevance weighting is a key dimension for advertising because it addresses the wants and needs of consumers. Experiment 4 (Shanteau and Ptacek 1978) provides a good example of this type of influence. That study revealed that situations have a very strong influence on consumer cognitive processes and that the weight of a product attribute can vary widely across different usage situations. As illustrated in figure 8-2, these weight shifts produced pronounced changes in preference ordering for brands of batteries. Thus, averaging has several important implications for advertising.

Applications of Weights

The various applications of the weighting concept in consumer/advertising settings deserve further comment. One particularly interesting usage of averaging weights has been to explain the negativity effect. As has been reported frequently (for example, Levin et al. 1973), negative information often has more effect than positive information. Using an averaging approach, Riskey and Birnbaum (1974) were able to show that this effect can be accounted for by the weight parameter. Moreover, they found that in some situations, even a large amount of positive information never makes up for a single piece of negative information. The extension of this approach to consumer topics like image analysis (for example, Reich, Ferguson, and Weinberger 1977) would seem to be especially appropriate.

It is also worth noting the use of the averaging model to describe the initial opinions of consumers. The weight given to initial views can provide important insights into how consumers react to attribute information. In experiment 2, for instance, the initial weights provided a useful index of the reluctance of husbands and wives separately to make what they perceive to be joint decisions. In short, the weight parameter of the averaging model provides a useful measure of a number of important consumer-related issues.

Conclusions

This chapter presented evidence from a number of consumer studies that suggest that averaging is a very common psychological mechanism for processing consumer information. According to Anderson (1981), evidence for averaging processes has been found in so many situations that it seems reasonable to consider averaging as a basic component of cognitive behavior. Hence, the averaging model would seem to provide a valuable starting point for analyses of consumer cognitive processes in advertising.

Notes

1. As noted by Shanteau (1980), there have been a variety of definitions of what constitutes a weight. To a large extent, the differences in these definitions are arbitrary and reflect the particular interests and/or statistical tools of the various investigators involved (Anderson et al. 1981). The definition of weight used in information integration, however, has proved particularly useful in providing descriptions of a wide variety of decision and judgment tasks (for example, Anderson and Lopes 1974; Brien 1979; Norman 1976; Shanteau 1980).

2. In plots of factorial designs, weight is proportional to the slope of the lines; thus, for products described by a single attribute, the weight and therefore the slope should be maximal. With two attributes, however, the weight is split according to averaging, and so the slope should be less. In simple adding models, there is no trade-off of weights, and so the slope should be unchanged in going from one to two attributes.

3. The measurement procedures used in this research were based on what Shanteau (1980) has termed *impact* values. These values are a function of both the weight and the scale values of the averaging model. Since there was little evidence of any shift in scale values, however, the values in table 8-1 can be viewed as a direct function of the weights.

4. Both the sauces and the vegetable mixes were varied somewhat in constructing the prototypes. For instance, green beans in cream sauce was made up of green beans plus wax beans and red peppers in a heavy cream sauce, and corn in cream sauce consisted of corn plus pinto beans in a cream sauce. Thus, these combinations should not be viewed as representing a strict factorial design. Nonetheless, the results appear to be quite orderly. This suggests that the base vegetable and the sauce dominated the judgments and that there is a relatively systematic pattern to the combination judgments.

5. Constant-weight averaging should not be confused with an equal-weight model. A constant-weight model assumes that the weight on an attribute does not change as the scale values change. This assumption leads to the parallelism prediction demonstrated in figure 8-.1 An equal-weight model is based on placing equal weight on all attributes. Although equal weighting has been advocated for some purposes (for example, see Dawes and Corrigan 1974), it has little descriptive usefulness for the sort of judgments presented here.

Part III
Effects of Manipulating Advertising Variables on Consumer Psychological Processes

In the search for more-effective advertising, many researchers have looked to the structure of the advertising, manipulating variables such as copy content, visual or pictorial content, and the use of specific source characters (like well-known versus unknown spokespersons). The chapters in this part deal with two such areas: (1) the visual and verbal components of advertising and their impact upon cognitive measures and (2) the effect of time compression upon both cognitive and more-traditional advertising-effectiveness measures such as recall, believability, and interest. Each of these areas represents a new research stream for advertising (dating only from the late 1970s), although they enjoy a somewhat longer history in the psychology and communication literature. Also, each has shown the promise of providing significant improvements in our understanding of how variations in specific executional elements can increase the probability of more-effective advertising communication.

Chapter 9 reviews the work of Percy and Rossiter on the effect of variations in visual and verbal components upon information processing and cognitive responses to advertising. Building from a base in the imagery literature, a series of experiments is discussed that points to the interaction of both visual and verbal considerations in the mediation of both visual and verbal imaging responses to advertising. The impact of these responses is presented within the framework of broader processing and stored communication effects. The results appear to support the model; just as the work presented by Mitchell in chapter 10 seems to support a similar model. In addition, following a series of guidelines decocted from the literature of psycholinguistics, an effort is made to manipulate verbal grammatical and semantic structures but with apparently very little success.

Chapter 10 begins by reminding the reader that most research on persuasion has concentrated on the verbal component of advertising and this despite the fact that most advertising contains little, and sometimes no, verbal information. Mitchell presents a two-stage conceptual model of the information-acquisition process, where the first stage is oriented toward the focus of a receiver's attention and the second stage is the type of processing that occurs as the receiver attends to the stimuli. Hypothesizing that the visual elements of advertising may affect attitudes by helping a receiver to extract verbal information about the product from the visual element alone, the model suggests in addition that the visual components of an advertisement also may have an emotional component or may interact with the verbal component to produce an effect or attitude toward the advertising. Several specific studies are presented that explore this model, and much as Percy and Rossiter found, this research suggests that significant attitude formation may result simply from the visual elements in an advertisement.

Chapter 11 deals with the question of time compression in advertising. Interest in this area has been stimulated largely by the reported findings of MacLachlan and his colleagues, beginning with a *Journal of Advertising Research* article in 1978. They have reported a number of remarkable effects from their series of experiments. However, other studies have tended to raise a number of methodological questions associated with their work, as well as questions as to whether or not there really are any advantages attending to time compression. Lautman and Dean deal with these questions in chapter 11, defining time compression, reviewing the literature, and presenting the results of a comprehensive study that attempts to address many of the methodological weaknesses identified in earlier studies. Their findings essentially are at odds with the earlier work, suggesting that the advantages, if any, of time compression in advertising may be quite limited.

Mediating Effects of Visual and Verbal Elements in Print Advertising upon Belief, Attitude, and Intention Responses

Larry Percy and
John R. Rossiter

Advertising, regardless of media, employs words, pictures, or some combination of words and pictures to communicate a specific message. Along the way, however, many things occur as receivers process the stimuli contained in the advertising, always assuming the advertising is processed at all. Research in the applied area of advertising effectiveness typically utilizes only a recognition or recall measure as a dependent variable, while most research into the area of cognitive receiver response has centered only upon verbal processing. In fact, the general area of information processing, regardless of discipline, has relied heavily upon verbal information processing and has utilized recall measures as dependent criteria.

Studies by Rossiter and Percy (1978; 1980), Mitchell and Olson (1977; 1981), and Wright (1979) have addressed the notion of imagery in advertising communication, utilizing visual versus verbal stimulus elements, with beliefs, attitudes, and intentions as dependent variables. Interesting, and significant, relationships were found, suggesting a mediating role for visual imagery in increasing cognitive response to advertising.

Thus, while it would now seem that imagery affects not only verbal communication (as Paivio 1971 and others have shown) but also visual communications and that cognitive responses are involved as well as memory, a question occurs: Where do these imagery effects fall in relation to more-traditional processing considerations? In an effort to address this question, this chapter reviews the ongoing research of Rossiter and Percy in the area of visual imaging and psycholinguistic mediating effects upon cognitive responses to advertising. Both verbal and visual elements in advertising can stimulate imagery, and variations in words and pictures are known to have differentiating effects upon at least recall measures of communication.

A Hypothesized Advertising-Response Model

In an early paper, Rossiter and Percy (1977) introduced a theoretical model that predicted that visual-imaging ability will mediate the processing of both visual and verbal stimuli (see figure 9-1). The model assumes that the initial and primary reaction to a visual stimulus is some type of visual or iconic encoding, which is labeled a visual-imagery response. The initial and primary reaction to a verbal stimulus was hypothesized to consist of verbal-comprehension response where the verbal stimulus is decoded and understood. However, as the cross arrows indicate, either initial reaction may cue a subsequent verbal-comprehension or visual-imagery response.

It was well known that verbal stimuli simultaneously could evoke visual-imagery as well as verbal-comprehension responses. Reseachers such as Paivio (1969; 1971) and Hulse, Deese, and Egeth (1975) had shown a consistently more-powerful influence with the visual-imagery value of verbal stimuli on verbal learning than other verbal-comprehension factors such as the meaningfulness of the stimuli. For example, more-concrete words, sentences, or even larger textual units have been shown to have strong imagery value. For this reason, any initial covert information-processing response to a verbal element in advertising may initiate either a verbal-comprehension response or a visual-imagery response or both.

However, the subsequent response in processing the verbal cue holds the greater theoretical interest in understanding the persuasive impact of the verbal stimulus. If the verbally attended stimulus is decoded favorably, then one should expect verbal reinforcement to occur, and if a visual-imagery

Advertising Response Model I

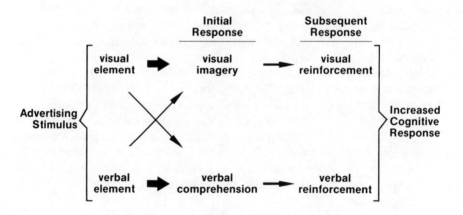

Figure 9-1. Advertising-Response Model I

response is associated with the verbal element, and if it, too, is favorable, one should also expect visual reinforcement as well. Note that the model we are discussing assumes that both visual and verbal reinforcement are possible from a verbal-only cue.

The verbal-reinforcement component of this hypothesis has a long history, beginning with the work of Staats and Staats (1957) who demonstrated that favorably evaluated words indeed can function as verbal reinforcers. As a result, when such verbal stimuli are associated with a product or brand, attitudinal response toward the product or brand can be increased.

Until the work of Rossiter and Percy (1978; 1980), there had been no support for the visual-reinforcement component of the verbal loop in the hypothesized advertising-response model. Unlike the affective learning involved in the Staats experiments, no one had investigated whether the visual-imagery value of verbal stimuli was related to cognitive response, only recognition or recall. Paivio (1971) had shown that with high-imagery words, improved verbal learning occurred regardless of the connotative value of the words, as long as the imagery values were equal. While this could be taken as an indication that verbal reinforcement is not involved in verbal learning but that some type of visual reinforcement mediated by the evoked image of the verbal element could be, this must be tempered by the fact that only a recall or recognition measure was used as a dependent variable. As we shall see in the discussion of the research, repair to more-cognitive-response-oriented dependent measures does support a dual-reinforcement model for verbal stimuli.

Although, as we have seen, some evidence did exist linking verbal-communication elements through both visual-imagery and verbal-comprehension responses to cognitive responses to advertising, no such evidence of a dual-coding phenomenon was available. There was, however, ample suggestion that visual imagery, at any rate, always occurs in response to visual stimuli. The classic experiment reported by Shepard (1967) revealed an incredible capacity for recognition of advertisements, even over time, for large sets of visual stimuli. His findings suggest that people do indeed store visual images of all visual stimuli they attend to.

Before going further, perhaps this is a good point to detail what we mean when referring to visual imagery. We follow the definition offered by Richardson (1969), who defines visual imagery as a consciously experienced, quasi-perceptual event. We also believe, as described by the model in figure 9-1 (and here we differ from Richardson somewhat), that subsequent visual-imagery responses made to the initial iconic image are capable of assuming reinforcing qualities. This view should be distinguished carefully from the imagery-coding theory advanced by Bugelski (1970; 1977). In his theory, Bugelski holds that all coding is imaginal, but he is not referring to a picturelike visual image when he uses the term *image*. We do mean to imply a picturelike visual image.

As indicated by the model, we also feel such a visual-imagery response is the most likely response to a visual element in advertising, although a verbal response is certainly possible. However, as with verbal stimuli, the subsequent responses to visual stimuli pose the more-difficult problem. Glanzer and Clark (1962), in advancing their "verbal loop hypothesis," suggest that although initial responses to visual stimuli may indeed be visual imagery, subsequent responses are verbal. However, such a theory would have a very difficult time explaining the results of Shepard's experiment.

Our contention is that subsequent responses to verbal stimuli may not pass through any verbal loop at all. In fact, as the model implies, we are suggesting a dual-loop theory in which both visual and verbal elements in advertising communication may mediate cognitive responses through both verbal comprehension and visual imagery—hence, a visual-verbal-loop hypothesis. This theory is an extension of Paivio's (1978) dual-coding theory of information processing. However, we are suggesting that with visual elements, a visual-imagery response is most likely and that subsequent responses may be entirely visual reinforcement with no verbal response at all. In contrast, verbal stimuli should result primarily in a verbal-comprehension response with subsequent verbal reinforcement.

A Framework for Processing Advertising

The role of visual elements in advertising communication has been discussed elsewhere in great detail (Rossiter and Percy, 1982). In that discussion, the authors developed a framework for illustrating the role of visual stimuli in relation to verbal cues during initial processing of the advertised message. This framework provides a logical extension for making operational the visual-verbal-loop model discussed in the previous section.

While it would be possible to explore auditory as well as visual advertising stimuli within this framework, we shall restrict ourselves only to the visual element, remembering that this also includes a linguistic component (in the form of written words and numbers). The complete advertising communication framework as advanced by Rossiter and Percy (1982) illustrates the role of visual phenomena as they are processed initially in short-term memory, leading to stored-communication effects in long-term memory, with eventual consumer behavior influenced by communication-effect retrieval. The parts of this framework with which we are concerned are illustrated in figure 9-2.

Initial Processing

Initial processing is conceptualized as consisting of three subprocesses, each with its own subcomponents. Attention is assumed to occur first and is

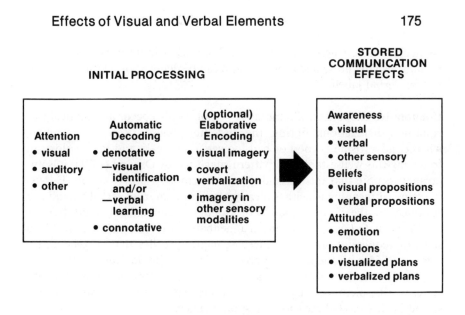

Figure 9-2. Advertising Communication Framework for Initial Processing and Stored-Communication Effects

regarded primarily as a sensory-focusing response or set of responses. As Kellogg (1980) has shown, this need not be active, or conscious, attention, but some sense-organ response is necessary. Next, we suggest that a process called decoding automatically occurs in which the stimulus is analyzed or evaluated for meaning in the manner proposed by Osgood, Suci, and Tannenbaum (1957) and Osgood (1971). Decoding consists of a denotative or identificatory response that may be visual, verbal, or both and a closely occurring connotative or emotional meaning response in which evaluation, potency, and activity features are registered automatically.

Denotative Responses. Denotative responses are essentially identificatory responses of the type "That is a _____." The identification may occur in any sensory modality, but the most common type of response is a verbal labeling or naming of the stimulus. Verbal labeling naturally occurs in response to linguistic stimuli, but as Pezdek and Evans (1979) have shown, it also occurs frequently in response to all but the most complex pictorial stimuli. However, denotative responses may also consist of an automatic image—for example, a mental snapshot if the input stimulus modality is visual (pictorial or linguistic), an echoic image if the stimulus is linguistic (visual or auditory), or even smelling, tasting, or feeling images for stimuli that are identified habitually through these other sensory modalities. Of particular interest here is the fact that linguistic stimuli in advertising (especially visually presented brand names) can be denoted by a visual image as well as verbal labeling.

Connotative Responses. Connotative responses also occur automatically as conditioned reactions during the decoding phase. Receivers evaluate whether advertising is good or bad, powerful or weak, and fast or slow. In following this well-established pattern suggested by Osgood (1971), it is important to note that this three-dimensional emotion-power-action (E-P-A) structure of meaning is neither merely a way of analyzing verbal stimuli nor confined to the verbal mode. For example, Tannenbaum and Kerrick (reported in Osgood, Suci, and Tannenbaum 1957) found that pictorial signs of (concrete) nouns produced semantic profiles that correlated, on average, .965 with the semantic profile of the graphological word: for example, the word *elephant* versus a picture of an elephant. Similarly, abstract words, pictures, music, and any other type of stimulus can be represented in this three-dimensional response space.

Finally, a third process called elaborative encoding may take place. However, we do not consider it a necessary condition for communication effects to occur. Elaborative encoding, if it does occur, and this depends upon previous learning as well as the recipient's current motivational state, may take the form of visual imagery, covert verbalizations or thoughts, or imagery in other sensory modalities, as in imagined tasting, smelling, or feeling responses. Elaborative encoding corresponds with what is often termed *cognitive responses*, except that we take a broader view of these responses by including imagery.

Cognitive responses in the current psychological and consumer research literature have been conceptualized as purely verbal. For example, Greenwald (1968) refers to cognitive responses as subjectively produced thoughts or arguments, and Olson and Dover (1978) refer to them as "internal subvocal" responses. Calder (1978) has been one of the few to recognize that cognitive responses also may be visual-imagery responses. In fact, cognitive responses may include imagery in any modality—for example, hearing a jingle suggested by a brand name, tasting a cold beer shown in an advertisement, smelling fresh baked cookies in an advertisement, or feeling the smoothness of just-washed hair in a shampoo commercial.

An additional theoretical point must be considered with elaborative encoding. With verbal cognitive responses, it is reasonably clear what "elaborative" means. Any covert verbalizations, reported overtly to the experimenter or written down as a protocol, that are not verbatim statements or close paraphrases of linguistic content in the advertisement or simple descriptions of pictoral content presumably would qualify as elaborative. Transferring this definition to visual-imagery responses, any visual images that are not iconic replays of the pictorial content, of an illustration in print advertising or a video sequence in television advertising, or of written words would qualify as elaborative visual imagery. However, an obvious problem arises in measuring elaborative visual imagery. To be recorded the imagery would have to be translated into a verbal description or else drawn visually on paper. Both methods involve expressive difficulties such that errors might tend to be counted mistakenly as elaborative (Evans 1980). While this is a significant measurement problem, it does not alter the theoretical distinction between iconic denotative visual imagery and the more-subjective imagery characteristic of elaborative encoding.

Stored-Communication Effects

Within the framework of advertising communication we are considering, stored-communication effects in the form of product-related responses are centered around awareness as a basic and minimal communication response. It may be visual like when a product is recognized at the point of purchase, it may be verbal like the recall of a brand name or product, or it may be both visual and verbal.

Attached to these basic awareness responses are various preferential responses including beliefs, attitudes (in the global-affect sense), and intentions. Beliefs and intentions, of course, may be stored as visual responses, although they are stored more often as verbal responses. Attitudes, in contrast, are purely emotional responses that do not contain visual or verbal components directly.

The research we review in this chapter goes byeond the traditional use of only an awareness response as a dependent variable for response to advertising and considers responses such as beliefs, attitudes, and intentions as dependent variables.

Imagery versus Processing Effects

While the research in the series of studies conducted by Rossiter and Percy deals with both verbal and visual stimuli, two response effects continue to be of interest, as reflected by the dual, visual-verbal, hypothesis. Certain verbal elements in advertising communication may be expected to produce either or both visual-imagery or verbal-comprehension responses, just as visual elements may be expected to stimulate either or both responses.

The specific considerations to be reviewed include visual and psycholinguistic consideration in particular areas of visual imagery and message processing. Visual-imagery responses center around concrete versus abstract and high-imagery-value words and picture size. Verbal-comprehension responses center around psycholinguistic principles such as sentence length and complexity, use of relative pronouns, and adjective versus adverb as well as color versus black and white in pictorial elements.

Visual-Imagery Responses

One of the more-consistent psycholinguistic findings has been the more-attractive power of concrete versus abstract words. Concrete words usually are described as those that refer to either objects, persons, places, or things that can be seen, heard, felt, smelled, or tasted. Abstract words refer to those things that cannot be experienced by our senses. Yuille and Paivio (1969) have found that concrete words are more effective than abstract words in communicating ideas, are better remembered, tend to be more meaningful, and as a result, are better comprehended. Others also have found that concrete words are more positively associated with comprehension (Begg and Paivio 1969; Sheehan 1970), and Paivio (1971) points out that both recognition and recall occur more accurately and faster for concrete words. We, along with Paivio, attribute this to imagery (if not always visual imagery).

Imagery value, according to Toglia and Battig (1978), is the extent to which a word arouses a sensory experience, such as a mental picture or sound, quickly and easily. As Paivio (1971) has pointed out, the imagery value of words is correlated highly with a word's concreteness; the two measures have about three-quarters of their variance in common. Therefore, while it is not, strictly speaking, impossible for more-abstract words to stimulate visual-imagery responses, it is much less likely unless learned specifically (Rossiter and Percy 1982).

Research on the imagery value of larger vebal units such as phrases, clauses, sentences, and so on has been rare. However, the few studies that have been done strongly suggest that imagery value improves communication. Jorgensen and Kintsch (1973), for example, have shown that high-imagery sentences can be evaluated significantly faster as true or false than low-imagery sentences, and Holyoak (1974) has found that sentences rated high in imagery value are significantly easier for receivers to understand than sentences rated low in imagery value. As we have found consistently, however, little or no research has attempted to link these larger verbal units with attitudinal responses.

Concrete versus abstract verbal stimuli have been an important part of much of our work, and we review the results in a later section. The visual stimulus with which we have been most concerned in visual-imagery response is picture size. Larger pictures or illustrations in print advertisements have been found to produce larger reported visual images, and these, in turn, produce better learning (Kosslyn and Alper 1977; Kosslyn 1981). Our work, again, moves beyond recognition and recall effects and measures, belief, attitude, and intention responses.

Verbal-Comprehension Responses

McGuire (1976) reminds us that the issue of comprehension obviously is related intricately to language and that indeed, until only recently was it simply assumed that one could comprehend what is perceived only to the extent that it was encoded linguistically. With the recognition that encoding may take place within a context of verbal imagery (Pollio 1974), much of the literature of psycholinguistics becomes relevant to the issue of comprehension (compare Deese 1970; Slobin 1971; Wason and Johnson-Laird 1972).

Percy (1982) related a number of psycholinguistic principles to advertising copy, but little experimental evidence exists isolating explicit advantages in mediating verbal-comprehension responses. Several such areas, however, have been studied and are reviewed later in this chapter. For example, we know not only that sentence length affects recall and comprehension (Wearing 1973) but also that it tends to be confounded by questions of sentence complexity. The addition of phrases and clauses not only increases grammatical complexity, but also causes processing to be more complex psychologically (Wang 1970). As sentence length increases, recall and comprehension become less a linear function of the number of words than of the grammatical complexity. For example, perhaps the most difficult sentence to recall or comprehend is one described as self-embedded, a sentence containing both an independent and a dependent clause. Within this context of self-embedded sentences, several studies (Hakes and Cairns 1970; Hakes and Foss 1970) have shown that the use of relative pronouns tends to facilitate recall and comprehension.

Also, of course, words that are found to be used more frequently are heard, read, and repeated faster and with fewer errors in tests of recognition (Paivio 1971). In tests of recall, a positive relationship has been found between word frequency and recall in both short- and long-term-memory tasks (Postman 1970).

While we have noted that visual elements in advertising tend to be more likely to mediate visual-imagery responses, we have suggested also that in certain cases they will stimulate verbal-comprehension responses. One such area is color versus black and white. Some evidence (Dooley and Harkins 1970) suggests that color's principal effect is motivational, whereas black and white is equally as effective as color as an information transmitter.

In a practical experiment, Sparkman and Austin (1980) found that one-color versions of newspaper ads generated 41 percent more sales volume than a matched black-and-white version. We have looked at this question in some detail, exploring its effects upon belief, attitude, and intention responses.

Research Review

The research reviewed in this section reports the results of four studies conducted from 1977 through 1981 by Rossiter and Percy. Each study examines one or more aspect of the visual-verbal-loop hypothesis, concentrating upon visual-imagery and verbal-comprehension responses to advertising stimuli and their mediating effects upon belief, attitude, and intention responses.

Study One

This first study has been reported elsewhere (Rossiter and Percy 1978; 1980) in some detail, largely as support for the visual-verbal-loop hypothesis and the mediating influence of visual-imaging ability in consumer response to advertising, both for visual- and verbal-stimulus content in advertising through visual reinforcement. In this discussion, we are looking at the results only as they relate to visual-imagery and verbal-comprehension responses.

Methodology. Four print advertisements were created and prepared professionally for a hypothetical brand of imported beer. The four ads varied in terms of high versus low visual emphasis and concrete versus abstract verbal emphasis. The advertisements were black and white, with picture size and copy type adjusted to reflect recommendations of a professional advertising art director while preserving the experimental conditions (see figure 9-3).

A two-by-two experimental design was implemented where subjects each were exposed to two of the four combinations such that each executional element was presented. Because of this dual presentation, two fictional brand names were required. Two equivalent and neutral names were selected through a pretest of nine candidate names among a sample of thirty male and thirty female beer drinkers. On the basis of this pretest, the two most equal and neutral names, Bauer and Laufer, were chosen.

Subjects in the study were eighty-eight adult beer drinkers (forty-four men and forty-four women), representing a broad age group, recruited and interviewed at a typical midwestern shopping center. Each subject was shown

BAUER BEER

Bavaria's number 1 selling beer for the last 10 years

Winner of 5 out of 5 taste tests in the U.S. against all major American beers and leading imports

Affordably priced at $1.79 per six-pack of 12 oz. bottles

LAUFER BEER

Bavaria's number 1 selling beer for the last 10 years

Winner of 5 out of 5 taste tests in the U.S. against all major American beers and leading imports

Affordably priced at $1.79 per six-pack of 12 oz. bottles

BAUER BEER

Bavaria's finest beer
Great taste
Affordably priced

LAUFER BEER

Bavaria's finest beer
Great taste
Affordably priced

Figure 9-3. Study One Stimulus Set

either a visually or verbally oriented advertisement containing either concrete or abstract copy according to the experimental condition. After reviewing the advertisement, they were presented a card with the appropriate brand name followed by four seven-point bipolar scales and asked: "As best you can judge, based on this advertisement, how would you rate this brand?" The scales—good-bad, inferior-superior, unpleasant-pleasant, and interesting-boring (with end adjectives in this order)—were selected from Osgood, Suci, and Tannenbaum (1957) and Fishbein and Ajzen (1975) for their high loadings on the semantic evaluation factor. Fishbein and Ajzen found these dimensions to yield a unidimensional measure of affect with reliability (coefficient alpha) of over .80. The scales were scored on a seven-point minus-three to plus-three system, with summated belief (range = −12 to +12) representing a dependent variable reflective of overall brand affect. Next, the subject was given a card containing an eleven-point scale for measuring an intention to buy the new brand. The process then was repeated for the second advertisement assigned to each subject's experimental condition: low visual if the original condition was high visual and concrete copy if the first advertisement contained abstract copy.

Results. The findings are summarized in table 9-1. They reveal that the high visual condition (that is, large versus small picture size) was significantly (p < .01) more effective in inducing positive brand attitude as reflected by summated belief evaluations and a significant (p < .05) advantage for concrete over abstract copy. In addition, a strong interaction was evident, with high visual and concrete copy outperforming low visual and abstract copy (p < .005).

While the expected order was replicated by the intention measure, the mean differences were not as pronounced as they were for summated belief product attitude. The interaction of high visual and concrete copy versus low visual and abstract copy, however, was significant at the .01 level.

Study Two

In this study two sets of rough ads with virtually no verbal content were used to test the impact of variation in visual content upon belief salience and intention to buy.

Table 9-1
Summated Belief Product Attitude and Intention, by Type of Advertisement

Type of Advertisement	Mean Summated Belief Product Attitude[a]	Mean Intention[b]
High visual	4.41	6.58
Low visual	2.60	5.95
Concrete copy	4.54	6.59
Abstract copy	2.50	5.94

[a]Summated belief product attitude range = −12 to +12.
[b]Intention range = 0 to 10.

Methodology. Five ads were rendered professionally for an existing brand of frozen prepared food. Three ads in the first set reflected a single illustration of a plated entrée, multiple illustrations of plated entrées, and multiple illustrations of people representing a variety of life stages and life-styles (see figure 9-4). Each advertisement had the same headline: "Everyone loves Stouffer's." The specific objective of this experiment was to see which illustration best communicated the target beliefs "Good for everyday meals" and "Ideal for most families."

The second set of two ads varied an illustration where in one the plated product dominated the ad with a secondary illustration of the same female source and the other execution, a female source dominated the ad with a secondary illustration of the plated product (see figure 9-5). The specific objective of this experiment was to determine which visual emphasis most strongly mediated evaluation beliefs toward the product, thus leading to the greatest intention to buy.

A sample of ninety adult homemakers was selected on an areawide cluster basis in three cities (Boston, Indianapolis, Phoenix). A total of thirty personal, in-home interviews were conducted in each city, five in each of six sampling locations reflecting middle and upper-middle socioeconomic areas. Subjects were shown randomly one of the three advertisements from the first set and were asked to read it as they would read any ad they might come across in a magazine. After looking at the test ad, it was removed from sight, and a series of questions was asked: first, what the subjects felt the advertiser was trying to communicate, aside from trying to persuade them to buy the product (a typical cognitive-response elicitation) and second, a series of belief scales reflecting the communication objectives of the advertising.

Results. We were interested particularly in whether the visual-imagery reinforcement of the verbal headline by the multiple-products versus multiple-people execution would influence more strongly the target beliefs. As the results in table 9-2 indicate, the traditional cognitive-response elicitations suggest that subjects perceive that the execution showing a variety of people reflects the advertiser's desire to communicate the notion that everyone loves the product and that the multiple-product execution is communicating the number and variety of products available. Each of these responses suggests a verbal-comprehension response to the advertising rather than a visual-imagery response, even though the advertising is almost wholly visual in orientation.

However, when asked specifically to rate their beliefs about the brand, the variety-of-products execution, and even the simple single-item execution (which reflected the current, and for several years prior, advertising approach for the brand), showed significantly more positive response than the variety-of-people execution for the targeted beliefs (see table 9-3).

Reprinted with permission of Stouffer Foods Corporation.

Figure 9-4. Study Two Initial Stimulus Set

Figure 9-5. Study Two Second Stimulus Set

Table 9-2
Summary of Cognitive Elicitations

Execution	Elicitation	Percent
Single item	Appetizing/delicious	37
	Tastes like homemade	33
	Looks good	27
	It is good	20
	Everyone likes	20
Variety of products	Large variety	60
	Appetizing/delicious	33
	Looks good	30
	Tastes like homemade	13
	Unusual/different dishes	13
Variety of people	Everyone likes	57
	Makes you feel happy/friendly	30
	For everyone	27

What these results suggest is that the more-concrete nature of the product-oriented visual executions had a greater effect upon the target beliefs as a result of stronger visual-imagery responses; this even though the subjects thought the variety-of-people execution was the advertisement that was trying to communicate the fact that everyone would like the brand. Without the reinforcement of the imagery response, the target beliefs were less likely to be affected.

After exposure to one ad from the first set, and completing the elicitation and belief scale question, each subject was asked to view one of the two executions from the second set. Here, the intent was to determine the extent to which a dominant source character versus product appeal in the visual execution would mediate beliefs and intention toward a hypothesized line extension. As the results in table 9-4 suggest, value-based beliefs were significantly stronger when the product was the dominant visual element in the advertising, even though more-general beliefs occasioned almost no difference.

This value response subsequently was reflected in the expressed intention to buy. Here, those seeing the execution where the product dominated

Table 9-3
Target Beliefs as a Function of Execution

	Percent Who Agree Strongly		
Belief	Single Item	Variety of Products	Variety of People
Good for everyday meals	40	50	30
Ideal for most families	23	40	20

Table 9-4
Beliefs about Product as a Function of Execution
(percent)

	Food Dominates		Woman Dominates	
Belief	*Agree Strongly*	*Disagree Strongly*	*Agree Strongly*	*Disagree Strongly*
High quality	39	20	39	17
Appetizing	32	24	28	25
Delicious	22	26	19	22
Good value	30	13	19	14
Best	20	22	14	28

were significantly more likely to express interest in the product: 45 percent were likely to buy versus 28 percent.

Clearly, the visual element in the execution has influenced the imagery response, which in turn has mediated belief and intention responses. Again, the more-concrete (or, as some have suggested, more-relevant—that is, showing product) visual component leads to a stronger positive response.

Study Three

This study extends study one by re-examining the picture-size phenomenon for a different product; by varying picture size through three levels; by varying only picture size in independent treatments—that is, with constant copy; by including brand beliefs as well as overall affect as dependent attitudinal measures; and by systematically adding a second visual-stimulus dimension, color. The color versus black-and-white selection is of obvious practical importance to advertisers, but it is also of theoretical importance since, as the earlier discussion points out, color should have a mediating effect upon verbal comprehension.

Methodology. The product category selected for this experiment was mineral water. A fictitious name, Esprit, was selected and presented as a possible new imported brand of mineral water. The stimulus ads in the study again were a professionally prepared rough execution. The advertisement consisted of the brand name, Esprit, at the top of the page, with a rendering of a bottle and glass beneath and a simple product claim at the bottom. Variations of this advertisement then were created by making color copies of the full picture, a 30 percent reduction of the picture (but not the brand name), and a 60 percent reduction of the picture. Black-and-white versions were created by simply reproducing the three ads with a conventional copier (see figure 9-6).

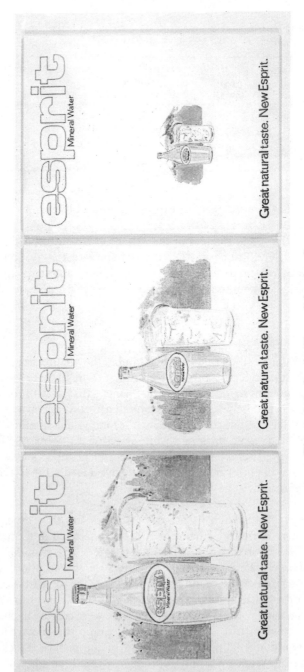

Figure 9-6. Study Three Stimulus Set

The study was conducted among ninety adult heads of household (forty-five men and forty-five women) randomly selected for personal mall-intercept interviews at a typical suburban shopping mall in a midwestern city. A broad range of demographics was represented. Each subject was assigned randomly to one of six cells representing the three sizes and the two color versus black-and-white conditions. The test was monadic, each subject seeing only one ad. The full experimental design thus was a three-by-two factorial with fifteen observations per cell. Statistical power considerations, and the exploratory nature of the study, suggested that the alpha level of significance be set at .10, although exact probabilities are reported.

Subjects were presented one of the advertisements and asked to look at it and read it as they normally would read an advertisement in a magazine. The ad was removed, and the subjects were asked a short series of elicitive probes in an attempt to gather imagery and cognitive-response data. Then, looking at the ad again, they were handed a card with eleven-point bipolar rating scales and were asked to rate the brand as socially acceptable-socially unacceptable, good tasting-poor tasting, expensive-cheap, natural-artificial, chic-"pseudo-chic." These attributes were selected from pilot research on the frequency of freely elicited attributes for the mineral-water category. In addition, subjects were asked to rate the personal importance of each of these attributes in choosing a mineral-water product, using a zero-to-ten scale (very unimportant to very important). Next, a measure of overall affect toward the brand was gathered over a seven-point scale for four of the same dimensions used in study one: good-bad, inferior-superior, unpleasant-pleasant, interesting-boring. Finally, each subject was asked how likely it would be that they would try this brand of mineral water, using a scale of zero to ten (would not try to would try).

In addition to considering the individual attribute beliefs, the five scales were summed for an overall measure of beliefs, and an expectancy-value measure of the beliefs and their corresponding importance weights was computed, along with an overall affective measure computed from the sum of the four evaluative measures.

Results. Significant effects were found for each dependent measure except summated belief. Although the main effect for the summated belief measure is not significant for picture size, the result does suggest a slight effect. The multi-attribute attitude measure, as modeled by the sum of beliefs weighted by importance, was influenced significantly by size ($p < .008$). These results are detailed further in table 9-5 and seem to support the earlier results of study one, which implied that a larger picture generated more-favorable brand attitude than a smaller picture.

It is interesting, however, as shown in table 9-6, that the measure of overall affect toward the brand showed no significant size main effect ($p = .697$),

Table 9-5
ANOVA Results for the Multi-Attribute Attitude Measure

Source of Variation	Sum of Squares	DF	Mean Square	F	p
Main effects	33324.511	3	11108.170	3.720	.015
Color	2912.711	1	2912.711	0.975	.326
Size	30411.800	2	15205.900	5.092	.008
Two-way interactions					
Color by size	4745.356	2	2372.678	0.794	.455
Explained	38069.867	5	7613.973	2.549	.034
Residual	250862.533	84	2986.459		
Total	288932.400	89	3246.431		

although it did show a significant color main effect ($p = .001$) and a color-by-size interaction ($p = .059$). Thus, the size effect worked only with color and not with black and white. This is surprising, since the affect measure used here is the same one used in the first study (Rossiter and Percy 1978; 1980). This suggests that the concrete versus abstract verbal elements contained in the advertisements used in the earlier study were a confounding factor in the interpretation of visual effects as measured by a multi-attribute formulation of overall affect.

Finally, while there was a moderate main effect for color ($p < .094$) on intention to buy the new brand of mineral water, there was none for size ($p < .325$).

Study Four

In this study, an effort was made to explore more fully the mediating effect of specific psycholinguistic characteristics upon verbal-comprehension re-

Table 9-6
ANOVA Results for Summated Affect

Source of Variation	Sum of Squares	DF	Mean Square	F	p
Main effects	204.289	3	68.096	4.620	.005
Color	193.600	1	193.600	13.135	.001
Size	10.689	2	5.344	0.363	.697
Two-way interactions					
Color by size	86.067	2	43.033	2.920	.059
Explained	290.356	5	58.071	3.940	.003
Residual	1238.133	84	14.740		
Total	1528.489	89	17.174		

sponses. A series of product copy claims was developed, reflecting several variables known to have impact upon recall and comprehension—for example, the number of words in a sentence, frequency of words occurring in everyday usage, level of concreteness, and the effect of relative pronouns in self-embedded sentences.

Methodology. The research was conducted as a part of a larger study on food and the meal. Three exercises were created where subjects were asked to evaluate hypothesized new lines of food products over the set of four affect measures used in studies one and three: good-bad, inferior-superior, unpleasant-pleasant, interesting-boring. In addition, an intention-to-try measure was taken using a zero-to-ten scale (would not try to would try).

In the first exercise, subjects were assigned randomly to one of four cells in a two-by-two experimental design, where each cell contained two moderate to highly concrete words within two descriptive clauses. They were then asked to imagine a new line of frozen prepared entrées that is described as follows:

Condition 1: "Easy cooking and for a real hunger";
Condition 2: "Easy to cook and for a real hunger";
Condition 3: "Easy cooking and when really hungry";
Condition 4: "Easy to cook and when really hungry."

In the second exercise, subjects were assigned randomly to one of four cells in a two-by-two experimental design, where each cell contained either a relative or demonstrative pronoun and nine or thirteen words. They were asked to imagine a new calorie-controlled food that is advertised as follows:

Condition 1: "It's food that tastes good in your mouth and looks good on you."
Condition 2: "It's food which tastes good in your mouth and looks good on you."
Condition 3: "It's good tasting food that looks good on you."
Condition 4: "It's good tasting food which looks good on you."

The final exercise placed subjects in one of two experimental conditions designed to reflect frequently versus infrequently used words. They were asked what they felt about a new dessert that was described as follows:

Condition 1: "Attractively, beautifully, deliciously, tasty?"
Condition 2: "Attractive, beautiful, delicious, taste?"

The study utilized personal, in-home interviews among a sample of 120 female heads of household selected on an areawide cluster basis. Six sampling points were utilized in each of five geographically diverse cities (Boston, Pittsburgh, Memphis, Denver, Seattle).

Results. The first experiment produced virtually no difference between conditions for overall product attitude. ANOVA results for the moderately concrete versus highly concrete conditions indicated no main effects—a fact not at all surprising when one sees the summated mean values in table 9-7. Intention, however, while providing an insignificant ANOVA, did produce means in the expected direction. Referring to table 9-8, we see the highly concrete mean of 5 is greater than the moderate mean of 4.14, with the two mixed means between at 4.23.

The fact that no significant main effects or interactions were found suggests that perhaps the stimuli must provide a clear concrete-versus-abstract distinction before expected mediational effects will be noticed. However, from an experimental standpoint, it is not easy to find similar pairs of statements that will reflect such a difference.

In the second experiment, the results indicate that the Hakes and Cairns (1970) and Hakes and Foss (1970) contention that relative pronouns facilitate comprehension of self-embedded sentences is supported, at least directionally, by the findings that both the overall affect and intention measures tend to be greater with the use of a relative pronoun (see table 9-9). However, once again, ANOVA results suggest no significant main effects ($p < .414$) for overall affect, and $p < .407$ for intention).

When considering the number of words used, we again found no significant main effect ($p < .583$ for overall affect, and $p < .815$ for intention). In addition, for both measures, the thirteen-word condition was stronger directionally than the nine-word condition. This finding was surprising. Both sentences were right branching; the only difference was the use of a compound right branch in the thirteen-word case. One possible explanation for this result could lie in the finding of Holms (1973), who found that for

Table 9-7
Summated Belief Product Attitude Scores, by Condition

	Cooking (4.83)	Cook (6.18)
Hunger (4.77)[a]	2.56	2.54
Hungry (3.92)	2.55	1.30

[a]Values in parentheses reflect concreteness ratings as reported by Brown and Ure (1969).
W.P. Brown and D.M.J. Ure, "Five Rated Characteristics of 650 Word Association Stimuli," British Journal of Psychology, 60, 23-249.

Table 9-8
Intention to Try Scores, by Condition

	Cooking (4.83)	Cook (6.18)
Hunger (4.77)[a]	4.23	5
Hungry (3.92)	4.14	4.23

[a]Values in parentheses reflect concreteness ratings as reported by Brown and Ure.

relatives, center-embedded sentences tended to be recalled more easily. Even though the thirteen-word condition was a right-branching self-embedded sentence with a compound branch, in terms of message processing, perhaps it was treated as a center-embedded sentence. To illustrate, consider the following example:

Right branching: "Its food (that/which) tastes good in your mouth and looks good on you"

Center embedded: "It's food (that/which) tastes good in your mouth helping you look good"

The problem is that even though some researchers (Miller 1973; Wearing 1973) found that shorter sentences should be easier to remember, the effects of length are not so simple or conclusive as this implies. Memory and comprehension are not so much determined by the number of words as by the grammatical complexity of some long sentences. Right-branching sentences, for example, have been found to be not as affected as other constructions by the number of subordinate clauses (Goldman-Eisler and Cohen 1971; Hamilton and Deese 1971). Length, therefore, should be a concern only when it affects the grammatical complexity of a sentence.

In the final exercise, the more frequently used set of descriptions (attractive, beautiful, delicious, taste) was found not to be significantly better

Table 9-9
Attitude and Intention by Condition

Condition	Mean Summated Belief Product Attitude	Mean Intention
That	3.30	7.11
Which	4.52	8.34

than the somewhat less frequently used set (attractively, beautifully, deliciously, tasty) in mediating overall affect ($t = -.96$) or intention ($t = .18$). Directionally, the results were mixed. Intention was found to be in the direction predicted (10.52 versus 10.15), although this difference is slight. However, the less frequently used adverbs generated a much greater overall affect (11.60 versus 9.07). Since the ANOVA results support the null hypothesis of no difference, perhaps frequency of use, unless greatly exaggerated in difference, while influencing recall (Paivio 1971; Postman 1970) may not mediate verbal-comprehension responses.

Discussion

The research reviewed in this chapter has attempted to deal with two major concerns: (1) the almost complete lack of cognitive-response variables such as beliefs, attitudes, and intentions as dependent variables in tests of visual and verbal mediating effects upon responses to advertising and (2) the distinction between visual-imagery and verbal-comprehension responses as a function of either visual or verbal stimuli (as outlined in figure 9-1).

We have argued extensively elsewhere for the importance of beliefs, attitudes, and intentions as communication objectives for advertising (Percy and Rossiter 1980; Rossiter and Percy 1982). Beliefs especially are an interesting theoretical issue in the study of communication effects for visual stimuli because of the strong verbal response involved in learning. The results of Mitchell and Olson (1977; 1981) provided perhaps the first test of the effects of visual elements alone on product beliefs. They found a strong mediating effect for visual-only advertising upon product beliefs, we would suggest owing to a visual-imagery and subsequent reinforcement response. Our research, reviewed under study three, looked at the effect of picture size upon product belief, and while not as significant as the Mitchell and Olson findings, we noted a modest effect ($p < .134$). These data would seem to suggest that a visual-imagery response, occasioned only by a visual stimuli, indeed can mediate product beliefs.

The results of study two, although somewhat less rigorous, dealt specifically with manipulations of elements in an advertisement for an established brand (and hence an a priori and well-developed set of beliefs). In each experiment the researchers found that variation in visual content significantly affected targeted belief saliences. Again, this would appear to support the notion of visual-imagery response leading to a specific belief response.

Attitude as a communication objective is obviously important, particularly in cases where consumers select products on some overall evaluative rating rather than on the basis of one or two attribute beliefs. For this reason, we operationalized attitude as an overall or global evaluative response in the expectancy-value mode, following Fishbein and Ajzen (1975). Mitchell and Olson (1977; 1981) also included measures of overall product attitude in their work and found positive relationships between visual elements in advertising and product attitude. In studies one and three, the effect of picture size upon overall product attitude was measured, and in each case a significant positive effect was noted: Larger picture sizes stimulate significantly more-favorable attitudes than the same picture reduced in size.

The ability of visual elements in advertising to mediate product attitude independently (that is, exclusive of verbal elements) has been established clearly by these studies. Verbal elements also appear to be capable of mediating product attitude through a visual-imagery response. Study one found a significant advantage ($p < .05$) for concrete versus abstract copy in generating positive brand attitudes; and consistent with Paivio's dual-code theory, there was a large interaction effect between the visual and verbal components.

Study four examined a number of verbal stimuli, with inconclusive results. Overall attitude was measured for moderate versus highly concrete words, and no effect was found. Here, we were expecting a visual-imagery response. With frequency of word use and number of words in a sentence, where verbal-comprehension responses were expected, no significant mediating effects were noted. Comparing relative versus demonstrative pronouns. A slight predicted directional advantage for relative pronouns was measured (4.52 versus 3.30), although this difference was not statistically significant. So, while we did note a concrete-versus-abstract difference in study one, this was confounded (perhaps) by the strong interaction with the visual stimuli. The purely verbal study four was unable to measure any significant mediating effect for either visual-imagery or verbal-comprehension responses; the latter is in contradiction to expectations raised by the psycholinguistic literature.

Intention, the final dependent variable considered, was measured in all four studies, as well as by Mitchell and Olson (1977; 1981) and Wright (1979). In each case, while some significant mediating effects were noted, the effects for intention usually were weaker than for attitudes. As we have remarked elsewhere (Rossiter and Percy 1980), this may result because intention to act is an operant rather than a classically conditioned response and as such is under the control of variables outside the content of the advertising (for example, price, distribution, and so forth).

Specifically, our research indicated an advantage for larger pictures in the high visual condition of study one but not for picture size in study three; concrete versus abstract verbal stimulus led to an expected advantage for concrete, along with a significant interactive effect ($p < .01$) with picture size in study one, plus a directional (5 versus 4.14), albeit not significant, effect in the moderate versus highly concrete verbal-only condition of study four. Study two, which examined intention to try a line extension for an established product, found that the more-concrete-oriented visual combination mediated a significantly greater intention to try the advertised product (45 versus 28 percent). Again, it would seem that visual-imagery responses to both visual and verbal stimuli can mediate intention responses significantly, although not as strongly as attitudinal responses.

The verbal-only exercises in study four again revealed no significant effects for intention, although relative versus demonstrative pronouns were significant directionally as predicted (8.34 versus 7.11). The problems throughout this study of verbal-only copy claims not conforming significantly (if at all) to the verbal-comprehension response implied by traditional studies in psycholinguistics perhaps simply reflect the difficulty in creating matched pairs of linguistically different constructs. This problem is compounded by the issue of grammatical complexity.

We have avoided mentioning the color-versus-black-and-white issue researched in study three to this point because of the admittedly difficult task of classifying response to that variable as either visual imagery or verbal comprehension. Because of the nature of this variable, and particularly, its use within this study, we tend to hypothesize it as a visual stimulus generating a verbal-comprehension response. This hypothesis is reinforced by the suggested motivational nature of its effect (Dooley and Harkins 1970) and by the Sparkman and Austin (1980) finding of a strong, direct relationship to sales. Regardless of the response, there is ample evidence in our research of color having a significant mediating effect upon beliefs, attitudes, and intentions. Although not reported in the discussion of study three, a significant ($p < .08$) effect was found for a taste belief (one of five measured), suggesting that where relevant, color can mediate belief salience. For both overall product attitude ($p < .001$) and intention ($p < .094$), color was found to have a significant mediating effect.

In summary, the Rossiter and Percy research to date has found varied and significant visual-imagery responses for both visual and verbal stimuli in mediating belief, attitude, and intention responses to advertising. The important influences of visual-only and interaction of visual with verbal elements in stimulating visual-imagery responses to advertising is certainly of practical significance to advertising. The difficulty in isolating verbal-comprehension responses as implied by verbal-only examples of psycholinguistic principles known to mediate recall and comprehension remains a concern. While some results were in the predicted direction, none was statistically significant. Furture efforts must better discriminate the verbal stimuli over a larger range and must attempt to minimize the confounding influence of grammatical complexity.

10 The Effects of Visual and Emotional Advertising: An Information-Processing Approach

Andrew A. Mitchell

Most of the research on persuasion has emphasized verbal or written communications. Consequently, most of the models of persuasion that have been developed are based primarily on the verbal responses made by individuals to advertisements. The cognitive-response approach to persuasion, for instance, has focused on the verbal thoughts made by individuals during exposure to a persuasive communication (for example, Greenwald 1968; Wright 1973), while the cognitive-structure approach has emphasized the product-attribute beliefs that are formed or changed after an exposure to a persuasive communication (Lutz 1975; Olson and Mitchell 1975).

Very few advertisements, however, contain only verbal information. Most advertisements, in fact, contain very little verbal information. In addition, many advertisements seem to contain very little verbal or visual information about the advertised product and seem instead to be designed primarily to evoke an emotional response in the consumer. Examples of these types of advertisements are those for McDonald's and AT&T long-distance calling. How do visual and emotional advertisements work? Do they have an effect on consumer behavior? If so, how? These issues have generated considerable interest recently among advertising researchers (for example, Rossiter 1982; Rossiter and Percy 1982; Kisielius 1982; Edell 1982).

In this chapter, I explore these issues by first examining a conceptual model of the information-acquisition process and then reviewing a study that examined the effects of visual and emotional advertisements. The results of this study raise a number of issues that I examine with the conceptual model and the results of three additional experiments.

Conceptual Model

Information-Acquisition Process

During the information-acquisition process, data from the environment are encoded, and a representation of this encoded information is stored in long-

197

term memory. The mental processes that occur during exposure to the data from the environment will determine what information will be stored in long-term memory and how it will be represented. Two critical factors affect these mental processes—attention and the processing strategy that is used. These factors, in turn, are affected by other variables such as the stimulus, knowledge about the stimulus, and the current goals of the individual (Mitchell 1982a).

The first factor, attention, has limited capacity. This has two important implications. First, we can attend to only a limited number of stimuli at one time. Second, we can devote only a limited amount of attention to each stimulus. Consequently, in the information-acquisition process, what stimuli are attended to and the amount of attention devoted to each stimulus are of critical importance. We are exposed to a large number of stimuli at any given time but focus our attention on only a small number of these stimuli. Observers believe that stimuli that are attended to are represented in long-term memory and can be recalled if the appropriate retrieval cues are available (Krugman 1977; McGuiniss 1980).

During exposure to a stimulus, we must also decide how much attention to devote to that stimulus. We may devote full attention to the stimulus or we may try to devote attention to more than one stimulus at a time. The amount of attention that we devote to a stimulus will be related to the second factor, processing strategy.

While attending to a stimulus, a number of different mental processes may occur. Many of these processes are low-level processes that occur automatically (Posner and Snyder 1975; Schneider and Shiffren 1977). Shapes are recognized as horses and semantic meaning is attached to words. These processes require little, if any, attentional capacity and usually cannot be overridden even though it may be in the individual's best interests to do so.

Higher-level, or controlled, processes require attention and, usually, the activation of appropriate knowledge structures for their execution. Examples of these higher-level processes are the generation of inferences and counterarguments. The individual's knowledge about the stimulus and his or her goals while exposed to the stimulus will determine these higher-level processes. For instance, making inferences about the performance of a particular automobile may require knowledge of how the weight of the automobile and the size of the engine affect acceleration.

The differences between these lower- and higher-level processes are evident in text comprehension. In reading a story or an advertisement, individuals organize their understanding of the information at different levels. Phrases and sentences are read and understood at one level, and then these sentences and phrases are organized and integrated into an understanding of the text at a higher level (for example, Fredrickson 1975;

Kintsch and Van Dijk 1978). The reading and understanding of phrases and sentences are largely automatic; however, the processes involved in organizing and integrating these sentences and phrases are control processes. Reading a story or an advertisement to achieve different goals will result in different higher-level processes (Kintsch and Van Dijk 1978). For instance, reading a story for pleasure as opposed to reading the same story to analyze the writing style or the structure of the story will result in very different higher-order processes.

Long-Term Memory

Most of the current experimental evidence strongly supports an associative network model of long-term memory (for example, Wickelgren 1981; Anderson 1976). Within this model, the nodes of the network represent ideas or concepts, and the links are the associations among concepts. These links differ in the strength so that some concepts are more strongly associated than others.

Information retrieval in this model occurs through spreading activation. Specific nodes within the network are activated, and activation then spreads to the nodes linked to the activated node (Collins and Loftus 1976). The stronger the association between two nodes, the more likely the activation of one node will result in the activation of a related node. After the activation of a particular node exceeds a threshold level, the information at the node is recalled. Higher-order, or controlled, processing essentially adds and strengthens links between two nodes in memory (Anderson and Reder 1979; Mandler 1979).

Information Acquisition from Visual
and Verbal Stimuli

Research on the acquisition of information from visual and verbal stimuli in cognitive psychology has indicated two important findings. First, a number of studies have indicated that there are two different channels in the information-acqusition process—a verbal and a visual channel (for example, Brooks 1968; Posner 1969; Posner et al. 1969); that is, if a subject is given a verbal-distractor task that effectively blocks the verbal channel while he or she is exposed to a stimulus, the subject may still acquire information about the stimulus through the visual channels (Mitchell 1982c).

The second important finding is that subjects can recognize and recall visual stimuli better than verbal stimuli (for example, Paivio 1971). For instance, if subjects are shown a series of words (for example, *dog, cat, fish*) or a picture of a well-known stimulus (for example, picture of a horse) and are later asked to recall the items, the subjects consistently will recall a significantly greater percentage of the stimuli presented as pictures than as words. In addition, words that represent specific objects (for example, *car*) are recalled better than words that represent abstract concepts (for example, equity).

The ability to recall a visual stimulus, however, seems to depend upon whether or not a semantic interpretation was given to the stimulus (for example, Bower and Karlin 1974; Wiseman and Neisser 1974). For instance, Klatzky and Rafnel (1976) showed subjects nonsense pictures and either provided them with no labels, meaningful labels, or meaningless labels. Recall of the pictures with meaningful labels was superior to recall of pictures with no labels or with meaningless labels. Recall in the latter two conditions was about the same.

Paivio (1971) has presented a dual-code theory to explain these results. According to this theory, stimuli can be represented in memory using a verbal code, a visual code, or both. Information presented pictorially is most likely to be represented using both a verbal and visual code; concrete words are less likely to be represented using both codes, and abstract words normally are represented with only a verbal code. Since the use of each code has an additive effect on the probability of recalling the item, the theory predicts the standard finding that items presented pictorially are recalled better than items presented verbally and that concrete words are recalled better than abstract words.

The semantic interpretation of a pictorial stimulus seems critical in facilitating the recall of that stimulus. This interpretation or labeling response, within a network model of memory, would provide a link between the visual representation and a semantic node in memory. In addition, the creation of a visual image of a word also seems to facilitate recall.

Social psychologists have suggested that vivid information has a stronger effect on judgments than pallid information (Nisbett and Ross 1980). Although Nisbett and Ross do not provide a precise definition of "vividness," they suggest that vivid information is "(a) emotionally interesting, (b) concrete and imagery-provoking and (c) proximate in a sensory, temporal, or spacial way" (p. 52). However, after reviewing a number of studies that examined the effect of vividness, Taylor and Thompson (1982) concluded that vividness primarily affects whether or not the individual attends to the stimuli. Included in this literature review were three studies that examined the presentation of information visually and verbally. All three studies found no differences in the verbal responses made to the verbal or the visual presentation of information.

Effects of Processing Strategy

Differences in how individuals process the information from advertisements will affect what information is represented in memory and how it is represented. These differences in how individuals process the information will be determined by the goals of the individual that, in turn, will affect the knowledge structures that are activated while exposed to the advertisement. If an individual has a goal of learning about or forming an evaluation of the advertised brand, the text-processing literature (for example, Kintsch and Van Dijk 1978; Graesser 1981) suggests that he or she first will form a verbal representation of what the advertisement is communicating about the product. Fishbein and Ajzen (1975) refer to such representation as message belief. This should occur whether the information is verbal or visual. For instance, we find that in studies where we give our subjects the goal of evaluating the advertised brand in advertisements that are primarily visual, the concurrent protocols indicate that the subjects use the visual information to form a verbal understanding of the advertised brand (for example, Mitchell 1982c).

This verbal understanding then is used to generate higher-order thoughts or elaborations like counterarguments. Theoretically, if an individual forms the same verbal understanding of messages that are presented verbally and visually, the resulting higher-order thoughts should be the same. This may be why the three studies cited by Taylor and Thompson (1982) found no difference in the verbal responses to information presented verbally and visually.

With brand processing, an individual probably will form a node for the advertised brand in memory, if one does not already exist, and the higher-level or elaborative thoughts will form linkages between the concepts and the brand node (for example, Anderson and Reder 1979). A representation of the advertisement also probably will be linked to the brand node.

If an individual looks at an advertisement with other goals like trying to identify the music used in an advertisement, very different higher-level processes will occur (Mitchell, Gardner, and Russo 1981). In these situations, the individual probably will not form a verbal representation of the information in the advertisement and will not activate the knowledge structure for the brand or product while processing the information. If the advertisement is primarily verbal, some automatic processing of the verbal information will probably occur so bits and pieces of the information may be available in memory. Less information, however, will be acquired under these conditions than with a brand strategy (Mitchell, Gardner, and Russo 1981). In addition, linkages may not be formed between the acquired information and the brand node in memory.

The type of processing that occurs during exposure to an advertisement will affect how the information from the advertisement is represented in memory. If the individual attends to the advertisement, then a mental representation of the advertisement will exist in memory. However, in order to retrieve that mental representation, links will need to be formed between the mental representation of the advertisement and other structures in memory. The types of links that are formed will depend upon the type of higher-level processing that has occurred. For instance, a Schlitz beer commercial has a scene about soaring in the Alps. If an individual executes a brand-processing strategy while exposed to the commercial, links should be formed between the mental representation of the commercial and the node for Schlitz beer (figure 10-1). However, if the individual executes a nonbrand-processing strategy by activating his or her knowledge structures about soaring, linkages probably will be formed between the mental representation of the commercial and the soaring node (figure 10-2). If the advertisement is not labeled as a Schlitz beer advertisement, linkages will not be formed between the representation of the advertisement and the Schlitz beer node. If these links are not formed, activation of the Schlitz beer node would not result in the activation of the representation of the television commercial.

Emotion

Emotion has been conceptualized as having both a physiological component and a cognitive component (for example, Schachter and Singer 1962; Schachter 1964; Mandler 1975). Mandler, for instance, has suggested that the physiological component is the level of autonomic arousal and is undifferentiated across emotions. The cognitive component provides a label for the emotion based on the perceived cause. Evidence for this model is based on a number of studies where arousal is induced artificially and then potential sources of the arousal are manipulated. These manipulations have been found to result in different labelings on the emotion (for example,

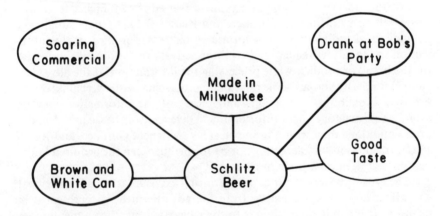

Figure 10-1. Linkage of Soaring Commercial to Schlitz-Beer Node after Brand Processing

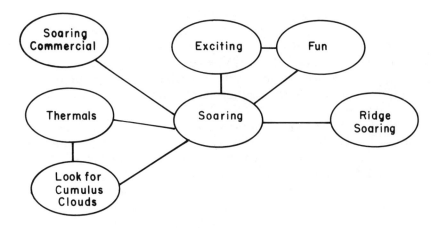

Figure 10-2. Linkage of Soaring Commercial to Soaring Node after Non-brand Processing

Schachter and Singer 1962). A number of different cognitive typologies that may form the basis for labeling emotions have been developed (for example, Roseman 1979; Weiner 1982).

Research has indicated that moods and emotions can affect a number of different information-processing activities. First, moods have been found to affect problem solving. Individuals in a pleasant mood have been found to be more creative in problem solving, but they are also more likely to use heuristics in obtaining a solution (Isen et al. 1982). Second, moods have been found to affect the retrieval of information. Individuals who learn information while experiencing a particular mood are better able to retrieve that information when they are experiencing the same mood (for example, Bower, Monteiro, and Gilligan 1978). In addition, individuals experiencing a pleasant mood are more likely to recall pleasant experiences, while individuals experiencing an unpleasant mood are more likely to recall unpleasant experiences (Bower 1980). Third, emotion may affect judgments and evaluations. For instance, individuals in a pleasant mood are more likely to evaluate the products they own more favorably (Isen et al. 1978) and to make more-optimistic judgments about the occurrence of particular events (Johnson and Tversky 1982).

The effect of mood and emotion on problem solving can be explained partially by examining the effect of the physiological component of emotion, autonomic arousal, on the factors affecting information acquisition. Kahneman (1973) has suggested that arousal may affect the allocation of attention. Low arousal may result in low levels of attention to the stimulus, while high arousal may cause a narrowing of attention on the dominant elements of the stimulus (Easterbrook 1959) or the arousal state (Mandler 1975). These effects on attention are thought to be responsible for the inverted-U-shaped relationship usually found between arousal and performance (for example, Broadhurst 1957; Malmo 1959). Consequently, moods and emotions that generate low levels of arousal may improve performance on a task, while moods and emotions that generate high levels of arousal may be detrimental.

The effect of emotion on information retrieval, judgment, and evaluation can be explained partially by assuming that emotional information also may be represented in memory by nodes (for example, Clark 1982; Clark and Isen 1982; Bower 1980; Bower and Cohen 1982). In these models, the emotional feeling associated with an event or concept may be linked to the concept or event in memory. These emotional nodes may be activated directly or through the associated event or concept. For instance, if I am currently in a happy mood and I try to recall specific events in my life, I am more likely to remember pleasant events because my happy state activates emotional nodes representing happiness. Since activation also spreads through the related semantic links, happy events will receive more activation than unhappy events so happy events are more likely to be recalled. Within this model, emotion may be generated also by activating a node (for example, my Uncle Bill) that has an emotional node attached to it.

This information suggests that emotional advertising may have an effect on consumers in the following way. An advertisement may generate an emotional response either through an emotional episode experienced by someone in the advertisement (for example, AT&T long-distance calling) or through emotional symbols (for example, pictures of kittens). If emotional symbols are used, these symbols may activate a particular knowledge structure that contains an emotional node through partial pattern matching (for example, Hayes-Roth 1978). This emotional response may increase the level of autonomic arousal that, in turn, may increase attention levels. The emotional response would be represented in memory by a node connected to the representation of the advertisement in memory or the advertised brand node. In addition, the increase in attention levels may result in the formation of a more-extreme attitude either directly or through the generation of additional thoughts (for example, Tesser 1978; Fiske 1981).

Emotional advertisements that cause high levels of arousal may reduce effectively the amount of verbal response to the advertisement. This may affect the ability of the advertisement to change attitudes and may reduce the number of linkages formed in memory between the advertisement and other concepts. This would make it difficult to retrieve a representation of the advertisement, which may account for the lower levels of recall frequently found with emotional advertisement (for example, Zielske 1982).

If an emotional node has been connected in memory to the brand node, either directly or through the representation of the advertisement, this emotional node may become activated whenever the brand node is activated. This would result in the same emotional feeling although probably at a somewhat less-intense level than was created in the advertisement. So, for instance, if an advertisement created a happy feeling, this happy feeling may be activated whenever the individual thought about or used the advertised product.

Attitude toward the Advertisement

Mitchell and Olson (1981) examined the effect of visual and emotional advertising on the second, or processing, stage of the information-acquisition process. Their research strategy was to test alternative theories of attitude formation and change against the verbally oriented Fishbein model that posits that belief formation precedes attitude formation. The two alternative theories were the mere-exposure hypothesis suggested by Zajonc (1980) and the classical conditioning of attitudes (Staats and Staats 1956). Consequently, the resulting study manipulated repetition and the content of the advertisement. This latter manipulation included four different advertisements for hypothetical brands of facial tissues. Three of the advertisements contained a picture that varied in the amount of information presented about the brand and in emotional content. The pictures were of kittens, a sunset, and an abstract painting. The kitten advertisement was hypothesized to convey softness and positive affect, the sunset only positive affect, and the abstract painting only neutral feelings. The fourth advertisement contained only a headline stating that "Brand X facial tissues are soft."

The results of the study indicated no repetition effects but strong effects due to message content. Both the kitten and sunset advertisements created more positive brand attitudes than advertisements with the verbal message or the abstract painting. An analysis of covariance using predicted attitude scores from the Fishbein model did not remove all the reliable differences among brand attitudes, indicating that the beliefs about the brands that were formed were not the only mediator of the effect of the advertisements on brand attitudes. A second construct was formed by factor analyzing a series of scales that measured the subjects' reaction to the advertisements, such as believability and interest in the advertisement. One of the resulting factors was clearly an evaluative factor, and the sum of the scales that loaded highly on this factor was used as a measure of the subjects' attitude toward the advertisement. This measure and the predicted attitude from the Fishbein model did remove all the reliable differences among brand attitudes for the different products (table 10-1). This suggest that both the beliefs that were formed during exposure to the advertisements and the subjects' feelings about the advertisement may mediate the effects of emotional and visual advertisements on the formation of brand attitudes.

In the Mitchell and Olson (1981) study, however, the authors used only structured scales to measure beliefs. Consequently, it is possible that the authors failed to measure all the salient product-attribute beliefs. Therefore, it is possible that if these unmeasured beliefs had been measured, their inclusion in the Fishbein model would have eliminated all the attitudinal differences among the brands.

Conceptually, this does not appear to be a very plausible explanation, and the empirical evidence confirms this implausibility. Three different studies (Gardner 1981; Edell 1982; Mitchell 1982c) have found also that attitude toward the advertisement has a significant effect on brand attitudes after controlling for the prediction of attitudes from the Fishbein model. In two of the studies (Mitchell 1982b; 1982c), elicited beliefs were used to predict attitudes. Consequently, the effect seems to be quite strong, and the attitude-toward-the-advertisement construct does not appear to be a surrogate measure for unmeasured reliant beliefs.

Based on these results, Mitchell (1980; 1982a) has suggested that the two mediators—attitude toward the advertisement and the predicted attitude from the Fishbein model—may represent two different channels in the information-acquisition process. The first channel, represented by the predicted attitude from the Fishbein model, is a verbal channel representing thoughts and beliefs about the advertised product. The second channel, represented by attitude toward the advertisement, is less clearly understood in terms of

Table 10-1
Effect of Covariants on the F-Ratio for the Main Effect of Advertising Content

Dependent Variable	No Covariant	Covariant (s)			
		$\Sigma\, b_i e_i$	$\Sigma\, b_i e_i$ and A_{ad}	A_{act}	A_{act} and A_{ad}
A_o	27.43[a]	16.03[e]	0.13	—	—
A_{act}	14.54[a]	3.18[b]	0.86	—	—
BI	15.62[a]	—	—	3.61[a]	2.47

Source: Reprinted from Andrew A. Mitchell and Jerry C. Olson, "Are Product Attribute Beliefs the Only Mediator of Advertising Effects on Brand Attitudes?," *Journal of Marketing Research* 18 (August 1981):318-332. Copyright 1981 by the American Marketing Association. Reprinted with permission.
[a]$p < .001$.
[b]$p < .05$.

causes and causal mechanisms. It may represent the effect of the previously discussed nonverbal channel on attitudes, or it may be based on the emotional reaction to the visual element of an advertisement if it generates an emotional response. In the latter case, it may represent a separate emotional system (Zajonc 1980).

Empirical support for the conceptualization of the verbal channel was reported in a study that found that the number of counterarguments and support arguments generated and the predicted attitude from the Fishbein model explained approximately the same variance in brand attitudes that were formed after exposure to advertisements for hypothetical brands (Mitchell 1982c).

During exposure to an advertisement, then, an individual may generate verbal thoughts about the advertised brand and form beliefs about it. These thoughts and beliefs will explain part of the variance in the brand attitudes that were found. Also, during exposure to the advertisement, the individual may make an affective response to the advertisement, and this affective response may explain an additional part of the variance in the brand attitudes that were formed. This affective response might be thought of as a node in memory that is attached to the memory trace of the advertisement. As discussed previously, this memory trace may or may not be connected to the brand node in long-term memory. If it is attached to the brand node, the memory trace of the advertisement might be thought of as simply another concept associated with the brand and the attitude toward the advertisement as an evaluation of that memory trace (Mitchell and Olson 1981).

Issues

The results of the Mitchell and Olson (1981) study indicate that the attitude-toward-the-advertisement construct may mediate the effects of emotional and visual advertising. However, the study also raises a number of issues concerning this construct. The first issue concerns whether the attitude-toward-the-advertisement effects are transitory or whether they persist over time. It is entirely possible that an individual's attitude toward the advertisement may affect brand attitudes immediately after exposure to the advertisement; however, if attitudes are measured some time after exposure to the advertisement, these effects may disappear. Attitudes then may be based only on the beliefs that are formed.

Second, there is some question as to whether attitude toward the advertisement will have an effect on brand attitudes when the advertisements also contain verbal information about the product. In the Mitchell and Olson study, three of the advertisements contained only pictures, and we might argue that attitude toward the advertisement will have an effect only in these impoverished conditions. In more-realistic advertisements, which also contain verbal copy, these effects may disappear.

The final issue concerns the nature of the channel represented by the attitude-toward-the-advertisement construct and the factors that affect it. It appears to be tapping something other than the verbal product thoughts or beliefs. However, as discussed earlier, the exact nature of this channel is unclear. Is it essentially a nonverbal channel or does it also include verbal thoughts about the advertisement? Also, it is unclear exactly what components of the advertisement affect attitude toward the advertisement. Do only the visual elements of an advertisement affect it, or is attitude an affective reaction to the entire advertisement?

Results

In this section I discuss the results from a series of experiments that shed some light on the issues that were discussed. Here, I present only the parts of the experiments pertaining to the issues. The first experiment addresses the issue of whether or not the attitude-toward-the-advertisement effects were transitory. The second experiment examines the effect of pairing the same affect-arousing photographs with different verbal copy for different products. The third experiment examines causes of attitude-toward-the-advertisement effects.

Experiment One

In the first experiment (Mitchell and Dasgupta 1982), we showed subjects advertisements with photographs that differed in the affective feelings they generated. Pretests were used to select two photographs that generated positive feelings and two photographs that generated negative feelings. These photographs were used in advertisements for four hypothetical brands in different product categories—toothpaste, deodorant, facial tissues, and ball-point pens. The pen and facial-tissue brands were paired with positively evaluated photographs, while the toothpaste and deodorant brands were paired with negatively evaluated photographs. Some verbal copy was included in the advertisements; however, the information provided in the copy was for relatively unimportant product attributes. For instance, the copy for the deodorant discussed how the deodorant was packaged.

In the first condition, the subjects ($n = 19$) saw the four advertisements and, then, after a short filler task that was used to clear short-term memory, completed a questionnaire. This questionnaire was used to obtain measures or attitude toward the advertisement (A_{ad}), brand attitudes (A_o), and standard Fishbein measures of beliefs (b_i) and the evaluation of the belief (e_i). The scales and procedures were the same as those used by Mitchell and Olson (1981). In the second condition, subjects ($n = 19$) saw the four advertisements and then were asked to write on separate sheets of paper their feelings about each product. This was done to ensure that the subjects had formed an attitude toward the products. Then they were asked to return in two weeks to participate in a second experiment. When they reported two weeks later, they were given the same questionnaire that the first group received.

Consequently, the resulting design has two factors: a time factor with two levels (immediate, delayed measures) and an advertising-content factor with four levels (two advertisements with positively evaluated pictures and two advertisements with negatively evaluated pictures). Time is a between-group factor, and advertising content is a within-subject factor.

An ANOVA for attitude toward the brand (A_o), attitude toward the act of purchasing and using the brand (A_{act}), and attitude toward the advertisement (A_{ad}) indicated main effects for the advertising-content factor ($p < .001$). The time factor was significant only for attitude toward the brand ($p < .05$), and none of the interactions was significant. The means for the brand attitude are plotted in figure 10-3. The two brands paired with the negatively evaluated photographs (deodorant and toothpaste) have significantly lower attitudes than the two brands paired with the positively evaluated photographs (pen and facial tissue). The brand attitudes for three of the four products showed slight declines over the two-week period, which accounted for the significant effect on this factor.

The attitude-toward-the-advertisement measures for the four brands showed the same pattern as the brand attitudes (figure 10-4). The attitudes toward the advertisement for the two products paired with the negatively evaluated photographs (deodorant and toothpaste) were significantly lower than the same measures for the two products paired with the positively evaluated photographs (pen and facial tissue). However, the time factor and the interaction were not significant ($p > .05$).

Regression analysis was used to examine if attitude toward the advertisement has a significant effect on brand attitudes in both conditions. The results indicated that it did. After controlling for the effect of the predicted attitude from the Fishbein model, the coefficient on the attitude toward the advertisement was significantly different than zero ($p < .001$) in both conditions. These results, then, indicate that attitude-toward-the-advertisement effects persist over time.

Readers should note, however, that the regression results do not provide any insights into the cognitive mechanisms underlying the brand-attitude measures in the delayed condition. Since both brand attitudes and the at-

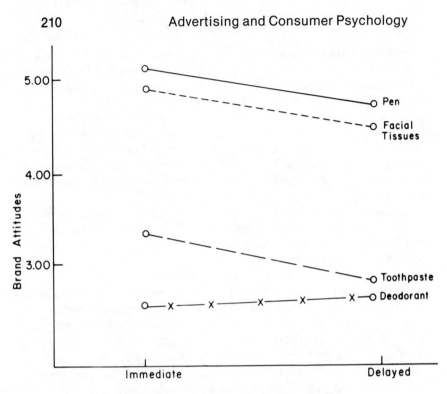

Figure 10-3. Stability of Brand Attitudes

titude toward the advertisement were relatively stable over the two-week period, it was not clear whether subjects in the delayed condition simply accessed their previously formed attitudes or whether they recombined their beliefs about the products and their feelings about the advertisement to form a brand attitude.

Experiment Two

In the second experiment (Mitchell 1982b), the same positively, neutrally, and negatively evaluated photographs were paired with verbal copy for four different products (deodorant, pen, cola, and toothpaste). The copy for each advertisement was approximately fifty to fifty-five words in length. In addition, for each product, a fourth condition contained only the verbal copy. The resulting design was a latin square where four groups of subjects saw four advertisements for the four different products.

    An ANOVA for brand attitudes indicated main effects for product and picture type ($p < .01$). Except for the pen, the brand attitudes indicate similar profiles across the picture-type condition. The brand attitudes are highest

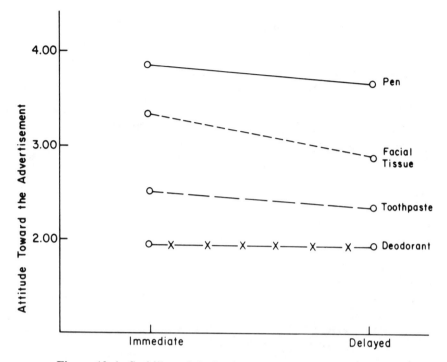

Figure 10-4. Stability of Attitude toward the Advertisement

in the condition where the advertisement contained the positively evaluated photograph and lowest in the condition with the negatively evaluated photograph. For the toothpaste product, however, the profile differs slightly since the brand attitude in the copy-only condition was higher than the neutral-photograph condition (see figure 10-5). For the pen, the condition in which the advertisement was paired with the neutral photograph had the most positive brand attitude. This attitude was significantly more positive than the condition in which the advertisement contained the positively evaluated photograph.

An ANOVA for attitude toward the advertisement also indicates main effects for product and picture type ($p < .01$). The means for the attitude toward the advertisements by condition are presented in figure 10-6. A comparison of figures 10-5 and 10-6 indicates that the brand-attitude and attitude-toward-the-advertisement measures are mirrored almost exactly across conditions. Except for the toothpaste brand, the differences among the brands on the two measures are almost identical across conditions. Even with the pen, where the advertisement with the neutral photograph produced the most positive attitude, the attitude toward the advertisement was also highest.

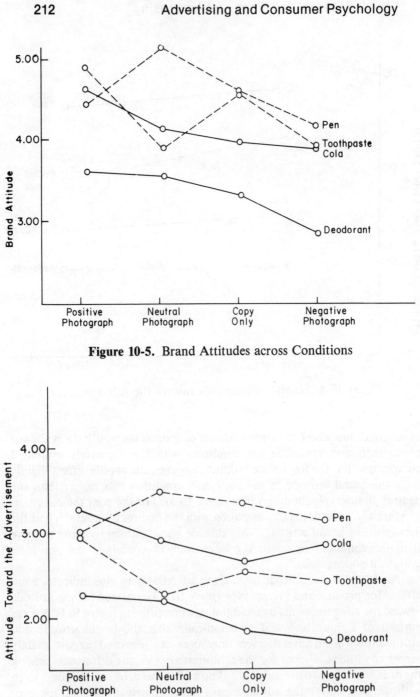

Figure 10-5. Brand Attitudes across Conditions

Figure 10-6. Attitude toward the Advertisement across Conditions

The significant main effect was due to product because the attitude toward the advertisement and the differences on this measure across products for for advertisements that contain the same photograph suggest that the attitude toward the advertisement is not based solely on the subjects's evaluation of the photograph. For instance, in the advertisements with the negatively evaluated photograph, the attitude toward the advertisement for the deodorant brand was significantly lower than the attitude toward the advertisement for the three other products ($p < .01$). If the photograph was the primary cause of the resulting attitude toward the advertisement, then all the advertisements that contained the same photograph should result in similar attitudes toward the advertisement. This did not occur, suggesting that the attitude toward the advertisement is based on all the components of the advertisement, not simply the photograph.

Experiment Three

In the third experiment (Mitchell 1980; Mitchell 1982c), subjects examined eight different advertisements under four different processing conditions. In the first condition, subjects were asked to examine the advertisements and to evaluate the advertised products. In the second condition, subjects were asked different questions about the structure of the advertisements. Examples of these questions are How many boats are there in the advertisement? and How many words are there in the copy? The third condition was a distraction condition. Here the subjects were asked to evaluate the advertised products, but at the same time they had to watch flashing lights and raise their hand whenever the red light flashed. Finally, in the fourth condition, subjects were asked to evaluate the advertised product, but at the same time they were given a three-digit number and had to count backward by threes. The purpose of this task was to block any verbal processing of the information in the advertisement.

There were fifteen subjects in each of the four conditions. After examining all of the advertisements, the subjects filled out a questionnaire from which measures of brand attitudes and the attitudes toward the advertisement were taken. In addition, in conditions one and three, concurrent protocols were taken while the subjects examined the advertisements. Of the eight advertisements seen by the subjects, four were primarily verbal and four were primarily visual. The visual advertisements contained positively evaluated photographs.

Two results of this study are of interest here. The first concerned the ability of the verbal protocols to predict the resulting attitude toward the advertisement. To examine this, the verbal protocols were coded into counterarguments and support arguments and into positive and negative statements about the advertisements. These four categories were mutually exclusive. These categories of statements from condition one then were used to predict attitude toward the advertisement using multiple regression analysis. The results are presented in table 10-2. We can see that both the positive and negative statements about the advertisement have a significant effect on attitude toward the advertisement and that the signs of the regression coefficients are in the right direction. The coefficient associated with the number of positive advertisement thoughts is positive, and the coefficient associated with the number of negative advertisement thoughts is negative. These regressions explain slightly under 20 percent of the variance in the attitude toward the advertisements.

A separate regression was run for the visual and the verbal advertisements. These results also are shown in table 10-2. The coefficients in both regression equations are remarkably similar, and in each equation, the positive and negative advertisement statements explained around 20 percent of the variance. However, when the subjects' feelings about the photographs are included, the percentage of the variance explained increases to 40 percent. In this latter equation, the coefficient on the number of positive advertisement statements becomes insignificant. This suggests that this measure and the subjects' feelings about the photograph are correlated highly. Since all the photographs were evaluated positively, it appears that these photographs generated primarily positive advertisement statements.

The second result that is of interest is whether the attitude-toward-the-advertisement measures for each advertisement were different across the four different processing conditions. An analysis of variance indicated no differences for any of the products by processing conditions.

In summary, then, the number of positive and negative thoughts about the advertisement had a significant effect on the attitude toward the advertisement. However, the subjects' attitude toward the pictures in the adver-

Table 10-2
Regression Models for Predicting Attitude Toward the Advertisement

Type of Advertisement	Beta Weights			
	Negative Ad Statements	Positive Ad Statements	Attitude toward the Picture	R^2
All advertisements	−0.284[a]	0.311[a]	—	.18
Verbal advertisements	−0.281[a]	0.299[a]	—	.17
Visual advertisements	−0.303[a]	0.281[a]	—	.20
	−0.267[a]	0.121	0.474[a]	.40

[a]$p < .001$.

tisements had a stronger effect. No differences in the attitude toward the advertisement were found across processing conditions. These results suggest that the attitude toward the advertisement is, at best, mediated only partially by verbal responses. Verbal responses explained only part of the variance in the attitude toward the advertisement, and the blocking of verbal responses in two of the conditions did not result in any differences in this construct.

Discussion

In examining the effects of visual and emotional advertising, we have conceptualized the information-acquisition process as consisting of two stages. The first stage concerns the focus of attention, or what stimuli in the environment receive attention. The second stage concerns the type of processing that occurs while the stimuli receive attention. Previous research has suggested that visual and emotional advertising may affect both stages. Taylor and Thompson (1982), for instance, suggest that more-vivid stimuli are likely to receive more attention, and the research discussed here suggests that the attitude toward the advertisement may mediate visual and emotional effects at the second stage.

The research discussed here also provides a better understanding of the attitude-toward-the-advertisement mediator and its effects over time. The results indicate that the attitude-toward-the-advertisement effects also occur with advertisements that contain verbal copy and that these effects do not appear to be transitory. Although statistically significant differences were found on attitude toward the brands (A_o) over the two-week period, attitude toward the advertisement still had a significant effect on attitude toward the brand two weeks later. The significant differences in attitude toward the brands over the two-week period were caused by a decay in this measure for three of the four products.

Evaluative verbal responses about the advertisements were found to explain around 20 percent of the variance in the attitude-toward-the-advertisement measures. When the subject's evaluation of the photograph in visual advertisements was included in the prediction equation, the amount of variance explained increased to 40 percent. However, in an experiment where the verbal responses made by subjects were manipulated, no differences were found in the attitude toward the advertisement across processing conditions. This suggests that the formation of the attitude toward the advertisement is based only partially on the evaluative verbal statements made about the advertisement.

At this point then, attitude toward the advertisement appears to mediate visual and emotional effects and may represent a primarily nonverbal channel. This channel appears to be based on an interaction between the visual and verbal elements of an advertisement. For instance, individuals may extract verbal product information from visual elements of an advertisement, and the verbal elements of the advertisement may affect the resulting attitude toward the advertisement (figure 10-7).

A similar model has been proposed by Rossiter and Percy (1978). In their model, individuals also may use the verbal information in the advertisement to create visual imagery, and this effect is transmitted through an alternative channel. One direction for future research is to examine if visual-imagery effects would be captured with the attitude-toward-the-advertisement construct.

The visual elements of advertisements, then, may affect brand attitudes in two different ways. First, individuals may be able to extract verbal information about the product from the visual element. For instance, a photograph of a kitten in a facial-tissue advertisment may result in the individual inferring that the facial tissues are very soft. Second, the visual element may have an emotional component or may interact with the verbal component to produce an effect on attitude toward the advertisement.

The type of processing strategy used during exposure to an advertisement may have an effect on the relative influence of the two channels in the formation of brand attitudes. A study by Gorn (1982) suggests that with a brand-processing strategy, the verbal channel may have a stronger influence on attitude formation but that with a nonbrand-processing strategy, the strength of the influence may be reversed.

Other issues that were discussed were the cognitive representation of attitude toward the advertisement and the causal mechanisms that are the basis of the attitude-toward-the-advertisement effect. First, we suggested that the emotional response to an advertisement might be represented as a node in a network model of memory. This node would be attached to a representation of the advertisement in memory or to a node representing the advertised brand. This emotional node may be activated directly (for example, think of pleasant advertisements) or through the activation of connecting nodes.

Finally, alternative causal mechanisms for the attitude-toward-the-advertisement effects were discussed. Originally, Mitchell and Olson (1981)

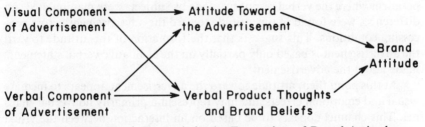

Figure 10-7. Dual Channels in the Formation of Brand Attitudes

suggested that attitude-toward-the-advertisement effects might occur through classical-conditioning mechanisms where a pleasant stimulus (the advertisement) is paired with the brand name. With our better understanding of cognitive mechanisms, a more-precise model of how these effects occur should be available. Two different models were discussed, but the empirical evidence presented did not support either. The first model suggested that an emotional advertisement may create a sympathetic emotional response in the individual. The emotional response in the individual would include autonomic arousal that, in turn, may increase attention levels. This increase in attention levels may result in the creation of more-extreme attitudes to the advertised brand, either directly or through the generation of more thoughts (for example, Tesser 1978; Fiske 1981). Under the second model, the visual element of the advertisement would activate a particular knowledge structure that contained an emotional node through partial pattern matching (for example, Hayes-Roth 1978). The emotional node would be activated, creating a similar emotional response in the individual, and an emotional node then would be attached to the representation of the advertisement or to the node representing the advertised brand. Both of these models would predict that the advertisement with the most positively evaluated visual element would result in the most favorable brand attitude. This did not occur consistently in the second study. One possible reason why this did not occur is that individuals may have overridden these effects with controlled process (Mitchell 1982b).

Finally, this discussion has indicated that there will be a positive relationship between attitude toward the advertisement and brand attitudes. This suggests that only advertisements that consumers like will be effective. However, some evidence indicates that a J-shaped relationship exists between the liking of an advertisement and its effectiveness (for example, Silk and Vavra 1974)—that is, the most effective advertisements are those that are liked very much or disliked very much; the least effective advertisements are those that are neither liked nor disliked.

Although these two positions seem irreconcilable, they really are not since the positive relationship between attitude toward the advertisement and brand attitudes was found only for the second stage, while the J-shaped relationship includes both the first and second stages. Whether the advertisement is liked or disliked may have a strong effect on the first stage, whether or not the advertisement is attended to. Consequently, a U-shaped relationship may exist at the first stage, and a positive linear relationship exists at the second stage, resulting in an overall J-shaped relationship for both stages.

11 Time Compression of Television Advertising

Martin R. Lautman and
K. Jeffrey Dean

Largely as a result of research by MacLachlan and his colleagues (MacLachlan and LaBarbera 1978; LaBarbera and MacLachlan 1979; Mac-Lachlan and Siegel 1980) and the development of new speech-compression equipment such as the Lexicon Varispeech II and the TCS recorder, the process of time compression has received much publicity in advertising circles (for example, Dougherty 1979) as a technique for saving commercial time. It is not surprising that, given the escalation in media costs for commercial time, advertisers have looked to time compression as a technique for making better use of their advertising dollars. In fact, MacLachlan has claimed that nineteen of the twenty largest advertising agencies have tested or broadcast time-compressed television commercials (MacLachlan 1980).

What Is Time Compression?

Time compression is a process by which commercials are condensed while their audio and visual quality at a broadcast level are preserved. Specifically, the time-compression process consists of accelerating the speed of the film (tape) while still maintaining the normal pitch and timbre of the human voice. This is accomplished by an electronic process that capitalizes on voice-wave redundancies, deriving from the fact that the duration of most phonemes is longer than is needed for speech comprehension. Small periodic bits (snippets) of about one-fiftieth of a second are cut from a tape, and the remainder is spliced together to form a continuous tape. The snipping procedure is programmed to improve intelligibility by deleting sounds from certain vowels and consonants (such as *e, m,* and *s*), leaving sounds of others (such as *t* and *b*), keeping the beginning of words, and preserving the pauses between words.

Theoretically, one can compress commercials about as much as one would like. Practically, however, the compression should not exceed 25 percent (MacLachlan 1980) although compressions of up to 40 percent have been cited as possible (MacLachlan and LaBarbera 1978) and those of up to 50 percent have been described as not noticeable (LaBarbera and MacLachlan 1979).

The authors thank Ms. Carol Vohsen for her assistance in designing this study and Ms. Ann Pelovitz for her assistance in coordinating the project and summarizing the data.

Early Research

Research on time compression has been in progress for over twenty-five years, with studies of speech rate beginning even earlier. Variation in reported rates of speech in the research literature can be traced to factors such as verbalizing a written passage versus conversational speaking, type of material, and reader style. For example, the average number of words per minute (wpm) reported by Lumley (1933) for radio announcers was 162 wpm, by Nichols and Stevens (1957) for conversational speaking was 125 wpm, and by Foulke (1967) for oral reading was 174 wpm. In general, texts on speech have reported speaking rates ranging from 120 to 180 wpm (Miller et al. 1976).

The early work on compressed speech concentrated on the effects of compression on comprehension. Foulke and Sticht (1969) summarized this research by stating that comprehension declines slowly (linearly) until 275 wpm (regardless of the compression that may have occurred to achieve that rate) and declines at an accelerated rate thereafter.

Once the effect of compression on comprehension was established, this paradigm was applied to a number of populations and subpopulations in an attempt to generalize the findings. No significant differences were observed as a function of sex (Orr and Friedman 1964; McCracken 1969), intelligence (as measured by I.Q.) of children (Fergen 1955), or language used (Myerson 1974). However, a positive relationship between intelligence and comprehension has been observed for adults (Fairbanks, Guttman, and Miron 1957b; 1957c).

One of the potential advantages of time compression is the ability to use the time saved. Several researchers have sought to determine if the additional time could be used to increase the amount of information learned over that learned with uncompressed messages. Studies with technical materials by Sticht (1969a) and Fairbanks, Guttman, and Miron (1957b), where compressed messages were repeated twice in the same amount of time required to listen to the uncompressed message once, showed a slight improvement, at best, over the uncompressed material. Similarly, augmentation of selected facts that were elaborated on (Fairbanks, Guttman, and Miron 1957b) or presentation of new but related information (Sticht 1971) in compressed messages did not increase the amount of learning compared to what obtained with one presentation of the uncompressed version. What was accomplished in the Fairbanks and co-workers (1957c) study, however, was a shifting of learning to the additional content, probably because the added emphasis caused the respondents to consider it as more important to learn.

Research has been conducted also on the relationships of rate of speech with attitude shifts and with persuasion. Wheeless (1971) investigated the effects of time compression on persuasion and source characteristics. Three levels of compression of a 1,141-word message designed to solicit purchase orders for a how-to-study booklet were tested among college students. The normal-rate recording was 145 wpm with compressed rates of 204 wpm (41 percent compression), 239 wpm (65 percent compression), and 296 wpm (105 percent compression) tested. Four criterion measures were used: (1) purchase orders, (2) attitudes toward the message, (3) source authoritativeness, and (4) source character. The three nonpurchase criteria were measured on semantic differential rating scales.

Neither frequency of purchase nor attitude toward the message was affected by rate. Source authoritativeness and character, however, were rated higher for the normal-rate conditions.

Miller et al. (1976), in two well-controlled field studies designed to expand on some earlier laboratory studies (Baeber and Miller 1976), found that rapid speech leads to increased speaker credibility and greater persuasion. These results were observed to be independent of initial source credibility. It should be noted, however, that the 300-to-400-word messages used in these studies were not designed to sell or promote purchases.

Current Research

MacLachlan and his colleagues have reported three empirical studies involving time compression and advertising commercial interest and recall. Each of these studies is reviewed briefly and is followed by a critique of the methodologies employed. The issues raised in that critique serve as the basis for the study reported in this chapter.

In the first reported study of time compression and commercials, MacLachlan and LaBarbera (1978) tested six television commercials at both normal and compressed (25 percent) speeds. Following exposure, each of the commercials was rated for interest on a six-point semantic differential scale, ranging from very dull to very interesting. Two days after exposure, without any pre-alerting, respondents were asked an unaided brand-recall question. The results showed "that in five of the six cases the faster version was reported as the most interesting." Unaided brand recall, however was not appreciably different for the compressed and normal-rate commercials.

In 1979, LaBarbera and MacLachlan extended their studies to radio commercials. Six radio commercials were tested at both normal and compressed (30 percent) speeds. Once again, the dependent measures were interest and recall. Recall here, however, was obtained two hours after exposure.

Although the instructions to the respondents indicated that interest would be measured on all six commercials, data from only five are presented, and unaided recall is presented for five commercials and aided recall from three commercials. The results showed that in every case the faster commercial was rated more interesting. With respect to the recall measure, in all five instances unaided recall was higher for the faster commercials, and aided recall was higher in all three tests (LaBarbera and MacLachlan 1979).

The third empirical study reported was by MacLachlan and Siegel (1980). Respondents were exposed to either time-compressed (25 percent) or normal-rate versions of the same commercials embedded in a program context. The time-compressed program context included two additional time-compressed commercials (actually, one thirty-second commercial was compressed into two twelve-second segments). Respondents were shown one of the two programs and were told that it would serve as the basis for a classroom discussion that day. Two days later, unaided and aided commercial-recall data were obtained.

In terms of unaided recall, it was reported that all commercials performed better when time compressed and that, "on the average, recall for the time-compressed versions was 36 percent greater than recall for the normal versions." Proven aided recall was obtained by having respondents write down all they could remember about the commercials after having been given the brand names. Once again, the time-compressed versions performed better, and the researchers found "that commercials gain an average of 40 percent in their 'Burke score' when the compressed versions are compared with scores for their normal versions."

While at first glance the results of MacLachlan and his colleagues are intriguing, the reader should note a number of methodological issues relating to these studies.

Respondents

All of MacLachlan's studies involved students in what appears to be a classroom environment. With this type of population in this type of environment, one always must question the demand characteristics of the situation and the effects of that environment on motivation to comply with the experimenter. Second, we might also argue that students are more capable and/or motivated than the general population, especially when memory-related tests are concerned. Last, it is unlikely that the target market for the commercials tested was students and others of their age group. As such, it is difficult to predict the effects on this group of commercial interest on recall scores.

Multiple Stimuli

All respondents exposed to time-compressed commercials were exposed to more than one commercial, making it difficult to tease apart commercial contrast effects, cumulative impact effects, and so forth. Furthermore, in two studies (MacLachlan and LaBarbera 1978; LaBarbera and MacLachlan 1979), respondents were exposed to both time-compressed and normal-rate commercials, making the assessment of any pure time-compression effects difficult.

Established Brands

All of the commercials tested had been aired previously and were for established products and services, confounding brand awareness/usage and commercial interest/familiarity effects.

Recall Procedures and Measures

The procedures followed for obtaining recall measures have the potential for contamination since they could have allowed for interrespondent interaction between exposure and recall, did not make use of individual interviews with individual interviewers recording verbal responses, did not use standard questioning sequences and methods for recording responses, and did not employ a typical home-viewing environment for obtaining recall.

Statistics

MacLachlan reports statistical significance on the basis of one-tailed tests, assuming that the time-compressed version of a commercial will always outperform the normal-rate version. Yet, in his first article on time compression (MacLachlan and LaBarbera 1978), two commercials exposed at normal rates scored higher on unaided recall than their respective time-compressed versions, and the only commercial showing a statistically significant increase in unaided brand recall was the one where the normal-speed version was recalled better than the time-compressed version. Also, a careful examination of the three cases in which interest was higher for one of the two versions of a commercial reveals that in one case interest was significantly higher in favor of the normal version.

These results would suggest that assuming directionality in statistical tests of time-compression data is not warranted and that the more-conservative two-tailed tests are in order.

A second example of a lack of conservatism relates to the reporting of improvement with time compression in terms of percentages. For example, in the MacLachlan and Siegel (1980) study, the finding of a 36 percent increase in unaided recall scores is highlighted, eventually being cited in the popular press (Dougherty 1979). Careful examination of the results, however, shows that for unaided recall, in only one of four tests does the time-compressed commercial outperform the regular version at statistically reliable levels. The 36 percent average largely reflected the score of one commercial and included two commercials where the actual recall scores were so low that a small absolute change (1 or 2 percent) gave rise to large (and unreliable) percentage increases in recall (26 and 23 percent respectively).

Testing How Advertising Works

Perspective on Testing

Testing of advertising requires some assumptions (a model, if you will) of how advertising works. Figure 11-1 shows a stepwise approach relating to advertising development and pretesting. This approach assumes that assessment of advertising effectiveness begins with the setting of objectives (criteria) against which advertising performance can be measured.

Separate objectives need to be set for each of the two major (and assumed independent) factors involved in advertising—attention/recall/awareness and communication/persuasion. In the case of attention/recall/awareness, the objective usually is expressed in terms of some percentage of a target market that must demonstrate recognition/recall of the advertising. Typically, in the case of communication/persuasion, these objectives are phrased in terms of advertising-strategy messages that must be recalled and some measure of shift in attitude, behavioral intent, or actual behavior that must occur.

The sequence of events in figure 11-1 shows communication and persuasion testing preceding attention/recall testing. This reflects our thinking that given the current trend of exceptionally heavy media budgets, people will be exposed to and will recall advertising messages, assuming any reasonable level of attention; that it is easier to modify commercials in order to assure communication of key advertising-strategy messages than it is to affect commonly used attention/recall measures; and that it is better to have a commercial that is average in attention/recall but right on target in terms of communicating an effective strategy than one that is high on attention/recall but that communicates only a mediocre strategy. The popular literature contains numerous references to commercials scoring below normative levels on an attention/recall test but scoring well in the marketplace in terms of product sales (Honomichl 1981; McMaham and Kile 1981).

Although tangential to the purpose of this study, one other differentiation made in figure 11-1 should be noted. We distinguish between advertising strategy and advertising tactics in the form of print ads and commercials.

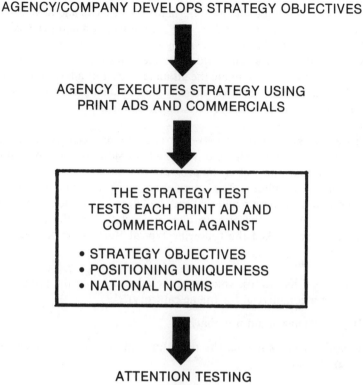

AGENCY/COMPANY DEVELOPS STRATEGY OBJECTIVES

AGENCY EXECUTES STRATEGY USING
PRINT ADS AND COMMERCIALS

THE STRATEGY TEST
TESTS EACH PRINT AD AND
COMMERCIAL AGAINST

• STRATEGY OBJECTIVES
• POSITIONING UNIQUENESS
• NATIONAL NORMS

ATTENTION TESTING
RECALL

Figure 11-1. The Advertising-Development and Testing Progression

It is clear to us that one can have a strong advertising strategy with weak execution of it in the form of commercials and print ads (tactics). Too often the recognition of weak tactical executions results in the discarding of strategies that may or may not be weak.

The Performance-Measuring Techniques

What are the effects of time compression on commercial-recall scores? What are the effects of time compression on commercial communication, believability, interest, appeal, and persuasion? Different methodologies with different respondents in different cities were used to answer these questions. Both of these methodologies have normative data bases and have been subject to extensive reliability studies. The communication and persuasion test (The Strategy Test) also has shown high correlations between advertising messages recalled in the real world and under controlled testing conditions. That test is designed to simulate the ultimate impact of advertising achieved through repeated real-world viewings by employing a paradigm of multiple forced exposures in a controlled testing environment.

On-Air Recall Test. In our twenty-four-hour on-air recall test, respondents were prerecruited by telephone to watch a television program the following day. Twenty-four hours after the program was aired, the respondents were recontacted by telephone. The interviewer confirmed that they had been able to watch the program and that they had been in the room for the entire program. After several warm-up questions relating to the program, the respondents were asked the following typical Burke-type day-after-recall questions:

"Next, I'd like to ask you about the advertising in the program. Did you see a commercial for (name category)?"

If yes: "What brand was that?"

If no: "While watching the program, did you see a commercial for (name brand)?"

Communication and Persuasion—The Strategy Test. Over the past ten years, ARBOR has employed a technique called The Strategy Test as a method for the testing of communication and persuasion of commercials and print ads. The Strategy Test is an updated version of the Motivated Learning Procedure (MLP) initially developed by John Dollard while he was at DuPont. It has been reported on and utilized in a number of different types of studies (Grass, Winters, and Wallace 1971; Lautman, Percy, and Kordish 1978).

Target-market respondents are screened and recruited in a central location test facility to participate in an advertising test. No attempt is made at tricking or fooling the respondents as to the purpose of the study. No distracting stimuli or other commercials are employed. Respondents are told that they will see a commercial three times in succession and then will be asked questions concerning what they learned. The interviewing procedure is one on one and face to face.

Underlying this technique is the assumption that if respondents cannot learn the advertising strategy under this motivated scenario, they never will learn it, given the clutter environment on television, interruptions at home, and so forth. It is a test to determine the potential effectiveness of an advertising execution, assuming that people pay attention to it. As such, The Strategy Test serves as a maximum learning-potential measure. An extensive normative data base is available relating to communication, believability, interest, appeal, and motivation/persuasion.

In order to measure communication with The Strategy Test, it is necessary to define message objectives in a hierarchical fashion according to the advertising-communication strategy. The following list shows the message objectives for the three commercials tested:

Primary Message Objectives
Brand name
Product type
Product attribute (Commercials A and B)
End benefit
New (Commercials A and B)

Secondary Message Objectives
Support for end benefit

Tertiary Message Objectives
Line-extension slogan (Commercial A)
Product-attribute slogan (Commercial B)
End-benefit slogan (Commercial C)

The partitioning of the advertising strategy into primary, secondary, and tertiary message objectives is based on the facts that all messages are not of equal importance to the advertiser; that messages of primary importance are critical and, if not learned at normative levels or better, the commercial cannot be considered successful regardless of any other messages learned; and that since all messages are not of equal importance, they will receive differential advertiser attention within the commercial and will not be learned at equivalent levels, resulting in different normative levels.

The Test Stimuli and Research Questions

Ten test cells were constructed to answer five questions. There were separate groups of respondents in each cell. Table 11-1 shows the ten cells, three with each of two commercials (A and B) and four with one commercial (C).

Question 1: What Are the Effects of Time Compression on Animatics? Of particular concern to advertisers is the question, Is the (presumed) effect of time compression apparent with animatics? Animatics are television

Table 11-1
Test Stimuli

| | New Product X | | | | | |
| | Commercial A | | | Commercial B | | |
Version	1	2	3	1	2	3
Finished (F)/ Animatic (A)	A	A	A	A	A	A
Length (seconds)	30	26	30	30	26	30
Compressed	No	Yes	Yes	No	Yes	Yes
Augmented	No	No	Yes	No	No	Yes
Addition/Reiteration	—	—	Addition	—	—	Reiteration

| | Established Product Y | | | |
| | Commercial C | | | |
	1	2	1	2
Finished (F)/ Animatic (A)	F	F	A	A
Length (seconds)	30	26	30	26
Compressed	No	Yes	No	Yes
Augmented	No	No	No	No

commercials that include artist drawings but no action scenes. Given that a large amount of commercial pretesting is done with animatics (for us, at ARBOR, it is over 50 percent of all tests) and the fact that commercials that do not survive pretesting are not produced in finished form, it is important to determine if time compression will work at this level of execution.

Comparing version 1 and version 2 for each of the three commercials should enable us to quantify this effect for both new and established products.

Question 2: What Are the Effects of Time Compression on Finished Commercials? This question is answered by comparing versions 1 and 2 for commercial C.

Question 3: Do the Effects of Time Compression Translate from Animatics to Finished Executions? This question is related to question 1. Clearly, if the effects are translatable within animatics but cannot be extrapolated to finished versions of the same commercial, then from a practical perspective, the utility of the technique will be nominal. This question is answered by comparing the finished and animatic, time-compressed version (version 2) for commercial C.

Question 4: What Is the Effect of Using the Extra Seconds Provided by Time Compression for Emphasizing Product Benefits? Along with the potential usefulness of cutting down commercials of over thirty seconds to thirty seconds, there is also the potential utility of shortening a thirty-second commercial and using the extra time to reiterate product benefits promoted in the commercial. Comparing the three versions of commercial B allows us to test this possibility.

Question 5: What Is the Effect of Using the Extra Seconds Provided by Time Compression for Introducing New Information to the Consumer? This question is a variation on question 4 and examines an alternative use for the extra seconds that might become available by compressing a thirty-second commercial. To evaluate this possibility, we compare the three versions of commercial A.

Sample

For the on-air test, a total of 400 respondents (female, heads of household) were recruited to watch each commercial, giving a total of 4,000 recruited respondents. For The Strategy Test portion of the study, 100 target-market respondents were screened and recruited, giving a total of 1,000 respondents. Interviewing was conducted in four widely dispersed geographic areas.

Interviewing, Coding, and Tabulating

All interviewing, coding, and tabulating were conducted by professional staff without knowledge as to the purpose of this study or the type of commercial being tested.

Results

Recall

Table 11-2 shows the related recall data projected to a nonprerecruited sample. The average (normative level) commercial in this test tends to score 24 percent on related recall. There were slight differences at best in recall for the commercials tested between normal, time-compressed, and time-compressed and augmented versions. Furthermore, this was true regardless of whether the normal commercial tested was below average, average, or slightly above average on recall.

Although not related to the purpose of this study, one other interesting finding is the comparable scores of animatic and finished versions of the same commercial.

Table 11-2
On-Air Recall Data Projected to Nonprerecruited Samples
(percent)

Version	Not Compressed (30 Seconds)	Compressed (26 Seconds)	Compressed and Augmented (30 Seconds)
Commercial A			
Base Number of Respondents	139	150	132
Recall	24	24	24
Commercial B			
Base Number of Respondents	131	138	145
Recall	19	14	17
Commercial C, finished			
Base Number of Respondents	134	120	—
Recall	29	28	—
Commercial C, animatic			
Base Number of Respondents	146	144	—
Recall	29	29	—

Communication

Table 11-3 shows the percentage of respondents for each commercial who were primary message learners; that is, they learned all of the primary messages (see list in previous section). The extra time provided by the time compression was used in the augmented version of commercial B to reiterate a product attribute categorized as a primary message. This clearly had a positive impact, with more respondents qualifying as primary message learners. As we would expect, the new information provided in the augmented version of commercial A that was not related to primary messages did not increase the number of primary message learners.

Table 11-3
Percentage of Respondents Who Were Primary Message Learners

Version	Number of Messages	Not Compressed	Compressed 26 Seconds	Compressed 30 Seconds
Commercial A	5	20	13	18
Commercial B	5	22	13	26
Commercial C, finished	3	73	66	—
Commercial C, animatic	3	58	60	—

Note: Difference is significant at the 95 percent level of confidence for number in box.

In table 11-3, the percentages of primary message learners is the same for the animatic and finished versions of commercial C, consistent with the contention that communication scores can be predicted from animatic to finished versions of commercials.

Table 11-4 shows the communication (percentage recalling the message) of the tagline for commercial A and the reinforced product attributes of commercial B. Top-of-mind communication refers to the percentage of respondents who played back a message in response to the first question asked: "Please describe briefly everything you saw and heard in the commercial." Probe Once: "Anything else?" Total communication refers to the percentage of consumers who played back a message in response to any of a series of open-ended unaided questions designed to elicit every aspect of the commercial recalled. Communication of the new tagline in the extra seconds of commercial A clearly had an impact at least on total communication. The fact that there was recall of the tagline in the two nonaugmented versions probably was a result of the fact that the tagline was really not new and had been used to introduce other new products by this company.

Augmenting the time-compressed version of commercial B through additional emphasis on two product attributes was observed to affect only one product attribute, and that only for total communication relative to the

Table 11-4
Percentage of Respondents Recalling Message Communication

	Not Compressed (30 Seconds)	Compressed (26 Seconds)	Compressed and Augmented (30 Seconds)
Commercial A Tag-line communication			
Total	28	13	44
Top of mind	1	1	12
Commercial B Product attributes (reinforced twice)			
Product attribute 1			
Total	42	46	40
Top of mind	13	21	19
Product attribute 2			
Total	28	21	39
Top of mind	3	3	12

nonaugmented time-compressed commercial. Thus, simply reiterating a message did not necessarily insure an increase in its communication.

Believability, Interest, and Appeal

Table 11-5 shows for each commercial the percentage of respondents considering it believable or interesting or citing a specific feature as appealing or unappealing in response to a direct probe to that effect.

The results of these tests of believability, interest, and appeal are presented in terms of the five questions raised earlier.

Question 1. Comparisons between the time-compressed and normal versions of commercials A, B, and C in animatic form show that only for commercial A is there a significant effect in the predicted direction. In that case,

Table 11-5
Overall Effects of Time Compression on Animatics:
(percentage of respondents)

Communication Version	Believability	Interest	Specific Mentions	
			Appealing Features	Unappealing Features
Commercial A				
Not compressed	73	47	64	56
Compressed (26 seconds)	73	61	63	37
Compressed and augmented	80	57	60	47
Commercial B				
Not compressed	71	69	75	35
Compressed (26 seconds)	67	61	67	38
Compressed and augmented	74	55	64	40
Commercial C				
Animatic not compressed	88	79	68	34
Animatic compressed (26 seconds)	83	69	62	37
Finished not compressed	66	79	76	20
Finished compressed (26 seconds)	78	69	78	19

interest was higher, and fewer unappealing features were mentioned for the compressed version. Small differences were observed for believability or appealing features. The overall conclusion would seem to be that in most cases, the time-compressed and normal versions of commercials did not differ on believability, interest, and appeal.

Question 2. Comparing the results for the finished version of commercial C in time-compressed and normal versions shows no significant differences. Thus, we can conclude that, as with the animatics, time-compressed and normal versions of finished commercials did not differ on believability, interest, and appeal.

Question 3. The question relating to the translation of the benefits of time compression from animatics to finished versions assumed that such benefits would occur. The absence of such effects makes this question moot.

Question 4. The effect of using the extra seconds provided by a time-compressed thirty-second commercial for reiterating product benefits previously mentioned in the commercial was tested with commercial B. No differences were observed in believability or appeal among the normal, time-compressed, and time-compressed and augmented versions of commercial B. Contrary to previous findings with time compression, interest in the normal commercial was higher than that in the time-compressed and augmented version. Thus, we could conclude that time compression and augmentation in the form of reiteration of a previously mentioned benefit had no effect on commercial believability and appeal and, if anything, caused a decrease in commercial interest.

Question 5. The effect of using the extra seconds provided by time compression to introduce new information was tested with commercial A. Although the time-compressed version showed the predicted higher interest and lower unappealing scores, when the time-compressed commercial was augmented by new information, this effect was diluted. Thus, in comparing a normal-rate commercial with its time-compressed version augmented by new information to bring it back up to thirty seconds, no significant effects were observed for believability, interest, and appeal.

Purchase Intent

No significant differences were observed among the mean purchase-intent scores (five-point scale) for any of the commercial comparisons used to test the five questions outlined earlier. In every case, however, the normal version had higher purchase-intent scores over the compressed version. Furthermore, figure 11-2 shows that if one looks at only the definitely-will-buy cell (see Lautman, Edwards, and Farrell 1981), a trend across all four commercials is apparent; that is, time compression alone seems to depress purchase interest, and augmentation seems to rejuvenate it up to the level of the normal-rate commercial.

Discussion and Conclusions

From the results of this study, it would seem that time compression does not produce the gains promised by its proponents. Neither increases in recall scores nor systematic increases in interest, believability, and appeal levels were observed across all test conditions. Furthermore, although time-compression resulted in a slight (but not statistically significant) loss in persuasion, reinforcing and adding information seemed to counter the effect and pull purchase intent back up to the levels observed in the normal-rate versions.

While time compression did not produce the predicted results consistently, there did not seem to be consistently detrimental effects in terms of recall, communication, believability, interest, and appeal. Thus, it appears to us that time compression may be an effective editing technique. However, expectations of a significant improvement in commercial performance because of the use of time compression do not seem warranted.

Why were our results different from that of MacLachlan and his colleagues? Along with the procedural issues cited earlier, probably the most obvious difference was that we used a compression of about 15 percent while MacLachlan and his colleagues have used a minimum of 25 percent. An attempt was made to use 25 percent compression in our study, but the executional results were less than satisfactory. The characters in the commercials moved around in a style reminiscent of the Keystone Cops, and brand management saw no reason to test such markedly inferior commercials.

The 15 percent level of compression seems particularly suited to the inclusion of taglines, as was done in commercial A. In fact, that level of compression seems quite consistent with that currently being employed by MacLachlan. In his 1980 article in *Video Systems*, he stated, "More than 50 time-compressed commercials have been produced. . . . Most of these have been standard 30 second commercials that were reduced . . . for taglines. Usually the taglines are four or five seconds long" (p. 53). Thus, the tests with commercial A reported here seem to be particularly important given current practice.

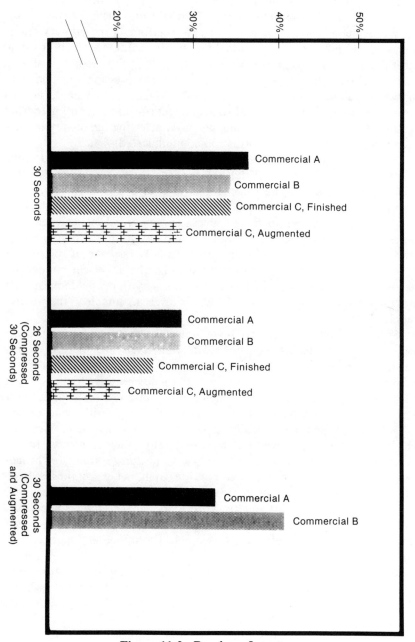

Figure 11-2. Purchase Intent

Using the extra time in commercial B after time compression for reiterating product attributes also seems to be consistent with MacLachlan's (1980) recommendations in that same *Video Systems* article. He states, "the extra time made available may be used for reinforcing the primary selling message, and not for . . . additional points" (p. 56). Once again, it would seem that to accomplish this reinforcement, four or five seconds is all that would be needed. This would result in a rate of compression about equal to that employed in our study. In this case of message reinforcement, the purpose of the compression would be to help direct consumer attention to what is most important in the advertising message, affecting the quality but not necessarily the amount of information communicated.

We can suggest three possibilities as to why the predicted time-compression effects on recall did not appear. First, as noted earlier, the level of compression may have been too little to have been noticeable. While overly speeding up the commercial may create a novelty effect, heightening attention, there was considerable concern among brand management that while this may have heightened recall it would have reflected poorly on the brand's quality image. Thus, unless a particularly fast rate of speed-up is done with a specific strategy motive in mind (like that in the current Federal Express commercial where the message itself is speed), it would appear that the compression will have to be done within levels acceptable to the creative people.

Second, given the relatively low-involvement nature of the products tested, it is possible that consumer attention levels in a natural home-viewing environment were too low to discern the compression. Finally, it is possible that the recall test used was not sufficiently sensitive to measure the effect. A recognition test, for example, might have identified differences that a recall method might not have had sufficient sensitivity to detect.

Not investigated in this study is the type of commercial problem for which time compression was proposed originally—the commercial that is too long in length and that must be cut down to thirty seconds for broadcast. Although we cannot say for certain, we would not expect the results to differ from those reported here. However, we do agree with Pringle (1980) that "no one should start out to write a spot longer than 30 seconds. Rather, the objective should be the most persuasive copy possible, and if time compression can be effectively used in its execution, all the better" (p. 10).

In the final analysis, we expect that the hoopla about time compression will die down and that it will become just one more technique used by editors and producers to develop the most effective and best commercials they can create. Over time they will learn with which content areas, types of commercials, types of scenes, and so on time compression will work best, and they will use it accordingly.

Part IV
Brain-Wave Response
to Advertising

The two chapters in part IV include reviews of the progress that has been made in assessing brain-wave and other physiological responses to advertising. Some research milestones of physiological responses to communications from the third century B.C. to 1982 are identified.

In chapter 12, Rothschild and Thorson review brain-wave research that complements the research reported in chapter 13. They report results of data-based research of brain-wave studies in advertising and offer a number of specific recommendations for doing brain-wave research. For research on commercials, testing only new commercials that elicit low-involvement responses is recommended to control for prior-exposure effects and responses other than electroencephalographic information.

In chapter 13, Ray and Olson describe their research programs of psychophysiology—that is, relating those patterns of electrical activity to psychological processes and states. The authors give the details of how their experiments were conducted in 1981-1982. An outline is provided at the end of chapter 13 that should be referenced in research on psychophysiological responses to advertising.

12

Electroencephalographic Activity as a Response to Complex Stimuli: A Review of Relevant Psychophysiology and Advertising Literature

Michael L. Rothschild and *Esther Thorson*

The notion that electroencephalographic (EEG), or brain-wave, data can help advertising managers was suggested first by Krugman (1971). In the past few years this idea has become intuitively appealing to many in the academic and practitioner community although to date a limited amount of writing and research has been done to support the notions.

This chapter reviews the relevant psychophysiology, advertising, and consumer-behavior literature and derives some conclusions concerning the future of brain-wave research for advertising research. We discuss the key variables and methodological conventions in brain-wave research, psychophysiological knowledge that seems transferable to advertising research, and an evaluation of work that has attempted to relate brain waves to advertising and consumer behavior.

One of the emerging streams of research in consumer behavior over the past five years has been concerned with the concept of low involvement. This work has led to a re-examination of issues related to information processing and, as a result, a re-examination of advertising strategies concerned with the learning of product information and the development of product purchase behavior. This, in turn, has led to a re-examination of the techniques used in the measurement of advertising.

Recall has long been the dominant measure of advertising effectiveness. Recall, however, implies learning under high-involvement conditions in which learning is stored in a highly organized structure (for example, Kintsch 1970; Martin and Noreen 1974).

Recognition has become more popular as a measure of advertising effectiveness recently, in part because of its relevance to low-involvement tasks. Recognition can occur whether or not learning is organized (for example, McCormack 1972).

The authors gratefully acknowledge the assistance of Robert Goldstein and Brian Koenig and the financial support of Bruzzone Research Company, McCollum/Spielman, Marketing Science Institute, and the University of Wisconsin on the project discussed in this chapter.

EEG data, however, have the intuitive appeal of being measurable under even lower conditions of involvement, in that attention can be measured (at least in theory) without the need for any questions to be asked. This implies a measurement of something related to learning but no cognitive structure needs to be verbalized. Recall, recognition, and EEG data map some dimensions of attention and have been shown to be related to one another.

In addition, EEG data have the virtue of being gathered in a continuous manner as the stimulus is being received. Therefore, one can observe the ability of the stimulus to hold attention as it is received by an audience. This continuous record of attention can be used to diagnose the various scenes within the commercial. In sum, EEGs differ from recall, recognition, and other verbally mediated responses in three ways:

1. EEG measures are ongoing and continuous.
2. They allow viewers to respond to commercials without first processing the response through a verbal system.
3. They provide a response measure even when the viewer is uninvolved and/or shows low levels of learning of the content of the message.

The remainder of this chapter reviews key issues relating the EEG to advertising research. The chapter is not intended to be comprehensive but to serve as an introduction for those wishing to begin an exploration of this area.

Review of Psychophysiology Literature

Electroencephalographic activity was reported first in 1875 by Caton (1875) who named it "electric currents of the brain." By 1913, two types of rhythms, now known as alpha and beta, had been distinguished in dogs (Prawdica-Weminski 1913), and these patterns were seen later in humans (Berger 1929). Berger also observed that the alpha rhythms were suppressed or disrupted by a visual stimulus. These rhythms were different sine-wave frequencies of electrical activity.

EEG activity is a measure of the power and frequency of electrical activity taking place below a particular location on the skull. It is measured typically at the surface of the scalp and is amplified and recorded.

Measured frequencies are typically in the range of 1 to 100 hertz (although one usually is concerned with frequencies under 30 hertz). Amplitude (or power) is recorded within predetermined frequency ranges (discussed in the section on frequency analysis), While there is some understanding of what EEG wave patterns signify, there is little knowledge of their genesis (Stern, Ray, and Davis 1980).

Location of Activity

Activity normally is recorded from one or more locations on the scalp. These locations have been standardized through use of the 10-20 system proposed by the International Federation of Societies for Electroencephalography and Clinical Neurophysiology (Jasper 1958). Twenty-one standard positions are spaced approximately equally across the skull.

EEG patterns recorded from widely spaced scalp electrodes are quite diverse. This variability is due to the structural and functional differences between brain sites underlying the electrodes. As brain tissue varies in its activity patterns, so do the manifestations of these activities on the scalp. There is no unanimity among experimenters as to the most appropriate electrode placements at this time.

The different locations have varying advantages and disadvantages. Early investigators recorded from occipital (rear) leads because alpha activity is greatest at the occiput and eye-movement and muscle artifacts are smaller (Galin 1979). Temporal and parietal sites are preferred sometimes because they show hemispheric lateralization most clearly (Galin and Ornstein 1972). In another study, Galin, Johnstone, and Herron (1978) reported strongest asymmetry at the central sites. Gevins et al. (1979a) found no differences across occipital, parietal, and central sites but did find minor differences when these sites were compared to frontal sites. Frontal sites seem to be most affected by muscle and eye-movement artifacts (Greenfield and Sternbach 1972). In another study, Davidson et al. (1979) have shown affect. In this study, positive affect was seen in the left frontal site; negative affect was seen in the right frontal site. Affect was in response to a television program. Parietal sites showed no differences.

To sum up, the frontal areas seem to be most vulnerable to artifacts but may also exhibit affect-related EEG. Mid-areas show hemispheric lateralization most clearly. Rear areas show overall alpha most clearly and are least vulnerable to muscular and/or eye-movement artifacts. We should note that these findings concerning frontal areas are recent and need replication. The findings in the rear areas have been replicated more often.

Frequency Responses

As mentioned, frequencies of less than 30 hertz seem to be most relevant to the processes being examined. Alpha frequency varies between 8 and 13 hertz, with waves of 25 to 100 microvolts appearing mainly from parietal and occipital derivations. Alpha rhythms are recordable from at least 85 percent of humans. Researchers often have observed that the level of alpha rhythm is related negatively to many types of cognitive activity (Greenfield and Sternbach 1972).

The nature of alpha is that it is suppressed momentarily by the onset of a visual stimulus. (Auditory stimuli produce much less suppression of alpha, faster recovery, and more-rapid habituation.) This involuntary response can be observed by placing a subject in a dark room and then turning on a light; it can also be observed with either subtler or more-complex visual stimuli. Alpha recovery will begin immediately following its suppression. The rate of recovery is related to the content of the stimulus and interest in this stimulus.

Alpha suppression and recovery have been studied most often in event-related potential work (ERP, discussed in a later section) but can be useful also in analyzing an ongoing stimulus like a television commercial.

Repetition of a stimulus also has an impact on the recovery of alpha (Warren, Peltz, and Hauter 1976; Mulholland 1978; Thompson and Obrist 1964). While any visual stimulus leads to alpha suppression, repetition of that stimulus leads to more-rapid alpha recovery. This more-rapid recovery may occur because less cognitive activity and attention are needed with successive repetitions.

Because of the well-documented inverse relationship between alpha and cognitive activity/attention, alpha frequency is the most often studied and reported dependent variable when examining various types of cognitive activity, tasks, and stimuli. It has also been the key dependent variable in studies of hemispheric lateralization (discussed in a later section) because one can observe an unequal suppression of alpha in the two hemispheres as a function of task or stimulus.

Beta frequency varies between 14 and 30 hertz and is second only to alpha in its occurrence in human EEG patterns. Beta is prominent in the central and frontal areas and has an amplitude of 2 to 20 microvolts. Some studies have shown the power of beta to be about one-half the power of alpha (Doyle, Ornstein, and Galin 1974).

Some observers feel that beta varies positively with attention or that beta is a result of alpha suppression (Greenfield and Sternbach 1972). There are also data to show that beta varies with alpha (Doyle, Ornstein, and Galin 1974; Gevins et al. 1979b), and this finding has led to speculation that beta often may be artifactual and may be a spillover from, or harmonic of, alpha (Doyle, Ornstein, and Galin 1974). There is no clear agreement as to what beta signifies; therefore, alpha has remained the most commonly observed waveform.

There are also a number of less-common waveforms. Of these, researchers feel that theta frequency rhythms (4-7 hertz) may have some potential usefulness in the study of normal adults. Other waveforms are found rarely and are only useful in the diagnosis of pathological medical cases.

Frequency Analysis

The EEG represents a continuous timegraph of the electrical-potential difference between a location of activity and a neutral reference point. Because of its continuous nature, a tremendous amount of response information is acquired in a very short time. This amount increases, of course, when observations are made at several locations simultaneously. A third dimension (in addition to time and location) that increases the amount of data concerns the several possible frequency bands from which one can sample.

To aid in controlling the volume of data, several steps can be taken. First, the EEG signal can be passed through a set of filters that limits the data. For example, if alpha and beta were being considered, 8- to 30-hertz data would be kept and other frequencies filtered out.

Second, a Fourier transformation (Thompson and Patterson 1974) can be performed on the data. This converts activity within a predetermined frequency range(s) to a measure of power. The power measure can be in voltage units or arbitrary units, but in either case, it is easier to evaluate than the original time-based data. Power is a measure of aggregate activity in a location and/or frequency band. Finally, the data that are now limited in frequency ranges and transformed to power units can be aggregated over time. In this way one can see units of power per frequency range per period of time. The minimum period of time must be great enough to allow the lowest frequency to be observed adequately.

Data Analysis

The data reduction discussed previously can be continued by adding an across-subject dimension. Averaging across subjects is a conservative technique since features that survive the averaging are those that are present most persistently. High variance across subjects may cause weak findings to be discarded.

Several data transformations have been suggested in the literature to reduce the impact of outlier and/or artifactual data and to normalize distributions. Most common here are log (Galin, Johnstone, and Herron 1978) and *Z* (Ehrlichman and Wiener 1980) transformations. Other suggestions include eliminating outlier data that may be caused by eye-movement and/or muscle-movement artifacts and the use of a geometric mean to discount outliers (Doyle, Ornstein, and Galin 1974). An addition and/or alternative is to use the median rather than the mean as a measure of central tendency since the median will be less affected by outliers (Rothschild et al. in press). Measures of central tendency and transformation can be used in combinations to clarify the hazy picture created by aggregation. Since EEG patterns are unique across individuals, variance can be extremely large. Appropriate transformations may be necessary to clarify the data structure.

Hemispheric Lateralization

Much evidence has been accrued over the past two decades that demonstrates that the two hemispheres of the brain are not functionally equivalent. In a very simplified view, one could describe the left hemisphere as supporting verbal and analytic processing, while the right hemisphere supports spatial, holistic, nonverbal processing.

These gross statements were derived initially from research on commissurotomized (Gazzaniga 1970; Sperry 1974), hemispherectomized (Smith 1972), or lesioned patients (Milner 1974) and later from a large number of studies done using unidimensional tasks or unidimensional stimuli in a population of normal subjects (see Galin and Ornstein 1972, for a review of this work).

In studies dealing with commissurotomized subjects, the corpus callosum (the major link between the hemispheres) had been severed surgically to treat extreme cases of epilepsy. While these individuals seemed to function normally, researchers learned much about the brain by studying these people with separated hemispheres. For example, the left hemisphere was unable to do symbolic, nonverbal processing, while the right hemisphere was unable to do verbal processing. Hansen (1981) provides an introductory summary of work in this area and some potential implications for advertisers.

Unfortunately, it is unclear at this time as to what hemispheric relationship exists in normal subjects who are asked to do complex tasks or are exposed to complex stimuli. In these situations there is often a suppression of alpha in both hemispheres. It is not known if this indicates unrelated, competing, or parallel cognitive activity. As a result, it seems unreasonable to generalize from either commissurotomized subjects or from simple tasks to normal subjects and complex tasks (Galin 1979).

Other studies, which consider EEG data as they relate to more-complex tasks (Gevins et al. 1979b; Gevins et al. 1980), have found no evidence for lateralization of different cognitive functions across several complex tasks.

In studies involving normal subjects, the research paradigm is one where the subject is given a task presumed to involve one or both hemispheres and then EEG activity is observed. This paradigm focuses on ongoing EEG activity in which frequency domain parameters, shown as power levels over some frequency band width, are gathered. These usually compare the relative levels of alpha activity in the two hemispheres across locations or over time.

Hemispheric data are reported as either left/right (Galin, Johnstone, and Herron 1978; Gevins et al. 1979b; Galin and Ornstein 1972; McKee, Humphrey, and McAdam 1978) or left-right/left + right (Ehrlichman and Wiener 1980; Morgan, MacDonald, and Hilgard 1974). These ratios differ less than 15 percent between right-dominant and left-dominant tasks (Donchin, Kutas, and McCarthy 1977); such a slight difference in the best of situations leads one to speculate that it would be difficult to find dominance in complex tasks. This speculation has been supported by Gevins et al. (1979b; 1980) who find little hemispheric dominance in subjects asked to do a complex task.

Other studies show two to five times greater hemispheric effect in the alpha band than across the entire band of 1-35 hertz (Doyle, Ornstein, and Galin 1974). Furthermore, the asymmetry found by Doyle shows the activity of both hemispheres moving in the same direction but the hemisphere primarily engaged in the cognitive activity developing proportionately less power.

Subject-Related Variables

A number of subject variables must be considered in brain-wave research. These include age, sex, handedness, recent drug ingestion, amount of sleep, English as a native language, history of seizures and unconsciousness, and stage in the menstrual cycle (Perry and Childers 1969; Shagass 1972; Galin, Johnstone, and Herron 1978; Regan 1972). A lack of control over these variables has been shown to affect EEG patterns. Given the complexity of data gathering, one should attempt to deal with a homogenous sample in early studies so that data are not overwhelmed by across-subject differences that could have been controlled.

Event-Related Potentials

Another category of studies analyzes the EEG primarily in the time domain. These studies are concerned with the waveforms of event-related potentials (ERP) and report data in terms of amplitude and latency of the waveform following the eliciting event. In studies of this type, a brief auditory or visual stimulus interrupts a task. Experimenters measure EEG activity following interruption to see what types of activities were affected. Dominant areas of task-related activity are least likely to be affected by interruption, while areas of the brain not involved in the task will show alpha suppression in response to the ERP stimulus.

ERP data seem to be less useful than EEG because of the time dependence related to the ERP stimulus. Data can be gathered only intermittently (in response to the discrete ERP stimulus) and, as a result, are less complete (Galin 1979). This is especially a problem for studying long, complex tasks when any single ERP data-collection period covers only several hundred milliseconds. Osborne and Gale (1976) also comment on the inappropriateness of the ERP when studying a continuous complex task because the sampled periods are too brief. This chapter does not pursue ERP methods.

This section reviewed cursorily the psychophysiology literature as it relates to electroencephalographic activity. We attempted to indicate some of the complexities associated with doing research in this area and to provide an introduction to the reader so we can assess the advertising-related literature.

Review of Advertising Literature

The use of electroencephalographic data in the field of advertising has a short history with a very limited amount of work. We present the review of this work first theoretically and then empirically.

Theory Speculation

The non-data-based work in this area is strongly interrelated with the concept of low-involvement learning and with the views of Krugman. In several papers, Krugman (1977a; 1977b; 1978) has developed a number of interesting speculations concerning hemispheric lateralization and frequency bands. He feels that print advertising is a left-hemisphere-dominant stimulus, while television commercials are right-hemisphere-dominant stimuli. Topics/products that elicit high involvement are left dominant; those that elicit low involvement are right dominant. Recall, reading, and speaking are left-hemisphere tasks; recognition and perception are right-hemisphere tasks.

Krugman also discusses the meaning of alpha and beta frequency-band EEG activity. For these he postulates that the two bands are correlated inversely and that, as beta activity increases, cognitive activity is occurring.

Hansen (1981) also has written in the area of hemispheric lateralization and consumer behavior. His work reviews studies dealing with the functional specializations of the right and left brain and is useful to the introductory reader in that it provides more detail than other papers in this region. Hansen begins with the work by Krugman and proceeds to outline a large number of studies that support the lateralization notions he has put forth. He concludes with a series of hypotheses relating lateralization and consumer behavior and discusses future potential research strategies.

Along with the optimistic predictions of Krugman and Hansen, one should consider also the more-pessimistic views of Katz (1980), who feels that speculation concerning lateralization has been overstated. He bases his conclusions on the fact that the optimistic reports are founded on studies of subjects with separated hemispheres. Since these subjects are not normal, he feels we should not generalize from them to normally functioning people. He goes on to cite studies that show that the hemispheres complement one another and that the notions of hemispheric dominance need to be considered more carefully, as discussed earlier.

Furthermore, Krugman's views of the meaning of beta also may not be consistent with more-recent work where alpha and beta seem to be correlated positively (discussed earlier). It seems too early to attach meaning to beta; interpretation of alpha seems clearer and here Krugman's views seem more on target.

In summary, Krugman's three papers are thought provoking but not always based on the most current psychophysiological literature. The hypotheses derived need to be tested since the issues related to low-involvement learning also are just beginning to be tested; clearly, low-involvement learning differs from high-involvement learning. It is unclear when recall is an appropriate measure, but it is also unclear what other measures are appropriate in these low-involvement cases and how learning from television occurs. EEG data have the potential to provide insight into these areas. Krugman is correct in raising the EEG as a potentially useful research paradigm and should be supported for his speculative papers, but the reader should be made aware of the bounds of knowledge in assessing the work.

Data

Data-based work examining EEG activity as a response to advertising stimuli also is limited. The first data-based paper to consider EEG and advertising was written by Krugman (1971). In this study he collected EEG data from one subject who read a magazine and watched television in an isolated room. His finding was that the print stimulus elicited more beta activity than alpha; slow waves (similar to theta) occurred least. Television elicited mostly theta activity and least beta with an intermediate amount of alpha. With repetition of commercials, beta diminished. However, the single-subject design of this study limits its generalizability.

Weinstein and co-workers published two papers in this area (Appel, Weinstein, and Weinstein 1979b; Weinstein, Appel, and Weinstein 1980).

In the first experiment, small groups of subjects viewed television commercials that had been aired previously and tested for recall. Commercials were for both high- and low-involvement products. Each subject saw a high- and a low-recall commercial for each of ten products, and each subject saw this ordering of twenty commercials three times in succession. There was no distracting program content. Findings were as follows:

> Lower alpha occurred for television commercials than for a blank television screen. (This is consistent with the psychophysiology literature.)

> No significant difference in alpha appeared across hemispheres although slightly greater alpha occurred in the right hemisphere. (No difference is consistent with the current psychophysiology literature although not consistent with Weinstein's hypothesis. The directional tendency is counter to Weinstein's hypothesis.)

> High-recall commercials led to lower levels of alpha. (This finding is consistent with that found in a large number of psychophysiology studies that show a negative relationship between alpha and attention.

As Krugman (1980) pointed out, there is another interesting finding in Weinstein's data set in that left dominance deteriorates with repetitions of the message. This is consistent with Dimond and Beaumont's (1973) view that the left hemisphere is more active in novel situations and less active in routine cases. Krugman (1979) has published other criticism of this study elsewhere. Appel, Weinstein, and Weinstein (1979a) have responded.

In the second study (Weinstein, Appel, and Weinstein 1980), subjects saw previously aired commercials for high- and low-involvement products embedded in program content (television) or with editorial content (magazine). Each subject was exposed to both television and magazine (randomly ordered). Findings were as follows:

> Greater levels of beta occurred for print than for television. (This is consistent with Weinstein's hypothesis and Krugman's work. The psychophysiology literature is ambivalent with regard to beta activity.)

> Left-hemisphere beta activity is greater for print than for television in one part of the study but is not replicated in a later part. (Where there is a difference, it is consistent with the hypothesis; the psychophysiology literature is tending toward the view that complex stimuli are processed in both hemispheres and will not show a dominance.)

> High-recall print ads led to greater beta activity than low-recall ads. This finding did not hold for television commercials. In the first study

high-recall television commercials had been associated with lower alpha levels. One study shows no beta differences; one shows alpha differences.

In another study, Rockey, Greene, and Perold (1980) showed a sixty-minute program with embedded commercials to twenty-four subjects. Commercials were selected so that eight well-known brands were represented; each brand had two commercials; one commercial was high recall and one was low recall based on prior tests done by Gallup and Robinson. Some commercials were quite well known (for example, Mean Joe Greene for Coca Cola); others were unknown animatics.

The data showed significant differences between program and commercials for measures of attention but no differences between high- and low-recall commercials; the EEG data did not relate to the recall data.

Some of the commercials were repeated. The data show a marginally significant increase in attention during the second viewing within the hour. Again, the results did not differ by high- and low-recall commercials.

Results may have been clearer if more-consistent stimuli had been used. Some commercials were well known; others were not. Some were finished; others were animatics. Some were for high-involvement products; others were for low. Without controlling for these factors it would be hard to come up with meaningful results, and this was indeed the case here.

In another study, Cacioppo and Petty (1982) introduce what they term *social psychophysiology,* or the study of affect through physiological methods. In this paper they examined the relationship between hemispheric dominance of alpha activity and affect as measured in paper-and-pencil tests. They found a significant inverse relationship between left-hemisphere EEG activity and affective polarization and a positive relationship between right-hemisphere EEG activity and affective polarization.

Ray and Olson have been working in the area of EEG response to advertising for about a year. Their work appears as chapter 13.

Rothschild and Thorson have attempted to control for the lack of homogeneity of stimuli and lack of acclimation of subjects. All commercials were finished and were for low-involvement products not found in the test-market area. Subjects saw the commercials embedded in program materials and viewed extraneous materials for thirty minutes before the test commercials were shown (for details, see Rothschild et al. in press).

This study showed a strong negative correlation between alpha activity and immediate (thirty-minute) recall, immediate recognition, and delayed (two-week) recognition. Delayed recall scores were too low to analyze. Adjective factors correlated in the hypothesized directions (positive adjectives: negative correlation; negative adjectives: positive correlation) but were not significant.

The main goal of this study was to examine the change in alpha levels over the course of the commercials. The data show that different scenes have different capabilities of eliciting a drop in alpha and maintaining that lower level. Some scenes do not cause a drop in alpha (the scenes do not elicit this involuntary physiological response); some scenes cause a drop in alpha, but the drop is followed by rapid recovery of alpha (they elicit an involuntary increase in attention but do not maintain interest); some scenes cause a drop in alpha and a slow recovery of alpha (the eventual recovery of alpha is also involuntary but can occur with varying degrees of rapidity).

Data in this study are consistent with the psychophysiology literature. Alpha should correlate negatively with paper-and-pencil measures of cognitive activity. The onset of visual stimuli should cause a sudden drop in alpha that is followed by recovery with various rates of rapidness.

Conclusions

Advertisers have become very interested in considering EEG measures as a set of responses to commercial stimuli. Their interest is founded upon psychophysiology results that indicate a strong relationship between certain types of stimuli and certain types of EEG responses.

It is also clear, though, that these findings will transfer only with difficulty to the relationship between advertising-commercial stimuli and learning-response measures. As noted in the psychophysiology literature, findings become more difficult to observe as stimuli become more complex. This complexity has been overlooked in many of the advertising-related studies and may be a major contributor to a lack of meaningful findings.

To overcome these complexities requires a concerted effort at simplification in a number of areas. This calls for a homogeneity within variables. Subjects must be as similar as possible in the current stage of research; this chapter lists some variables to control.

Stimuli must be similar in some dimensions. Commercials vary in a myriad of ways that cannot be accounted for but also vary in a few that should be controlled. Level of respondent involvement with the product class is crucial. This involvement may effect the entire method of processing that may in turn impact upon electrical activity. While an involving product will elicit varying levels of response involvement depending on factors such as need or stage in the purchase process, less-involving products rarely elicit high response involvement regardless of need. Therefore, it is felt that low-involvement cases lead to more-homogeneous processing.

Old versus new stimuli also can be controlled easily. Old stimuli can elicit a wide range of responses depending upon prior exposure (which is impossible to control). New stimuli produce a more-consistent response since the novelty is equal for all subjects.

Combining two variables would suggest that new commercials for products that elicit low-involvement responses would lead to the least variance among respondents. Such a logic may be crucial when dealing with EEG data in the early stages of investigation.

Most data reported at this time have shown aggregation of electrical activity over a thirty-second interval. Thirty seconds is a very long time in a field where data are reported in thousandths of seconds. By aggregating in this way, it is possible that important data are never observed. The appropriate unit of analysis may be the scene rather than the entire commercial.

Krugman has made a similar argument for simplicity by urging the study of one commercial as it is viewed by one subject. We do not agree with this method, but we do agree with his call for simplicity and homogeneity in observation.

The study of EEG responses to advertising stimuli is fascinating but will not survive without careful observation of events. Much more work is needed before stimuli as complex as thirty-second commercials can be evaluated in a meaningful sense.

13

Perspectives on Psychophysiological Assessment of Psychological Responses to Advertising

William J. Ray and
Jerry C. Olson

In the 1970s, a group of leading scientists and philosophers was asked to write chapters for a book entitled the *Encyclopaedia of Ignorance* (Duncan and Weston-Smith 1977). As the title reflects, their purpose was to delineate interesting but unanswered questions and to identify problems that remain to be solved in their areas of expertise. For instance, Roger Sperry (1974) discussed problems in the evolution of brain function. Other authors pointed to unanswered questions in the nature of the immune system, particle physics, and the mechanics of evolution and to philosophical issues regarding our conception of time. We have adopted this style to some extent in this chapter. Instead of discussing what we already know about psychophysiological assessment,[1] we emphasize what we see as important dimensions of our ignorance regarding psychophysiological measures of psychological responses (for example, information-processing activity). We think that solutions to these issues are necessary for this work to be useful in advertising research. We also present our conceptual perspective for developing these solutions by describing our program of research in psychophysiological measurement as applied to advertising.

A Brief History of Psychophysiological Assessment

The idea of using physiological responses as indicators of psychological states dates back at least to the third century B.C. (Mesulam and Perry 1972). Men such as Erasistratos and Galen are associated with early experimental use of physiological measures. For instance, Galen related a case involving insomnia on which he was asked to consult. When the woman was

The research program described in this chapter has been supported by Young and Rubicam, Inc., and by a grant from the Marketing Science Institute. Olson served as a visiting research professor at MSI in 1981-1982, during which time this chapter was written.

253

unwilling to discuss her problems, Galen turned to physiological measures, in this case her heart rate, as a means of understanding the problem. Using a fairly systematic series of observations of the woman's heart rate over a period of days, Galen was able to demonstrate that the cause of her insomnia was her love for a male dancer in the court. From the early experimental studies of Galen to anecdotes about Eastern merchants who could tell a customer's feelings by looking at the pupils of their eyes, physiological responses came to be interpreted as representing the window to the soul.

Similar claims are echoed today in areas ranging from psychophysiological assessment of clinical disorders to lie detection to advertising research. Where lie the promises and where lie the problems in these claims? We believe it is critically important for those interested in using physiological measures in advertising research to develop an accurate and reasonably sophisticted perspective on psychophysiology and what it can tell us about people's behaviors.

The Language of Psychophysiology

To begin to get a handle on this complex issue, consider the following metaphor. Assume that each psychophysiological measure—such as brain waves (EEG), heart rate (EKG), electrodermal activity (EDA, previously referred to as skin conductance or GSR), muscular activity (EMG), and so forth—represents a language of its own. Assume further that measures of psychological states and processes (for example, emotions, beliefs, attention) and overt behaviors are also separate languages. This metaphor suggests several questions. How are we to understand each language? How does one physiological language like EEG activity translate into another language like EKG activity? How does a psychophysiological language translate into other, quite different languages of human behavior such as emotional or feeling responses, or overt motor acts, or cognitive behavior such as information processing or thinking?

Many (perhaps most) of us probably would agree with the assumption that a (knowable) relationship exists between different physiological measures, and we probably also believe there is an association between physiological measures and thoughts, feelings, and acts. Thus, the basic issue involves the nature of the translation from one language to another. A simple proposition (that got many people interested in this field in the first place) is that direct transformational rules relate physiological measures with each other and with response measures at the other levels. In its simplest form, a one-to-one mapping relationship was assumed, which implied that each thought, feeling, or action could be determined from the appropriate physiological measure. Moreover, it was assumed that the language of any one physiological response was the same as that of any other response. As a recent example, Krugman (1981, p. 8) has suggested that it does not matter which physiological measure one uses "since they all measure the same thing." The same thing being measured was arousal. Current neuropsychological speculation and evidence, however, are inconsistent with such a simple interpretation. In the next section, we consider the idea of arousal in greater detail and point out problems with the idea that all physiological measures are measuring the same construct, as well as the idea that physiological measures measure constructs.

Arousal

Since the early part of this century, arousal has been used as an intervening variable to help explain performance differences. For example, the Yerkes-Dodson law of 1908 postulated an inverted U-shaped function by which performance was related to arousal. Thus, persons who were underaroused performed poorly, as did subjects who were overaroused. Maximal performance was expected from subjects who were moderately aroused. In this simple relationship, physiological and behavioral processes were seen to parallel each other. Later, with the discovery of the electrical activity of the brain cortex (EEG) and of the reticular activating system, it became possible to speak of the brain as aroused or activated. More recently, Duffy (1962) has suggested an arousal continuum, ranging from coma to sleep to intense emotional excitement. Despite the usefulness of an arousal, or activation, concept for certain research questions, its treatment as a unitary construct capable of describing both brain and behavior responses and their interrelationships has led to a number of problems.

Problems with Unitary Arousal Theory

In a review written in 1959, John Lacey outlined the problems with the unitary approach. He addressed the question of how psychophysiological measures might be used to evaluate and assess psychotherapy, an application similar to the psychophysiological assessment of advertising effects. Perhaps the most telling criticism of unitary arousal theory was the discovery of patterns of physiological responding, usually referred to as directional fractionation. This is the case in which a person evidences a consistent patterning of physiological responses that are directionally different. For example, if you ask people to look at a slide, you may observe decreases in their heart rates and skin resistance. However, if you give them a math problem to solve in their heads, you may again see a decrease in skin resistance but an increase in heart rate. Here is a situation in which two physiological indicators, both of which are presumed to measure arousal, evidence different patterns of covariance, depending upon the task. It is not true that any physiological measure necessarily will give you the same information as any other. As another example, consider the dissertation research by Brad Hatfield recently conducted in our laboratory. Hatfield examined EEG and EKG changes in Olympic-class marksmen as they prepared to fire at targets. He found that as these elite marksmen moved from a resting state to a performance state, there were changes in heart rate but not in EEG alpha activity.

Such patterns of covariance are inconsistent with a simple unitary arousal continuum and present difficulties for those who seek to conceptualize all physiological measures as indexes of arousal. One theoretical alternative is to speak of types of arousal. For instance, Lacey (1959) suggested that arousal be divided into cortical arousal, autonomic arousal, and behavioral arousal. A similar distinction is supported also by research in anxiety in which cognitive and somatic components are shown to differ (compare Borkovec, 1976). The suggestion that there is more than one type of arousal has several implications. One is the need to record a physiological response that corresponds to the particular type of arousal of interest. However, since we are not always certain which arousal type is being measured, another implication is the need to measure multiple physiological responses and to examine the patterns of covariance among them.

Further illustrations of the problems of a unitary arousal theory are provided in the review by McGuinness and Pribram (1980) and in the critique by Vanderwolf and Robinson (1981) of arousal theory as related to animal EEG research. The latter article delineates many of the problems with using EEG activation or deactivation as a simple index of arousal. The authors also pointed out the various (and sometimes separate) biochemical systems involved in behavior. In doing so, they provided substantial evidence against the notion that all arousal is mediated biochemically through adrenaline (compare Krugman 1981). In addition, Tucker (1981) has suggested that the two hemispheres of the human brain may produce different types of arousal, with the left being more influenced by dopaminergic processes and the right more influenced by serotonin and norepinephrine.

In sum, arousal is seen no longer as a simple, unitary construct. Thus, we might expect to find in any advertising study a complex set of relationships between psychophysiological measures and other (psychological) measures of human responsiveness. Given that a simple arousal theory seems to have serious problems, how then might we theoretically proceed? An important beginning is to differentiate our terms clearly.

Types of Arousal

Words such as *emotionally, activation,* and *arousal* seemingly are used interchangeably in consumer research. Part of this confusion may stem from
the fact that the early experimental work was performed on animals and
that overt motor activity such as running, fighting, and so on was used to
index these arousal states. In the process, some of the traditional finer-
grained distinctions that previously had been applied to human behavior
were abandoned. Now, however, it seems important to reestablish these
distinctions.

Harkening back to the nineteenth century, William James (1890) suggested that the concept of attention requires differentiation into several
types, including whether the attention is immediate or derived, passive or
active, and takes as its object a thought or a sense experience. For our purposes, it may be useful to examine the passive/active distinction in greater
detail. For James, passive attention was a reflexive, nonvoluntary, effort-
less form of arousal. One's passive attention can be invoked when a novel
stimulus comes into view, upon hearing one's name, or on exposure to an
instinctual stimulus like a person in a sexual pose. Passive attention is conceptually similar to Sokolov's orientating response in which a person responds to novelty with a physical orientation toward the stimulus (for example, head turning) higher sensitivity of the sense organs, increased beta-
level EEG activity, skin-conductance increases, slowing of the heart rate,
vasoconstriction in the limbs, and vasodilation in the head (Lynn 1966).

Conversely, active attention for James was a voluntary process. This
type of attention is illustrated by those controllable activities required to
listen to a speech, to read a book, or to maintain a focus during a problem-
solving activity. James made two interesting observations concerning the
concept of active attention. First, voluntary attention cannot be sustained
for more than a few seconds at a time. Although we may seem to listen to a
talk or focus on a problem continuously, according to James we are making
successive efforts to bring the topic back to mind. James's second observation concerning active attention is that no one can attend continuously to
an object that does not change. Recent research suggests this limitation may
be truer for the left hemisphere than the right (Dimond and Beaumont
1973).

Sharpless and Jasper (1956) made a distinction similar to James's but
from a more-physiological basis. They suggested that aspects of the central
nervous system associated with arousal (or attention, as James called it)
could be divided into two parts. One aspect rapidly habituates to a stimulus,
while the other habituates more slowly. McGuiness and Pribram (1980)
have suggested that the first, more-phasic component lasts one to three

seconds and is reflexive in nature. Such arousal might be produced by a mismatch of incoming information with previously established neural traces (for example, memories). For example, this short-term attention is produced when you expect a particular set of stimuli but receive another; it is stimulus sensitive. The second type of attention is slower to habituate and is considered to be more under a person's control. Thus, it is more related to interest and motivational factors.

Similar distinctions have been made in current cognitive psychology and neuropsychology. For instance, Posner (1978) discussed parallel versus serial processes, Donchin (1979) contrasted stimulus evaluation with response selection, and Broadbent (1977) described preattentive and attention processes. Of particular relevance, McGuinness and Pribram (1980) distinguished between arousal and activation. They saw short-term arousal as addressing the question What is it?, whereas the more-tonic activation addresses the question What is to be done?[2] Finally, in a review of neurophysiological mechanisms in arousal theory, Vanderwolf and Robinson (1981) suggest that short-term reflexive or phasic arousal is sensitive to cholingeric innervation, whereas the more-tonic arousal is aminergic, thus suggesting biochemical as well as psychological differences in these processes.

Although many of these researchers are interested in the neurophysiological and biochemical processes involved in these types of arousal/attention, the overall distinction between short- (one to three seconds) and long-term (over three seconds) phasic versus tonic arousal and the psychological processes and states associated with each are relevant for consumer researchers. For example, certain parts of a television commercial might produce phasic, short-term arousal but not tonic, longer-term activation. Or, a consumer who is particularly interested in a certain product might reveal toniclike activation responses to parts of a commerical for that product that are otherwise dull and unarousing (in a phasic sense).

Psychophysiological Research in Advertising

Historically, many applied studies, whether in the area of consumer behavior or clinical processes, have avoided the important issues discussed here. In such studies the researchers often began with a simplifying assumption like changes in heart rate equal changes in arousal. Such a perspective leads to the use of a limited research design in which only heart rate (or whatever) is measured. Any observed changes in heart rate (especially those that are covariant with the experimental treatments) then are interpreted in terms of the original assumption. Consider an example in which several consumers are shown segments from television shows. Since heart rate normally varies, it is quite likely that some changes in heart rate will be contemporaneous with changes in the program segments. Thus, it will be possible to claim that certain segments of the show are more arousing than others.

Note, however, that such data do not provide any support for the arousal theory on which the study was based. The original assumption that arousal changes equal heart-rate changes was never tested. By basing the study on this naive theory of arousal and by measuring only heart rate, it is difficult to learn anything new about arousal. We might note also that commercial tests measuring (only) simple hemispheric lateralization based on EEG ratios (for example, right-hemispheric alpha activity divided by left) have the same logical problems as the simple heart-rate-and-arousal illustration. Little, if anything, new can be learned, and the basic assumptions that form the basis for the study are not tested in any rigorous sense.

What happens next? Often the researcher attempts to modify the original material in order to increase (or decrease) arousal, or hemispheric imbalance, or whatever measure is of interest. However, he or she usually discovers that this approach is more difficult than originally supposed. This is so because, for any given stimulus manipulation, the physiological measures do not always (ever?) vary as the simple assumption predicts. At this point, some researchers conclude that physiological measurement is too complicated and drop the research. In fact, several corporate researchers who supported such research have reported to us that they did so only once or twice with limited success.[3] Perhaps the subsequent realization of the great complexity of this type of research may explain why so few long-term research programs can be found in applied psychophysiology. Thus, the published literature is replete with one or two attempts by researchers to test empirically specific theoretical conceptualizations using psychophysiological measures.

We would like to propose a different approach to applied psychophysiological research. Our alternative involves a programmatic examination of the psychophysiological and psychological responses of individuals to complex stimuli in general and to television programming and commercials in particular. We admit that this approach is more complex than the current alternatives and may appear at times to be making slower progress. We begin with questions and not with simple answers. Conceptually, we assume that the relationships between psychophysiological measures and thoughts, feelings, and actions are quite complex. We further assume that different measures and levels of analysis represent somewhat separate languages, and our task is to develop a means of translating from one to another. Finally, we do not see our task as an easy one or one that is guaranteed to produce short-term results that are understood or applied easily to advertising-research issues.

When we first decided to examine the relationships between measures of psychological and psychophysiological responses (especially EEG activity) to television commercials, we reviewed the literature in both consumer behavior and psychophysiology/neuropsychology. Few studies in the basic psychophysiological literature were related to television studies. Although some studies examined the relationships between various psychophysiological measures and the presentation of information through film, these were of minimal value. In the next section, we briefly consider the EEG research in psychophysiology and advertising. This research is also reviewed by Rothschild and Thorson in chapter 12 (see also Weinstein 1980).

A Brief Overview of Psychophysiological Measures of Advertising Effects

A number of psychophysiological measures ranging from heart rate (EKG) to electrodermal activity (EDR) to pupillary responses have been used in connection with advertising research (see Watson and Gatchel 1979; or Stewart and Furse 1982, for review). Recent interest, however, has focused on electrocortical measures of brain activity, recorded using EEG methods.

One of the most often cited studies of EEG and advertising was conducted by Krugman (1971). Krugman recorded EEG from a woman (Sidney Weinstein's secretary) while she either looked at television commercials or read magazine ads. The overall conclusion of this research report was that print ads produced more high-frequency EEG activity (beta, at 12.3-31.8 hertz) than television commercials. In contrast, television commercials produced more lower-frequency activity (delta and theta at 1.5-7.5 hertz, alpha at 7.6-12.33 hertz), at least for this individual than print ads. Krugman interpreted these findings in terms of his concept of low-involvement learning (for example, Krugman, 1965).

In this and other papers, Krugman proposed a kind of imitation model of television viewing; that is, he hypothesized that exposure to material via television "typically produces changes in behavior prior to changes in attitude" (1977, p. 7). He further argued for a nonverbal form of memory storage that may be evoked when an appropriate stimulus or internal state is presented at a later time. This type of memory should be measured best by recognition tasks, not verbal recall. In fact, if indeed the information is stored in a totally nonverbal form, then verbal recall would be difficult, perhaps impossible. Thus, Krugman's arguments lead to the conclusion that assessing advertising effects requires nonverbal measures, of which EEG is one example. Krugman's ideas also suggest that more-primitive forms of physiological processing occur during television viewing than the higher-level cortical functioning we tend to associate with verbal behavior and analytical reasoning.

Associated with the interest in EEG measures of advertising effects is the recent excitement regarding the hemispheric-lateralization hypothesis (compare Hansen 1981; Hecker 1981). Hemispheric lateralization refers to the proposition that the two brain hemispheres evidence differential functioning. This idea dates back at least 100 years to the work of Hughlings Jackson (Taylor 1958). In recent years, however, development of radical brain-surgery procedures for the treatment of epilepsy and the subsequent psychological analysis of these patients produced a renewed interest in the area (compare Sperry 1974). The general hemispheric-lateralization formulation suggests that the right hemisphere of the human brain is specialized for holistic, gestalt, or visual-spatial processing, whereas the left hemisphere is specialized for analytic and verbal processing (Sperry 1974; Semmes 1968; see Harnad et al. 1977; Kinsbourne 1978; Levy 1980, for general reviews of this area). This proposition is supported by research results obtained from both brain-damaged and normal subjects, using a variety of techniques including dichotic listening, tachistoscopic presentations, lateral eye movements, blood-flow studies, and electrocortical recordings. Electrocortical results using both evoked potentials and EEGs suggest that differential electrical activity indicative of differential cognitive activity may be observed in the two hemispheres during verbal and spatial tasks (see Donchin, Kuts, and McCarthy 1977, for a review).

In some initial studies, EEG activity has been recorded in a wide band (approximately 0-30 hertz), and differential hemispheric activation was reported for verbal as opposed to spatial tasks (Galin and Ornstein 1972), especially for men (Ray et al. 1976). Time-series analysis suggested that the change in overall EEG was related directly to changes in the alpha band (Doyle, Ornstein, and Galin 1974). Since alpha activity (waves of slow frequency and high amplitude) traditionally has been considered to have an inverse relationship with mental activity (Adrian and Matthews 1934), most researchers have assumed that the presence of alpha in a given hemisphere denotes cortical deactivation and, thus, a lack of cognitive processing in that hemisphere. However, Walters (1964), among others, has emphasized that not only cognitive activity but also other factors such as anxiety and anticipation can produce changes in alpha and may confound observed relationships. A direct interpretation of the alpha/cognitive-processing relationship may not be as serious a problem in highly controlled laboratory studies that involve discrete, cognitively simple tasks. However, in advertising research, where the type of material and the variation in the responses of interest may vary greatly, such a simple interpretation of alpha may be problematic.

The hemispheric hypothesis has been examined in recent EEG advertising research. Appel, Weinstein, and Weinstein (1979) studied responses to ten pairs of television commercials for which recall had been predetermined. These ads were shown to a sample of thirty right-handed women ranging in age from eighteen to forty-nine. EEG was recorded, but the analysis was in terms of alpha activity only. Comparing total alpha activity (both hemispheres averaged together) during the initial baseline period (blank television screen) with the first, second, and third presentation of the commercial showed significantly more alpha activity during the blank-screen condition. No differences were obtained between the first, second, and third presentations of the commercials. When these data were analyzed by hemisphere, no support was found for the researchers' hypothesis that television viewing would produce more right-hemispheric activity. Likewise, there was no support for the idea that recall would be associated with left-hemispheric alpha. However, recall was correlated with overall alpha (across both hemispheres).[4]

In a later EEG study, Weinstein, Appel, and Weinstein (1981) included differential stimulus materials by comparing television commercials with print advertisements. Eight thirty-second television commercials were presented to thirty women in two groups of four within an action adventure movie. The print ads were embedded in a mock-up of a magazine including editorial material. The authors concluded that their results demonstrated greater left-hemispheric involvement for print than television advertisements. However, given that the authors changed both their measure (from alpha to beta) and their method of analysis (from number of seconds of alpha to percentage of beta) in the second study, it is difficult to compare the results of both studies. For our purposes, it is not necessary to examine these two studies critically at a deeper level. Others have done so and have raised a number of interesting questions (see Krugman 1980; Rossiter 1980; chapter 12).

However, it may provide a useful perspective to note that the early Krugman papers seem to have been motivated by an interest in using measures of physiological processes as a means of understanding low-involvement and nonverbal processing. In contrast, the two studies reported by the Weinstein group seem to be focused on active processing of the advertisement and verbal recall of information in the ads. Thus, although both Krugman (for example, 1981) and Weinstein (1980) emphasize the importance of physiological research for advertising, they seem to have rather different underlying rationales for advocating such measures. It is almost as if a given physiological measure can have different meanings depending upon the particular question being asked. Moreover, it seems that the psychophysiological measures used to assess psychological variables are selected based on simple, essentially intuitive ideas about arousal. In contrast, our approach is based on the assumption that things are much more complex than that. The next section describes the research program we have begun.

A Research Program in Psychophysiological Assessment

How can we characterize the state of the art in psychophysiology? Certainly, many skilled researchers are studying a variety of problems at several different levels of analysis. Some are concerned with more-or-less pure physiology—electrochemical processes at a very micro (molecular, neural) level. Others are interested in these same types of phenomena but for larger-scale brain structures. Others are involved in recording (via electrodes on the scalp) the electrocortical activity from rather large regions of the brain. A subset of these latter researchers is interested, as we are, in psychophysiology—that is, in relating those patterns of electrical activity to psychological processes and states.

Perhaps because relatively few physiologists have such interests, the field does not have a large-scale theory, or even a general conceptual framework, for organizing and explaining the mass of discrete research findings that have been produced. Such a model would be immensely valuable. Not only could it help us to understand the data we have collected thus far, but also it could direct our future research. For example, it could provide useful guidelines for deciding what to do in an EEG study—for example, what kinds of brain-activity responses should we measure, in what location, and for how long should we record? Instead of such a global model, at present we have several interesting, but rather general, almost intuitive, notions about smaller-scale issues—for example, the hemispheric-lateralization idea or propositions about localization of brain functions. As yet, these separate ideas have not been integrated into a larger-scale model. Thus, they can provide only general guidance as to what to do in our research program.

Lacking an overall conceptual framework, we are faced with the difficult, somewhat distasteful task of conducting a research program without the clear boundaries and direction provided by a comprehensive theory. Note that a desirable theoretical model should be specified at a level that will be relevant for explaining physiological (and psychological) responses to complex, natural stimuli like advertisements. Developing such a theory will be difficult, in part because the field has not yet produced much empirical evidence regarding the variables of interest. In fact, there is precious little good descriptive data about how measures of the various physiological and psychological factors vary (and that are covariant) in response to changes in natural stimulus variables. Thus, the initial efforts in our research program have been devoted toward generating such a data base.

General Approach

We have begun to measure a variety of physiological and psychological responses to a wide variety of stimuli, some of which are very complex, like television commercials, while others are simpler, like mental arithmetic or visual imaging. In these initial studies we have taken two related approaches. In the experimental approach, we examine how both the physiological and psychological variables are affected by our manipulations of the stimuli (for example, different types of advertising execution strategies, for different product categories, for different numbers of exposures). We also examine the effects of subject factors (for example, age, sex, past experience) and external factors such as time of day or the program material surrounding the commerical. Our correlational approach seeks to identify consistent patterns of relationships between the physiological measures and between them and the psychological variables. To do this we use various types of correlational analyses like factor analysis, as well as less-familiar techniques like coherence analysis (to measure the extent to which electrocortical activity recorded from various regions of the brain are coherent or consistent with each other).

Our overall goal is to develop generalizations about psychophysiology based on our experience with such data sets. We are trying, in a basic inductive manner, to develop tentative propositions about the relationships between physiological and psychological responses. Of course, these preliminary ideas will be influenced by and ultimately combined with other theories. From these initial conceptual models, we may be able to deduce propositions and to subject them to empirical tests using our data sets. Particularly promising ideas then can be subjected to tests using new data from specially designed studies. By this bootstrapping approach—a kind of spiral process of induction-deduction-test-induction-and so on—we hope eventually to develop some useful generalizations about the relationships between physiological and psychological responses to complex stimuli, including advertising. We expect this process to take several years. We hope that others will join in attempting to develop this area.

Specific Features of Our Research Program

During 1981, we have conducted two major studies of advertising effects that provide the first entries for our data base. Since both studies were quite similar in overall design, we discuss their major characteristics together. Neither of these studies has been anlayzed completely as yet; therefore, we do not intend to present any details of the complex results. Rather, our goal is to describe our conceptual rationale and empirical approach as manifested in the beginnings of our psychophysiological research program.

Advertisements. Thus far, we have examined consumer responses to thirty-second television commercials only, although we intend to include print advertisements in subsequent research. We attempted to select commercials for testing that represented distinctions of both theoretical and practical interest. Previous studies have not made clear distinctions among types of commercials. In both studies we contrasted commercials that emphasized product or brand characteristics (attribute) with advertisements (usually for the same brand) that said little or nothing about product features. Typically, the latter commercials showed the product being used by particular types of people in specific situations (image) or included emotional scenes in which the product had some relevance (emotional). Such differences in executional style or strategy are of interest to the advertisers. In addition, they might be expected on theoretical grounds to produce different types of psychological (and physiological) responses. Multiple commercials (six and twelve) were included in the two studies.

Subjects. In both studies we examined the responses of both male and female adults between the ages of eighteen and fifty-five. Previously published research has included only women as subjects (Appel et al. 1979; Weinstein et al. 1980; chapter 12); thus, we know very little about possible sex differences. All subjects were right handed and heads of their households, and most were at least occasional users of the product categories portrayed in the advertisements.

Exposure Environment. In both sudies we tried to make the exposure environment as natural as possible. Of course, the physiological recordings were conducted in our laboratory, not in people's living rooms. Subjects were run individually in a small room adjacent to the lab (in some studies, subjects were run in small groups; see Weinstein et al. 1980). Subjects were seated in a large comfortable chair. A television program was playing during the fifteen to twenty minutes it took to attach and check all the electrodes to give subjects a chance to get used to the exposure environment. The commercials were presented in pairs, embedded within real television programs about forty minutes long (a sports documentary and a talk show were used). We also recorded brain response to selected aspects of the program material.

Physiological Measures. In the two studies conducted so far, we have concentrated on measuring brain-wave activity in terms of EEG rather than other physiological responses (for example, EDR). Our approach has been to record brain responses at several different sites on the scalp in order to explore the extent to which different brain regions respond similarly. For example, in the second study we recorded from the frontal, temporal, and parietal areas in both hemispheres (six recording sites). Most previous advertising research has recorded from only one region, often the parietal area.

In our analyses, we have considered a wider range of EEG frequencies (more levels of activity) than is usual. In previous work, researchers commonly have examined only a portion (for example, only alpha or beta) of the traditional EEG frequency range of 0.5 to 30 hertz. In both of our studies we resolved the EEG signals, via an on-line fast-Fourier-transform analysis, into these standard frequency bands: delta (0.5-4 hertz), theta (4-8 hertz), alpha (8-12 hertz), beta$_1$ (12-16 hertz), and beta$_2$ (16-28 hertz). Thus, we have information on the full spectrum of electrocortical (brain-wave) activity from several separate areas of the brain. Although this makes our analyses more complex than in previous research, it allows us to check for consistencies in the patterns of covariance across sites and across frequencies.

Psychological Measures. Whereas most previous research examined only a limited number of other, psychological responses to television commercials (for example, only recall) against which to relate the few physiological measures that were taken, we have included measures of several types of psychological responses. In both studies we measured ad recall taken via telephone interviews twenty-four to forty-eight hours after exposure. We also measured cognitive responses (self-reported thought protocols) to several of the commercials. These will be scored in terms of their content—for example, thinking about brand, the ad, or something else—and related to the multiple measures of brain activity. We also had subjects rate the commercials on an extensive set of scales (liking, interest value, entertaining, and so forth), and these will be related with the brainwave response variables. In sum, we measured a variety of psychological responses, most of which are similar to the measures commonly taken in commercial-advertising research. By carefully examining the pattern of relationships between these variables and the physiological measures, we hope to be able to infer aspects of the meaning of the brainwave response measures.

Future Research

What does the conceptual and methodological research program outlined in this chapter imply about the direction of future research in psychophysiology? We have assumed that psychophysiological assessment of information processing in advertising is a very complicated problem, akin to translating simultaneously among multiple languages. Our approach is to recognize explicitly that complexity and to attempt to deal with it both conceptually and empirically. As yet we do not have answers to the major questions about psychophysiology. However, in the style of the *Encyclopaedia of Ignorance*, we offer some concluding thoughts about specific issues that we believe are important dimensions of our current ignorance about psychophysiology. We intend to address many of these topics in our research. These issues are organized in measurement, person characteristics, stimulus factors, and context domains. We should emphasize that although most of these issues are presented as simple main effects, we fully expect to find complex interactions among measure, subject, stimulus, and context factors.

I. Measurement Issues
   A. Parametric Factors
      1. What brain-wave frequencies should be analyzed (delta, theta, alpha, beta, or total activity)?
      2. How should the electrocortical activity be quantified (absolute or relative activity, normalized against a baseline measure, or Z transform)?
      3. What techniques should be used to analyze the EEG record (for example, Fourier, coherence)?
      4. What recording sites (that is, areas of the brain) should be used? How many sites are needed?
      5. How long should a segment or epoch of brain activity be (that is, one-, two-, five-, ten-, or thirty-second segments)?
   B. Empirical/Conceptual Questions
      1. What is the relationship between different EEG frequencies, both within and across recording sites (for example, how are alpha and beta activity related)?
      2. What is the relationship between different recording sites, both within and across hemispheres?
      3. Is the coherence between sites a useful indicator of processing activity?
      4. How are the various EEG indexes at covariance with other physiological indicators (for example, heart rate, skin conductance)?
      5. How are brain-activity measures related to other levels of analysis such as information processing (for example, thoughts, feelings), memory states (beliefs, attitudes, recall), and motor acts (purchase activities)?

II. Person Factors
   A. Stable Factors
      1. What is the effect on physiological responses of factors such as sex, age, and personality characteristics?
      2. How does a person's past experience—his or her cognitive structures of product-related knowledge stored in memory— affect physiological response?
   B. Fluctuating Factors
      1. What effects do motivational goal states (for example, viewing commercials for entertainment versus active interest in product, self-involvement versus neutral involvement) have on physiological responses to advertisements?
   C. Group versus Individual Data
      1. On what bases can we aggregate data from individuals?
      2. What different things can we learn from individual-level responses as opposed to group-level responses?

3. How do certain demographic factors (for example, socioeconomic status) mediate or moderate physiological responses?

III. Stimulus—Commercial—Characteristics
   A. How does the executional strategy of a commercial affect people's physiological and psychological responses (for example, hard versus soft sell, emotional versus attribute)?
   B. How does physiological response vary as a function of specific features within the commercial (sudden cuts, models, music, colors, and so on)?

IV. Context Factors
   A. How does the content of the program (vehicle) influence physiological responses to the commercials? What effects do adjacent commercials have?
   B. In what ways does the exposure environment (for example, distractions) determine the manner in which the information is processed, and how is this reflected by physiological responses?

Conclusion

This chapter began with a reference to the relative state of ignorance about psychophysiology. We feel this sense of ignorance rather keenly. It has provided an overall direction to our research program in applied psychophysiology, primarily through establishing a set of important questions that we feel need to be answered and through its influence on the style of our research approach. We have pointed out some of the problems of psychophysiological research as we see them and have described briefly how we intend to deal with some of them. The major unanswered questions we identified include the interrelations among alternative measures of physiological responses; the relationship of physiological responses to responses at other levels such as thoughts, feelings, and actions; and the conceptualizations of psychological constructs such as arousal, attention, activation, thinking, and effort, in terms of physiological factors. The present literature in the neurosciences offers hints and some direction but no definite answers to these important issues. We briefly described our research approach in terms of television advertising and psychophysiology and identified some of the specific issues in that domain that need to be addressed. Other viable approaches exist, of course. Our goal was to give a sense of what we feel is important for developing an understanding of these complex and fascinating issues. We hope others will become interested enough to develop their own research programs and to contribute to the solution of these questions so that our next chapter does not have to begin with a reference to the *Encyclopaedia of Delusions* (Duncan and Weston-Smith 1979).

Notes

1. The reader who is interested in a general introduction to psychophysiological methods might consult a general review of research by Andreassi (1980), an introduction to autonomic nervous system functioning by Van Toller (1979), a general introduction to recording techniques by Stern, Ray, and David (1980), or a more-advanced discussion of recording techniques by Brown (1967) or Martin and Venables (1980). Discussion of specific EEG techniques may be found in these works as well as in EEG texts (compare Cooper, Osselton, and Shaw 1974; Thompson and Patterson 1974). The relationship of psychophysiology to other fields such as clinical psychology (for example, Ray, Cole, and Raczynski 1983) and social psychology (for example, Cacioppo and Petty 1983; Stern and Ray 1983) have implications for consumer research.

2. Note the similarity of these distinctions to the ideas proposed by Krugman (1972) in his three-exposure theory of advertising repetition.

3. It is also true, as Krugman (1981) pointed out, that many researchers oversell the value of physiological measures to companies and agencies. Subsequently, they are unable to deliver what they promised, and the sponsors become disillusioned with psychophysiological research.

4. This last finding seems to point out an inconsistency in how alpha was viewed in this research, unless we assume that a person best recalls the information that is processed cognitively (that is, thought about) the least. It should be pointed out also that unlike previous psychophysiological studies, this study did not present what are referred to as right-hemispheric problems like spatial tasks or left-hemispheric problems like verbal manipulation. The subjects were told only to watch the commercials as they would normally. Thus, in essence, the study had only one type of task, watching television, and we are not sure how to categorize TV viewing in terms of hemispheric activation.

Part V
Structures of
Psychological
Responses to
Advertising

This final part contains five chapters that deal with innovative approaches to a better understanding of how to evaluate the effectiveness of advertising. Most evaluative techniques utilized today in advertising tend to be some variation of either recognition or recall tests, measures of belief or attitude change, or some form of cognitive-response protocol analysis. The authors of these chapters utilize many of these familiar dependent variables; however, they offer more-interesting and -useful applications. In addition, they present new ways of modeling advertising effectiveness, with the seemingly greater potential for understanding what constitutes effective communication.

Chapters 14 and 15 build upon psycholinguistic principles in an attempt to evaluate advertising executions better. One of the points made by Percy and Rossiter in chapter 9 was the importance of the specific words used by a copywriter in creating advertising. Their discussion outlined how the grammatical and semantic properties of words and sentences affect the way in which both verbal and visual encoding occurs. In a similar manner, we may suppose that the way in which receivers use words when talking about advertising also can provide insight into what they really feel about the advertising. Alwitt explores this question in chapter 14. As she points out, when one expresses oneself in words, one does not always say exactly what one means. Utilizing three linguistic variables, protocols generated from a typical cognitive-response exercise for six rough commercials are analyzed, and the results are discussed. In general, Alwitt shows that looking at receiver descriptions of advertising in this way can be an effective tool in learning more about how receivers are likely to respond to advertising.

Despite the fact that recognition and recall measures of advertising are overused or even misused as evaluative tools in accessing the effect of advertising, they nonetheless remain influential criteria among advertising practitioners. In chapter 15, Thorson and Rothschild decompose commercial scripts and receiver cognitive-response data into a propositional structure via a text-comprehension model along the lines of the Kintsch and Van Dijk model. Utilizing a series of regression analyses, they attempt to predict immediate and delayed recall. Overall, while their general hypothesis held, recognition was not predicted as well as recall, and immediate recall was predicted better than delayed recall. It is interesting that they found different variables entering the various predictive equations, in keeping with an intuitive feel that more ad-specific variables should predict recognition while more-global characteristics of response would predict recall.

The final three chapters move from specific evaluative models of advertising effectiveness and deal more generally with processing models. In chapter 16, Madden approaches the question of how persuasive communication influences behavior through an application of latent structure analysis. Within the concept of a hierarchy-of-effects model similar to McGuire's information-processing paradigm, a belief-based model is presented where reception and yielding (in McGuire's terms) are viewed as latent factors rather than observed factors. In attempting to deal with advertising effectiveness in terms of an attitude toward the advertising, his results tend to suggest the viability of the proposed latent structure.

Chapter 17 departs from the more cognitively oriented approaches that fill this book (and the literature generally in this area), as Wilton and Tse discuss an approach based upon a process model of consumer satisfaction. The thesis advanced is that since a receiver, in responding to a message, undergoes a perceptual and psychological process, it is necessary to access this process rather than the state. Their findings, contrasted with the more usual pre- and postattitude measures, suggest at least some promise with such an approach.

The final chapter by Lastovicka reports an interesting study of responses to repetitive television advertising. While the study examines Krugman's notion of three-exposure sufficiency, perhaps of more interest is the mode of analysis. Lastovicka uses a rather creative application of multimode factor analysis in an attempt to provide direct support to Krugman's theory. While in many ways exploratory and often ambiguous, the findings do tend to provide a direct link in support of the theory.

14 What Do People Mean When They Talk about Advertising?

Linda F. Alwitt

One common method used to evaluate the effect of advertising is to expose a commercial and simply ask a viewer open-ended questions such as What were your thoughts and feelings when you saw this commercial? What went on in the commercial you just saw? The responses to these questions typically are content analyzed as to what was said. However, when we express ourselves in words, we do not always say what we mean. The gap between what we mean and what we say is due both to the way our language is structured and to the way each of us personally uses our language. Meaning is carried in both the words we use—the semantic aspects or the vocabulary—and in the way the words are organized—the grammar or the structure of language.

We may be able to understand more of the meaning that motivates and underlies a verbal response to questions about advertising by looking at the structure of those responses—that is, by looking at how a response is worded. By delving beneath the surface to see some part of the deep structure, we may be able to extract additional meaning from what people say when they react to advertising.

This chapter includes three examples of how this way of thinking about people's verbal reactions to advertising can allow us to know more about what they mean:

1. A case grammar approach to richness of detail, where the verb is considered the pivot of an intended meaning and the arguments of that verb constitute details;
2. The use of personal pronouns as markers of personal involvement with advertising;
3. Direct and indirect references to a brand as a marker of what people think about the brand.

These examples were developed in a practical context that has several implications for the research to be reported here. Two of them are:

I thank Harriet Stahl Wulfstat, who coded most of the response protocols; Esther Thorsen's shop, which coded brand mention; and Leila Green and Melody Douglas-Tate for their comments on a draft of the chapter.

1. The characteristics of the products and advertising are not necessarily balanced; that is, some products use product-substantive advertising and other products use mood advertising.
2. The coding schemes were developed to be taught easily to analysts and to be used for a variety of types of advertising.

Sixty people viewed one of six different rough commercials (line-drawing storyboards) and then answered two questions:

1. Now I'd like you to tell me what happened to you as you were looking at the commercial. What thoughts or ideas went through your mind and what feelings did you have?
2. In your own words, please describe what went on and what was said in the commercial.

Each question was probed only once with "Anything else?," and the interviewers recorded each response verbatim.

In addition, respondents indicated whether or not they agreed with fifty-two statements about the advertising and the product, using a six-point rating scale (Schlinger 1979). The responses to the two open-ended questions were content analyzed in the following ways:

Richness of details,

Personal involvement,

Brand mentions,

Evaluation of the product and the execution,

Verbosity.

Three of the commercials were for established products, and three were for new products. There were commercials for one food product, one personal-care product, and four beverages.

Richness of Detail

The first example of examining the structure of language in response protocols deals with richness of detail. The more a person talks about details of an event, the more he has processed the event, tied it to his previous knowledge, and should be able to recall it (for example, Kintsch and Van Dijk 1978). Richness of detail in response protocols was coded by considering the verb as the pivot of an utterance. The noun phrases associated with that verb may be considered as arguments of a verb. Each argument of a verb may be called an idea, and this is the basis for so-called idea coding. Idea coding, then, is a way to quantify the richness of detail when a respondent recalls a commercial. For example, a respondent might describe a commercial by saying, "The man in the ad liked the drink." That description has fewer arguments of the verb *like* than the description, "The man dressed like Superman liked the sugar-free grape drink."

A sentence uttered by a respondent may contain ideas based on the action of the verb, who performed the action, the object or recipient of the action, the locale, and so forth. An idea, in general, answers the questions: Who? What? Whom? When? Where? How? Recall protocols 1 and 2 are hypothetical examples of idea coding:

Recall Protocol 1

The <u>man</u> <u>walked</u> in on the <u>cook</u>. The cook <u>showed him</u> <u>how they made the</u>
   1   2   3   4   5
<u>dough</u> by <u>kneading</u> it. I remember the <u>package</u> and they named it <u>Brand</u>
          6   7   8
<u>Name</u>, and to tell the truth it seemed like the same setting as when they sell

other products—just a different product.

Recall Protocol 2

I can't remember where the <u>guy</u> was from. He was <u>French</u> and he <u>talked</u> to
                            1   2   3
the <u>cook</u>. He said he <u>just came back from France</u>, and the cook <u>said</u> he had
    4   5   6
a <u>new product</u>, and they <u>showed how they made it</u> in the <u>oven</u>, and they
   7   8   9
showed <u>three varieties</u>. I remember the <u>picture</u> and the <u>special flavor</u>.
      10   11   12

Note than an idea is a proposition about the content of the commercial. It is neither a proposition that evaluates the commercial nor that describes a personal experience triggered by the commercial.

Three questions are asked of any test: Is it reliable? Is it sensitive? Is it valid? Those questions also can be asked of idea coding. Interrater reliability on thirty response protocols was .82, which gives us some confidence in the clarity of the coding method. As for sensitivity, idea coding has been used successfully to discriminate between two advertising executions for the same brand, between two populations of respondents, and between a speeded-up versus a regular-time version of the same commercial (Schlinger et al. in press).

Idea coding is reliable and sensitive in some situations, but what does it mean? How can we define its validity? To attempt to answer this question, we carried out a multiple regression to predict the number of ideas from ten attitude scales and from content analyses of open-ended questions using the other coding methods mentioned earlier (evaluation, personal involvement, verbosity, and brand mention). Table 14-1 shows sample items for each of the ten attitude scales.

The major results of this analysis follow. A summary of the regression parameters for selected predictor variables is shown in table 14-2. First,

Table 14-1
Attitude Scales

Scale	Sample Item
Stimulation	The commercial was lots of fun to watch and listen to. Exciting.
Relevance	The commercial showed me the product has certain advantages. Important for me.
News	The commercial gave me a new idea. I would be interested in getting more information about the product.
Identification	I liked the commercial because it was personal and intimate. The commercial was very realistic— that is, true to life.
Antagonism	That ad insults my intelligence. In poor taste.
Brand reinforcement	I know that the advertised brand is a dependable, reliable one. What they said about the product was dishonest. (Negative)
Familiarity	I saw this ad before. I am familiar with this ad.
Confusion	It required a lot of effort to follow this commercial. It was too complex. I wasn't sure what was going on.
Brand interest	The commercial told about a product I think I'd like to try. I will definitely buy the brand in the commercial.
Negative to claim	The commercial made exaggerated claims about the product. I don't see how the product has much to do with what was being shown in the commercial.

Table 14-2

Regression Parameters for Richness of Detail (Verbosity Removed) for Selected Predictor Variables

Predictor Variable	Beta Weight	Unique Contribution[a]	Simple Correlation	Tolerance[b]
News	$.21^c$	.018	$.17^c$	0.41
Confusion	$.20^c$	.031	$.18^c$	0.74
Unfavorable evaluation of execution	$-.19^c$	.017	.00	0.46

$R^2 = .13$, $F(21, 275) = 1.99$, $p < .006$.

[a] Squared semipartial correlation.

[b] A tolerance of 1 indicates no collinearity. Tolerance $= 1 - R^2$ when predictor variables are the other variables in the regression.

[c] Significantly greater than zero at $p < .05$.

respondents used richer detail the more they talked about the advertising they had just viewed. This result means that verbosity, the number of words a person uses to answer a question, must be controlled in order to examine what influences richness of detail. Second, richness as measured by idea coding was not well predicted by attitudes toward advertising or toward the product. Only 13 percent of the variance in richness could be accounted for by attitudes and by the other content-analysis methods used. Richness, then, appears to reflect cognitive aspects of information processing rather than attitudinal or evaluative aspects. This result is, of course, partly a result of the way we defined idea coding; it is limited to descriptions of the content of the commercial. This way of measuring richness of ideas might be considered a summary measure of recall.

Even though in general attitudes did not predict richness of details about the content of the advertising very well, two specific attitude scales did predict richness. First, people mentioned more details when they were not confused by the commercial. As mentioned earlier, confusion is indexed by agreement with statements like "It required a lot of effort to follow the commercial." Second, people mentioned more details of the content of the commercial when they felt that the commercial told them something new. They agreed with statements like "The commercial gave me a new idea."

Since people recall more details when they feel there is new information in the advertising, one might expect richer descriptions of the content of a commercial for new compared to established products. This hypothesis was tested by comparing richness of detail for two commercials for a new product versus two commercials for an established product. Respondents gave richer response protocols for the two new-product commercials (mean = 9.02) than for the two established-product commercials [mean $= 7.95$, $t(238) = 2.55$, $p < .01$]. This advantage of new-product commercials in richness of recalled detail is consistent with the result that people remember more details when they feel the commercial tells then something new.

In sum, richness of detail in recalling the content of a commercial has been quantified by a coding scheme based on the verb as the pivot of a sentence and the associated noun phrases as arguments of the verb, or ideas. The coding is reliable and sensitive in certain situations. It reflects cognitive responses to the advertising and is improved in reaction to an unconfusing execution and in executions that present new information to the viewer.

Personal Involvement

Here is a second example of how the structure of language may tell us more about people's reactions to advertising. When people watch television advertising, they sometimes relate the message or the execution to their own lives. This "personal connection," as Krugman (1967) has called it, is evidence that the advertising has penetrated the attention barrier and, the advertiser hopes, has entered the inner space of memory. One clue that there is indeed a relationship between the advertising and a person's values or knowledge is that the respondent refers to herself when she talks about the advertising. The use of personal-pronoun coding to indicate personal involvement has been used previously in advertising research (Leavitt, Waddell, and Wells 1970; Krugman 1967). On our coding, we first identified clauses that included a personal pronoun such as I, me, my, we, and so on and then classified the clauses as to their content. For the present analysis, clauses that contained personal pronouns were categorized as concerning either the execution or the product or message or either a positive or a negative comment. The interrater reliability of personal-pronoun coding for thirty verbal protocols was .89, which is sufficiently high to encourage confidence in the measure.

This method of coding personal involvement with a commercial can, of course, be used to evaluate the differences between competitive executions. However, it can be used also to examine general questions on how people talk about advertising. For example, when people talk about advertising, is there a trade-off between involvement with the product or message and with the execution or do people get involved with both the product and the execution? This question was approached by regression analysis.

Two multiple regressions were carried out, one to predict personal involvement with the product or message and the other to predict personal involvement with the execution. The predictor variables were the ten attitude scales shown in table 14-1, evaluation of the advertising, personal involvement with the execution (for the product regression) or the product (for the execution regression), and brand mention. How much a person talks about a commercial is correlated positively with personal involvement with both the product ($r = .33$) and the execution ($r = .54$) but to different degrees. This means that personal involvement should be evaluated independently of verbosity. To do this, the multiple regressions were run on residuals of personal involvement after verbosity was removed. Summaries of regression parameters for selected predictor variables are shown in tables 14-3 and 14-4.

Several results of these analyses are of interest. First, about half of the variance in personal involvement with either the execution or the product could be accounted for by the predictor variables. This suggests that the influence of the predictor variables is indeed important in interpreting personal involvement. Second, in general, personal involvement with either the execution or the product is not highly related to people's attitudes toward the advertising. Only 4 percent of the variance in product personal involvement and 10 percent of the variance in execution involvement is accounted for by attitude alone. For each of the regressions, on product and on execution personal involvement, only one attitude scale had a significant influence (beta weight). Specifically, respondents who were less accepting of the advertised brand (low on brand reinforcement) tended to make more personal comments about the execution. Respondents who were confused by the advertising tended to make more personal comments about the product. It appears that people talk about what they feel comfortable talking

Table 14-3
Regression Parameters for Personal Involvement with the Execution (Verbosity Removed) for Selected Predictor Variables

Predictor Variable	Beta Weight	Unique Contribution[a]	Simple Correlation	Tolerance[b]
Brand reinforcement	$-.21^c$	.014	$-.24^c$	0.32
Favorable evaluation of execution	$.22^c$	.036	$.11^c$	0.72
Unfavorable evaluation of execution	$.36^c$	.082	$.41^c$	0.62
Personal involvement with product	$-.18^c$	.020	$-.22^c$	0.64
Indirect reference to brand	$-.19^c$	.030	$-.25^c$	0.83

$R^2 = .57$, $F(21, 275) = 17.70$, $p < .0001$.
[a]Squared semipartial correlation.
[b]A tolerance of 1 indicates no collinearity. Tolerance $= 1 - R^2$ when predictor variables are the other variables in the regression.
[c]Significantly greater than zero at $p < .05$.

Table 14-4
Regression Parameters for Personal Involvement with the Product
(Verbosity Removed) for Selected Predictor Variables

Predictor Variable	Beta Weight	Unique Contribution[a]	Simple Correlation	Tolerance[b]
Confusion	$-.25^c$	.049	$-.12^c$	0.81
Favorable evaluation of execution	$.11^c$	.008	$.16^c$	0.67
Favorable evaluation of product	$.36^c$	.009	$.33^c$	0.76
Unfavorable evaluation of product	$.30^c$	.071	$.26^c$	0.78
Personal involvement with execution	$-.20^c$	.026	$-.20^c$	0.65
Number of brand mentions	$.16^c$	.023	$.13^c$	0.86

$R^2 = .54$, $F(21, 275) = 15.33$, $p < .0001$.
[a]Squared semipartial correlation.
[b]A tolerance of 1 indicates no collinearity. Tolerance $= 1 - R^2$ when predictor variables are the other variables in the regression.
[c]Significantly greater than zero at $p < .05$.

about; that is, people talk about what they know or what is positive and therefore does not subject them to the onus of making a negative statement. Alternatively, this result could be idiosyncratic to the specific advertising used in the analysis.

Third, personal comments about either the product or the execution are associated with both positive and negative evaluations. The use of a personal pronoun does not necessarily imply a positive personal-involvement, as shown in figure 14-1. There were more personal-pronoun mentions for respondents who were above the median in favorable evaluations of the advertising as well as above the median in unfavorable evaluations of the advertising.

Fourth, there is a negative correlation ($r = -.24$) between personal involvement with the execution and with the product, even when the effects of verbosity are removed from each of the two kinds of personal involvement. This means that when more personal-involvement comments are made about the execution, fewer are made about the product or message and vice versa. Thus, there is a trade-off between personal involvement with the product and with the execution when people talk about advertising they have just seen. The question of whether it is better to have personal involvement with the product or with the execution depends, of course, upon the goal of the particular commercial. We might want to see more personal involvement with the product for product-substantive advertising and more personal involvement with the execution for image advertising.

In summary, we have developed a method for coding personal involvement with advertising. This method of categorizing the way people use

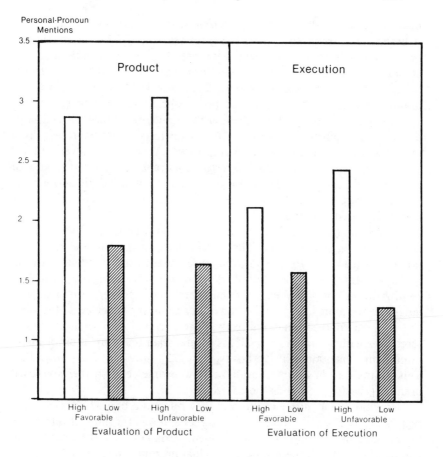

Figure 14-1. Personal-Pronoun Mentions for Favorable and Unfavorable
Evaluations of Advertising

personal pronouns when they talk about advertising has yielded some insights into what they mean. People talk about topics that are comfortable to
talk about, and they concentrate on either the execution or the product
rather than on both of those aspects of advertising. People are not necessarily positive when they are involved personally with advertising; that is, they
use personal pronouns when they have either favorable or unfavorable comments to make about the product or the execution.

Brand Reference

There is a third way in which the structure of language used by respondents to
talk about advertising can help us better understand what those respondents

mean. Since a brand is an object, it is represented in our minds as a concept. A brand can be referred to directly as, for example, 7UP or indirectly as it or the brand. In content analyzing responses to open-ended questions, it is common to count direct brand mentions, but indirect references to the brand often are ignored. Since both direct and indirect references to the brand are made to the same concept, the brand, they both can tell us something about how people feel about the brand. What they tell us may be different. The purpose of the third analysis is to compare the roles played by direct and indirect references by respondents to the brand advertised in a commercial. People may refer indirectly to a brand as it merely because of grammatical convention. The more you talk about a brand, the more likely you are to say it after the first reference. For example, "The ad was for Cheer. It's a good brand."

Direct and indirect references to the brand were coded for five of the six commercials in our data set. There were more indirect references to the brand, it (mean = 2.76 ± 2.13), than direct uses of the brand name (mean = 1.64 ± 1.47) when people talked about the advertising they had just seen. Also, as one would expect from experienced speakers of the English language, the more a respondent had to say about the advertising, the more she referred to the brand indirectly. The correlation of indirect brand references with verbosity, $r = .38$, is greater than the correlation of direct brand-name mention with verbosity, $r = .22$, $[t(297) = 2.06, p < .05]$. This means that in order to evaluate how people refer to the advertised brand, verbosity again must be controlled.

How do people differ in the way they refer to a brand? Two multiple regressions were carried out, one for direct and one for indirect references to the advertised brand. The independent variables were the ten attitude scales (table 14-1), richness of detail, evaluation comments, and personal involvement. The effects of verbosity were removed from the direct and indirect references to the brand.

For direct brand-name mentions, the predictor variables accounted for 23 percent of the variance. Summaries of the regression parameters are presented in tables 14-5 and 14-6. People tended to mention the brand name more when they were highly involved with the product and when they infrequently used the word *it* to refer to the brand. However, they also tended to mention the brand name more when they showed little positive involvement with the advertising and when they judged the advertising to be irrelevant.

For indirect references to the brand, the predictor variables accounted for 21 percent of the variance. People tended to refer indirectly to the brand more when they were highly involved with the product, evaluated the product favorably, and did not use the brand name directly. Indirect and direct references are similar in these ways. In addition, however, people who used more indirect references to the brand tended to be involved positively with

Table 14-5
Regression Parameters for Direct Mention of Brand (Verbosity Removed)
for Selected Predictor Variables

Predictor Variable	Beta Weight	Unique Contribution[a]	Simple Correlation	Tolerance[b]
Product involvement	.36[c]	.059	.19[c]	0.45
Indirect reference to brand	−.24[c]	.049	−.17[c]	0.82
Positive involvement with advertising	−.20[c]	.014	−.06	0.35
Relevance	−.27[c]	.016	−.23[c]	0.22

$R^2 = .23$, $F(21, 275) = 3.92$, $p < .0001$.
[a]Squared semipartial correlation.
[b]A tolerance of 1 indicates no collinearity. Tolerance $= 1 - R^2$ when predictor variables are the other variables in the regression.
[c]Significantly greater than zero at $p < .05$.

the advertising. Although verbosity was removed from indirect brand reference, people may still have talked more about the brand when they referred indirectly to the advertised brand. The results of the indirect-reference regression suggest that the more people talked about a brand, the more positive they were about both the brand and the advertising.

Direct and indirect references to the brand do not always mean the same thing, at least for the commercials in this analysis. That point can be demonstrated in a different way. Direct and indirect references to the adver-

Table 14-6
Regression Parameters for Indirect Reference to Brand (Verbosity Removed)
for Selected Predictor Variables

Predictor Variable	Beta Weight	Unique Contribution[a]	Simple Correlation	Tolerance[b]
Product involvement	.18[c]	.014	.23[c]	0.43
Favorable evaluation of product	.21[c]	.025	.32[c]	0.57
Brand-name mention	−.25[c]	.052	−.17[c]	0.81
Positive involvement with advertising	.16[c]	.009	.20[c]	0.35

$R^2 = .21$, $F(21, 275) = 3.46$, $p < .0001$.
[a]Squared semipartial correlation.
[b]A tolerance of 1 indicates no collinearity. Tolerance $= 1 - R^2$ when predictor variables are the other variables in the regression.
[c]Significantly greater than zero at $p < .05$.

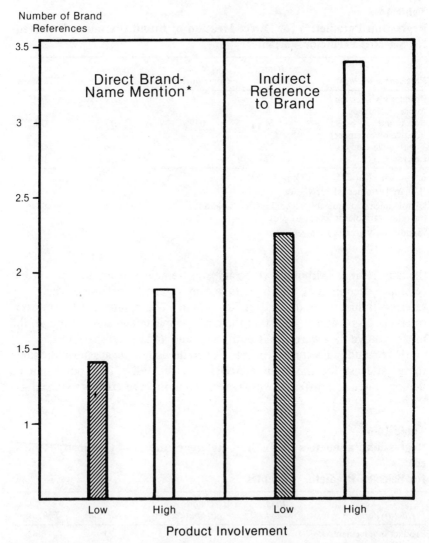

Number of Brand
References

Product Involvement

p < .10.

Figure 14-2. References to the Brand for Low (Below Median) and High
(Above Median) Involvement with the Product

tised brand are similar in one way. Figure 14-2 shows that when people are
highly involved with the product, they are more likely to refer to the brand
both directly and indirectly.

However, direct and indirect references to the brand differ in other
ways. Figure 14-3 shows three ways in which direct and indirect references
to a brand are associated with different attitudes. When there is a highly

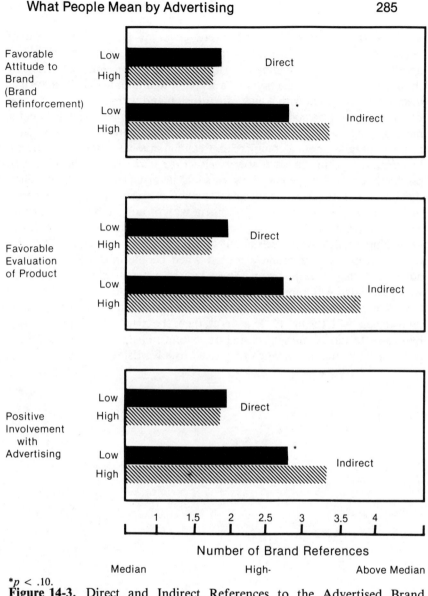

Figure 14-3. Direct and Indirect References to the Advertised Brand Related to Three Attitudes

(above median) favorable attitude toward the brand, there are more indirect (but not direct) references to the brand. When there is a highly (above median) favorable evaluation of the product, there are more indirect (but not direct) references to the brand. When people show high (above median) positive involvement with the advertising, there are more indirect (but not more direct) references to the brand.

In summary, three examples were given of how the structure of language can be used to extract extra meaning from people's verbalizations about advertising. Idea coding is a way to quantify the richness of details by thinking of the verb as the pivot of a sentence and arguments of the verb as ideas. It is associated with a lack of confusion and with the perception that new information was presented in the commercial. Personal involvement is measured by categorizing the way personal pronouns are used when a respondent talks about a commercial. Personal involvement does not necessarily imply a positive attitude toward either the advertising or the advertised product. Also, when people show personal involvement with the product, they tend not to show involvement with the execution and vice versa; that is, there is a trade-off in involvement with product and with execution. The way a person refers to the brand advertised in a commercial can tell us something about how he feels about that product or commercial. More indirect references to a brand are used when people talk more about the advertising they have just seen. These indirect references, in our data set, were associated with more positive attitudes toward both the brand and the advertising. Direct brand-name mentions were associated only with positive involvement with the brand. In general, then, the structure of language used by people to talk about advertising does seem to help us understand more about what people mean when they react to advertising.

15 Recognition and Recall of Commercials: Prediction from a Text-Comprehension Analysis of Commercial Scripts

Esther Thorson and
Michael L. Rothschild

Although recall remains the most frequently used memorial index of commercial effectiveness, there recently has been some discussion about recognition as an alternative (for example, Bettman 1979; Krugman 1972; Berger 1981). Most of this chapter centers around assumptions about whether recall and recognition index different processes in the response to commercials. These assumptions need to be subjected to empirical research. Because recall and recognition are measured by differing tasks, direct comparison of the two is not possible. For that reason, this chapter compares the two types of measures by examining how they are predicted from psycholinguistic analyses of the verbal content in commercials. Specifically, three questions are posed and tested: (1) Are recall and recognition measures equally well predicted from psycholinguistic analyses of the verbal content of commercials? (2) Do the same aspects of verbal content serve as the best predictors for recall and recognition? and (3) Does the time of delay between commercial presentation and memory performance differentially affect the prediction equations for recall and recognition?

Three Empirically Supported Generalizations about Recall and Recognition

Psychologists' research in memory and cognition, for several years, has included studies of the relationships between recall and recognition (for example, Brown 1976; Craik and Tulving 1975). This literature can serve as a useful guide to hypotheses about remembering commercials. In fact, three main generalizations about the relationships of recall and recognition find considerable support in this literature and determine the direction of our study.

The first generalization is that recall and recognition tasks involve different cognitive operations (Kintsch 1977; Klatzky 1980; Seamon 1980).

Recall, on the one hand, involves both a memory search for the location where required information is stored, and a pattern-matching process at that location to determine whether the found information is appropriate to report (Anderson and Bower 1972; Kintsch 1970). Recognition, on the other hand, requires only the pattern-matching process. This is because the information is presented and, therefore, need not be retrieved.

The second generalization is a result of the first. Since a key process in recall is retrieval of the storage area, the tasks of organizing and inter-relating items are a prime necessity for successful recall. However, organization of information is less important for recognition. Instead, because the pattern-matching process is primary, it is necessary to acquire the kind of information about items that will allow them to be discriminated from each other. Indeed, organization of information frequently has been shown to affect recall strongly but to have little or at least less impact upon recognition (for example, Kintsch 1970; Martin and Noreen 1974; McCormack 1972; Tulving 1962).

Consistent with the notion that recognition requires learning to discriminate among stimuli is our third generalization, that recognition depends greatly upon repetitions of stimulus items (or larger amounts of study time per item), while recall does not. Stated another way, the simple maintenance of items in short-term memory that occurs with repetitions of key words or ideas aids the learning of discriminating features (for example, Woodward, Bjork, and Jongeward 1973). This maintenance does not, however, necessitate that the stimulus items will be organized (Hogan and Kintsch 1971) and therefore is not particularly important for recall.

Before these generalizations can be used to make specific predictions about differences between recall and recognition of commercials, a system for deriving predictive linkages between commercials and memory is needed. A set of good candidates for such a system are the text-processing models (for example, Bower, Black, and Turner 1979; Kintsch 1974; Rumelhart 1975). These psycholinguistic models were developed to describe the complex semantic interrelationships in texts and films and to predict memory for them.

One text-processing model that has proved to be a successful predictor of memory is that of Kintsch and van Dijk (1978), and therefore, we turn to that approach. Further, a modified version (called an advertising language model, ALM) of Kintsch and van Dijk's model has been applied with some success to predicting recall for commercials (Thorson and Snyder 1981), and that success seemed to warrant using the ALM to compare recall and recognition. Therefore, prior to applying further the three generalizations about recall and recognition to memory for commercials, a brief description of the ALM text-processing variables is in order.

The ALM: Prediction of Memory
from Text-Processing Variables

The ALM defines two levels of meaning in the verbal content of a commercial. One level consists of *micropropositions*, which represent individual ideas. The other level consists of *macropropositions*, which are the main ideas of the text. Micro- and macropropositions are composed of the same components: a relational term and one or more arguments. Relational terms serve a predicate, descriptive, or connective function. Arguments are concepts acted upon by a relational term. For example, the sentence "Handsome Harry hit the ball and ran" would be represented at one level of meaning by the three micropropositions shown in table 15-1. The first microproposition exemplifies the descriptive function, the second is a predicate, and the third serves a connective function. Depending upon the text in which the sentence was embedded, any of the three micropropositions could serve also as a second, more-generalized kind of meaning, the macroproposition. Assuming that the third microproposition represents a main idea in the text, it is circled to indicate its dual status as a micro- and a macroproposition.

An interrelated set of micropropositions forms a cluster. Each microproposition, represented by a number, is linked to others by its semantic relations to them. Connective micropropositions are placed to the left of the predicate micropropositions they connect. Descriptive micropropositions are placed to the right of the micropropositions they describe. The cluster structure for "Harry hit the ball and ran" is shown also in table 15-1. The location of macro- and micropropositions in clusters is identified by their distance from the left-hand side of the cluster, with the location farthest to the left called level 1; the next location, level 2; and so on. Represented by a circle, the macroproposition for the sample sentence of table 15-1 is located at level 1.

To allow application of propositional structure to commercials, each macroproposition is identified as belonging to one of three meaning classes.

Table 15-1
Micro- and Macropropositions and Clusters

Microproposition	Macroproposition	Cluster	
		Level 1	Level 2
(Harry, handsome)			1
(hit, 1, ball)		3	
			2
(and. 2, ran)	(and. 2, ran)		

The first class includes macropropositions related to executional aspects of commercials. The second class contains information about product characteristics, and the third class contains the brand name. Thus, every macroproposition is either executional (EX MA), related to product characteristic (PC MA), or related to brand name (Brand).

In examining recall for commercials, the ALM analysis is applied both to the commercials and to what viewers remember of the commercials (free-recall protocols). These analyses result in values for each of the dependent (recall) and predictor variables shown in table 15-2. In addition to ALM-defined dependent measures, others can be and are, as in the present study, included in the list of dependent measures. These variables, primarily

Table 15-2
Dependent and Predictor Variables

Dependent Variables	Predictor Variables
Free-recall task	
Micropropositions per viewer	Number of micropropositions (MI)
Product-characteristic macro-propositions per viewer	Mean micropropositions per cluster (MI/CL)
Executional macropropositions per viewer	Number of macropropositions (MA)
Clusters per viewer	Mean macropropositions per cluster (MA/CL)
Percent viewers with related free recall	Repetitions per macroproposition (MA Rep)
Percent free recall of brand	Number of product-characteristic macropropositions (PC MA)
Percent free recall of claim	Mean product-characteristic macro-propositions per cluster (PC MA/CL)
Percent free recall of scene	Repetitions per product-characteristic macroproposition (PC MA Rep)
Recognition task	Number of executional macropropositions (EX MA)
Product category	Mean executional macropropositions per cluster (EX MA/CL)
Brand	Repetitions per executional macro-proposition (EX MA Rep)
Major claim	Number of brand macropropositions (Brand)
Package	Ratio of brand macropropositions to micropropositions (Brand/MI)
	Ratio of brand macropropositions to macropropositions (Brand/MA)
	Cluster level of first brand macroproposition (Brand Lev)

percentages of viewers with correct recall or recognition responses, also are listed in table 15-2.

Text-processing variables have been shown to be critical to memory for texts (for example, Kintsch and van Dijk 1978; Vipond 1981), and similarly, ALM variables predict memory for commercials (Thorson and Snyder 1981). The exact combination of variables that predict different memory-dependent measures seems to vary with the specifics of the task (for example, Vipond 1981). Nevertheless, some general relationships between text-processing variables and memory typically have held. For example, larger numbers of micro- and macropropositions in a text (or commercial) have predicted poorer recall (Kintsch 1974), as have larger numbers of propositions per cluster (Thorson and Snyder 1981). In contrast, repetitions of brand macropropositions have had a positive effect on recall (Thorson and Snyder 1981).

One final addition was made to the text-processing variables. Because nearly half the tested commercials involved singing of text, music was added and treated as a dummy variable. Intuitively, it seemed that when text was sung, the tune likely would serve as a distractor and effective storage would become less probable.

To obtain specific best fitting predictions for each memory measure, the intercorrelations of individual ALM commercial measures and memory measures are examined, and the subsets of significantly correlated commercial measures are combined via multiple linear regressions. The resulting regression equations form the link between commercials and memory in that they essentially identify what aspects of commercial organization combine to determine various aspects of what is remembered.

As can be seen, then, the ALM defines a set of variables that both characterizes the verbal content of commercials and predicts recall of commercials. With this approach and the psycholinguistic model that guides it in mind, we can return to the three generalizations about recall and recognition discussed earlier, and from them, we can derive specific hypotheses about the ALM predictor equations.

Five Hypotheses about Recall and Recognition

Hypothesis 1. In light of the generalization that recall depends upon the organization of stimulus materials, a first hypothesis is that the free recall of commercials should have significant portions of their variances explained by linear regressions combining ALM variables. The previous success of Thorson and Snyder (1981) in predicting day-after recall of commercials lends further plausibility to this hypothesis.

Hypothesis 2. Similarly, to the extent recognition is not dependent on the organization of stimuli, less of the variance in recognition scores should be explained by linear regression equations combining ALM variables.

Hypothesis 3. In light of the generalization that recall and recognition tasks require different cognitive processes, it is hypothesized that the ALM variables in best fitting regression equations for recall and recognition measures will differ. Those ALM variables that reflect global aspects of the organization of ideas in the commercial (for example, the number of micro- and macropropositions and the number of micro- and macropropositions per cluster) should be likely to enter the recall equations. Those ALM variables indexing the occurrence (and repetition) of specific information (for example, measures based on executional, product characteristic, and brand-name macropropositions) should be likely to enter the recognition equations.

Hypothesis 4. Next, also in light of the generalization that recall and recognition tasks require different cognitive processes, it is hypothesized that recall and recognition measures will not be highly correlated. Thus, a commercial that has high recall scores is not necessarily expected to have high recognition scores since verbal content advantageous to one measure of memory is not necessarily advantageous to the other measure.

Hypothesis 5. Finally, a differential relationship between the accuracy of predictions for recognition and recall as a function of delay is hypothesized. Because recall requires both retrieval and pattern recognition, this difficult task should show significant loss over time, and there should be a corresponding loss of accuracy in the predicting of recall with delay (floor effect). In contrast, the recognition tasks, requiring only a simple pattern-discrimination process, would be expected to show ceiling effects with immediate testing (Singh and Rothschild 1982), resulting in poorer predictions (since all commercials should show undifferentially high recognition scores). With a lowering from the ceiling performances as a function of the delay, the ALM predictor equations should be able to show improved accuracy of prediction.

These hypothesis were tested in a fairly natural situation in which viewers watched commercials embedded in programming they were told they were to evaluate. Memory for the commercials was measured in recall and recognition tasks performed at two delay intervals. The ALM analysis was applied to the commercials and free-recall protocols, and the derivation of best fitting multiple regression equations predicting each memory measure in table 15-2 formed the data base for evaluation of the hypotheses.

Method

Eighteen thirty-second commercials for convenience and package products not available in the test area were embedded in two half-hour situation comedies, "Phyllis" and "The Brady Bunch." Three commercials were placed in each of the three commercial breaks in each program. Three videotapes were made so that the order of the commercials could be counterbalanced partially across and within breaks.

Eighty-two women aged twenty to fifty were recruited from a local church. Payment for their services was donated to the church.

Design and Procedure

Recall and recognition were measured within subjects. Delay, either one-half hour (immediate) or two weeks (delay), was a between-subjects variable.

At their recruiting, subjects were instructed that they would be participating in two experimental sessions, during both of which they would be evaluating two situation-comedy programs. Only the delay-condition subjects participated in two separate sessions. The evaluation of television programming was stressed to encourage typically high attention to the programming and low attention to the commercials.

The subjects in the immediate condition viewed the first situation comedy and then were given a short questionnaire to evaluate the program. At the end of the second program, subjects again evaluated the program and then were told they would be asked to recall the commercials. They were given the free-recall questionnaires that asked them to list, for each commercial they could recall, the appropriate product category, brand name, and the claims made for the product and the scenes, actors, and stories in the commercial. They were to include any item of information recalled from a commercial, even if they could not recall all of the categories of information. They were also informed that a bonus of 10°, in addition to their participation fee, would be added for each commercial they recalled. This bonus was used in an attempt to motivate as much recalling effort as possible.

After completion of the recall questionnaire, subjects returned it to the experimenter and received recognition questionnaires. For each commercial there were four recognition pages. On the first page were listed five product categories, only one of which was viewed in a commercial. On the second page were listed five product categories, only one of which was viewed in a commercial. On the second page were listed five brand names, on the third page five claims, and on the fourth page five drawings of product packages with the brand name shown. On each page the subject was to select the item that she recognized from a commercial. Subjects were not allowed to return to completed pages. Upon completion of the recognition questionnaire, subjects were thanked, paid, and excused.

Subjects in the delayed condition also viewed the commercials and two situation comedies during their first session. After each program, delay subjects were given questionnaires asking them to evaluate the programs. After the second questionnaire, the subjects were reminded to return in two weeks and were excused. Upon their return after two weeks, the delay-condition subjects were given the same instructions and the same free-recall and recognition questionnaires the immediate-condition subjects had received. Upon completion of the questionnaires, the subjects were thanked, paid, and excused.

Variables and Scoring

Each commercial script was translated into lists of micropropositions and clusters. Next, executional and product-characteristic macropropositions were located in the clusters, and for each commercial, the values of each variable listed in table 15-2 were calculated.

Subjects' responses to the questions about claim and execution on the free-recall questionnaires also were analyzed into lists of micropropositions and clusters. Executional and product-characteristic macropropositions were located in the clusters.

Results

Since the unit of analysis was individual commercials, mean values for all of the dependent and predictor variables listed in table 15-2 were calculated for each of the eighteen commercials.

Intercorrelations were computed among predictor and dependent variables, and those correlations significant at $p < .05$ determined what predictor variables were used in the regression equations for each dependent measure. The regression results are shown in tables 15-3 to 15-6. Only the ALM variables with regression coefficients shown in the tables were entered into the equations.

Because of the small number of observations and correlations among the predictor variables, the structure of the regression equations would not be expected to generalize identically to a large-number case. Nevertheless, the general form of the predictions provides some insight into how well the text-comprehension variables predict memory performance. We should note that although treating commercials as the unit of analysis led to analysis of

Table 15-3
Regression Predictions for Immediate Free Recall

Predicted Recall Measure	Predictor Variables						Evaluative Statistics			
	Brand	MI	MA	MA Rep	MA/CL	Music	R^2	F	DF	p
	Standardized Regression Coefficients									
Micropropositions per viewer	.19	—	—	—	$-.89^a$	-1.01^a	.83	23.3	(3,14)	.00
Clusters per viewer	—	—	—	—	$-.44^a$	$-.29^a$	.60	11	(2,15)	.00
PC macropropositions per viewer	$.06^b$	$.01^b$	—	—	—	—	.47	4.14	(2,15)	.05
EX macropropositions per viewer	—	—	—	$-.08$	—	$-.25^b$	.33	3.71	(2,15)	.05
Percent viewers with some free recall	—	—	-10^a	—	1.06^a	—	.66	14.4	(2,15)	.00
Percent recall of brand	—	$-.004^b$	—	—	$-.021$	—	.45	6.07	(2,15)	.01
Percent of claim	.02	—	—	$-.04$	—	$-.06$	.33	2.34	(3,14)	.12
Percent recall of scene	.02	—	—	$.06^b$	$-.05^b$	—	.44	3.69	(3,14)	.03

Note: Regression coefficients were evaluated with *t*-tests.
[a] $p < .01$.
[b] $p < .10$.

Table 15-4
Regression Predictions for Delayed Free Recall

Predicted Recall Measure	Predictor Variables					Evaluative Statistics		
	MA Rep	MA/CL	PC MA/CL	Brand/MI	R^2	F	DF	p
		Standardized Regression Coefficients						
Micropropositions per viewer	—	.02ᵃ	—	.52	.33	3.62	(2,15)	.10
Clusters per viewer	—	.01ᵃ	—	—	.19	3.71	(1,16)	.10
Percent viewers with some free recall	—	—	.05ᵃ	.45ᵃ	.38	4.54	(2,15)	.03
Percent recall of brand	1.04	—	—	8.11	.26	2.57	(2,15)	.11

Note: Regression coefficients were evaluated with *t*-tests.
ᵃ$p < .10$.

Table 15-5
Regression Predictions for Immediate Recognition

Predicted Recognition Measure	Predictor Variables					Evaluative Statistics		
	EX MA Rep	PC MA/CL	Brand/MI	Music	R^2	F	DF	p
	Standardized Regression Coefficients							
Product category	-.28[a]	.03	—	-.14[b]	.60	6.91	(3,14)	.00
Package	—	—	.99[b]	-.15[b]	.32	3.51	(2,15)	.06

Note: Regression coefficients were evaluated with t-tests.
[a] $p < .01$.
[b] $p < .10$.

Table 15-6
Regression Predictions for Delayed Recognition

Predicted Recognition Measure	Predictor Variables				Evaluative Statistics			
	EX MA	EX MA Rep	Brand/MI	Brand Lev	R^2	F	DF	p
	Standardized Regression Coefficients							
Product category	-.02[a]	-.26[a]	—	—	.40	4.95	(2,15)	.02
Brand	—	—	1.01[a]	—	.18	3.43	(1,16)	.08
Claim	—	—	—	.18[a]	.29	6.56	(1,16)	.02
Package	—	—	1.02[a]	—	.19	3.77	(1,16)	.07

Note: Regression coefficients were evaluated with t-tests.
[a]$p < .10$.

only eighteen cases, each case is based upon forty-one observations and therefore can be assumed to show considerable stability (Langbein and Lichtman 1978).

Table 15-3 shows the best fitting linear regressions for prediction of immediate free recall. In support of hypothesis 1, seven of the free-recall measures have significant percentages of their variance accounted for by the equations. An eighth measure, the percentage of subjects who recalled claim, falls only slightly short of significance at the .10 level. As we can see in table 15-3, brand macropropositions has, as predicted, a positive effect on recall measures. With two exceptions, the effects of the number of micro- and macropropositions per cluster and music were also, as predicted, negative. Contrary to predictions, however, the effects of repetitions per macroproposition were negative in two cases out of three.

Hypothesis 5 predicted that the accuracy of ALM predictions for delayed recall would be less than for immediate, and as we can see in table 15-4, this prediction was supported. Only four of the recall measures had significant portions of their variance predicted by ALM variables, and for those variables with significant equations, the R^2 values were much lower than recognition values. Like the equations for immediate recall, measures of macropropositional structure and brand-name use served as the primary predictors. Unlike the equation for immediate recall, however, the number of macropropositions per cluster had a positive effect on delayed recall.

Turning to the predictions for recognition performance, we can see by comparing tables 15-5 and 15-6 to tables 15-3 and 15-4 that, with the exception of product-category recognition, the R^2 values for the recognition equations are considerably less than those for recall. This result supports hypothesis 2. Hypothesis 5, the tenet of which was that the predictions for delayed recognition would be better than those for immediate recognition, was not supported in that the R^2 values in the immediate condition are higher than the comparable measures for the delayed condition. Conversely, the hypothesis did receive support in that the equations since all four of the delayed measures accounted for significant portions of the variance, whereas only two immediate-recognition equations were significant.

Hypothesis 3 stated that the ALM variables predicting recognition would be different from those predicting recall. Although two variables, the ratio of brand macropropositions to micropropositions and the occurrence of music, showed overlap, recognition measures showed greater dependence upon the more-specific executional and product-characteristic macropropositions. Recall, however, showed significant dependence upon the more-global measures of numbers of micro- and macropropositions.

Hypothesis 4, predicting that recall and recognition scores for a commercial would not be high, also was supported. Tables 15-7 and 15-8 show

Table 15-7
Intercorrelations of Immediate Recall and Recognition Measures

Recognition Measures	Recall Measures							
	MI/ Viewer	PC MA/ Viewer	EX MA/ Viewer	CL/ Viewer	Percent Free Response	Percent Brand	Percent Claim	Percent Scene
Product category	.58[a]	.48[a]	.41[a]	.58[a]	.58[a]	.29	.51[a]	.41[a]
Brand	.26	.12	.20	.18	.11	.13	.09	.09
Claim	.35	.29	.27	.07	−.06	−.30	.30	.16
Package	.17	−.09	.21	−.06	−.13	.00	−.18	−.19

[a] $p < .10$.

Table 15-8
Intercorrelations of Delayed Recall and Recognition Measures

Recognition Measures	Recall Measures							
	MI/ Viewer	PC MA/ Viewer	EX MA/ Viewer	CL/ Viewer	Percent Free Response	Percent Brand	Percent Claim	Percent Scene
Product category	.82[a]	.45[a]	.75[a]	.80[a]	.81[a]	.02	.53[a]	.65[a]
Brand	.28	−.02	.22	.25	.29	.29	.18	.23
Claim	−.02	.09	.00	−.03	−.19	−.08	.28	−.08
Package	.39	.10	.30	.36	.38	.24	.24	.28

[a] $p < .10$.

the intercorrelations of recall and recognition. As we can see, only recognition of product category correlated significantly with how well aspects of the commercials were recalled. It is interesting that the significant product-category correlations are higher for the delayed conditions than for the immediate.

Discussion

In large part, the five hypotheses about the relations between predictor equations for recall and recognition were supported. The predictive power for immediate free recall was high, while prediction of delayed recall was lower. Overall, recognition was not as well predicted as recall, and the delay effect for recognition was just the opposite of that for recall. This latter result is consistent with the intuitive notion that recognition becomes, with delay, a more-useful indicator of memory for commercials and that recall is a more useful indicator with short delays.

The fact that different ALM variables entered the recall and recognition equations can be interpreted as indicating that different aspects of commercial verbal content affect the two memory processes. Given the specificity of the five alternatives in the recognition task, it seems reasonable that particulars of execution and product characteristics would affect recognition. Likewise, given the openness of the free-recall task, it seems reasonable that global characteristics of commercials (for example, numbers of micro- and macropropositions) would determine recall.

That product-characteristic recognition was correlated significantly with the recall measures and was predicted more successfully with the ALM equations are results that deserve further investigation. It is plausible that storage of product category is highly integrated with brand name, product characteristics, and executional aspects of the commercial, and for that reason, the recognition of product category is a process much different from recognition of brand, claim, or visual representation of the package. Why product-category recognition is correlated highly with all measures of free recall seems more difficult to explain. A possibility is that effective propositional organization of the information in a commercial leads to good recall of execution and product characteristics, and because the identification of product category is inherent in that information, it will also show high accuracy of recognition.

Finally, the results of this study support the predictive utility of the ALM. The magnitude of the R^2 values for recall indicate that the ALM captures much of what makes commercials recallable. Although the ALM predictions for recognition are less strong than those for recall, the amount of variance accounted for nevertheless ranges from around 20 percent to 60 percent. These values are sufficient to indicate noteworthy explanatory strength for the ALM and to encourage further investigation of its utility.

16 Latent Structure Analysis of Message Reactions

Thomas J. Madden

Marketing researchers have a noted history of attempting to understand the process by which persuasive communications influence consumer behavior. In particular, the emergence of the hierarchy-of-effects model (Lavidge and Steiner 1969), in conjunction with the DAGMAR method developed by Colley (1962), stirred a great deal of interest among advertising researchers and marketing academics concerning the measurement of message effectiveness.

Typically, persuasive communications have been evaluated using measures of recall and/or attitudes. These measures assess the impact of the message-related arguments but neglect any impact of the message (that is, a reaction or attitude toward the commercial).

The purpose of this chapter is to incorporate both product-specific beliefs and message beliefs within a particular hierarchy-of-effects model. The model tested here is similar to McGuire's (1978) information-processing paradigm; however, here reception and yielding are viewed as latent factors rather than observed factors.

Information-Processing Approach

Hierarchy-of-effects models, along with the more-recent information-processing models, purport to represent a sequence of mental processes in which the individual moves closer to an overt action. Inspection of the mental processes typically specified in these models demonstrates the congruence of these approaches with the Yale communication-research program under the direction of Dr. Carl I. Hovland. A basic assumption underlying the approach specified by Hovland and his colleagues was that message effectiveness depends upon the extent to which the message is attended, comprehended, and accepted.

McGuire (1978) has advocated utilizing an information-processing paradigm for the development and appraisal of advertising communications. He states, "The gist of this approach is to view the individual exposed to a persuasive communication as an information-processing machine which must proceed through a chain of behavioral steps, each probabilistically linked to the preceding one" (p. 156).

Symbolically, McGuire's model is represented as:

$$P(P) \rightarrow P(A) \rightarrow P(C) \rightarrow P(R) \rightarrow P(Y) \rightarrow P(B),$$

where
$P(P)$ = Probability of presentation,
$P(A)$ = Probability of attention,
$P(C)$ = Probability of comprehension,
$P(R)$ = Probability of retention,
$P(Y)$ = Probability of yielding,
$P(B)$ = Probability of behaving on basis of beliefs.

As shown by the constructs comprising the behavioral chain, McGuire's approach is quite similar to that advocated by Dr. Hovland and his colleagues.

Typically, what these models assess is the amount of attention, comprehension, retention, and yielding to the product-specific attributes and/or benefits proffered by the commercial; that is, what is the effect(s) of the commercial on consumers' attitude toward the advertised brand? Shimp (1981) suggests that attitudes toward the advertisement should be assessed as well as attitudes toward the advertised brand. The notion behind this suggestion is that attitudes toward the advertisement could have a mediating effect on brand choice operating through brand attitudes.

Attitude toward the Advertisement

One diagnostic method of measuring an advertisement's effectiveness is to determine postexposure attitudes toward the object of the communication. However, these evaluative-scale attitude-type measures can neglect "self-generated" cognitions (Petty, Ostrom, and Brock 1981). These cognitions typically are measured via message-evoked thoughts or cognitive responses; that is, subjects are asked to verbalize their thoughts as they listened to the commercial. These cognitive responses are considered to mediate the persuasion process:

> To the extent that the persuasion situation elicits thoughts that are favorable, attitude change in the direction advocated should be facilitated; but if negative thoughts are elicited, attitude change should be inhibited. [Petty, Ostrom, and Brock 1981, p. 29]

Recently, marketers (Shimp 1981; Mitchell and Olson 1981; MacKensie and Lutz 1982) have investigated the impact of consumers' attitudes toward an advertisement (ATT_A) on brand choice. Mitchell and Olson interpret ATT_A measures as accurate reflections of consumers' evaluations of the overall advertising stimulus. This construct ATT_A is conceptualized as being distinct from either brand-attribute beliefs or brand attitudes (Mitchell and Olson 1981, p. 327). Shimp (1981) has argued that the construct is comprised of two relatively distinct dimensions, one cognitive and the other emotional, and that these dimensions, because of different underlying mechanisms, have nonequivalent impacts upon consumers.

The recent empirical analyses of attitude toward the ad (Shimp 1981; Mitchell and Olson 1981; MacKensie and Lutz 1982) provide support to the notion that the construct has a mediating or indirect impact on behavior, or some surrogate measure of behavior, through product-related attitudes. MacKensie and Lutz tested four alternative specifications and found the best fitting model contained an indirect effect of attitude toward the ad on intention, through attitude toward the brand, but there was no statistically significant direct effect of attitude toward the ad on intention.

Research Model

McGuire (1978), in his two-factor model, has condensed the preceding specification by combining attention and comprehension into one factor (reception) and purports that the persuasion process can be characterized succinctly by reception and yielding alone. He advocates that for simple messages (for example, those typically communicated in commercials), comprehension can be assumed given the individual has attended to the message.

The model proposed and tested here is consistent conceptually with McGuire's two-factor model; however, reception and yielding are made operational as latent factors. A latent factor is one that is not observed directly but that is inferred from observations (measurements) on reflective and/or formative variables. These observed variables usually are called manifest variables. Lazarsfeld and Henry state:

> We realize that in the real world we are surrounded by indicators, and we observe their covariation, and we ask whether the patterns of covariation we observe may not tell us something about the defining nature of a concept. [1968, p. 3]

Figure 16-1 presents the path-diagram representation of the model. The model proposed in figure 16-1 is tested using latent structure analysis. A thorough discussion of the use of latent class models is not provided since it is beyond the scope of this chapter, but we refer the interested reader to either Clogg (1979), Goodman (1974), and/or Lazarsfeld and Henry (1968) for an explanation of the technique. In essence, a latent class is considered to exist if when the tth level of the latent variable is held constant, the relationship(s) among the manifest variables vanishes. For example, first assume

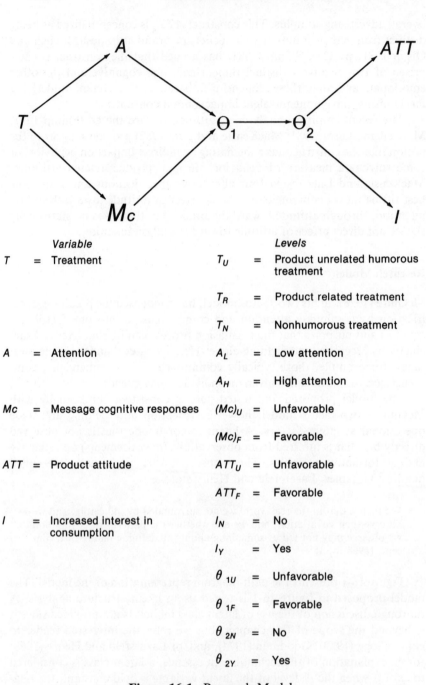

	Variable			Levels
T	= Treatment		T_U	= Product unrelated humorous treatment
			T_R	= Product related treatment
			T_N	= Nonhumorous treatment
A	= Attention		A_L	= Low attention
			A_H	= High attention
Mc	= Message cognitive responses		$(Mc)_U$	= Unfavorable
			$(Mc)_F$	= Favorable
ATT	= Product attitude		ATT_U	= Unfavorable
			ATT_F	= Favorable
I	= Increased interest in consumption		I_N	= No
			I_Y	= Yes
			θ_{1U}	= Unfavorable
			θ_{1F}	= Favorable
			θ_{2N}	= No
			θ_{2Y}	= Yes

Figure 16-1. Research Model

that three manifest variables (A, B, and C) show association (the model of independence does not fit). If, within each class of the latent factor, these manifest variables are independent, then the latent factor is said to explain the original association among the manifest variables. Interpretation of the latent factor, in a manner analogous to the factor analytic model, is determined by inspection of the association of the manifest variables with the latent factor. This is accomplished using the estimated conditional probabilities (for example, $\pi_{it}^{\bar{A}X}$); that is, the probability of being in the ith level of manifest variable A given that the observation is in the tth level of the latent factor.

In figure 16-1, Θ_1 and Θ_2 are the two latent factors reception and yielding, respectively. The reception factor (Θ_1) has three formative indicators: the commercials (T), attention (A), and cognitive responses (Mc). The cognitive responses reflect positive or negative thoughts about the commercial, not the product being advertised. The cognitive responses were coded by two independent judges. The interjudge-reliability assessment (r = .82) indicated similar coding by the two judges.

The yielding factor (Θ_2) has one formative indicator, the estimated latent factor reception (Θ_1), and two reflective indicators of product attitudes (ATT) and interest in consumption of the product (I). Hence, in this specification, beliefs about the commercial are considered as formative indicators of reception and, in combination with the commercials and attention, are a formative indicator of yielding. Product attitudes are specified as reflective indicators of yielding.

The Experiment

We designed an experiment to assess subjects' reactions to humorous versus nonhumorous commercials (Madden 1982). The following section briefly describes the procedural aspects of the experiment.

Sample

One hundred sixty-four undergraduate students, equally divided between men and women, were recruited as subjects. Subjects were not informed of the intent of the study, and a follow-up or briefing confirmed that the objective of the experiment had been well disguised. Subjects were assigned randomly to treatment groups.

Treatment Conditions

The manipulations of humor pertained to three different sixty-second radio commercials for a new dairy product, not yet marketed in the area at the time of the study. Two of the radio commercials utilized humor. The humorous commercials differed in the contiguity of the humor to the product. In one commercial, the humor was product related, while in the other the humor was unrelated—that is, extraneous—to the product. The third radio commerical presented the information in a nonhumorous—that is, serious—format. The information content delivered in each radio commercial was identical. Extensive pretesting of the treatment groups was undertaken to insure that the radio commercials differed only with respect to the method of delivery. Finally, the radio commercials were produced professionally in order to maintain consistent quality across the treatment groups.

Procedure

Test commercials and unrelated dummy advertising were integrated into a fifteen-minute radio program. Subjects were required to listen to the entire broadcast in individual booths. In the course of each broadcast, subjects were exposed to two executions of the same treatment. Immediately following the broadcast, subjects were administered a questionnaire that asked for information about what they heard.

Results and Discussion

The first step in the analysis was to fit a two-class model to the cross classification of treatment (T), attention (A), and message-related cognitive responses (Mc). The following restrictions were imposed on the two classes: Favorable message-related cognitive responses in class one would equal unfavorable-message cognitive responses in class two, and high attention in class one would equal low attention in class two.

Hence, if the likelihood of being in latent class one, given favorable-message cognitive responses, is high, then the likelihood of being in latent class two, given favorable-message cognitive responses, must be low. (The same interpretation holds for the attention variable.)

Table 16-1 reports the parameter estimates, latent class proportions, and conditional probabilities for the two-class model. The goodness-of-fit measures indicate that the two-class latent model provides a statistically better fit than the model of independence; the change in the likelihood ratio chi square was 26.31 with 3 degrees of freedom ($p < .001$). Moreover, with 4 degrees of freedom the model fit the data quite well ($p > .10$).

The conditional probabilities reported in table 16-1 indicate that class one is a favorable dimension; that is, high attention and favorable-message cognitive responses. Class two is an unfavorable dimension represented by

Table 16-1

Latent-Class Parameters for a Two-Class Model Involving Treatment (T), Attention (A), and Message Cognitive Response (Mc)

Manifest Variables	Latent Class	
	1	2
T_U	.52	.11
T_R	.42	.12
T_N	.06	.76
A_L	.35	.65
A_H	.65	.35
$(Mc)_U$	.26	.74
$(Mc)_F$	.74	.26
Class probabilities	.61	.39

low attention and unfavorable-message cognitive responses. Moreover, inspection of the conditional probabilities for the treatment variable indicates that the two humorous treatments (T_U, T_R) are associated with the favorable dimension (class one), while the nonhumorous treatment (T_N) is associated with the unfavorable dimension (class two).

The yielding dimension was fit by reclassifying subjects into the two latent classes of reception, based on modal probabilities, and cross-classifying reception with attitudes and increased interest. To test the hypothesis that a person who yields to the message exhibits favorable reception, favorable attitudes, and increased interest in consumption of the product, a restricted model was fit. The first class of the two-class yielding dimension was restricted to exhibit favorable reception, favorable attitudes, increased interest.

Table 16-2 presents the parameter estimates for the yielding two-class model. The two-class model provides a good fit to the data ($p > .25$) and fits the data significantly better than the model of independence ($p < .05$). Because of the imposed restrictions, examining the log odds of being in class one of the latent factor, given the subject is at a particular level of a manifest variable, provides an assessment of the association of each manifest variable with yielding. For example, $\pi^{\bar{R}\Theta_2}$ was restricted to equal .90, which indicates a strong association between favorable reception and the restricted favorable class. However, if $\pi^{\bar{R}\Theta_2}$ also equals .90 or some value close to .90, then the log odds will be zero or close to zero, indicating little association between reception and yielding. These log odds also are represented in table 16-2.

Notice that for all variables, the odds of being in the first class are positive. Therefore, we can consider this class to reflect yielding to the message, whereas the second class reflects no yielding to the message.

Table 16-2

Latent-Class-Parameter Estimates for a Two-Class Model Involving Reception (*R*), Attitudes (*Att*), and Interest in Consumption of the Product (*I*), with the Log Odds in Favor of Yielding

	Latent Class		
Manifest Variable	1	2	Log Odds
R_F	.90	.63	0.36
R_U	.10	.37	−1.31
$(ATT)_U$	.10	.75	−2.01
$(ATT)_F$	.90	.25	1.28
I_N	.10	.82	−2.10
I_Y	.90	.18	1.61
Class probabilities	.14	.86	

Of particular importance are the log odds in favor of yielding given reception. The reception variable is a composite variable of treatment, attention, and message-related cognitive responses. Remember that favorable reception was characterized by high attention, favorable cognitive responses pertaining to the commerical, and exposure to the humorous treatments, whereas unfavorable reception was characterized by low attention, unfavorable cognitive responses pertaining to the commercial, and exposure to the nonhumorous commercial. If reception, and consequently thoughts about the commercial itself, are associated with yielding, then the probability of yielding to the message should be greater for those subjects in the favorable level of reception than for those in the unfavorable level.

The log odds reported in table 16-2 indicate that the probability of yielding is greater for those subjects classified as having favorable reception of the message than for those classified as having unfavorable reception.

An alternative method for analyzing the association between the two latent factors, reception and yielding, is to cross classify the two latent variables and subsequently to analyze the percentage of responses for each level of each manifest variable for the different profiles. Cross classifying reception (favorable, unfavorable) and yielding (yes, no) produces four profiles: favorable reception/yielding (11); favorable reception/no yielding (12); unfavorable reception/yielding (21); and unfavorable reception/no yielding (22).

Table 16-3 presents the percentage of responses for each level of each manifest variable for the different profiles. Notice that profile 21, unfavorable reception/yielding contained no subject. The profiles most interesting are 11 and 22—that is, favorable reception and yielding versus unfavorable reception and no yielding respectively. Notice that profile 11 is represented

Table 16-3
Cross Classification of Four Response Profiles with Manifest Variables
(percent)

	Profile			
Manifest Variable	*11*	*12*	*21*	*22*
Number of Subjects	20	90	0	54
Treatment				
Unrelated humor	55	54	0	0
Related humor	45	46	0	0
Nonhumor	0	0	0	100
Attention				
Low	10	49	0	67
High	90	51	0	33
Message cognitive responses				
Unfavorable	5	38	0	67
Favorable	95	62	0	33
Attitude				
Unfavorable	0	77	0	72
Favorable	100	23	0	28
Interest in consumption of product				
No	0	80	0	85
Yes	100	20	0	15

by the humorous treatments, high attention, favorable-message cognitive responses, favorable attitudes, and increased interest. Profile 22, in marked contrast, is represented by the nonhumorous treatment, low attention, unfavorable attitudes, unfavorable-message cognitive responses, and no increased interest. Hence, if we conceive of persuasion as being represented by profile 11 and the lack of persuasion being represented by profile 22, then the idea of a chain relationship among the manifest variables appears to be supported.

Further evidence of this chain relationship is evident from the examination of profile 12, favorable reception/no yielding. This profile is characterized predominantly by unfavorable attitudes and no increased interest, the two reflective factors of the yielding dimension. However, neither is attention low nor are the messages' cognitive responses unfavorable. It appears that the persuasion process was initiated but then truncated after the formation of unfavorable attitudes. Note that the message cognitive responses were classified only with respect to the commerical, not the advertised product. Thus, it is possible that negative product cognitive responses induced the elicited unfavorable product attitudes.

The subjects classified as being persuaded (profile 11) were exposed to the humorous treatments, whereas the subjects classified as not being persuaded (profile 22) were exposed to the nonhumorous treatment. A potential explanation is that for those people who enjoyed the humorous commercials, a positive halo was established that was carried over to the product and/or product-consumption measures; that is, because of a general liking for the message, the individuals were persuaded, but this was not necessarily based upon the product-specific information proffered. However, for those individuals that did not have strong favorable beliefs about the message, the processing of the product-specific information did not create a favorable attitude, and with no other facilitator, persuasion was hindered.

To investigate this notion, the two profiles were cross classified for various dimensions representing structured evaluations of the message. In addition, profile 12 (favorable reception/no yielding) also is presented. These subjects were exposed also to the humorous commercials; however, they were less likely to exhibit high attention or favorable-message cognitive responses than subjects exposed to profile 11. Table 16-4 presents these cross classifications. Inspection of the percentages in the table indicates that for all the dimensions, those subjects in profile 11 were disposed more favorably to the commercial than either of the other two profiles.

Summary

This research incorporated cognitive responses and standard attitude measures into a hierarchy-of-effects paradigm. The persuasion process, as typified by the hierarchy-of-effects paradigm proposed here, was considered to be characterized by two latent factors. The hypothesized latent structure proved to fit the data well and was clearly interpretable.

Table 16-4
Evaluation of Commercials, by Subjects Classified into Profiles
(percent)

	Profile		
Dimension	*11*	*12*	*22*
Artful	70	40	24
Believable	80	37	54
Interesting	80	47	15
Witty	65	44	20
Candid	60	30	44
Honest	85	33	54
Informative	85	59	83
Uninsulting	60	28	48

Cross classifying the two latent factors reception (favorable, unfavorable) and yielding (yes, no) rendered four profiles. Inspection of the favorable reception/yielding profile and the unfavorable reception/no yielding profile provided support for the notion of persuasion being conceptualized as the scalar product of hierarchical cognitive factors. Those subjects in the favorable reception/yielding profile had positive responses to all the cognitive factors, whereas those subjects in the unfavorable reception/no yielding profile had negative responses to all the cognitive factors.

The message cognitive responses, which would be antecedent to any measure of attitude toward the advertisement, clearly were associated with the two previously mentioned profiles. Hence, this research indicates that these types of measures or more-formal measures of attitude toward the advertisement should be included in models proposed to assess the effectiveness of advertisements.

17 A Model of Consumer Response to Communication and Product Experiences

Peter C. Wilton and
David K. Tse

In two review articles, Holbert (1977) and Watson and Gatchel (1979) discuss several trends in the measurement of advertising effectiveness. While many methods have been used, the basic question of what measure best predicts behavior remains unanswered.

Two authors, Wright (1973) and Mitchell (1980), attempt to explain advertising effects in terms of cognitive processes. This process perspective is, in our opinion, an important conceptual recognition. In this chapter, we propose an extended-process measurement system for asessing the effects of advertising. Rather than the conventional single perceptual (recall, recognition, and so on) or evaluative measure (preference, attitude, and so on), the tool we advocate is a process system. In responding to a message, consumers experience a psychological process. In order to capture this underlying process, therefore, measures that reflect the process rather than the state are needed.

In this chapter, we present a paradigm for studying the response of consumers to communication and product experiences and discuss the results of a laboratory-based experiment that tested the proposed approach. The results, contrasted with the well-accepted pre- and post-attitude measures, strongly suggest the usefulness and promise of our proposed process system.

Throughout the development of advertising research in laboratory settings, four basic measurement approaches have been suggested. The first type is the perceptual (or cognitive) measure. This includes measuring the subject's recall, recognition, attention, and comprehension of the advertisement to which he or she is exposed. The second type of measure is the affective (or evaluative). This includes subject's acceptance, attitude, or preference toward the advertised product. The third type of measure corresponds to the behavioral element of the advertising effect and includes, for example, buying intention, actual buying in simulated stores, and brand loyalty (Aaker and Myers 1975). A totally different set of measures that overlaps the cognitive and affective approach is that of physiological-response measures. Based on hypothetical relationships between physiological responses and psychological processes, these measures include pupillary response, electrodermal response, heart rate, and so forth (Watson and Gatchel 1979).

By making use of these measures, the experimenter can develop a number of designs to assess the effects of a particular advertisement. The most commonly used designs are the pre- and postdesign and test-control-group design. There are noted problems associated with measures obtained from such designs. The first problem concerns pre- and postmeasures of similar constructs (for example, attitude). This design is often a strong inducement toward demand bias. The second problem relates to the prediction of sales or buying behavior. In a survey of advertising agencies conducted in 1977 (Fletcher and Bowers 1979), users of advertising research consistently report dissatisfaction with the sales and behavioral prediction of existing measures. The third problem is associated with measures of the effect of multiple exposures to the message. The difficulty of assessing the effect accurately still is unresolved (Cuba 1978).

An alternative approach to the assessment of message effects is to recognize that response to the message is an element of an extended process that includes (inter alia) development of product expectations, actual in-use experience, and a variety of postusage compensatory behaviors. Some of these constructs have been addressed in the literature on consumer satisfaction. To date, however, the construct of consumer satisfaction appears fraught with both theoretical and methodological problems. In part, we hypothesize, these problems are due to the failure of satisfaction researchers to recognize the construct as a process. The work of Oliver (1977; 1980) represents a notable exception to this criticism.

In this chapter, we propose a more-complete process model of consumer satisfaction and response behavior. The constructs (and measures) developed in this model are an attempt to capture the important psychological and behavioral process experienced by consumers in a hypothetical exposure/purchase situation.

A Proposed Paradigm

Conceptually, a process consists of a subject motivated by some specific goal and engaging in some activities on an object. The activities will be associated with changes in psychological feeling. The process also includes a feedback system that transmits the results of each and every activity to the subject for subsequent activities.

The framework in figure 17-1 summarizes the process experienced by a subject in a typical message and product situation. The framework is divided into two parts. The upper half represents the model we propose. The lower

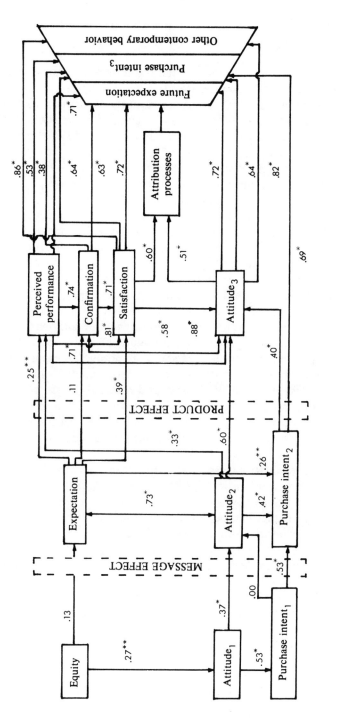

Figure 17-1. A Model of Consumer Response to Communication and Product Experiences

*$p \leq .01$
**$p \leq .05$

half represents the traditional pre- and postattitude shift design. We deliberately place the approaches together so that they might be contrasted and compared more easily.

Figure 17-1 casts the key variables in the framework of a process, in which, unlike traditional attitude measures, the constructs being measured vary at each stage of the process. A traditional, attitude-theory approach to evaluating the success of a particular message is given in the lower half of the figure. This approach consists of measuring the attitude of the consumer (usually through some form of linear-additive or linear-compensatory model) and the associated buying intention, at several intervals in the behavior process—namely, before exposure to the message, after exposure to the message but before product trial, and finally, after product trial. Any changes in attitude or buying intention then are attributed to changes in either the evaluations (importance) or the beliefs surrounding one or more attributes of the product, at each stage in the process. However, the key feature (and perhaps limitation) of this approach is the reliance upon the same measure—namely, attitude—to represent all mental states of the consumer, regardless of stimuli or process stage.

A process-based approach, however, differs in that it spans the entire response experience, with unique measures capturing unique components of the process at each stage. The upper half of figure 17-1 illustrates these measures. Prior to any evaluative message about the product, the consumer holds a set of general expectations for the product, based upon previous experience with the class of products, if any, and reasonableness—that is, equity. Equity expectations are likely unique to a "satisficing" decision/behavior process; ideal expectations of product performance are mediated by consideration of the implied trade-offs among attributes, especially price/performance.

With exposure to evaluative message(s) about the product, these general expectations may develop into a set of informed, though context specific, product expectations. Some readers may wish to argue that a measure of expected product performance can be represented equivalently by the expectancy component of expectancy-value, linear-additive attitude models, and that the attitude model is thus the more-powerful measure at this stage. We do not contest this argument here, since it is not central to the thrust of the paradigm, which states simply that (a unique measure is appropriate to each stage in the process, and that at the pre-exposure stage, the appropriate measure is expected product performance independent of attribute value or importance.

During and after actual product trial, these pretrial expectations may be either confirmed or disconfirmed by the consumer's perceptions of product performance, thereby leading to different levels of motivation for subsequent behavior. This level also will vary with the process used by the individual to assign responsibility for the experience (that is, the attribution process employed). One such process might be to assign responsibility for an unfavorable experience to a misleading message, for example. In addition, the confirmation/disconfirmation and attribution processes will act to determine a set of future expectations and behaviors, including (in addition to future buying intention) future product expectations and compensatory behavior—that is, behavior that manifests the level of satisfaction/dissatisfaction experienced by the consumer.

These distinctions lead to at least three important questions that underly the proposed paradigm:

1. Can consumer satisfaction be distinguished from postexperience attitude, or are the two constructs essentially equivalent?
2. If consumer satisfaction and postexperience attitude represent different constructs, do they result from the same, or different, psychological processes?
3. Which approach, process or attitude based, more meaningfully explains the underlying psychological and behavioral response to communication messages?

Methodology

In order to test the proposed approach, we designed an experiment in which we asked subjects (student volunteers from advanced courses in marketing management at the University of California, Berkeley) to act as potential purchasers for a new electronic hand-held record player. A complete description of the product is available from the authors. The procedure was as follows.

Subjects entered the laboratory and were instructed to enter one of six individual sound-proof cubicles, where the instruments and experimental manipulations were to be administered. After reading a brief description of the tasks involved and signing a consent agreement, subjects were given a one-page description of the new product and its potential applications. When they had finished reading this description, subjects provided information on a set of pre-exposure measures including equity expectations, attribute importance for each of twenty-six product attributes, ideal level of product performance, overall attitude, and a dollarmetric-scaled measure of purchase intention. A dollarmetric-scaled measure asks a subject how much price would have to increase in the brand preferred by the subject to cause a switch to another brand.

They then were instructed to read an evaluation of the new product by an independent consumer testing laboratory. This evaluation represented one of two manipulations in the experiment. For half the subjects (chosen at random), the evaluation reported favorably on the product; for the remaining subjects, the evaluation reported unfavorably. Copies of the two evaluations are available from the authors. The purpose of this (forced, single-exposure) message was to establish product-expectation differences among subjects, necessary in order to test fully the satisfaction hypotheses. After reading this evaluation, subjects provided information on a set of post-exposure measures including expected performance of the product, subjective probability of performance, revised overall attitude, and dollarmetric-scaled purchase intention.

At this stage, subjects received instructions on how to operate the product, together with the player. In order to ensure that subjects read the instructions fully (necessary to minimize the likelihood of an unsatisfactory experience due to unfamiliarity with product operating procedures), they were not given the miniature discs until reading of instructions had been completed.

The product experience represented the second manipulation of the experiment. Two versions (good and poor) of the product were employed to produce perceived product-performance differences among subjects. The good version of the product consisted of an advanced version of the product supplied by the manufacturer and not modified by the experimenters. The poor version of the product consisted of an earlier model, modified additionally by the experimenters to ensure poor performance during use. This modification involved offsetting (or jamming) a device within the player used to center the miniature discs. With the centering device offset, consistent record speed and sound quality were impossible to obtain from the product. The product-performance treatment was assigned randomly to subjects in both expectation groups. Thus, the experiment represents a two-by-two factorial, with repeated measures on subjects.

Final cell sizes were fifteen subjects in each of the two favorable-expectation treatment groups and sixteen subjects in each of the two unfavorable-expectation groups, for a total sample size of sixty-two.

As subjects were handed the product, they were told they would be able to use it (during the experiment) for as long as they wished. Any subjects assigned to the poor-product-performance treatment who complained to the experimenter about not being able to get the product to perform properly were told simply to return to the instructions and to try again or to stop if they wished. After the trial, subjects provided information on a set of posttrial measures including perceived product performance, confirmation/disconfirmation of expected performance, stated satisfaction, (revised) overall attitude, attribution for the overall level of satisfaction, (revised) dollarmetric-scaled purchase intention, likelihood of future behavior for each of nine possible compensatory behaviors, and finally, overall future product expectation.

Results

In the following sections, we present results concerning the effects of the experimental treatments, together with findings on the broad questions (identified previously) underlying the process approach. Before presenting these results, however, we should note that tests of the pretreatment equivalence of the four experimental groups were conducted using a series of multiple discriminant analyses on each of the pre-exposure measures. While not reported in detail here, these tests were strongly supportive of a homogeneous population. Only one discriminant function out of a total of thirty and three independent variables out of a total of eighty-two were capable of discriminating among the four experimental groups at a confidence level of .05 or better. Thus, initial responses of the sample would appear to contain only random error.

Given a sample initially equivalent in terms of its expectations of, and attitudes toward, a product, an important question is to determine to what extent different messages (one favorable, one unfavorable) are capable of separating the sample into two independent subsamples, each with a different (revised) expectation of the product. An answer to this question is provided in table 17-1. The table gives the beta coefficients (and associated significance levels) obtained by coding the message and product manipulations as two dummy variables and regressing these against the postexposure variables of overall expectation, overall attitude, and buying intention in a series of separate ordinary least squares (OLS) regressions. As expected, a significant effect is found for the message manipulation on all three postexposure dependent measures. By contrast, and also in conformance with the design, a nonsignificant effect is obtained for the product manipulation in each case.

Note also from table 17-1 that of the three dependent variables tested (overall expectation, attitude, and purchase intention), the variable most

Table 17-1
Dummy-Variable Regression of Message-Manipulation Verification

Dependent Variable	Beta Coefficients		Multiple r
	Independent Variable		
	Message	Product Performance	
Overall expectation	1.59	.23	.808
	(.000)[a]	(.145)	(.00)
Overall attitude	.97	.31	.555
	(.000)	(.120)	(.00)
Purchase intent	.67	.13	.257
	(.05)	(.710)	(.14)

Note: All dependent measures are postexposure to message.
[a]Significance levels are in parentheses.

significantly influenced by the message (as measured by the multiple r) is the overall expectation for the product ($r = .81$), while the variable least influenced by the message is stated purchase intent ($r = .26$). The weaker relationship between the message manipulation and purchase intent is not necessarily discouraging evidence for managers interested only in measuring the success of a message in terms of future behavior patterns. In the present example, the low correlation can be explained, at least in part, in terms of a low felt need for the product among the members of the sample, quite independent of the message.

A further result from table 17-1 that is perhaps even more interesting is the difference in the strength of the relationship observed between the message and overall expectation and the message and overall attitude ($r = .56$). The difference between these scores would imply that the two constructs, expectation versus attitude, are not the same construct and, further, that expectation is a superior measure for capturing the effects of different messages.

These results would imply that the message manipulation has been highly effective in establishing different expectations of the product for the two groups. The nature of these differences can be seen in table 17-2. The strongest differences are, not unexpectedly, on the product expectation measure, with a mean response of 3.9 for subjects exposed to the favorable message and 2.3 for those exposed to the unfavorable message. This difference is over 50 percent larger than the difference observed between the groups on the measure of overall attitude. Similarly, the measure of stated purchase intent would suggest only a weak effect for the message.

Additional results from a series of multiple discriminant analyses (not reported in detail here) further indicate that the message manipulation

Table 17-2
Means and t-Values for Message Treatment Groups

| | Treatment Group | | |
| | Favorable | Unfavorable | |
Dependent Variable	Message	Message	t-Value
Overall expectation	3.9	2.3	10.2 (.00)[a]
Overall attitude	3.6	2.6	4.9 (.00)
Purchase intent	2.8	2.2	2.0 (.06)

[a]Significance levels are in parentheses. All dependent measures are postexposure to message. The scores shown represent the mean response for each group on five-point bipolar scales for the product-expectation and attitude measures and a six-point scale for the purchase-intent measure. In all cases, higher scores denote more-favorable response.

created consistent differences in expectations on thirteen of a total of fourteen individual attributes discussed in the message and failed to establish differences in expectations on nine of a total of twelve individual attributes not discussed in the message.

Although discussed in greater detail later in the chapter, results of tests conducted to verify the product manipulation of the experiment are presented briefly in this section. Table 17-3 gives the results of an analysis of variance of scores on a variety of post-product-trial measures (overall satisfaction, confirmation, perceived product performance, attitude, future expectation, and purchase intent), according to experimental treatment.

We can draw several interesting observations from table 17-3. First, the product manipulation appears to have been highly successful. The objective product experience has established differences between the two treatment groups on all variables tested, except posttrial purchase intent (refer to the previous section); that is, following the usage experience, subjects exposed to the good product have significantly higher scores than subjects exposed to the poor product on satisfaction, perceived product performance, overall attitude, and performance confirmation.

Further, there appears to be no interaction between the product and the message manipulations. The two treatments have independent effects on the posttrial measures. The only posttrial measures to reflect any effect of the message are overall attitude and future expectations of product performance. This result is especially noteworthy since it indicates the difficulty of separating the effects of a message from the effects of usage experience,

Table 17-3
ANOVA Results of Product-Manipulation Verification

Dependent Measure	F-Ratios Treatment Effect			Multiple r
	Message	Product	Interaction	
Overall satisfaction	3.37	23.63	.025	.56
	(.07)[a]	(.00)	(.88)	
Overall confirmation	.65	16.20	1.97	.47
	(.42)	(.00)	(.17)	
Overall attitude	5.25	12.31	.00	.48
	(.03)	(.00)	(.98)	
Purchase intent	1.92	3.45	.46	.31
	(.17)	(.07)	(.55)	
Overall perceived performance	.80	50.05	.90	.67
	(.38)	(.00)	(.35)	
Overall future expectation	5.18	9.23	.57	.43
	(.03)	(.00)	(.45)	

Note: All measures are post-product trial.
[a]Significance levels are in parentheses.

using only attitude as the measure of effect. Under a satisfaction paradigm, separate constructs are necessary to capture the effects at different stages. At the posttrial stage, the appropriate measures are overall satisfaction, overall performance confirmation, and perceived product performance. There is no reason to expect these measures to differentiate significantly the effects of the message. The results shown in table 17-3 support this approach.

Finally, examining the correlations between the treatments and the dependent measures indicates that the variable most influenced by the joint treatment appears to be perceived product performance and that the variable least influenced is, again, purchase intent. Note also that a measure of overall satisfaction is superior to a measure of overall attitude in capturing the joint effect of the two treatments.

Table 17-4 shows the means for each of the four treatment groups on the posttrial measures discussed earlier. The results provide rich insight into the nature of the response process. As anticipated, subjects who are exposed to a message that is inclined favorably toward the product and then who experience a poor product trial perceive the product as performing poorly, worse than expected, and overall, unsatisfactorily. Their future expectations of the product under normal, in-use conditions, however, are nonnegative. Thus, this group considers the trial experience unrepresentative of the extended-usage experience.

Table 17-4
Means and *F*-Values for the Four Treatment Groups on Selected Post-trial Measures

	Treatment				
	Favorable Message		Unfavorable Message		
Dependent Measure	*Good Product*	*Poor Product*	*Good Product*	*Poor Product*	*F-value*
Overall satisfaction	3.2	2.1	2.8	1.7	8.7 (.00)[a]
Overall confirmation	3.1	1.7	2.9	1.9	9.2 (.00)
Overall attitude	3.4	2.5	2.8	2	6.1 (.00)
Purchase intent	2.4	1.5	1.7	1.3	2.3 (.09)
Overall perceived performance	3.6	1.7	3.2	1.8	17.5 (0)
Overall future expectation	3.4	2.9	3.1	2.1	4.6 (.00)

Note: All measures are post-product trial. All measures were obtained using five-point bipolar scales (with the exception of the purchase-intent measure that is based upon a six-point scale), with higher numbers denoting more-favorable response.
[a]Significance levels are in parentheses.

It is interesting that the surprise effect of encountering a product that performs poorly when initial expectations are high is not well captured by a measure of overall attitude; overall confirmation/disconfirmation, in contrast, shows a marked response to this effect, as evidenced by the low score of 1.7 for this group on the confirmation variable. This result illustrates one of the complexities of attempting to model the consumer-satisfaction process arising out of the multidimensionality of the construct. On one dimension, dissatisfaction may reflect disconfirmation of positive (favorable) dispositions; on another, it may reflect reinforcement of negative (unfavorable) initial dispositions. It is unlikely that these two manifestations of dissatisfaction are psychologically equivalent. In terms of the results shown in table 17-4, dissatisfaction arising from confirmation of unfavorable initial expectations appears to result in a higher level of dissatisfaction (mean scores, 1.7 versus 2.1).

A similar result can be observed in the two conditions intended to establish satisfied responses. The mean level of overall stated satisfaction is higher (3.2) for subjects receiving a favorable message followed by a well-performing product than for subjects receiving an unfavorable message followed by a well-performing product (2.8). These results suggest that where the product experience is consistent with the expectations created by the message (regardless of the direction of the expectations), the level of satisfaction/dissatisfaction will be intensified.

The combined effects of the message and product experiences can be seen also in the attribution behavior of subjects. Perhaps of greatest concern to advertising managers is the effect of the combined experiences on subsequent evaluation of the message. According to figure 17-1, the postusage evaluation of an advertising message can be represented as one form of the attribution process. The relevant question is To what extent do subjects consider the message responsible for their postusage level of satisfaction/dissatisfaction?

The responses provided by subjects to this question (using a five-point bipolar scale where higher numbers denote greater responsibility) show marked differences between treatments. Subjects exposed to a favorable message followed by a poor product experience are least inclined to attribute their postusage level of dissatisfaction to the message (mean, 2.5). This result is not surprising, especially considering the objective nature and source of the product message (an independent consumer-testing group). Given an unsatisfactory product performance, subjects in this condition may find it difficult to argue against the report and, instead, may elect to blame either the product or their own inexperience for the outcome.

Conversely, subjects receiving an unfavorable evaluation of the product followed by poor performance consider the message directly responsible for their feelings of dissatisfaction (mean, 3.8). This is an interesting result, a possible explanation for which might be that subjects, expecting the product to perform poorly, find the claims of the report to be exaggerated and consider the usage experience better than expected. However, this explanation must be rejected for several reasons. First, if this phenomenon does occur, it should be associated also with a low level of dissatisfaction, if not some mild positive satisfaction, a hypothesis that is not supported by the mean stated satisfaction score for this group. Second, the phenomenon should be associated also with high disconfirmation of initial expectations. The mean disconfirmation score for this group (1.9) implies that the product performed worse than expected. The explanation for this score notwithstanding, the implications for subsequent message evaluation are clear. Unfavorable initial expectations followed by an unfavorable usage experience lead to strong re-evaluation of the message.

Subjects exposed to a favorable message followed by either a well-performing product or a poorly-performing product have message attribution scores of 2.9 and 3.3 respectively. This is the more-typical consumer-trial scenario, where the consumer responds favorably toward the product after seeing the message and ultimately decides to try the product. The results show quite simply that, if the product does not meet initial expectations, the message will be held at least partially responsible.

Given successful message and product manipulations, we now can turn our attention to three basic questions that underlie the proposed paradigm.

Can Satisfaction Be Distinguished from Attitude?

The conceptual arguments favoring a separation of the attitude construct from satisfaction are a fundamental premise of this chapter. However, the validity of these arguments might be determined also empirically. Figure 17-1 contains the pairwise product-moment correlations between relevant variables obtained from the current sample. At first glance, the satisfaction and post-product-trial attitude constructs would appear to be very similar ($r = .88$). However, analysis of the relationship of these two constructs to other measures in the model indicates the constructs to be quite separate. In particular, satisfaction and overall attitude differ in their ability to explain both the attribution processes and compensatory behavior patterns used by subjects in response to the experience.

An example of this difference is given in table 17-5, which shows the partial correlation coefficients for satisfaction with each of eight individual compensatory behavior items, after controlling for attitude differences.

If attitude and satisfaction are equivalent constructs, then the association observed between either of the variables and any other measure in figure 17-1 should be identical. More important, if the constructs are equivalent, then controlling for the effect of one (either satisfaction or attitude)

Table 17-5
Partial Correlation Coefficients for Satisfaction and
Compensatory Behavior

Compensatory Behavior Item	r	Significance
Tell family	− .04	.39
Tell friends	.14	.15
Suggest others purchase	.41	.00
Suggest others not purchase	− .42	.00
Buy as a gift	.23	.04
Complain to manufacturer	− .27	.02
Return product for refund	− .33	.00
Complain to consumer group	− .38	.00
Commend manufacturer	.06	.31

Note: $n = 57$.

also will control for the effect of the other. In this case, the controlled variable would contribute little, if anything, to the explanation of other measures in figure 17-1, and thus, we should observe a nonsignificant association between the controlled variable and any other variable in the model.

In table 17-5, after controlling for the effect of attitude differences in the sample, the satisfaction construct continues to exhibit a strong and significant association with six of the nine individual compensatory behavior items included in the experiment. This would seem to suggest that the two constructs, satisfaction and attitude, are contributing uniquely, and not interchangeably, to the prediction of compensatory behavior. (An equivalent analysis, controlling for satisfaction differences and testing the association remaining between attitude and the nine compensatory behavior items, yielded only one significant correlation.) A similar result, though not as strong, is obtained with respect to individual attribution items, as well as future expectations for the product ($r = .26$, significance, .02).

What Are the Causes (Determinants) of
Satisfaction and Attitude?

In essence, this question is inseparable from the previous question. If there is no difference between the two constructs, then it may be possible to infer they both reflect the same determinants; the converse would also be true. Thus, interpretation of these two questions should not be independent.

From figure 17-1, the determinants of the satisfaction construct are identified as perceived product performance and confirmation/disconfirmation, as mediated through product expectation and usage experience.

Though not shown in the figure, for purposes of comparison, we will adopt a linear-additive, compensatory model of attitude structure. This class of attitude models has been reviewed adequately elsewhere (Wilkie and Pessemier 1974) and so is not discussed in detail in this chapter. Using these two models, the structure of the two constructs can be written as follows:

$$\text{Satisfaction} = f (\text{perceived performance, confirmation}) \qquad (17.1)$$

where

$$\text{Confirmation} = g (\text{perceived performance, expectation, objective product experience}) \qquad (17.2)$$

and

$$\text{Perceived performance} = h (\text{expectation, objective product experience}). \qquad (17.3)$$

$$\text{Attitude} = f (\text{importance, perceived performance of product attributes}) \qquad (17.4)$$

where, according to the current design, perceived performance is determined as in equation 17.3.

Table 17-6 gives the results obtained by applying the satisfaction model specified here to the current data. The results were obtained by coding the objective product experience (product manipulation) as a dummy variable and running the series of independent ordinary least squares regressions specified earlier. (Again, interpretation of the regression coefficients may be confounded due to the presence of multicolinearity among the dependent measures.)

The findings strongly support the basic premise. Equation 17.1 shows overall product satisfaction to be related significantly to both perceived product performance and overall performance confirmation/disconfirmation. The directions of the relationships are also consistent with the model. Equation 17.2 also shows a strong relationship between the hypothesized variables and overall performance confirmation. However, the measures of product expectation and objective product experience are not, of themselves, significant. This finding needs to be interpreted in the light of the results for equation 17.3, which show the objective product experience to

Table 17-6
Determinants of Satisfaction

Dependent Measure	Independent Measures			Multiple r
Overall satisfaction	Perceived performance	Confirmation		
	.56	.25		.82
	(.00)	(.03)		(.00)
Overall confirmation	Expectation	Perceived performance	Product experience	
	−.06	.58	.06	.74
	(.54)	(.00)	(.31)	(.00)
Perceived performance	Expectation	Product experience		
	.19	.39		.70
	(.10)	(.00)		(.00)

Note: Significance levels are shown in parentheses.

be the key determinant of perceived product performance. Thus, in equation 17.2, objective product experience fails to explain a large portion of the (residual) variance in confirmation scores since the variable to which it is related most closely (perceived product performance) already has explained most of the variance. Failure of overall expected product performance to contribute to equation 17.2 suggests that the usage experience may outweigh the effects of the message in determining confirmation. Alternatively, the result may indicate a measurement problem. As phrased, for expectation to be related to confirmation scores, there would need to be differences among those who expected it to perform poorly and those who expected it to perform well, in terms of the likelihood of the expectations being confirmed. Clearly, this likelihood is influenced only by the product manipulation.

Although not reported in detail here, results of the same tests conducted on individual attributes indicate the pattern holds in almost every case.

To compare this satisfaction model with a weighted-beliefs (linear-additive) attitude model using identical procedures, it would be necessary to regress overall perceived performance and overall importance against overall attitude and to examine the coefficients and relationship strength. However, since a measure of overall importance has no intuitive meaning in a multi-attribute context, this comparison is not possible. Instead, the linear-additive structure of attitude is tested by estimating a predicted attitude score for the individual, using the model, and comparing this against the posttrial stated attitude for the same individual. This in itself illustrates one of the major measurement limitations of the attitude construct—namely, the reliance on an attribute-based structure. Without reference to product attributes, it is not possible to measure, or interpret, the affective component of the construct.

The predicted attitude for a subject is obtained by multiplying the stated importance weight for an attribute by the perceived performance of the product on that attribute (posttrial) and summing across all attributes. It should be noted that this is not a strong test of the weighted-beliefs model since it is reasonable to expect the stated attribute importances to change following either exposure to an evaluative message for the product or to actual usage. The data available from the current experiment include only the pre-exposure importances. It is, of course, possible to derive the posttrial attribute importances by regressing perceived performance (by attribute) against stated liking. Sample size permitting, the validity of the attitude model then could be tested by predicting scores for a hold-out sample, using the derived importances, and comparing these scores against the stated. In the present experiment, the limited sample size precludes this option.

This problem notwithstanding, the attitude scores predicted by the model, when regressed against the stated posttrial attitude, give a correlation coefficient of .37, significant beyond .003. Thus, a linear-additive model of attitude structure would appear to be supported by the results of the experiment.

While neither model can be rejected by the data, the analysis does indicate a clear conceptual distinction between the two constructs, attitude and satisfaction. Only one component, perceived product performance, is common to both measures. Further, the satisfaction construct explicitly allows for a measure of confirmation/disconfirmation, which can itself be considered a subprocess. Although not explicitly tested here, according to figure 17-1, overall, stated satisfaction also will be influenced by future product expectations, which in turn, are affected by the process of attribution and the ability to take some form of compensatory action (behavior). The importance of these conceptual distinctions rests upon management's desire for understanding the complexities of the response process (that is, the level of refinement desired) and the ability to support the complete model empirically. To this end, a simultaneous equations analysis of the satisfaction model outlined in figure 17-1 is currently in process.

Which Construct, Satisfaction or Attitude,
Better Captures the Response Process?

The model of consumer response to communication and product-usage experiences, presented in figure 17-1, implies that in order to understand the process, the manager must be able to identify the unique effects of the different inputs to the process. In this experiment, two measures are available for separating the effects of a message from the effects of the usage experience: attitude and satisfaction (or its components). In the section on manipulation verification, we presented evidence to suggest the superiority of the satisfaction paradigm for capturing both effects. Further examination of figure 17-1 reinforces that assertion.

Under an attitude-based approach to assess the effects of the message, the manager would compare the attitudes of consumers pre- and postexposure to the communication; to assess the effects of product usage, postexposure and post-product-trial attitudes would be compared. A similar analysis could be conducted using stated purchase intent instead of attitude as the measure of effect. Under either measure, a strong effect might be indicated by a large difference in scores, pre- and postinput to the process.

In figure 17-1, the zero-order correlation between pre- and postexposure attitude is shown as .37, and between pre- and postexposure purchase intent it is .53, indicating some change in attitude, but less in purchase intent, following exposure to the message. Between pre- and post-product-trial attitude, the zero-order correlation is .60, and between pre- and posttrial, purchase intent is .69. Two explanations are possible for these reasonably high correlations (and apparent lack of change in attitude or purchase intent) following product trial. First, it is possible that the input to the process was not significant, and the measures validly reflect this by remaining stable. Second, it is also possible that the input to the process is significant but that the attitude and purchase-intent measures fail to detect the effect.

One way of addressing this question is to examine the attitude and purchase-intent scores, in the light of the satisfaction measures appropriate to the same stage. Referring to figure 17-1, the zero-order correlation between the premessage measure of equity and the postmessage measure of expectation is only .13. Similarly, the correlation between expectation and (posttrial) product performance is only .25. These low correlations indicate weak correspondence between the satisfaction measures prior to and following each input to the process. In contrast to the attitude and purchase-intent measures, the satisfaction measures suggest a marked effect for both the message and the product experience.

Thus, if the objective is to be able to separate the unique effects of different inputs, satisfaction again would appear to offer additional information. In a broad context, satisfaction also contributes to the description and understanding of the consumer-response process through the specification of unique constructs for separate inputs to the process.

If the interest of the manager is not primarily to understand the process of response to communication and usage experiences but rather simply to predict future behavior (either future purchase, or other compensatory behavior), then the process measure is again appropriate. Reference to figure 17-1 shows postusage satisfaction to correlate at least as highly as, if not higher than, postusage attitude with all measures of future behavior and future expectation.

Conclusion

In this chapter, we have outlined the need for considering consumer response to evaluative messages as a component of the broader process of consumer response. The chapter has presented a paradigm for identifying the key measures necessary to evaluate consumer response from the process perspective and compared these measures with the more-traditional attitude-based approaches. Results of a laboratory experiment testing the proposed approach reveal major differences in the ability of the two constructs, attitude and satisfaction, both to explain and predict the response of individuals to message and product-usage experiences.

The satisfaction approach, when viewed in a process framework, appears to offer the manager or researcher an integrated, and more-complete, analysis of response to communication and product experiences. Consumer response to advertising does not end with message exposure, but instead, it is integrated closely with the usage, and postusage, experience. Evidence of this assertion can be found throughout this chapter, but it is most directly visible in the tendency of some consumers to assign responsibility for their felt level of dissatisfaction to the communication message. Under such an (extended) model of response, measures that look simply at part of the process (namely, pre-/postexposure changes in cognition or affect) are, by definition, incomplete. The appropriate approach is to examine the effects of the message only as they are mediated by the usage, and postusage, experience.

A Pilot Test of Krugman's Three-Exposure Theory

John Lastovicka

Knowing how much advertising repetition is too much or too little is a continual and vexing problem for advertising planners. Although management-science models can simulate what proportion of an audience is exposed one time, two times, three times, and so on by different media schedules (Headen, Klompmaker, and Teel 1976; 1977), advertising managers are described as relying on subjective judgment to evaluate if a given simulated media schedule contains the right amount of frequency (Ray and Sawyer 1971; Scissors and Petray 1976).

The real problem, therefore, is that advertisers lack a verified theoretical structure to explain the effects of message repetition on audience response. This problem seems widely recognized in the advertising industry. For example, Schultz' (1979) survey of advertisers and agencies found that the media area perceived as most in need of investigation and study is that of advertising-frequency effects.

This chapter addresses this problem with an empirical laboratory test of one theory that accounts for the effect of advertising repetition on audience response. The theory, Krugman's (1972; 1975) three-exposure theory, has the virtues of being intuitively appealing and of being designed especially to explain how repetitive advertising works. This theory, however, lacks direct evidence. Krugman's expositions of three-exposure theory contain only indirect support.

An Exposition of Three-Exposure Theory

Krugman argues that within the potentially dozens of times that an audience is exposed to a given advertisement, there are essentially only three psychological exposures or periods of actual exposures. Each psychological exposure is characterized by a different receiver response.

The first psychological exposure, which corresponds to the first or more exposures to a message, is typified by the receiver's unfamiliarity with the

This research reported in this chapter was supported by grants from the University of Kansas General Research Fund and from the University of Kansas School of Business Research Fund, provided by the Fourth National Bank and Trust Company. The ideas and opinions expressed herein are solely those of the author.

message. A What is it? type of cognitive response is said to dominate as the receiver decodes the advertising message.

Depending upon message difficulty and receiver ability and motivation, the second psychological exposure may begin as early as the second exposure or as late as (or later than) the tenth exposure. Due to familiarity with the message, the second psychological exposure contains a recognition response. Unique, however, to this exposure is an evaluative What's in it for me? response. This stage is characterized by a comparison of the decoded message to the receiver's needs.

The third psychological exposure serves as a reminder (if there are behaviors yet to be taken as the result of the earlier evaluation in the second exposure) and/or as a reinforcer of the earlier evaluations. Further, during the third psychological exposure comes the beginning of the viewer disengagement of attention from the commercial message about the product. At this stage, the viewer may still react to an ad's message style in an irritated manner, with a What do they think I am, a moron? response, or (due to the perceived entertaining nature of an ad) an opposite response may be elicited.

Krugman (1975) suggests three-exposure theory provides a good starting point for evaluating the effects of repetitive advertising. He claims it useful in estimating the amount of frequency in a media schedule that is either too little or too great.

A Method for Testing Three-Exposure Theory

A repetitive-advertising, forced-exposure laboratory experiment was designed to examine the following questions:

Can audience responses across repeated exposures be summarized or characterized as representing only three types of exposures?

If three exposure types provide an adequate summary, does each exposure type correspond with the characterization of cognitive responses suggested by Krugman in three-exposure theory?

To what degree are the considerations in the first and second questions dependent upon the advertising message format or the product advertised?

These research questions were investigated with a four-dimensional data matrix, as shown in figure 18-1, which consisted of a set of individuals' responses to repetitive advertising stimuli on a battery of Likert-type items. More specifically, twenty-seven undergraduate student subjects were exposed (as a group) to a set of six different finished television advertisements, on five separate exposure occasions over a month's time. After each exposure to every advertisement, the subjects responded to a battery of sixteen different

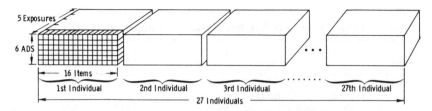

Figure 18-1. Four-Dimensional Data Matrix

items designed to measure viewer reaction to television advertising. The items, all of which used a one-to-six-point strongly disagree-strongly agree scale, were selected from a larger battery of items known as the viewer-response profile (Leo Burnett Company 1977; Schlinger 1979). Table 18-1 contains the items used in the research. The advertisements were shown by themselves under forced-exposure conditions.

The six commercials were selected to represent both a variety of advertised goods and services and a variety of message styles. Two of the advertisements, "Fender Bender" and "Chicago," were for Allstate Auto Insurance; two others, "Duke of Klaxton" and "Fox Hunt," were for the Audi Fox automobile; and the pair, "Big Day" and "Mother Country," was for United Airlines. The message treatments ranged from slice of life to a plain-speaking spokesman to travelogues filled with scenery, music, and dance. In addition, pretests of a large pool of commercials with different, but similar, student samples suggest that the likelihood of exposure to the six test commercials prior to the study was very low. Further, since the six television commercials were from past and discontinued advertising campaigns (at the time of the study), the test sample would not have been subject to additional exposures of the six commercials from their regular television viewing.

The small convenience sample employed in this research can be justified several ways. First, all the members of the student sample classified themselves as regular TV viewers in a battery of questions asked after all the exposures to the six test commercials. Consequently, since this sample has had regular experience with repetitive television advertising, it was relevant to this research. Second, although the sample size may seem low, it is adequate for the method used to analyze the data. In fact, the computational procedures for the particular psychometric model used to summarize the data would be hard pressed to handle a much larger data base. Third, this study is not meant to be the definitive test of three-exposure theory. The results of this exploratory study should be viewed as no more than tentative generalizations that may be confirmed in further studies.

The four-dimensional data matrix shown in figure 18-1 was analyzed with Lastovicka's (1981) four-mode component analysis. This multivariate

Table 18-1
Varimax Rotated Scale Mode-Component Loadings Matrix: D*

Item Number	Item	I_{r*}	II_{r*}	III_{r*}
2	During the commercial I thought how the product might be useful to me.	.435	− .037	− .049
3	I felt as though I was right there in the commercial experiencing the same thing.	.314	− .038	− .140
6	The commercial was meaningful to me.	.446	.043	.040
8	The ad did not have anything to do with me or my needs.	− .439	− .055	− .210
11	The commercial gave me a good idea.	.306	− .006	− .126
14	As I watched I thought of reasons why I would or would not buy the product.	.418	− .044	.042
5	I clearly understood the commercial.	.136	.366	.072
7	The commercial was too complex. I was not sure what was going on.	− .001	− .536	− .011
12	I was not sure what was going on in the commercial.	− .009	− .531	− .006
15	I was so busy watching the screen, I did not listen to the talk.	.083	− .339	.024
16	The commercial went by so quickly that it just did not make an impression on me.	.070	− .405	.074
1	The commercial was lots of fun to watch and to listen to.	.076	.003	− .438
4	I have seen this commercial before.	.095	.056	.372
9	I have seen this commercial so many times that I am tired of it.	.013	− .050	.434
10	I thought the commercial was clever and quite entertaining.	.050	.036	− .428
13	The ad was not just selling—it was entertaining me. I appreciated that.	.051	− .002	− .448

Note: Salient loadings used in interpretation are underlined.

procedure treated all of the dimensions of the data (subjects, exposures, ads, and question items) in a symmetric fashion by decomposing each dimension into a set of basic latent components; that is, with these data, the four-mode procedure developed a person typology (as in Q-factor analysis), an exposure typology, an advertisement typology, and a set of question or scale components (as in R-factor analysis). Further, the four-mode procedure specifies the interrelations among the subject, exposure, ad, and question components in what is termed a *core* matrix.

The Four-Mode Model

Four-mode factor component analysis is applied to a four-dimensional data matrix Y that has cell entries $y_{i'j'k'l'}$ such that $i' = 1, 2, 3 \ldots i;$

$j' = 1, 2, 3 \ldots j$; $k' = 1, 2, 3 \ldots k$; and $l' = 1, 2, 3 \ldots l$. For the current analysis, the i, j, k, and l correspond to individuals, exposure occasions, advertisements, and items respectively. Consequently, the four-dimensional data matrix in figure 18-1 contained the elements $y_{i'j'k'l'}$ such that $i' = 1, 2, 3, \ldots 27$; $j' = 1, 2, 3, 4, 5$; $k' = 1, 2, 3, 4, 5, 6$; and $l' = 1, 2, 3, \ldots 16$.

The fundamental four-mode component analysis model is as follows:

$$y_{i'j'k'l'} \cong \hat{y}_{i'j'k'l'} =$$

$$\sum_{m'=1}^{m} \sum_{p'=1}^{p} \sum_{q'=1}^{q} \sum_{r'=1}^{r} \left(a_{i'm'} \, b_{j'p'} \, c_{k'q'} \, d_{l'r'} g_{m'p'q'r'} \right) \qquad (18.1)$$

The data, the $y_{i'j'k'l'}$s, are modeled by approximations, the $y_{i'j'k'l'}$s. The approximations are based on four modes (m, p, q, and r), which are thought to be more basic conceptually than the dimensions employed in collecting the original data. Each of these more-basic modes corresponds to one of the dimensions in the original data matrix Y: m corresponds to i, p to j, q to k, and r to l. The four-mode component-analysis model, like all component models, is essentially a data-reduction technique. Therefore, we hope that $m \ll i$, $p \ll j$, $q \ll k$, and $r \ll l$. Each of the basic modes represents the number of components in the domain of the corresponding dimension in the original data.

The coefficients $a_{i'm'}$, $b_{j'p'}$, $c_{j'p'}$, and $d_{l'r'}$ are elements in component-loading matrixes A, B, C, and D respectively. For example, if the i dimension in a four-dimensional data matrix represents responses to a set of i questionnaire items, then the coefficient $a_{i'm'}$ would represent the loading of question i' on the latent component m'. Alternatively, the basic modes can be interpreted as idealized entities, types, or clusters.

The coefficient $g_{m'p'q'r'}$ is an element in the four-dimensional core matrix G. The core matrix describes the interrelationships between the components found in each of the four dimensions of the original data matrix. In a sense, the core matrix can be thought of as a set of component scores. In the original four-mode data matrix, Y, each element represents a particular cross classification of some level of each of i, j, k, and l dimensions. In the same way, every element in the core matrix, G, represents a particular cross classification of each of the m, p, q, and r basic modes.

As in standard principal-component analysis, it is possible to consider varimax rotations or other types of transformations of the four-mode loading matrixes. These transformations can be represented in these matrix equations as follows:

$$A^* = AT_{m^*} \qquad (18.2a)$$

$$B^* = BT_{p^*} \qquad (18.2b)$$

$$C^* = CT_{q^*} \qquad (18.2c)$$

$$D^* = DT_{r^*} \qquad (18.2d)$$

where A^*, B^*, C^*, and D^* are the transformed loading matrixes and T_{m^*}, T_{p^*}, T_{q^*}, and T_{r^*} are square, nonsingular transformation matrixes.

If rotations have been performed, then this requires a four-mode model that takes into account not only the rotated loading matrixes but also core-matrix values that reflect the transformations. Following the form of equation 18.1, the effect of the transformations is as follows:

$$y_{i'j'k'l'} \cong \hat{y}_{i'j'k'l'} = \qquad (18.3)$$

$$\sum_{m'=1}^{m} \sum_{p'=1}^{p} \sum_{q'=1}^{q} \sum_{r'=1}^{r} \left(a^*_{i'm'} \, b^*_{j'p'} \, c^*_{k'q'} \, d^*_{l'r'} \, g^*_{m'p'q'r'} \right)$$

where $g^*_{m'p'q'r'}$ is an element in a transformed core matrix G^* and the coefficients $a^*_{i'm'}$, $b^*_{j'p'}$, $c^*_{k'q'}$, and $d^*_{l'r'}$ are elements in the transformed loading matrixes defined in equations 18.2a-18.2d.

Results

By applying procedures suggested by Lastovicka (1981), we estimated the coefficients specified in equation 18.1. Figure 18-2 contains a graphical representation of the estimated model. This figure shows the relationship among the core matrix, the loading matrixes, and the original four-dimensional data matrix illustrated in figure 18-1. The order of the loading matrixes in figure 18-2 clearly shows that considerable data reduction has taken place. Indeed, figure 18-2 suggests that a four-mode component model with four idealized viewer types, three exposure types, two advertisement types, and three response scales adequately represents the data. An assessment of goodness of fit of the model to the data shows the simple product-moment correlation between the $\hat{y}_{ijkl}$ and the y_{ijkl} coefficients, .88, to be high.

To ease the interpretation of the results, varimax transformation or rotation matrixes were applied to the component loading matrixes in the manner suggested by equations 18.2a-18.2d. The varimax rotated component

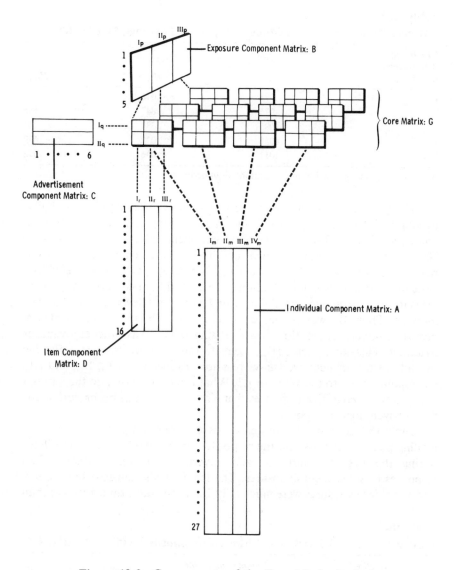

Figure 18-2. Components of the Four-Mode Analysis

loadings matrixes for the item, exposure, and advertisement modes are shown in tables 18-1, 18-2, and 18-3. Since the individual-mode loadings matrix would add little to understanding the current analysis, it is not presented. The individual-mode loading matrix, like the other loading matrixes, was also varimax rotated.

Table 18-2
Varimax Rotated Exposure Mode-Component Loadings Matrix: B*

Number of Advertising Exposures	I_{p*}	II_{p*}	III_{p*}
1	.991	− .016	.027
2	.076	.842	− .195
3	− .095	.534	.271
4	.036	.072	.639
5	− .013	− .036	.692

Note: Salient loadings used in interpretation are underlined.

The rotated item components, or scales, shown in table 18-1 are similar to major dimensions regularly found in advertising-response data (for example, Schlinger 1979). The first item component reflects the degree viewers claim to perceive an advertisement and its advocated consumer product as relevant to their needs. Component I_{r*}, therefore, may be interpreted as a scale measuring personal evaluation. The second item component seems to measure the degree viewers claim to understand a television commercial's message. Thus, II_{r*} was labeled comprehension. The third latent scale appears to characterize reactions to advertising exposure as either enjoyable or irritating. This component, III_{r*}, seems to tap emotive response, reflecting overall positive or negative viewer reaction. Respectively, I_{r*}, II_{r*}, and III_{r*} correspond nicely to the What of it?, What is it?, and What do they think I am, a moron? cognitive responses that Krugman suggests occur during different psychological exposures.

Table 18-2 contains the rotated-exposure-mode component matrix. The loading pattern suggests that the responses on the sixteen Likert-type items during the first exposure to each advertisement were different than responses to subsequent exposures. The loadings also suggest that the second and third exposures were much alike but at the same time different than

Table 18-3
Varimax Rotated Advertisement Mode-Component Loadings Matrix: C*

Product Advertised	Commercial Name	I_{q*}	II_{q*}
United Airlines	Big Day	.337	.145
	Mother Country	.594	− .164
Audi Fox	Duke of Klaxton	.467	.096
	Fox Hunt	.560	− .045
Allstate Auto Insurance	Fender Bender	.015	.681
	Chicago	.027	.691

Note: Salient loadings used in interpretation are underlined.

other exposures. Similarly, the fourth and fifth exposures were alike but different from other exposures. Such a loading pattern is consistent with three-exposure theory. Therefore, it may be appropriate to interpret $I_{p\bullet\bullet}$, $II_{p\bullet\bullet}$, and $III_{p\bullet}$ as Krugman's first, second, and third psychological exposures respectively. Correspondence of $I_{p\bullet}$, $II_{p\bullet}$, and $III_{p\bullet}$ to the psychological exposures will be tested further in the core matrix. Since the core matrix describes the interrelationships among the components found in each of the four dimensions of the original data matrix, an examination of the core will show if the exposure components ($I_{p\bullet}$, $II_{p\bullet}$, and $III_{p\bullet}$) relate to the item, or scale, components ($I_{r\bullet}$, $II_{r\bullet}$, and $III_{r\bullet}$) as theory predicts. For example, what is tentatively interpreted as the second psychological exposure, $II_{p\bullet}$, should be characterized with intense personal evaluation as measured by $I_{r\bullet}$.

The rotated loading matrix for the advertisement mode in table 18-3 suggests two advertisement types. $I_{q\bullet}$ appears to represent a group of four different ads for two different products, an airline and an imported automobile, while $II_{q\bullet}$ is a pair of ads for a single product, an automobile insurance. Besides the consumer product being promoted, the two sets of advertisements also differed in other important ways. For instance, in comparison to the insurance advertisements, the airline and automobile advertisements contained a more-complex message and made more use of drama, comedy, and music in their creative treatments.

Corresponding to the number of components retained for the individual, exposure occasion, advertisement, and item modes, the core matrix for this analysis is of order four by three by two by three. The core matrix, transformed to reflect varimax rotations on all four modes, is shown in table 18-4. The four-dimensional matrix G* can be thought of as containing scores of the four idealized viewer types on pairs of components representing combinations of different types of advertisements, psychological exposures, and response scales; that is, the core-matrix elements indicate the reactions (on three scales) of four different types of idealized viewers to two different groups of advertisements at three fundamental repetitive-exposure levels.

Interpretation of core-matrix elements will follow the convention of observing the trends or patterns of relative change in the columns of the core matrix presented in table 18-4. Because the distribution of core-matrix values in multimodal component analyses have unknown properties, this simple heuristic is used when interpreting the core matrix (Levin 1965; Vavra 1973).

The comprehension scores in the second and fifth columns of the core matrix in table 18-4 suggest that with increased repetition, the respondents claimed to know relatively more about the contents of the advertisements. This pattern of increased comprehension with additional exposures is consistent with Krugman's theory. The comprehension scores also show differences

Table 18-4
Transformed Core Matrix: G*

| | | Airline and Automobile Ads: I_{q^*} | | | Insurance Ads: II_{q^*} | | |
		Personal Evaluation[a]: I_{r^*}	Comprehension[b]: II_{r}	Emotive Response[c]: III_{r^*}	Personal Evaluation: I_{r^*}	Comprehension: II_{r^*}	Emotive Response: III_{r^*}
Respondent	Psychological Exposure						
Idealized respondent one: I_{m^*}	First psychological exposure: I_{p^*}	−.156	.120	.096	−.058	−.002	.004
	Second psychological exposure: II_{p^*}	−.100	.004	.075	−.011	.098	.070
	Third psychological exposure: III_{p^*}	−.187	.120	.053	−.187	.146	.083
Idealized respondent two: II_{m^*}	First psychological exposure: I_{p^*}	−.217	−.044	.018	−.274	.084	.187
	Second psychological exposure: II_{p^*}	.460	−.270	.080	.594	.198	−.069
	Third psychological exposure: III_{p^*}	−1.438	.845	.405	−.784	.263	.135
Idealized respondent three: III_{m^*}	First psychological exposure: I_{p^*}	.314	−.378	−.221	.107	−.146	.027
	Second psychological exposure: II_{p^*}	.630	−.242	−.176	.390	−.201	−.228
	Third psychological exposure: III_{p^*}	−.002	−.042	−.003	.089	−.319	−.140
Idealized respondent four: IV_{m^*}	First psychological exposure: I_{p^*}	.277	−.206	.114	.194	−.161	−.081
	Second psychological exposure: II_{p^*}	.305	−.187	−.149	.156	−.203	−.104
	Third psychological exposure: III_{p^*}	.510	−.347	−.170	.316	−.257	−.121

Note: Core-matrix values presented have been multiplied by ten.
[a]Higher numerical values on the personal-evaluation scales represent relatively higher perceived relevance.
[b]Higher numerical values on the comprehension scales represent relatively higher perceived understanding.
[c]Higher numerical values on the emotive-response scales indicate relatively higher irritation with the ad as a whole.

in respondent types. For example, types I and II claimed to understand the advertisements more than types III and IV.

Inspection of the personal-relevance scores in the first and fourth columns of G* in table 18-4 shows an almost universal phenomenon. In almost every pair of respondent and advertisement type, viewer questioning of advertisement-message content relevance was most intense during the second exposure. Although this result is inconsistent with cognitive theories of perception that claim information is evaluated first in terms of its pertinence, it is consistent with three-exposure theory. Krugman (1981) argues that, while message content is decoded during the first psychological exposure, evaluation of message relevance primarily occurs during the second psychological exposure. Differences between respondent types I and II versus III and IV are also apparent on personal evaluation. Across advertisement types, respondent types III and IV viewed the messages as having more personal relevance than respondent types I and II. When viewed simultaneously, columns one, two, four, and five of G* suggest that viewers think they know a good deal about the content of an irrelevant advertisement after a few exposures, while when viewers see the advertisements as relevant, they are viewed as not having precise or clear enough information.

The emotive response scores in the core matrix reveal individual differences in perceptions of the two different types of advertisements. For instance, whereas respondent type I found the airline and automobile advertisements more enjoyable with increased repetition and grew more annoyed with additional exposures to the insurance ads, respondent type II's emotive reactions to the advertisement types across exposures showed a reverse trend.

Discussion

With reference to the research questions raised in this study, we can report the following findings:

Within five forced repetitive exposures to television advertisements, there are three basic exposure periods.

The viewer responses that occur during the three basic exposure periods correspond with those suggested by three-exposure theory.

Neither the creative treatments nor the products advertised in this study had any direct impact on the quantity or the quality of the psychological exposures.

This study, however, provides only partial confirmation of Krugman's theory. For example, data were not collected for more than five exposures.

Consequently, we do not know if a sixth and seventh exposure would load on the third psychological-exposure component. Perhaps a fourth component would be required to model additional exposures. In addition, the obtained pattern of loadings in the exposure-component loading matrix may be due only to the simplex-like quality of the data, resulting from repeated measurements spaced over a relatively short period of time. Consequently, future investigations should consider nonrepeated-measure designs. Further, three-exposure theory is not limited to repetitive advertising in the television medium (Krugman 1975). Empirical research in other media settings is needed.

Despite these limitations, this study does provide direct evidence for three-exposure theory. Only when more-empirical investigations (using different methodologies) become available will advertising planners be able to use this theory confidently or to reject it as a basis in deciding how much advertising repetition is too much or too little.

References

Introduction

Allport, G.W., "Attitudes," *Handbook of Social Psychology*, ed. C. Murchison (Worcester, Mass.: Clark University Press, 1935), pp. 798-884.

Berelson, B., "What Missing the Newspaper Means," in *Communications Research, 1948-1949*, eds. P.E. Lazarsfeld and F.N. Stanton (New York: Harper & Row, 1949), pp. 217-246.

Britt, S.H., *Psychological Principles of Marketing and Consumer Behavior* (Lexington, Mass.: D.C. Heath and Company, Lexington Books, 1978).

Doob, L.W., *Communication in Africa* (New Haven: Yale University Press, 1961).

Ehrenberg, A.S.C., "Factor Analytic Search for Program Types," *Journal of Advertising Research* 8 (1968):55-63.

———, "Repetitive Advertising and the Consumer," *Journal of Advertising Research* 14 (1974):25-34.

Festinger, L., *A Theory of Cognitive Dissonance* (Stanford: Stanford University Press, 1957).

Hovland, C.I.; Janis, I.L.; and Kelley, H.H., *Communication and Persuasion* (New Haven: Yale University Press, 1953).

Insko, C.A., *Theories of Attitude Change* (New York: Appleton-Century-Crofts, 1967).

Krugman, H.E., "The Measurement of Advertising Involvement," *Public Opinion Quarterly* 30 (1967):583-596.

Lasswell, H.D., "The Structure and Function of Communication in Society," in *Communication of Ideas*, ed. L. Bryson (New York: Harper & Row, 1948), pp. 92-121.

Lipstein, B., and McGuire, W.J., *Evaluating Advertising: A Bibliography of the Communications Process* (New York: Advertising Research Foundation, 1978).

McGuire, W.J., "The Nature of Attitudes and Attitude Change," in *Handbook of Social Psychology*, vol. 3, 2d ed., eds. G. Lindzey and E. Aronson (Reading, Mass.: Addison-Wesley, 1968a).

———, "Personality and Susceptibility to Social Influence," in *Handbook of Personality Theory and Research*, eds. E.F. Borgatta and W.W. Lambert (Chicago: Rand McNally, 1968b).

———, "Persuasion, Resistance and Attitude Change," in *Handbook of Communication*, eds. I. De Sola Pool et al. (Chicago: Rand McNally, 1973).

_____ , "An Information-Processing Model of Advertising Effectiveness," in *Behavioral and Management Science in Marketing*, eds. H.L. Dans and A.J. Silk (New York: Roland Press, 1978), pp. 216-231.

McLuhan, M., *Understanding Media* (New York: McGraw-Hill, 1964).

Percy, L., and Rossiter, J.R., *Advertising Strategy: A Communication Theory Approach* (New York: Praeger, 1980).

Perloff, R.M., and Brock, T.C., "The Role of Own Cognitive Response in Persuasion: A Conceptual View," in *Advances in Consumer Research*, vol. 7, ed. J. Olson (Ann Arbor: Association for Consumer Research, 1980), pp. 741-744.

Pool, I. de Sola, "Communication Systems," in *Handbook of Communication*, eds. de Sola et al. (Chicago: Rand McNally, 1973), pp. 701-718.

Osgood, C.E.; Suci, B.M.; and Tannenbaum, P.H., *The Measurement of Meaning* (Urbana: University of Illinois Press, 1957).

Rossiter, J.R., and Percy, L., *Advertising and Sales Promotion Management* (New York: McGraw-Hill, forthcoming).

Wells, W.D., "The Rise and Fall of Television Program Types," *Journal of Advertising Research* 9 (1969):21-27.

Wright, P., "On The Direct Monitoring of Cognitive Response to Advertising," in *Consumer Buyer Information Processing*, eds. E.D. Hughes and M.L. Ray (Chapel Hill: University of North Carolina Press, 1974), pp. 52-66.

Wyer, R.S., *Cognitive Organization and Change: An Information Processing Approach* (Potomac, Md.: Lawrence Erlbaum Associates, 1974).

Zajonc, R.B., "Feeling and Thinking: Preferences Need No Inferences," *American Psychologist* 35 (1980):151-175.

Chapter 1

Abelson, R.P., "A Script Theory of Understanding, Attitude, and Behavior," in *Cognition and Social Behavior*, eds. J. Carroll and T. Payne (Potomac, Md.: Lawrence Erlbaum Associates, 1976), pp. 166-187.

Amstutz, A.E., *Computer Simulation of Competitive Market Response* Cambridge: MIT Press, 1967).

Anderson, N.H., "Integration Theory and Attitude Change," *Psychological Review* 78 (1971):171-206.

Apsler, R., and Sears, D.O., "Warning, Personal Involvement, and Attitude Change," *Journal of Personality and Social Psychology* 9 (1968): 162-168.

Bem, D.J., "Self-Perception: An Alternative Interpretation of Cognitive Dissonance Phenomena," *Psychological Review* 74 (1967):183-200.

Brock, T.C., "Communication Discrepancy and Intent to Persuade as Determinants of Counterargument Production," *Journal of Experimental Social Psychology* 3 (1967):296-309.

Brock, T.C., and Shavitt, S., "Cognitive Response Analysis in Advertising," in *Advertising and Consumer Psychology*, eds. L. Percy and A. Woodside (Lexington, Mass.: D.C. Heath and Company, Lexington Books, 1983).

Cacioppo, J.T.; Harkins, S.G.; Petty, R.E., "The Nature of Attitudes and Cognitive Responses and Their Relationships to Behavior," in *Cognitive Responses in Persuasion*, eds. R. Petty, T. Ostrom, and T. Brock (Hillsdale, N.J.: Lawrence Erlbaum Associates, 1981), pp. 31-54.

Cacioppo, J.T., and Petty, R.E., "Effects of Message Repetition and Position on Cognitive Responses, Recall, and Persuasion," *Journal of Personality and Social Psychology* 37 (1979):2181-2199.

_____ , "Persuasiveness of Communications Is Affected by Exposure Frequency and Communication Cogency: A Theoretical and Empirical Analysis of Persisting Attitude Change," in *Current Issues and Research in Advertising*, eds. J. Leigh and C. Martin (Ann Arbor: University of Michigan, 1980a), pp. 71-79.

_____ , "Sex Differences in Influenceability: Toward Specifying the Underlying Processes," *Personality and Social Psychology Bulletin* 6 (1980b):651-656.

_____ , "The Need for Cognition," *Journal of Personality and Social Psychology* 42 (1982):116-131.

_____ , "The Need for Cognition: Relationships to Social Influence and Self-Influence," in *Social perception in clinical and counseling psychology*, eds. J.H. Harvey et al. (Lubbock, Tex.: Texas Tech Press, in press).

Cacioppo, J.T.; Petty, R.E.; and Sidera, J.A., "The Effects of a Salient Self-Schema on the Evaluation of Proattitudinal Editorials: Top-Down versus Bottom-Up Processing," *Journal of Experimental Social Psychology* 18 (1982):324-338.

Chaiken, S., "Heuristic versus Systematic Information Processing and the Use of Source versus Message Cues in Persuasion," *Journal of Personality and Social Psychology* 39 (1980):752-766.

Chaiken, S., and Eagly, A.H., "Communication Modality as a Determinant of Message Persuasiveness," *Journal of Personality and Social Psychology* 34 (1976):605-614.

Chassin, L. et al., "Self Images and Cigarette Smoking in Adolescence," *Personality and Social Psychology Bulletin* 7 (1981):670-676.

Cialdini, R.B. et al., "Elastic Shifts of Opinion: Determinants of Direction and Durability," *Journal of Personality and Social Psychology* 34 (1976):663-672.

Cialdini, R.B., and Petty, R.E., "Anticipatory Opinion Effects," in *Cognitive responses in persuasion*, eds. R. Petty, T. Ostrom, and T. Brock (Hillsdale, N.J.: Erlbaum Associates, 1981), pp. 217-236.

Cialdini, R.B.; Petty, R.E.; and Cacioppo, J.T., "Attitude and Attitude Change," in *Annual Review of Psychology*, eds. M. Rosensweig and L. Porter (Palo Alto, Calif.: Annual Reviews Inc., 1981), pp. 310-346.

Cook, T.D., and Flay, B.R., "The Temporal Persistence of Attitude Change: An Evaluative Review," in *Advances in Experiential Social Psychology* (Vol. 11), ed. L. Berkowitz (New York: Academic Press, 1978).

Craik, F.M., and Lockhart, R.S., "Levels of Processing: A Framework for Memory Research," *Journal of Verbal Learning and Verbal Behavior* 11 (1972):671-684.

Eagly, A.H., "Comprehensibility of Persuasive Arguments as a Determinant of Opinion Change," *Journal of Personality and Social Psychology* 29 (1974):758-773.

Eibl-Ebesfeldt, I., "Similarities and Differences between Cultures in Expressive Movement," in *Nonverbal communication*, ed. R.A. Hinde (Cambridge: Cambridge University Press, 1972).

Engel, J.F., and Blackwell, R., *Consumer behavior*, 4th edition (Hinsdale, Ill.: Dryden Press, 1982).

Fazio, R.H., and Zanna, M.P., "Direct Experience and Attitude Behavior Consistency," in *Advances in experimental social psychology* (Vol. 14), ed. L. Berkowitz (New York: Academic Press, 1981), pp. 86-101.

Fishbein, M., and Ajzen, I., *Belief, attitude, intention, and behavior: An introduction to theory and research* (Reading, Mass.: Addison-Wesley, 1975).

Greenwald, A.G., "Cognitive Learning, Cognitive Response to Persuasion, and Attitude Change," in *Psychological foundations of attitudes*, eds. A. Greenwald, T. Brock, and T. Ostrom (New York: Academic Press, 1968), pp. 58-73.

Harkins, S.G., and Petty, R.E., "Effects of Source Magnification of Cognitive Effort on Attitudes: An Information Processing View," *Journal of Personality and Social Psychology* 40 (1981):401-413.

Hass, R.G., "Persuasion or Moderation? Two Experiments on Anticipatory Belief Change," *Journal of Personality and Social Psychology* 31 (1975):1155-1162.

Hovland, I.; Janis, I.L.; and Kelley, H.H., *Communication and Persuasion* (New Haven: Yale University Press, 1953).

Insko, C.A., *Theories of attitude change* (New York: Appleton-Century-Crofts, 1967).

Janis, I.L.; Kaye, D.; and P. Kirschner, P., "Facilitating Effects of 'Eating While Reading' on Responsiveness to Persuasive Communications," *Journal of Personality and Social Psychology* 1 (1965):181-186.

Judd, C.M., and Johnson, J.T., "Attitudes, Polarization, and Diagnosticity: Exploring the Effect of Affect," *Journal of Personality and Social Psychology* 41 (1981):26-36.

Kassarjian, H., "Consumer Psychology," in *Annual review of psychology* (Vol. 33), eds. M. Rosensweig and L. Porter (Palo Alto, Calif.: Annual Reviews Inc., 1982), pp. 192-213.

Kelman, H.C., "Processes of Opinion Change," *Public Opinion Quarterly* 25 (1961):57-78.

Kelman, H.C., and Hovland, C.I., "Reinstatement of the Communicator in Delayed Measurement of Opinion Change," *Journal of Abnormal and Social Psychology* 48 (1953):327-335.

Kiesler, C.A.; Collins, B.E.; and Miller, N., *Attitude change: A critical analysis of theoretical approaches* (New York: Wiley, 1969).

Krugman, H.E., "The Impact of Television Advertising: Learning without Involvement," *Public Opinion Quarterly* 29 (1965):349-356.

Laird, J.D.; Wagener, M.H.; and Szegda, M., "Remembering What You Feel: Effects of Emotion on Memory," *Journal of Personality and Social Psychology* 42 (1982):646-657.

Langer, E.; Blank, A.; and Chanowitz, B., "The Mindlessness of Ostensibly Thoughtful Action: The Role of Placebic Information in Interpersonal Interaction," *Journal of Personality and Social Psychology* 36 (1978):635-642.

Lutz, R.J., "A Functional Theory Framework for Designing and Pretesting Advertising Stimuli," in *Attitude Research Plays for High Stakes*, eds. J. Maloney and B. Silverman (Chicago: American Marketing Association, 1979), pp. 37-49.

Maddux, J.E., and Rogers, R.W., "Effects of Source Expertness, Physical Attractiveness, and Supporting Arguments on Persuasion: A Case of Brains over Beauty," *Journal of Personality and Social Psychology* 38 (1980):235-244.

Markus, H., "Self-Schemata and Processing Information about the Self," *Journal of Personality and Social Psychology* 35 (1977):63-78.

McGuire, W.J., "Inducing Resistance to Persuasion: Some Contemporary Approaches," in *Advances in Experimental Social Psychology* (Vol. 1), ed. L. Berkowitz (New York: Academic Press, 1964), pp. 54-76.

———— , "The Nature of Attitudes and Attitude Change," in *The Handbook of Social Psychology* (2nd ed), Vol. 3, eds. G. Lindzey and E. Aronson (Reading, Mass.: Addison-Wesley, 1969), pp. 372-398.

Miller, N., and Campbell, D.T., "Recency and Primacy in Persuasion as a Function of the Timing of Speeches and Measurements," *Journal of Abnormal and Social Psychology* 59 (1959):1-9.

Miller, N. et al., "Speed of Speech and Persuasion," *Journal of Personality and Social Psychology* 34 (1976):615-625.

Mills, J., and Harvey, J.H., "Opinion Change as a Function of When Information about the Communicator is Received and Whether He is Attractive or Expert," *Journal of Personality and Social Psychology* 21 (1972):52-55.

Nicosia, F., *Consumer Decision Processes* (Englewood Cliffs, N.J.: Prentice-Hall, 1966).

Norman, R., "When What is Said is Important: A Comparison of Expert and Attractive Sources," *Journal of Experimental Social Psychology* 12 (1976):294-300.

Petty, R.E., and Cacioppo, J.T., "Effects of Forewarning of Persuasive Intent and Involvement on Cognitive Responses and Persuasion," *Personality and Social Psychology Bulletin* 5 (1979a):173-176.

_____ , "Issue Involvement Can Increase or Decrease Persuasion by Enhancing Message-Relevant Cognitive Responses," *Journal of Personality and Social Psychology* 37 (1979b):1915-1926.

_____ , *Attitudes and Persuasion: Classic and Contemporary Approaches* (Dubuque, Iowa: Wm. C. Brown, 1981a).

_____ , "Issue Involvement as a Moderator of the Effects on Attitude of Advertising Content and Context," *Advances in Consumer Research* 8 (1981b):20-24.

_____ , "The Role of Bodily Responses in Attitude Measurement and Change," in *Social Psychophysiology: A Sourcebook*, eds. J.T. Cacioppo and R.E. Petty (New York: Guilford Press, 1983), pp. 415-441.

_____ , *Attitude Change: Central and Peripheral Routes to Persuasion* (New York: Springer/Verlag, in press a).

_____ , "The Effects of Involvement on Responses to Argument Quantity and Quality: Central and Peripheral Routes to Persuasion," *Journal of Personality and Social Psychology*, in press b.

_____ , "Motivational Factors in Consumer Response to Advertisements," in *Human Motivation: Physiological, Behavioral, and Social Approaches*, eds. R. Green, W. Beatty, and R. Arkin (Boston: Allyn & Bacon, in press c), pp. 73-92.

Petty, R.E.; Cacioppo, J.T.; and Goldman, R., "Personal Involvement as a Determinant of Argument-Based Persuasion," *Journal of Personality and Social Psychology* 41 (1981):847-855.

Petty, R.E.; Cacioppo, J.T.; and Heesacker, M., "The Use of Rhetorical Questions in Persuasion: A Cognitive Response Analysis," *Journal of Personality and Social Psychology* 40 (1981):432-440.

Petty, R.E.; Cacioppo, J.T.; and Schumann, D., "Central and Peripheral Routes to Advertising Effectiveness: The Moderating Role of involvement," *Journal of Consumer Research*, in press.

Petty, R.E.; Harkins, S.G.; and Williams, K.D., "The Effects of Group Diffusion of Cognitive Effort on Attitudes: An Information Processing View," *Journal of Personality and Social Psychology* 38 (1980):81-92.

Petty, R.E.; Ostrom, T.M.; and Brock, T.C., eds., *Cognitive Responses in Persuasion* (Hillsdale, N.J.: Erlbaum Associates, 1981).

Petty, R.E.; Wells, G.L.; and Brock, T.C. "Distraction can Enhance or Reduce Yielding to Propaganda: Thought Disruption versus Effort Justification," *Journal of Personality and Social Psychology* 34 (1976):874-884.

Regan, D.T., and Cheng, J.B., "Distraction and Attitude Change: A Resolution," *Journal of Experimental Social Psychology* 9 (1973):138-147.

Sandage, C.H.; Fryburger, V.; and Rotzoll, K., *Advertising Theory and Practice* 10th edition (Homewood, Ill.: Richard E. Irwin, Inc., 1979).

Schlenker, B.R., *Impression Management: The Self-concept, social identity, and interpersonal relations* (Monterey, Calif.: Brooks/Cole, 1980).

Schneider, W., and Shiffrin, R.M., "Controlled and Automatic Human Information Processing: I. Detection, Search and Attention," *Psychological Review* 84 (1977):1-66.

Sherif, C.W.; Sherif, M.; and Nebergall, R.E., *Attitude and Attitude Change: The Social Judgment-Involvement Approach* (Philadelphia: Saunders, 1965).

Sivacek, J., and Crano, W.D., "Vested Interest as a Moderator of Attitude-Behavior Consistency," *Journal of Personality and Social Psychology* 43 (1983):210-221.

Slamecka, N.J., and Graf, P., "The Generation Effect: Delineation of a Phenomenon," *Journal of Experimental Psychology: Human Learning and Memory* 4 (1978):592-604.

Smith, M.J., *Persuasion and human action* (Monterey, Calif.: Brooks/Cole, 1982).

Staats, A.W., and Staats, C.K., "Attitudes Established by Classical Conditioning," *Journal of Abnormal and Social Psychology* 57 (1958): 37-40.

Tesser, A., "Self-Generated Attitude Change," in *Advances in Experimental Social Psychology* (Vol. 11), ed. L. Berkowitz (New York: Academic Press, 1978).

Tesser, A., and Leone, C., "Cognitive Schemas and Thought as Determinants of Attitude Change," *Journal of Experimental Social Psychology* 13 (1977):340-356.

Wells, G.L., and Petty, R.E., "The Effects of Overt Head Movements on Persuasion: Compatibility and Incompatibility of Responses," *Basic and Applied Social Psychology* 1 (1980):219-230.

Wilkin, W.C., and Pessemier, E.A., "Issues in Marketing's Use of Multi-attribute Attitude Models," *Journal of Marketing Research* 10 (0000): 428-441.

Wood, W., "Retrieval of Attitude-Relevant Information from Memory: Effects on Susceptibility to Persuasion and on Intrinsic Motivation," *Journal of Personality and Social Psychology* 42 (1982):798-810.

Wright, P., "Message-Evoked Thoughts: Persuasion Research using Thought Verbalizations," *Journal of Consumer Research* 7 (1980): 151-175.

Wyer, R.S., *Cognitive organization and change: An information processing approach* (Potomac, Md.: Erlbaum Associates, 1974).

Yankelovich Monitor. *Technical Description/Appendix* (New York: Yankelovich, Skelly and White, 1981).

Zanna, M.P.; Kiesler, C.A.; and Pilkonis, P.A., "Positive and Negative Attitudinal Affect Established by Classical Conditioning," *Journal of Personality and Social Psychology* 14 (1970):321-328.

Chapter 2

Ackoff, R.L., and Emshoff, J.R, "Advertising Research at Anheuser-Busch, Inc. (1963-68)," *Sloan Management Review* (Winter 1975), pp. 8-9.

The Advertiser's Handbook, 2d ed. (Scranton, Penn.: International Textbook Co., 1921).

Amstutz, A.E., *Computer Simulation in Competitive Market Response* (Cambridge, Mass.: MIT Press, 1967).

Bartos, R., "Social Research Redefines Marketer's Target Audience," *Marketing News*, May 14, 1982.

Bass, F.M., "The Theory of Stochastic Preference and Brand Switching," *Journal of Marketing Research* 11 (February 1974):1-20.

Bettman, J.R., *An Information Processing Theory of Consumer Choice* (Reading, Mass.: Addison-Wesley, 1979).

Bogart, L., "Research Total Ad Environment as Media Choices Expand," *Marketing News*, May 14, 1982.

Bourne, F.S., "Group Influence in Marketing and Public Relations," in *Some Applications of Behavioral Research*, eds. R. Likert and S.P. Hayes, Jr. (Paris: UNESCO, 1957), pp. 207-257.

Brody, R., and Cunningham, S., "Personality Variables and the Consumer Decision Process," *Journal of Marketing Research* 5 (February 1968): 50-57.

Clark, L., ed., *Consumer Behaivor*, vols. 1 and 2 (New York: New York University Press, 1955).

——— , ed., *Consumer Behavior* (New York: Harper & Row, 1958).

Coleman, J.S., *Introduction to Mathematical Sociology* (London: Free Press, Collier-Macmillan, Ltd., 1964).

Engle, J.; Kollat, D.; and Blackwell, R., *Consumer Behavior* (New York: Holt, Rinehart and Winston, 1968).

Ferber, R., and Wales, H.G., eds., *Motivation and Market Behavior* Homewood, Ill.: Irwin, 1958).

Gatty, R., "Hormones, Body Rhythms, and Motivation," in *Proceedings of Division 23 American Psychological Association*, ed. R. Lutz (Los Angeles: Division 23, Consumer Psychology, American Psychological Association, 1981):54-55.

Gensch, D., "Computer Models in Advertising Media Selection," *Journal of Advertising Research* 8 (November 1968):137-148.

Haire, M., "Projective Techniques in Marketing Research," *Journal of Marketing* 14 (April 1950):649-656.

Hansen, F., *Consumer Choice Behavior: A Cognitive Theory* (New York: Free Press, 1972).

Harris, R.J., ed., *Information Processing Research in Advertising* (Hillsdale, N.J.: Erlbaum, 1982).

Howard, J.A., and Sheth, J.N., *The Theory of Buyer Behavior* (New York: Wiley and Sons, 1969).

Jacobson, R., and Nicosia, F.M., "Advertising and Public Policy: The Macroeconomic Effects of Advertising," *Journal of Marketing Research* 18 (February 1981):29-38.

Jacoby, J., "Personality and Consumer Behavior," *Purdue Papers in Consumer Psychology*, Working Paper #102 (Lafayette, Ind., 1969).

Kanter, D.L., "The Way You Test Advertising Depends upon the Approach the Advertising Itself Takes, Says Researcher," *Advertising Age*, July 15, 1957, pp. 61-62.

Kassarjian, H.H., "Personality and Consumer Behavior: A Review," *Journal of Marketing Research* 8 (November 1971):409-416.

Kelley, H.H., "The Psychotherapeutic Relationship," in *Clinical Psychology and Personality*, ed. B. Maher (New York: Wiley and Sons, 1969), especially pp. 216 and 219.

Koponen, A., "Personality Characteristics of Purchasers," *Journal of Advertising Research* 1 (September 1960):111-122.

Krech, D., and Crutchfield, R.S., *Theory and Problems of Social Psychology* (New York: McGraw-Hill, 1948).

Kroeber-Riel, W., "Activation Research: Psychobiological Approaches in Consumer Research," *Journal of Consumer Research* 5 (September 1979):240-250.

Kuehn, A.A., "Consumer Brand Choice—A Learning Process?," in *Quantitative Techniques in Marketing Analysis*, eds. R.E. Frank, A.A. Kuehn, and W.F. Massy (Homewood, Ill.: Irwin, 1962), pp. 390-403.

Lazarsfeld, P.F., "Sociological Reflections on Business: Consumers and Managers," in *Social Science Research on Business: Product and Potential*, eds. R.A. Dahl, M. Haire, and Lazarsfeld (New York: Columbia University Press, 1959), pp. 99-155.

Lazarus, R.S., "Thoughts on the Relations between Emotion and Cognition," *American Psychologist* 37 (September 1982):1019-1024.

Light, I., "The Era of Emotions," *Marketing News*, September 19, 1980.

Link, H.C., *The New Psychology of Selling and Advertising* (New York: Macmillan, 1932).

Lipstein, B., "A Mathematical Model of Consumer Behavior," *Journal of Marketing Research* 2 (August 1965):259-265.

Macoby, N., and Roberts, D.F., "Cognitive Processes in Persuasion," in *Attitude Research in Transition*, ed. R.I. Haley (Chicago: American Marketing Association, 1972), pp. 18-26.

Markin, R.J., Jr., *Consumer Behavior: A Cognitive Orientation* (New York: Macmillan, 1974).

Massy, W.F.; Montgomery, D.B.; and Morrison, D.G., *Stochastic Models of Buying Behavior* (Cambridge, Mass.: MIT Press, 1970).

Mayer, R., and Foote, N., "Technology, Affluence and Consumers: Searching for Useful Perspectives," in *Technological Change, Product Proliferation and Consumer Decision Processes*, vol. 5, ed. F.M. Nicosia (Washington, D.C.: National Science Foundation, 1975), pp. 58-71.

Mayer, R.N., and Nicosia, F.M., "Social Organization and Changing Consumer Values," in *Management under Differing Value Systems*, eds. G. Dlugos and K. Weirmair (Berlin: Walter de Gruyter, 1981), pp. 191-203.

McGuire, W.J., "An Information Processing Model of Advertising Effectiveness," in *Behavioral and Management Sciences in Marketing*, eds. H. Davis and A. Silk (New York: Wiley, 1978).

Moran, W.T., "Holding and Switching Strategies," in *Production Management Systems and Synthesis*, ed. M.K. Starr (Englewood Cliffs, N.J.: Prentice-Hall, 1972), pp. 191-217. See also Moran, "The Law of Conservation of Advertising Energy," in *Attitude Research Reaches New Heights*, eds. C.W. King and D.J. Tigert, Marketing Research Techniques, Bibliography Series Number 14 (Chicago: American Marketing Association, n.d.), pp. 57-69.

Morgan, J.N., "A Review of Recent Research on Consumer Behavior," in *Consumer Behavior: Research on Consumer Reactions*, ed. L.H. Clark (New York: Harper & Row, 1958), pp. 93-219.

Neisser, U., "On Social Knowing," *Personality and Social Psychology Bulletin* (December 1980).

Newman, J.W., *Motivation Research and Marketing Management* (Boston: Graduate School of Business Administration, Division of Research, Harvard University, 1957.

Nicosia, F.M., *Consumer Decision Processes: Marketing and Advertising Implications* (Englewood Cliffs, N.J.: Prentice-Hall, 1966).

————, "New Developments in Advertising Research: Stochastic Models," *Proceedings, American Association of Public Opinion Research*, Pacific Chapter, Annual Conference (February 1967), pp. 88-96.

————, "Advertising Management: Consumer Behavior and Simulation," *Journal of Advertising Research* 8 (March 1968):29-37.

————, "Brand Choice" (Paper presented to the Symposium on Behavioral and Management Science in Marketing, University of Chicago, December 1969).

———— , *Advertising, Management, and Society: A Business Point of View* (New York: McGraw-Hill, 1974).

———— , *Consumer Coping*, Research proposal, final report in preparation (Washington, D..C.: National Science Foundation, 1977).

———— , "Toward Behavioral-Behavioristic Models," in *Behavioral and Management Science in Marketing*, eds. H.L. Davis and A.J. Sink (New York: Ronald Press, 1978), pp. 136-154.

———— , "What Happened to Motivation in Consumer Psychology?," (Paper presented to the American Psychological Association, Eighty-seventh National Convention, New York, August 1979).

Nicosia, F.M., and Glock, C.Y., "Marketing and Affluence: A Research Prospectus," in *Marketing and the New Science of Planning*, ed. R.L. King (Chicago: American Marketing Association, 1968), pp. 510-527.

Nicosia, F.M., and Mayer, R.N., "Toward A Sociology of Consumption," *Journal of Consumer Research* 3 (September 1976):65-75.

Nicosia, F.M., and Rosenberg, B., "Substantive Modelling in Consumer Attitude Research: Some Practical Uses," in *Attitude Research in Transition*, ed. R.I. Healy (Chicago: American Marketiing Association, 1972).

Nicosia, F.M., and Wind, Y., "Emerging Models of Organizational Buying Processes," *Industrial Marketing Management* 6 (1978):353-369.

Nicosia, F.M., and Witkowsky, T.H., "The Need for a 'Sociology of Consumption'," in *Broadening the Concept of Consumer Behavior*, eds. G. Zaltman and B. Sternthal (Chicago: Association for Consumer Research, 1975), pp. 82-98.

Plummer, J., and Holman, R.H., "Communicating to the Heart and/or Mind," in *Proceedings of the American Psychological Association* (Los Angeles, 1981), pp. 59-62.

Poffenberger, A.T., *Psychology in Advertising* (Chicago and New York: A.W. Shaw Co., 1925).

Preston, I.L., "The Association Model of the Advertising Communication Process," *Journal of Advertising* 11 (1982):61-69.

Pribram, K., "The Biology of Emotions and Other Feelings," in *Emotions: Theory, Research, and Experience*, vol. 1 (New York: Academic Press, 1980).

Robertson, T.S., *Innovative Behavior and Communications* (New York: Holt, Rinehart & Winston, 1971).

Starch, D., *Principles of Advertising* (Chicago: A.W. Shaw, 1923).

———— , *Advertising Principles* (Chicago: A.W. Shaw, 1927).

Stouffer, S.A., et al., *The American Soldier: Adjustment during Army Life* (Princeton, N.J.: Princeton University Press, 1949).

Tetlock, P.E., and Levi, A., "Attribution Bias: On the Inconclusiveness of the Cognition-Motivation Debate," *Journal of Experimental Social Psychology* 18 (January 1982):68-88.

Timiras, P., "Concept of the Mind: From Ontogenesis to Old Age," *Proceedings* (Chicago: Annual Convention of the Association for Consumer Research, 1982), pp. 362-366.

Wells, W., "General Personality Tests and Consumer Behavior," in *On Knowing the Consumer*, ed. J. Newman (New York: Wiley, 1966).

White, P., *Advertising Research* (New York: D. Appleton & Co., 1927).

Zajonc, R.B., "Feeling and Thinking," *American Psychologist* (February 1980):7-36.

Zaltman, G., *Marketing: Contributions from the Behavioral Sciences* (New York: Harcourt, Brace, & World, 1965).

Zaltman, G.; Duncan, R.; and Holbek, J., *Innovations and Organizations* (New York: Wiley, 1973).

Zangwill, W.I. "Media Selection by Decision Programming," *Journal of Advertising Research* 5 (September 1965):113-119.

Chapter 3

DeLozier, M., *The Marketing Communications Process* (New York: McGraw-Hill, 1976).

Jugenheimer, D.W., and White, G.E., *Basic Advertising* (Columbus, Ohio: Grid, 1980).

Robertson, T.S., *Consumer Behavior* (Glenview, Ill.: Scott, Foresman, 1970).

Weilbacher, W.M., *Advertising* (New York: Macmillan, 1979).

Chapter 4

Cohen, J.B., "The Structure of Product Attributes: Defining Attribute Dimensions for Planning and Evaluation," in *Analytic Approaches to Product and Marketing Planning*, ed. A.D. Shocker (Cambridge, Mass.: Marketing Science Institute, 1979), pp. 54-86.

Geistfeld, L.V.; Sproles, G.B.; and Badenhop, S.B., "The Concept and Measurement of a Hierarchy of Product Characteristics," in *Advances in Consumer Research*, vol. 4, ed. K. Hunt (Ann Arbor, Mich.: Association for Consumer Research, 1977), pp. 302-307.

Gutman, J., "Uncovering the Distinctions People Make versus the Use of Multi-attribute Models: Do a Number of Little Truths Make Wisdom?," in *Proceedings of the Twenty-Third Annual Conference of the Advertising Research Foundation* (New York, 1977), pp. 71-76.

_____ , "A Means-End Chain Model Based on Consumer Categorization Processes," *Journal of Marketing* 46 (1982):60-72.

Gutman, J., and Reynolds, T.J., "A Pilot Test of a Logic Model for Investigating Attitude Structure," in *Moving Ahead with Attitude Research*, eds. Y. Wind and M. Greenberg (Chicago: American Marketing Association, 1977), pp. 19-28.

———— , "An Investigation of the Levels of Cognitive Abstraction Utilized by Consumers in Product Differentiation," in *Attitude Research under the Sun*, ed. J. Eighmey (Chicago: American Marketing Association, 1979), pp. 128-150.

Howard, J.A., *Consumer Behavior: Application and Theory* (New York: McGraw-Hill, 1977).

Kelly, G.A., *The Psychology fo Personal Constructs*, vols. 1 and 2 (New York: Norton, 1955).

Myers, J.H., and Shocker, A.D., "The Nature of Product Related Attributes" (Unpublished manuscript, 1980).

Olson, J.C., and Muderrisoglu, A., "The Stability of Responses Obtained by Free Elicitation: Implications for Measuring Attribute Salience and Memory Structure," in *Advances in Consumer Research*, vol. 6, ed. W.L. Wilkie (Ann Arbor, Mich.: Association for Consumer Research, 1979), pp. 269-275.

Rokeach, M.J., *The Nature of Human Values* (New York: Free Press, 1973).

Tolman, E.C., *Purposive Behavior in Animals and Men* (New York: Century Company, 1932).

Wickelgren, W.A. "Human Learning and Memory," in *Annual Review of Psychology* 32 (1981):21-52.

Young, S., and Feigin, B., "Using the Benefit Chain for Improved Strategy Formulation," *Journal of Marketing* 39 (July 1975):72-74.

Chapter 5

Bettman, J.R., *An Information Processing Theory of Consumer Choice* (Reading, Mass.: Addison-Wesley, 1979).

Brock, T.C., "Cognitive Restructuring and Attitude Change," *Journal of Abnormal and Social Psychology* 64 (1962):264-271.

———— , "Communication Discrepancy and Intent to Persuade as Determinants of Counterargument Production," *Journal of Experimental Social Psychology* 3 (1967):296-309.

Cacioppo, J.T.; Harkins, S.G.; and Petty, R.E., "The Nature of Attitudes and Cognitive Responses and Their Relationships to Behavior," in *Cognitive Responses in Persuasion*, eds. R.E. Petty et al. (Hillsdale, N.J.: Erlbaum, 1981), pp. 31-54.

Cacioppo, J.T., and Petty, R.E., "Effects of Message Repetition and Position on Cognitive Responses, Recall, and Persuasion," *Journal of Personality and Social Psychology* 37 (1979):97-109.

Cacioppo, J.T., and Petty, R.E., "Persuasiveness of Communication Is Affected by Exposure Frequency and Message Quality: A Theoretical and Empirical Analysis of Persisting Attitude Change," in *Current Issues and Research in Advertising*, eds. J.H. Leight and C.R. Martin (Ann Arbor: University of Michigan Press, 1980), pp. 81-88.

Cacioppo, J.T., and Petty, R.E., "Social-Psychological Procedures for Cognitive Response Assessment: The Thought Listing Technique," in *Cognitive Assessment*, eds. T.V Merluzzi, C.R. Glass, and M. Genest (New York: Guildford Press, 1981), pp. 114-138.

Cacioppo, J.T., and Sandman, C.A., "Psychophysiological Functioning, Cognitive Responding and Attitudes," in *Cognitive Responses in Persuasion*, eds. R.E. Petty et al. (Hillsdale, N.J.: Erlbaum, 1981), pp. 81-104.

Calder, B.J., and Sternthal, B., "Television Commercial Wearout: An Information Processing View," *Journal of Marketing Research* 17 (1980):173-186.

Cialdini, R.; Levy, A.; Herman, P.; Kozlowski, L.; and Petty, R.E., "Elastic Shifts of Opinion: Determinants of Direction and Durability," *Journal of Personality and Social Psychology* 34 (1976):663-672.

Cook, T.D., "Competence, Counterarguing and Attitude Change," *Journal of Personality* 37 (1969):342-358.

Eagly, A.H., "Comprehensibility of Persuasive Arguments as a Determinant of Opinion Change," *Journal of Personality and Social Psychology* 29 (1974):758-773.

Greenwald, A.G., "Cognitive Learning, Cognitive Response to Persuasion, and Attitude Change," in *Psychological Foundations of Attitudes*, eds. A.G. Greenwald, T.C. Brock, and T.M. Ostrom (New York: Academic Press, 1968).

Greenwald, A.G.; Leavitt, C.; and Obermiller, C., "What Is Low Consumer Involvement?" (Paper presented at the American Psychological Association Convention, Montreal, Canada, 1980).

Harkins, S.G., and Petty, R.E., "Effects of Source Magnification of Cognitive Effort on Attitudes: An Information-Processing View," *Journal of Personality and Social Psychology* 40 (1981):401-413.

Hovland, C.I.; Janis, I.L.; Kelley, H.H., *Communication and Persuasion* (New Haven: Yale University Press, 1953).

Hovland, C.I., and Weiss, W., "The Influence of Source Credibility on Communication Effectiveness," *Public Opinion Quarterly* 15 (1951): 635-650.

Janis, I.L., and Terwillinger, R., "An Experimental Study of Psychological Resistance to Fear-Arousing Communication," *Journal of Abnormal and Social Psychology* 65 (1962):403-410.

Keating, J.P., and Brock, T.C., "Acceptance of Persuasion and Inhibition of Counterargumentation under Various Distraction Tasks," *Journal of Experimental Social Psychology* 10 (1974):301-309.

Krugman, H.E., "The Measurement of Advertising Involvement," *Public Opinion Quarterly* 30 (1967):583-596.

Leavitt, C.; Waddell, C.; and Wells, W., "Improving Day-After Recall Techniques," *Journal of Advertising Research* 10 (1970):13-17.

Markus, H., "Self-Schemata and Processing Information about the Self," *Journal of Personality and Social Psychology* 35 (1977):63-78.

McGuire, W.J., "Personality and Attitude Change: An Information-Processing Theory," in *Psychological Foundations of Attitudes*, eds. A.G. Greenwald, T.C. Brock, and T.M. Ostrom (New York: Academic Press, 1968).

————, "The Nature of Attitudes and Attitude Change," in *Handbook of Social Psychology*, vol. 3, eds. G. Lindzey and E. Aronson (Reading, Mass.: Addison-Wesley, 1969).

Osterhouse, R.A., and Brock, T..C., "Distraction Increases Yielding to Propaganda by Inhibiting Counterarguing," *Journal of Personality and Social Psychology* 15 (1970):344-358.

Ostrom, T.M., and Brock, T.C., "A Cognitive Model of Attitudinal Involvement," in *Theories of Cognitive Consistency: A Sourcebook*, eds. R.P. Abelson et al. (Chicago: Rand McNally, 1968).

Padgett, V.R., "Cognitive Response Analysis of the Persuasiveness of Unintelligible Messages" (Ph.D. dissertation, Ohio State University, 1982).

Perloff, R.M., and Brock, T.C., "And Thinking Makes it So: Cognitive Responses to Persuasion," in *Persuasion: New Directions in Theory and Research*, eds. M.E. Roloff and G.R. Miller (Beverly Hills: Sage, 1980).

Petty, R.E., "A Cognitive Response Analysis of the Temporal Persistence of Attitude Change Induced by Persuasive Communications" (Ph.D. dissertation, Ohio State University, 1977).

Petty, R.E., and Brock, T.C., "Thought Disruption and Persuasion: Asssessing the Validity of Attitude Change Experiments," in *Cognitive Responses in Persuasion*, eds. R.E. Petty, T.M. Ostrom, and T.C. Brock (Hillsdale, N.J.: Erlbaum, 1981).

Petty, R.E., and Cacioppo, J.T., "Forewarning, Cognitive Responding, and Resistance to Persuasion," *Journal of Personality and Social Psychology* 35 (1977):645-655.

————, "Issue Involvement Can Increase or Decrease Persuasion by Enhancing Message Relevant Cognitive Responses," *Journal of Personality and Social Psychology* 37 (1979):1915-1926.

_____ , "Motivational Factors in Consumer Response to Advertisements," in *Human Motivation: Physiological, Behavioral, and Social Approaches*, eds. R. Geen, W. Beatty, and R. Arkin (Boston: Allyn & Bacon, 1983).

Petty, R.E.; Cacioppo, J.T.; and Goldman, R., "Personal Involvement as a Determinant of Argument-Based Persuasion," *Journal of Personality and Social Psychology* 41 (1981):847-855.

Petty, R.E.; Cacioppo, J.T.; and Keesacker, M., "Effects of Rhetorical Questions on Persuasion: A Cognitive Response Analysis," *Journal of Personality and Social Psychology* 40 (1981):847-855.

Petty, R.E.; and Ostrom, T.M.; Brock, T.C., eds., *Cognitive Responses in Persuasion* (Hillsdale, N.J.: Erlbaum, 1981).

Weiss, W., "Modes of Resolution and Reasoning in Attitude Change Experiments," in *Theories of Cognitive Consistency: A Sourcebook*, eds. R. Abelson et al. (Chicago: Rand McNally, 1968).

Wright, P.L., "Message-Evoked Thoughts: Persuasion Research Using Thought Verbalizations," *Journal of Consumer Research* 7 (1980): 151-175.

_____ , "Cognitive Responses to Mass Media Advocacy," in *Cognitive Responses in Persuasion*, eds., R.E. Petty, T.M. Ostrom, and T.C. Brock (Hillsdale, N.J.: Erlbaum, 1981).

Chapter 6

Assael, H., *Consumer Behavior and Marketing Action* (Boston: Kent Publishing Co., 1981).

Baddeley, A.D., "The Trouble with Levels: A Reexamination of Craik and Lockhart's Framework for Memory Research," *Psychological Review* 85 (1978):139-152.

Bettman, J.R., "Memory Factors in Consumer Choice: A Review," *Journal of Marketing* 43 (1979):37-53.

Britt, S.H., "How Advertising Can Use Psychology's Rules of Learning," *Printer's Ink* 252 (1955):74, 77, 80.

_____ , *Psychological Principles of Marketing and Consumer Behavior* (Lexington, Mass.: D.C. Heath and Company, Lexington Books, 1978).

Cermark, L.S., and Craik, F.I.M., *Levels of Processing in Human Memory* (Hillsdale, N.J.: Lawrence Erlbaum Associates, 1979).

Craik, F.I.M., and Lockhart, R.S., "Levels of Processing: A Framework for Memory Research," *Journal of Verbal Learning and Verbal Behavior* 11 (1972):671-684.

Craik, F.I.M., and Tulving, E., "Depth of Processing and the Retention of Words in Episodic Memory," *Journal of Experimental Psychology: General* 104 (1975):268-294.

Heller, N., "An Application of Psychological Learning Theory to Advertising," *Journal of Marketing* 20 (1956):248-254.

Hintzman, D.L., "Repetition and Memory," in *The Psychology of Learning and Motivation*, vol. 10, ed. G.H. Bower (New York: Academic Press, 1976), pp. 47-91.

Hyde, T.S., and Jenkins, J.J., "Recall for Words as a Function of Semantic, Graphic and Syntactic Orienting Tasks," *Journal of Verbal Learning and Verbal Behavior* 12 (1973):471-480.

Jacoby, L.L., Bartz, W.H., and Evans, J.D., "A Functional Approach to Levels of Processing," *Journal of Experimental Psychology: Human Learning and Memory* 4 (1978):331-346.

Krugman, H.E.,, "Why Three Exposures May Be Enough," *Journal of Advertising Research* 12 (1972):51-59.

_____ , "Memory with Recall Exposure without Perception," *Journal of Advertising Research* 17 (1977):7-12.

Lastovicka, J.L, "Questioning the Concept of Involvement Defined Product Classes," in *Advances in Consumer Research*, vol. 6, ed. W.D. Wilkie (Ann Arbor, Mich.: Association for Consumer Research, 1978), pp. 174-179.

Leavitt, C.; Waddell, C.; and Wells, W., "Improving Day-After Recall Techniques," *Journal of Advertising Research* 10 (1970):13-17.

Mowen, J.C., "The Availability Heuristic: The Effect of Imagining the Use of Product on Perceptions," *Proceedings of the American Marketing Association* 18 (1980):172-180.

Nelson, T.D., "Repetition and Depth of Processing," *Journal of Verbal Learning and Verbal Behavior* 16 (1977):151-171.

Olson, J.C., "Theories of Information Encoding and Storage: Implications for Consumer Behavior," in *The Effect of Information on Consumer and Market Behavior*, ed. A.A. Mitchell (Chicago: American Marketing Association, 1978), pp. 154-159.

Reid, L.N., and Soley, L.C., "Levels-of-Processing in Memory and the Recall and Recognition of Television Commercials," in *Current Issues and Research in Advertising*, eds. J.H. Leigh and C.R. Martin (Ann Arbor: Division of Research, Graduate School of Business Administration, University of Michigan, 1980), pp. 135-146.

Saegert, J., "A Demonstration of Levels-of-Processing Theory in Memory for Advertisements," in *Advances in Consumer Research*, vol. 6, ed. W.L. Wilkie (Ann Arbor, Mich.: Association for Consumer Research, 1978), pp. 82-84.

Saegert, J., and Young, R.K., "Comparison of Effects of Repetition and Levels of Processing in Memory for Advertisements," in *Advances in Consumer Research*, vol. 8, ed. L. Wilkie (Ann Arbor, Mich.: Association for Consumer Research, 1981), pp. 431-434.

Sawyer, A.G., "The Effects of Repetition," in *Buyer/Consumer Information Processing*, eds. G.D. Hughes and M.L. Ray (Chapel Hill: University of North Carolina Press, 1974), pp. 202-217.

Seamon, J.G., and Virostek, S., "Memory Performance and Subject-Defined Depth of Processing," *Memory and Cognition* 6 (1978):283-287.

"Should 200 Viewers' Memories Decide Whether Ads Live or Die?," *Wall Steet Journal*, July 24, 1980.

Wickelgren, W.A., "Human Learning and Memory," in *Annual Review of Psychology*, vol. 32, eds. M.R. Rosenzweig and L.W. Porter (Palo Alto, Calif.: Annual Reviews, Inc., 1981), pp. 21-52.

Wright, P.L., "On the Direct Monitoring of Cognitive Response to Advertising," in *Buyer/Consumer Information Processing*, eds. G.D. Hughes and M.L. Ray (Chapel Hill: University of North Carolina Press, 1974), pp. 220-248.

Young, R.K., and Saegert, J., "Further Experiments with Levels of Processing and Advertising Memory," Working Paper no. 18 (San Antonio: College of Business, University of Texas, 1982).

Chapter 7

Chay, R.F., "Single or Multiple Exposures in Measuring Ad Effectiveness: Which Offers Best Results?," *Marketing News* 15 (January 22, 1982):23.

Greenwald, A.G., "Cognitive Learning, Cognitive Response to Persuasion and Attitude Change," in *Psychological Foundations of Attitudes*, eds. A.G. Greenwald, T.C. Brock, and T.M. Ostrom (New York: Academic Press, 1968), pp. 181-203.

Hovland, C.I., "Changes in Attitude through Communication," *Journal of Abnormal and Social Psychology* 46 (1951):424-437.

Krugman, H.T., "The Measurement of Advertising Involvement," *Public Opinion Quarterly* 30 (1967):583-596.

Mitchell, A.A., "Involvement: A Potentially Important Mediator of Consumer Behavior," in *Advances in Consumer Research*, vol. 6, ed. W. Wilkie (Chicago: Association for Consumer Research, 1979), pp. 317-321.

Mitchell, A.A.; Russo, J.E.; and Gardner, M., "Strategy-Induced Low Involvement Processing of Advertising Messages," Working Paper series no. 34 (Chicago: Graduate School of Business, University of Chicago, 1981).

Petty, R.E.; Ostrom, T.M.; and Brock, T.C., "Historical Foundations of the Cognitive Response Approach to Attitudes and Persuasion," in *Cognitive Responses in Persuasion*, eds. R.R. Petty, T.M. Ostrom, and T.C. Brock (Hillsdale, N.J.: Erlbaum, 1981), pp. 5-29.

Wright, P., "Analyzing Media Effects on Advertising Responses," *Public Opinion Quarterly* 38 (1974):192-205.

_____ , "Factors Affecting Cognitive Resistance to Advertising," *Journal of Consumer Research* 2 (1975):60-67.

_____ , "Message-Evoked Thoughts: Persuasion Research Using Thought Verbalizations," *Journal of Consumer Research* 7 (1980):151-175.

Wright, P., and Rip, P., "Product Class Advertising Effects on First-Time Buyers' Decision Strategies," *Journal of Consumer Research* 7 (1980):176-188.

Chapter 8

Anderson, N.H., "Integration Theory and Attitude Change," *Psychological Review* 78 (1971):171-206.

_____ , *Foundations of Information Integration Theory* (New York: Academic Press, 1981).

Anderson, B.F.; Deane, D.H.; Hammond, K.R.; McClelland, G.H.; and Shanteau, J.C., *Concepts in Judgment and Decision Research: Definitions, Sources, Interrelations, Comments* (New York: Praeger, 1981).

Anderson, N.H., and Lopes, L.L., "The Psycholinguistic Aspects of Person Perception," *Memory & Cognition* 2 (1974):67-74.

Anderson, N.H., and Norman, A., "Order Effects in Impression Formation in Four Classes of Stimuli," *Journal of Abnormal and Social Psychology* 69 (1964):467-471.

Assmus, G., "NEWPROD: The Design and Implementation of a New Product Model," *Journal of Marketing Research* 39 (1975):16-23.

Bass, F.M., "A New Product Growth Model for Consumer Durables," *Management Science* 15 (1969):215-227.

Bettman, J.R., *An Information Processing Theory of Consumer Choice* (Reading, Mass.: Addison-Wesley, 1979).

Bettman, J.R.; Capon, N.; and Lutz, R.J., "Multiattribute Measurement Models and Multiattribute Attitude Theory: A Test of Construct Validity," *Journal of Consumer Research* 1 (1975):1-15.

Birnbaum, M.H., and Mellers, B.A., "Bayesian Inference: Combining Base Rates with Opinions of Sources Who Vary in Credibility" (Unpublished manuscript, University of Illinois, 1982).

Brien, M., "Consumer Involvement in Health Care Evaluation and Decision Making" (Ph.D. dissertation, Kansas State University, 1979).

Butzin, C.A., and Anderson, N.H., "Functional Measurement of Children's Judgments," *Child Development* 44 (1973):529-537.

Colley, R.H., *Defining Advertising Goals for Measured Advertising Results* (New York: Association of National Advertisers, 1961).

Dawes, R.M., and Corrigan, B., "Linear Models in Decision Making," *Psychological Bulletin* 81 (1974):95-106.

"Disposable Diapers," *Consumer Reports* (January 1968), pp. 36-38.

Ettenson, R.T., "The Acquisition of Expertise in Auditing: A Judgmental Analysis" (Master's thesis, Kansas State University, 1981).

Fishbein, M., and Ajzen, I., *Belief, Attitude, Intention, and Behavior: An Introduction to Theory and Research* (Reading, Mass.: Addison-Wesley, 1975).

Gaeth, G.J., and Shanteau, "Reducing the Influence of Irrelevant Information on Experienced Decision Makers," *Organizational Behavior and Human Performance*, 32, in press.

Gottman, J.M., *Marital Interaction: Experimental Investigations* (New York: Academic Press, 1979).

Gottman, J., and Reynolds, T.J., "A Pilot Test of a Logic Model for Investigating Attitude Structure," Working Paper no. 27 (Los Angeles: University of Southern California, 1975).

Haley, R.I., and Casey, C.B., "Testing Thirteen Attitude Scales for Agreement and Brand Discrimination," *Journal of Marketing* 43 (1979): 20-32.

Kotler, P., *Marketing Management Analysis, Planning and Control*, 4th ed. (Englewood Cliffs, N.J.: Prentice-Hall, 1980).

Krugman, H.E., "The Impact of Television Advertising: Learning without Involvement," *Public Opinion Quarterly* 29 (1965):349-356.

Lavidge, R.J., and Steiner, G.A., "A Model for Predictive Measurements of Advertising Effectiveness," *Journal of Marketing* 24 (1961):59-62.

Levin, I.P., "Averaging Processes in Ratings and Choices Based on Numerical Information," *Memory & Cognition* 2 (1974):786-790.

Levin, I.P., and Herring, R.D., "Functional Measurement of Qualitative Variables in Mode Choice: Ratings of Economy, Safety, and Desirability of Flying versus Driving," *Transportation Research* 15A (1981): 207-214.

Levin, I.P., and Louviere, J.J., "Psychological Contributions to Travel Demand Modeling," in *Human Behavior and the Environment: Current Theory and Research*, vol. 5, eds. I. Altman, P.B. Everett, and J.F. Wohlwill (New York: Pergamon Press, 1982), pp. 203-226.

Levin, I.P.; Wall, L.R.; Dolezal, J.M.; and Norman, K.L., "Differential Weighting of Positive and Negative Traits in Impression Formation as a Function of Prior Exposure," *Journal of Experimental Psychology* 97 (1973):114-115.

Louviere, J.J., and Kocur, G., *Analysis of User Cost and Service Tradeoffs in Transit and Paratransit Services*, Final report (Washington, D.C.: U.S. Department of Transportation (U.M.T.A.) Office of Service and Methods Demonstration, 1970), pp. 346-366.

Mahajan, V., and Muller, E., "Innovation Diffusion and New Product Growth Models in Marketing," *Journal of Marketing* 43 (1979):55-68.

McElwee, J.R., and Parsons, L.J., "The Cognitive Algebra of the Parametric Marginal Desirability Model: A Research Note," *Journal of Marketing Research* 14 (1977):257-260.

McGuire, W.J., "Some Internal Psychological Factors Influencing Consumer Choice," *Journal of Consumer Research* 2 (1976):302-319.

Meyer, R.J.; Levin, I.P.; and Louviere, J.J., "Functional Analysis of Mode Choice," *Transportation Research Record*, no. 673 (1978), pp. 1-7.

Norman, K.L., "A Solution for Weights and Scale Values in Functional Measurement," *Psychological Review* 83 (1976):80-84.

_____ , "Attributes in Bus Transportation: Importance Depends on Trip Purpose," *Journal of Applied Psychology* 62 (1977):164-170.

Oden, G.C., and Anderson, N.H., "Differential Weighting in Integration Theory," *Journal of Experimental Psychology* 89 (1971):152-161.

Park, C.W., "The Effect of Individual and Situation-Related Factors on Consumer's Selection of Judgmental Models," *Journal of Marketing Research* 13 (1976):144-151.

Phelps, R.H., "Expert Livestock Judgment: A Descriptive Analysis of the Development of Expertise" (Ph.D. dissertation, Kansas State University, 1977).

Ptacek, C.H., Personal communication on a proprietary report prepared in 1974.

Reich, J.W.; Ferguson, J.M.; and Weinberger, M.G., "An Information Integration Analysis of Retail Store Image," *Journal of Applied Psychology* 62 (1977):609-614.

Risky, D.R., and Birnbaum, M.H., "Compensatory Effects in Moral Judgment: Two Rights Don't Make up for a Wrong," *Journal of Experimental Psychology* 103 (1974):171-173.

Shanteau, J., "The Concept of Weight in Judgment and Decision Making: A Review and Some Unifying Propposals," Tech. rept. no. 228 (Denver: Center for Research on Judgment and Policy, University of Colorado, 1980).

_____ , "Cognitive Psychology Looks at Advertising: Commentary on a Hobbit's Adventure," in *Information Processing Research in Advertising*, ed. R.J. Harris (Hillsdale, N.J.: Erlbaum, 1973), pp. 302-319.

Shanteau, J., and Anderosn, N.H., "Test of a Conflict Model for Preference Judgment," *Journal of Mathematical Psychology* 6 (1969): 312-325.

Shanteau, J., and Ptacek, C.H., "Situation Determinants of Consumer Decision Making," in *Consumer Psychology Proceedings II*, ed. C. Leavitt (Columbus: APA Division 23, 1978):19-20.

Shanteau, J., and Troutman, C.M., "Commentary on Bettman, Capon, and Lutz," *Journal of Consumer Research* 1 (1975):16-18.

Shanteau, J.; Troutman, C.M.; and Ptacek, C.H., "Averaging Processes in Consumer Decision-Making," *Great Plains-Rocky Mountain Geographical Journal* 6 (1977):86-99.

Smith, R.E., and Swinyard, W.R., "Information Response Model: An Integrated Approach," *Journal of Marketing* 46 (1982):81-93.

Troutman, C.M., "Processes in Husband-Wife Decision-Making on Health Care Factors" (Ph.D. dissertation, Kansas State University, 1977).

Troutman, C.M., and Shanteau, J., "Do Consumers Evaluate Products by Adding or Averaging Attribute Information?," *Journal of Consumer Research* 3 (1976):101-106.

Wilkie, W.L., and Pessimier, E.A., "Issues in Marketing Use of Multi-attribute Attitude Models," *Journal of Marketing Research* 10 (1973): 428-441.

Chapter 9

Begg, I., and Paivio, A., "Concreteness and Imagery in Sentence Meaning," *Journal of Verbal Learning and Verbal Behavior* 8 (1969):821-827.

Brown, W.P. and Ure, D.M.J. (1969), "Five Rated Characteristics of 650 Word Association Stimuli," *British Journal of Psychology* 60, 233-249.

Bugelski, B.R., "Words and Things and Images," *American Psychologist* 25 (1970):1001-1012.

——, "Imagery and Verbal Behavior," *Journal of Mental Imagery* 1 (1977):39-52.

Calder, B.J., "Cognitive Response, Imagery, and Scripts: What Is the Cognitive Basis of Attitude?," in *Advances in Consumer Research,* vol 5, ed. H.K. Hunt (Ann Arbor, Mich.: Association for Consumer Research, 1978), pp. 630-634.

Deese, J.E., *Psycholinguistics* (Boston: Allyn & Bacon, 1970).

Dooley, R.P., and Harkins, L.E., "Functional and Attention-Getting Effects of Color Graphic Communications," *Perceptual and Motor Skills* 31 (1970):851-854.

Evans, G.W., "Environmental Cognition," *Psychological Bulletin* 88 (1980):259-287.

Fishbein, M., and Ajzen, I., *Beliefs, Attitude, Intention, and Behavior* (Reading, Massachusetts: Addison-Wesley, 1975).

Glanzer, M., and Clark, W.H., "Accuracy of Perceptual Recall: An Analysis of Organization," *Journal of Verbal Learning and Verbal Behavior* 5 (1962):289-299.

Goldman-Eisler, F., and Cohen, M., "Symmetry of Clauses and the Psychological Significance of Left Branching," *Language and Speech* 14 (1971):109-114.

Greenwald, A.G., "Cognitive Learning, Cognitive Response to Persuasion, and Attitude Change," in *Psychological Foundations of Attitudes,* eds. Greenwald, T.C. Brock, and T.M. Ostrom. (New York: Academic Press, 1968), pp. 147-170.

Hakes, D.T., and Cairns, H.S., "Sentence Comprehension and Relative Pronouns," *Perception and Psychophysics* 8 (1970):5-8.

Hakes, D.T., and Foss, D.J., "Decision Processes during Sentence Comprehension: Effects of Surface Structure Reconsidered," *Perception and Psychophysics* 8 (1970):413-416.

Hamilton, H.W., and Deese, J., "Comprehensibility and Subject Verb Relation in Complex Sentences," *Journal of Verbal Learning and Verbal Behavior* 10 (1971):163-170.

Holyoak, K., "The Role of Imagery in the Evaluation of Sentences: Imagery or Semantic Relatedness?" *Journal of Verbal Learning and Verbal Behavior* 13 (1974):163-166.

Hulse, S.H., Deese, J., and Egeth, H., *The Psychology of Learning,* 4th ed. (New York: McGraw-Hill, 1975).

Jorgensen, C.C., and Kintsch, W., "The Role of Imagery in the Evaluation of Sentences," *Cognitive Psychology* 4 (1973):110-116.

Kellogg, R.T., "Is Conscious Attention Necessary for Long-Term Storage?" *Journal of Experimental Psychology: Human Learning and Memory* 6 (1980):379-390.

Kosslyn, S.M., "The Medium and the Message in Mental Imagery: A Theory," *Psychological Review* 88 (1981):46-66.

Kosslyn, S.M., and Alper, S.N., "On the Pictorial Properties of Visual Images: Effects of Image Size on Memory for Words," *Canadian Journal of Psychology* 31 (1977):32-40.

McGuire, W.J., "Some Psychological Factors Influencing Consumer Choice," *Journal of Consumer Research* 2 (1976):302-319.

Miller, J.F., "Sentence Imitation in Preschool Children," Language and Speech 16 (1973):1-14.

Mitchell, A.A., and Olson, J.C., "Cognitive Effects of Advertising Repetition," in *Advances in Consumer Research,* vol 4, ed. W.D. Perrault, Jr. (Atlanta, Ga.: Association for Consumer Research, 1977), pp. 213-220.

———— , "Are Product Attribute Beliefs the Only Mediator of Advertising Effects on Brand Attitude?," *Journal of Marketing Research* 18 (1981):318-332.

Olson, J.C., and Dover, P.A., "Attitude Maturation: Changes in Related Belief Structures over Time," in Hunt, H.K. (ed), *Advances in Consumer Research,* vol. 5, ed. H.K. Hunt (Ann Arbor, Mich.: Association for Consumer Research, 1978), pp. 333-342.

Osgood, C.E., "Exploration in Semantic Space: A Personal Diary," *Journal of Social Issues* 27 (1971):5-64.

Osgood, C.E., Suci, G.J., and Tannenbaum, P.H., *The Measurement of Meaning* (Urbana: University of Illinois Press, 1957).

Paivio, A., "Mental Imagery in Associative Learning and Memory," *Psychological Review* 76 (1969):241-263.

_____ , *Images and Verbal Processes* (New York: Holt, Rinehart & Winston, 1971).

_____ , "A Dual Coding Approach to Perception and Cognition," in *Modes of Perceiving and Processing Information,* eds. H.I. Pick and E. Saltzman (Hillsdale, N.J.: Lawrence Erlbaum Associates, 1978), pp. 39-51.

Percy, L., "Psycholinguistic Guidelines for Advertising Copy," in *Advances in Consumer Research,* vol. 9, ed. A.A. Mitchell (Ann Arbor, Mich.: Association for Consumer Research, 1982).

Percy, L., and Rossiter, J.R., *Advertising Strategy: A Communication Theory Approach* (New York: Praeger, 1980).

Pezdek, K., and Evans, G.W., "Visual and Verbal Memory for Objects and Their Spatial Locations," *Journal of Experimental Psychology: Human Learning and Memory* 5 (1979):360-373.

Pollio, H.R., *The Psychology of Symbolic Activity* (Reading, Mass.: Addison-Wesley, 1974).

Postman, L., "Effects of Word Frequency on Acquisition and Retention under Conditions of Free Recall Learning," *Quarterly Journal of Experimental Psychology* 22 (1970):185-195.

Richardson, A., *Mental Imagery* (New York: Springer, 1969).

Rossiter, J.R., and Percy, L., "Visual Imagery Ability as a Mediator of Advertising Response," in *Advances in Consumer Research,* vol 5, ed. H.K. Hunt (Ann Arbor, Mich.: Association for Consumer Research, 1978), pp. 621-628.

_____ , "Attitude Change through Visual Imagery in Advertising," *Journal of Advertising* 9 (1980):10-16.

_____ , "Visual Communication in Advertising," in *Information Processing Research in Advertising,* ed. J.R. Harris (Hillsdale, N.J.: Lawrence Erlbaum Associates, 1982).

Sheehan, R., "The Relation of Visual Imagery to True-False Judgment of Simple Sentences" (Master's thesis, University of Western Ontario, 1970).

Shepard, R.N., "Recognition Memory for Words, Sentences, and Pictures," *Journal of Verbal Learning and Verbal Behavior* 6 (1967):156-163.

Slobin, D.I., *Psycholinguistics* (Glenview, Ill.: Scott, Foresman, 1971).

Sparkman, R., and Austin, L.M., "The Effect on Sales of Color in Newspaper Advertisements," *Journal of Marketing* 9 (1980):39-42.

Staats, C.K., and Staats, A.W., "Meaning Established by Classical Conditioning," *Journal of Experimental Psychology* 54 (1957):74-80.

Toglia, M.P., and Battig, W.F., *Handbook of Semantic Word Norms* (Hillsdale, N.J.: Lawrence Erlbaum Associates, 1978).

Wang, W.D., "The Role of Syntactic Complexity as a Determiner of Comprehensibility," *Journal of Verbal Learning and Verbal Behavior* 9 (1970):398-404.

Wason, P.C., and Johnson-Laird, P.N., *Psychology of Reasoning* (Cambridge: Harvard University Press, 1972).

Wearing, A.J., "The Recall of Sentences of Varying Length," *Australian Journal of Psychology* 25 (1973):155-161.

Wright, P., "Concrete Action Plans in TV Messages to Increase Reading of Drug Warnings," *Journal of Consumer Research* 6 (1979):256-269.

Yuille, J.C., and Paivio, A., "Abstractness and Recall of Connected Discourse," *Journal of Experimental Psychology* 82 (1969):467-471.

Chapter 10

Anderson, J.R., *Language, Memory and Thought* (Hillsdale, N.J.: Lawrence Erlbaum Associates, 1976).

Anderson, J.R., and Reder, L., "An Elaborative Processing Explanation of Depth of Processing," in *Levels of Processing in Human Memory,* eds. L.S. Cermak and F.I.M. Craik (Hillsdale, N.J.: Lawrence Erlbaum Associates, 1979), pp. 161-175.

Bower, G.H., "Mood and Memory," *American Psychologist* 36 (1980): 129-148.

Bower, G.H., and Cohen, P.R., "Emotional Influences in Memory and Thinking," in *Affect and Cognition*, eds. M.S. Clark and S.T. Fiske (Hillsdale, N.J.: Lawrence Erlbaum Associates, 1982), pp. 301-317.

Bower and Karlin, "Depth of Processing Pictures of Faces and Recognition Memory," *Journal of Experimental Psychology* 103 (1974):751-757.

Bower, G.H.; Monteiro, K.P.; and Gilligan, S.G., "Emotional Mode as a Context for Learning and Recall," *Journal of Verbal Learning and Verbal Behavior* 17 (1978):573-578.

Broadhurst, P.L., "Emotionality and the Yerkes-Dodson Law," *Journal of Experimental Psychology* 54 (1957):345-352.

Brooks, L.R., "Spacial and Verbal Components of the Act of Recall," *Canadian Journal of Psychology* 22 (1968):349-360.

Clark, M.S., "A Role for Arousal in the Link between Feeling States, Judgments, and Behavior," in *Affect and Cognition*, eds. M.S. Clark, and S.T. Fiske (Hillsdale, N.J.: Lawrence Erlbaum Associates, 1982), pp. 263-289.

Clark, M.S., and Isen, A.M., "Toward Understanding the Relationship between Feeling States and Social Behavior," in *Cognitive Social Psychology*, eds. A. Hastorf and M.A. Isen (New York: Elsevier North-Holland, 1982), pp. 302-320.

Collins, A.M., and Loftus, E.F., "A Spreading Activation Theory of Semantic Processing," *Psychological Review* 82 (1976):407-420.

Easterbrook, T.A., "The Effect of Emotion on Cue Utilization and the Organization of Behavior," *Psychological Review* 66 (1959):183-201.

Edell, J., "The Information Processing of Pictures in Print Advertisements" (Ph.D. dissertation, Graduate School of Industrial Administration, Carnegie-Mellon University, 1982).

Eysenck, M., *Attention and Arousal* (New York: Springer-Verlag, 1982).

Fishbein, M., and Ajzen, I., *Belief, Attitude, Intention, and Behavior* (Reading, Mass.: Addison-Wesley, 1975).

Fiske, S.T., "Social Cognition and Affect," in *Cognition, Social Behavior and the Environment*, ed. J.H. Harvey (Hillsdale, N.J.: Lawrence Erlbaum Associates, 1981), pp. 227-264.

Frederickson, C.H., "Effects of Context-Induced Processing Operations on Semantic Information Acquired from Discourse," *Cognitive Psychology* 7, (1975):139-166.

Gardner, M., "An Information Processing Approach to Examining Advertising Effects," (Ph.D. dissertation, Graduate School of Industrial Adminstration, Carnegie-Mellon University, 1981).

Gorn, G.J., "The Effects of Music in Advertising on Choice Behavior: A Classical Conditioning Approach," *Journal of Marketing* 46 (1982):94-101.

Graesser, A.C., *Prose Comprehension beyond the Word* (New York: Springer-Verlag, 1981).

Greenwald, A.G., "Cognitive Learning, Cognitive Response to Persuasion and Attitude Change" in *Psychological Foundations of Attitudes*, eds. Greenwald, T.C. Brock, and T.M. Ostrom (New York: Academic Press, 1968), pp. 147-170.

Hayes-Roth, F., "The Role of Partial and Best Matches in Knowledge Systems," in *Pattern-Directed Inference Systems,* eds. D.A. Waterman and F. Hayes-Roth (New York: Academic Press, 1978), pp. 557-576.

Isen, A.M.; Manns, B.; Patrick, R.; and Nowicki, G., "Some Factors Influencing Decision-Making Strategy and Risk Taking," in *Affect and*

Cognition, eds. M.S. Clarke and S.T. Fiske (Hillsdale, N.J.: Lawrence Erlbaum Associates, 1982), pp. 243-262.

Isen, A.M.; Shalker, T.E., Clark, M., and Karp, L., "Affect, Accessibility of Material in Memory and Behavior: A Cognitive Loop?," *Journal of Personality and Social Behavior* 36 (1978):1-12.

Johnson, E.J., and Tversky, A., "Affect, Generalization, and the Perception of Risk," *Journal of Personality and Social Psychology* vol. 40 (1982):54-61.

Kahneman, D., *Attention and Effort* (Englewood Cliffs, N.J.: Prentice-Hall, 1973).

Kintsch, W., and Van Dijk, T.A., "Towards a Model of Discourse Comprehension and Production," *Psychological Review* 85 (1978):363-394.

Kisielius, J., "The Role of Memory in Understanding Advertising Media Effectiveness: The Effect of Imagery on Consumer Decision Making," in *Advances in Consumer Research,* vol. 9, ed. A.A. Mitchell (Ann Arbor: Association for Consumer Research, 1982), pp. 182-186.

Klatzky, R.L., and Rafnel, K., "Labeling Effects on Memory for Nonsense Pictures," *Memory and Cognition* 4 (1976):717-720.

Lutz, R.J., "Changing Brand Attitudes through Modification of Cognitive Structure," *Journal of Consumer Research* 1 (1975):49-59.

Malmo, R.B., "Activation: A Neuropsychological Dimension," *Psychological Review* 66 (1959):367-386.

Mandler, G., "Organization and Repetition: Organizational Principles with Special Reference to Rote Learning," in *Perspectives on Memory Research,* ed. L. Nilsson (Hillsdale, N.J.: Lawrence Erlbaum Associates, 1979), pp. 291-328.

_____ , *Mind and Emotion* (New York: Wiley & Sons, 1975).

Mitchell, A.A., "Using an Information Processing Approach to Understand Advertising Effects," in *Advances in Consumer Research,* vol. 7, ed. J. Olson, (Ann Arbor: Association for Consumer Research, 1980), pp. 356-359.

_____ , "Cognitive Processes Initiated by Exposure to Advertising," in *Information Processing Research in Advertising,* ed. R. Harris (Hillsdale, N.J.: Lawrence Erlbaum Associates, 1982a).

_____ , "The Effect of Verbal and Visual Components in Advertisements on Attitude toward the Advertisement" (Working paper, Graduate School of Industrial Administration, Carnegie-Mellon University, Pittsburgh, 1982b).

_____ , "Variables Mediating Advertising Effects under Different Process-Conditions" (Working paper, Graduate School of Industrial Administration, Carnegie-Mellon University, Pittsburgh, 1982c).

Mitchell, A.A., and Dasgupta, N., "The Stability of Brand Attitudes Based on Attitude toward the Advertisement Effects'' (Working paper, Graduate School of Industrial Administration, Carnegie-Mellon University, Pittsburgh, 1982).

Mitchell, A.A.; Gardner, M.; and Russo, J.E., "Strategy-Induced Low Involvement Processing of Advertising Messages'' (Working paper, Graduate School of Industrial Administration, Carnegie-Mellon University, Pittsburgh, 1981).

Mitchell, A.A., and Olson, J.C., "Are Product Attribute Beliefs the Only Mediator of Advertising on Brand Attitudes," *Journal of Marketing Research* vol. 18 (1981):318-332.

Nisbett, R., and Ross, L., *Human Inference: Strategies and Short Comings of Social Judgment* (Englewood Cliffs, N.J.: Prentice-Hall, 1980).

Olson, J.C., and Mitchell, A.A., "The Process of Attitude Acquisition: The Value of a Developmental Approach to Consumer Attitude Research," in *Advances in Consumer Research*, vol. 2, ed. M.J. Schlinger (Chicago: Association for Consumer Research, 1975), pp. 240-246.

Paivio, A., *Imagery and Verbal Processes* (New York: Academic Press, 1971.

Posner, M.I., "Abstraction and the Process of Recognition," in *Advances in Learning and Motivation*, vol. 3, eds. J.T. Spence and G.H. Bower (New York: Academic Press, 1969), pp. 117-131.

Posner, M.I.; Boies, S.J.; Eichelman, W.H.; and Taylor, R.C., "Retention of Visual and Name Codes of Single Letters," *Journal of Experimental Psychology* 79 (1969):212-226.

Posner, M.I., and Snyder, C.R., "Attention and Cognitive Control," in *Information Processing and Cognition: The Loyola Symposium*, ed. R.L. Solso (Hillsdale, N.J.: Lawrence Erlbaum Associates, 1975), pp. 271-301.

Roseman, I., "Cognitive Aspects of Emotion and Emotional Behavior" (Paper presented at the Eighty-Seventh Annual Convention of the American Psychological Association, 1979).

Rossiter, J.R., "Visual Imagery: Applications to Advertising," in *Advances in Consumer Research*, vol. 9, ed. A.A. Mitchell (Ann Arbor: Association for Consumer Research, 1982), pp. 101-106.

Rossiter, J.R., and Percy, L., "Visual Imagining Ability as a Mediator of Advertising Response," in *Advances in Consumer Research*, vol. 5, ed. H.K. Hunt (Ann Arbor: Association for Consumer Research, 1978), pp. 621-629.

——— , "Visual Communication in Advertising," in *Information Processing Research in Advertising*, ed. R.J. Harris (Hillsdale, N.J.: Lawrence Erlbaum Associates, 1983, forthcoming).

Schachter, S., "The Interaction of Cognitive and Physiological Determinants of Emotional State," in *Advances in Experimental Social Psychology*, ed. L. Berkowitz (New York: Academic Press, 1964), pp. 62-63.

Schachter, S., and Singer, J., "Cognitive, Social and Physiological Determinants of Emotional State," *Psychological Review* 69 (1962):379-399.

Schneider, W., and Shiffren, R.M., "Controlled and Automatic Human Information Processing: I. Detection, Search, and Attention," *Psychological Review* 84 (1977):1-66.

Silk, A.J., and Vavra, T.G., "The Influence of Advertising's Affective Qualities on Consumer Response," in *Buyer/Consumer Information Processing*, eds. G.D. Hughes and M.L. Ray (Chapel Hill: University of North Carolina Press, 1974), pp. 157-186.

Staats, A.W., and Staats, C., "Attitudes Established by Classical Conditioning," in *Readings in Attitude Theory and Measurement*, ed. M. Fishbein (New York: Wiley & Sons, 1967), pp. 337-381.

Taylor, S.E., and Thompson, S.C., "Stalking the Elusive 'Vividness' Effect," *Psychological Review* 89 (1982):155-181.

Tesser, A., "Self Generated Attitude Change," in *Advances in Experimental Social Psychology*, vol 11, ed. L. Berkowitz (New York: Academic Press, 1978), pp. 289-338.

Weiner, B., "The Emotional Consequences of Causal Attributions," in *Affect and Cognition*, eds. M.S. Clark and S.T. Fiske (Hillsdale, N.J.: Lawrence Erlbaum Associates, 1982), pp. 185-210.

Wickelgren, W.A., "Human Learning and Memory," in *Annual Review of Psychology*, eds. M.P. Rosenzweig and L.W. Porter (Palo Alto: Annual Review, Inc., 1981), pp. 21-52.

Wiseman, G., and Neisser, U., "Perceptual Organization as a Determinant of Visual Recognition Memory," *American Journal of Psychology* 87 (1974):675-681.

Wright, P.L., "Cognitive Processes Mediating Acceptance of Advertising," *Journal of Marketing Research* 4 (1973):53-62.

Zajonc, R.B., "Attitude Effect of Mere Exposure," *Journal of Personality and Social Psychology Monograph Supplement* 9 (1968):1-27.

_____ , "Feeling and Thinking: Preferences Need No Inferences," *American Psychologist* 35 (1980):151-175.

Zielske, H.A., "Does Day-After Recall Penalize 'Feeling' Ads?," *Journal of Advertising Research* 22 (1982):19-24.

Chapter 11

Beaber, R.J., and Miller, N., "The Effects of Speech Rate on Attitude Change," (Unpublished manuscript, University of Southern California, 1974). Cited by Miller, N.; Maruyama, G.; Beaber, R.J.; and Valone, K., "Speed of Speech and Persuasion," *Journal of Personality and Social Psychology* 14 (1976):615-624.

Dougherty, P.H., "Condensing Commercial Lengths," *The New York Times*, May 29, 1979.

Fairbanks, G.; Guttman, N.; and Miron, M.S., "Auditory Comprehension of Repeated High-Speed Messages," *Journal of Speech and Hearing Disorders* 22 (1957a):20-22.

_____ , "Auditory Comprehension in Relation to Listening Rate and Selective Verbal Redundancy," *Journal of Speech and Hearing Disorders* 22 (1957b):23-32.

_____ , "Effects of Time-Compression upon the Comprehension of Connected Speech," *Journal of Speech and Hearing Disorders* 22 (1957c):10-19.

Fergen, G.K., "Listening Comprehension at Controlled Rates for Children in Grades IV, V and VI" *Dissertation Abstracts* 15 (1955):89.

Foulke, E., *The Comprehension of Rapid Speech by the Blind—Part III*, Interim Progress Report, Cooperative Research Project no. 2430 (Washington, D.C.: U.S. Department of Health, Education and Welfare, Office of Education, 1967).

Foulke, E., and Sticht, T.G., "Review of Research on the Intelligibility and Comprehension of Accelerated Speech," *Psychological Bulletin* 72 (1969):50-62.

Grass, R.C.; Winters, L.C.: and Wallace, W.H., "Communication Effectiveness of Advertising: A Method of Pretesting," *Proceedings of the 79th Annual Convention of the American Psychological Association* 6 (1971):659-660.

Honomichl, J.J., "TV Copy Testing Flap: What to Do about It?," *Advertising Age*, January 19, 1981, pp. 59-61.

LaBarbera, P., and MacLachlan, J., "Time-Compressed Speech in Radio Advertising," *Journal of Marketing* 43 (January 1979):30-36.

Lautman, M.R.; Edwards, M.T.; and Farrell, B., "Predicting Direct-Mail Response from Mall Intercept Data," *Journal of Advertising Research* 21 (1981):31-34.

Lautman, M.R.; Percy, L.H.; and Kordish, G.R., "Campaigns from Multidimensional Scaling," *Journal of Advertising Research* 18 (1978):35-40.

Lumley, F.H., "Rates of Speech in Radio Speaking," *Quarterly Journal of Speech* 19 (1933):393-403.

MacLachlan, J., "What People Really Think of Fast Talkers," *Psychology Today* (November 1979), pp. 113-117.

_____ , "Time-Compressed Commercials," *Video Systems*, (July 1980), pp. 20-23.

MacLachlan, J., and LaBarbera, P., "Time-Compressed Speech TV Commercials," *Journal of Advertising Research* 18 (August 1978):11-15.

_____ , "Time-Compressed Advertising: What Do We Know, Where Do

We Go?,'' *Proceedings of the AMA Educators Conference*, 1979, pp. 154-158.

MacLachlan, J., and Siegel, M.H., ''Reducing the Costs of TV Commercials by Use of Time-Compressions,'' *Journal of Marketing Research* 17 (February 1980):52-57.

McCracken, S.R., ''Comprehension for Immediate Recall of Time-Compressed Speech as a Function of Sex and Level of Activation of the Listener,'' *Proceedings of the Second Louisville Conference on Rate and/or Frequency-Controlled Speech,* October 22-24, 1969, pp. 313-319.

McMaham, H., and Kile, M., ''Testing Copy Research: An Old, Nasty Sore,'' *Advertising Age,* August 3, 1981, p. 40.

Miller, N.; Maruyama, G.; Beaber, R.J.; and Valone, K., ''Speed of Speech and Persuasion,'' *Journal of Personality and Social Psychology* 14 (1976):615-624.

Myerson, M.D., ''An Exploration of Comprehension Differences in Time-Compressed Japanese, Chinese, Hindi and English Speech,'' in *Time-Compressed Speech: An Anthology and Bibliography in Three Volumes*, vol. 2, ed. Sam Duker (Metuchen, N.J.: Scarecrow Press, 1974), pp. 716-729.

Nichols, P.G., and Stevens, L.A., *Are You Listening?* (New York: McGraw-Hill, 1957).

Orr, D.B., and Friedman, H.L., ''Research on Speeded Speech as an Educational Medium,'' (Progress report, grant no. 7-48-7670-203 (Washington, D.C.: U.S. Department of Health, Education and Welfare, Department of Education, 1964).

Pringle, L., ''Time-Compression,'' *BBDO Magazine* (May 1980), pp. 8-11.

Sticht, T.G., ''Comprehension of Repeated Time-Compressed Recordings,'' *Journal of Experimental Education* 37 (1969a):60-62.

———, ''Learning by Listening in Relation to Aptitude, Reading, and Rate-Controlled Speech,'' Human Resources Research Organization Technical report 69-23, December 1969b.

———, ''Learning by Listening in Relation to Aptitude, Reading and Rate-Controlled Speech: Additional Studies,'' Human Resources Research Organization Technical report 71-5, April 1971.

Wheeless, L.R., ''Some Effects of Time-Compressed Speech on Persuasion,'' *Journal of Broadcasting* 15 (1971):415-420.

Chapter 12

Appel, V.; Weinstein, S.; and Weinstein, C., ''Letters to the Editor,'' *Journal of Advertising Research* 19 (October 1979a):70.

_____ , "Brain Activity and Recall of TV Advertising," *Journal of Advertising Research* (August 1979b):7-15.

Berger, H., "Über das Elektrenkephalogramm des Menschen," *Archiv für Psychiatrie und Nervenkrankheiten* 87 (1929):527-570.

Cacioppo, J.T., and Petty, R.E., "The Relationship between Differential Hemispheric Alpha Adundance and the Affective Polarization of Thoughts about an Attitude Issue," *Advances in Consumer Research,* in press.

Caton, R., "The Electric Currents of the Brain," *British Medical Journal* 2 (1875):278.

Davidson, R.J.; Schwartz, G.E.; Bennett, J.; and Goleman, D.J., "Frontal Versus Parietal EEG Asymmetry during Positive and Negative Affect," *Psychophysiology* 16 (1979):202-203.

Dimond, S.J., and Beaumont, J.G., "Difference in the Vigilance Performance of the Right and Left Hemispheres," *Cortex* 9 (1973):259-265.

Donchin, E.; Kutas, M.; and McCarthy, G.; "Electrocortical Indices of Hemispheric Utilization," in *Lateralization in the Nervous System,* eds. S. Harnard et al. (New York: Academic Press, 1977).

Doyle, J.C.; Ornstein, R.; and Galin, D., "Lateral Specialization of Cognitive Mode: II. EEG Frequency Analysis," *Psychophysiology* 11 (1974):567-578.

Ehrlichman, H., and Wiener, M., "EEG Asymmetry during Covert Mental Activity," *Psychophysiology* 17 (1980):228-235.

Galin, D., "EEG Studies of Lateralization of Verbal Processes," in *The Neurological Bases of Language Disorders in Children: Methods and Directions for Research,* eds. C. Ludlow and M.E. Doran-Quine (Bethesda, Md.: National Institute of Health, 1979).

Galin, D.; Johnstone, J.; and Herron, J., "Effects of Task Difficulty on EEG Measures of Cerebral Engagement," *Neuropsychologia* 16 (1978):461-472.

Galin, D., and R.E. Ornstein, "Lateral Specialization of Cognitive Mode: An EEG Study," *Psychophysiology* 9 (1972):412-418.

_____ , "Individual Differences in Cognitive Style. I. Reflective Eye Movements," *Psychophysiology* 12 (1974):367-376.

Gazzaniga, M.S., *The Bisected Brain* (New York: Appleton-Century-Crofts, 1970).

Gevins, A.S.; Doyle, J.C.; Schaffer, R.E.; Callaway, E.; and Yeager, C., "Lateralized Cognitive Processes and the Electroencephalogram," *Science* 207 (1980):1005-1008.

Gevins, A.S.; Zeitlin, G.M.; Doyle, J.C.; Yingling, C.D.; Schaffer, R.E.; Callaway, E.; and Yeager, C.L.; "Electroencephalogram Correlates of Higher Cortical Functions," *Science* 16 (1977a):665-667.

Gevins, A.S.; Zeitlin, G.M.; Yingling, C.D.; Doyle, J.C.; Dedon, M.F.; Schaffer, R.E.; Roumasset, J.T.; and Yeager, C.L., "EEG Patterns during 'Cognitive' Tasks. I. Methodology and Analysis of Complex Behavior," *Electroencephalography and Clinical Neurophysiology* 47 (1976b):693-703.

Greenfield, N.S., and Sternbach, R.A., *Handbook of Psychophysiology* (New York: Holt, Rinehart & Winston, 1972).

Hansen, F., "Hemispheral Lateralization: Implications for Understanding Consumer Behavior," *Journal of Consumer Research* 8 (1981):23-36.

Jasper, H.H., "The Ten-Twenty Electrode System of the International Federation," *Electroencephalography and Clinical Neurophysiology* 10 (1958):371-375.

Katz, W., "The Split Brain Syndrome," *Journal of Professional Marketing Research Society* 1 (1980):14-18.

Kinstch, W., "Models for Free Recall and Recognition," in *Models of Human Behavior*, ed. D.A. Norman (New York: Academic Press, 1970).

Krugman, H.E., "Brain Wave Measures of Brain Involvement," *Journal of Advertising Research* (February 1971), pp. 3-10.

———, "Memory without Recall, Exposure without Perception," *Journal of Advertising Research* (August 1977a), pp. 7-12.

———, "Low Involvement Theory in Light of New Brain Research," in *Attitude Research Plays for High Stakes,* eds. J.C. Maloney and B. Silverman (Chicago: American Marketing Association, 1977b).

———, "Toward an Ideal TV Pre-Test" (Paper presented at the American Marketing Association Annual Advertising Research Conference, New York, 1978).

———, "Letters to the Editor," *Journal of Advertising Research,* October 19, 1979, p. 82.

———, "Sustained Viewing of Television" (Paper presented at the Conference Board, Council on Marketing Research, New York, 1980).

Martin, E., and Noreen, D.L., "Serial Learning: Identification of Subjective Consequences," *Cognitive Psychology* 6 (1974):421-435.

McCormack, P.D., "Recognition Memory: How Complex a Retrieval System," *Canadian Journal of Psychology* 26 (1972):19-41.

McKee, G.; Humphrey, B.; and McAdam, D.W., "Scaled Lateralization of Alpha Activity during Linguistic and Musical Tasks," *Psychophysiology* 10 (1978):441-443.

Milner, B., "Hemispheric Specialization: Scope and Limits," in *The Neurosciences Third Study Program*, eds. F.O. Schmitt and F.C. Worden (Cambridge, Mass.: MIT Press, 1974).

Morgan, A.H.; MacDonald, H.; and Hilgard, E.R., "EEG Alpha: Lateral

Asymmetry Related to Task, and Hypnotizability," *Psychophysiology*
11 (1974):274-282.

Mulholland, T., "A Program for the Study of Attention in Visual Communication," *Visual Learning, Thinking, and Communication*
(1978):77-91.

Osborne, K., and Gale, A., "Bilateral EEG Differentiation of Stimuli,"
Biological Psychology 4 (1976):185-196.

Perry, N.W., Jr., and Childers, D.G., *The Human Visual Evoked Response:
Method and Theory* (Springfield, Ill.: C.C. Thomas, 1969).

Prawdicz-Weminski, W.W., "Ein Versuch der Registrierung der elektri-
schen Gehirnerscheinungen," *Zentrablatt fur Physiologie* 27
(1913):951-960.

Regan, D., *Evoked Potentials in Psychology, Sensory Psychology and Clinical Medicine* (London: Chapman and Hall, 1972).

Rockey, E.A.; Greene, W.F.; and Perold, E.A., "Attention, Memory and
Attitudinal Reactions to Television Commercials under Single and
Multiple Exposure Conditions as Measured by Brain Research" (Paper
presented at ARF Twenty-sixth Annual Conference, New York, 1980).

Rothschild, M.L.; Goldstein, R.; Hirsch, J.; and Thorson, E., "Electro-
encephalic Activity, Recall and Recognition as Television Commercial
Response Measures," Madison, Wisconsin: University of Wisconsin,
Working Paper #43.

Shagass, C., *Evoked Brain Potentials in Psychiatry* (New York: Plenum
Press, 1972).

Smith, A., "Dominant and Nondominant Hemispherectomy," in *Drugs,
Development and Cerebral Function*, ed. W.L. Smith (Springfield, Ill.:
C.C. Thomas, 1972).

Sperry, R.W., "Lateral Specialization in the Surgically Separated Hemispheres," in *The Neurosciences Third Study Program,* eds. F.O.
Schmitt and F.C. Worden (Cambridge, Mass.: MIT Press, 1974).

Stern, R.M.; Ray, W.J.; and Davis, C.M.; *Pschophysiological Recording*
(New York: Oxford Unversity Press, 1980).

Thompson, L.W., and Obrist, W.D., "EEG Correlates of Verbal Learning
and Overlearning," *EEG and Clinical Neurophysiology* 16
(1964):332-342.

Thompson, R.F., and Patterson, M.M., *Bioelectric Recording Techniques.
Part B: Electroencephalography and Human Brain Potential* (New
York: Academic Press, 1974).

Warren, L.R.; Peltz, L.; and Hauter, E.S.; "Patterns of EEG Alpha during
Word Processing and Relations to Recall," *Brain and Language* 3
(1976):283-291.

Weinstein, S.; Appel, V.; and Weinstein, C., "Brain-Activity Responses to
Magazine and Television Advertising," *Journal of Advertising
Research* (June 1980), pp. 57-63.

Chapter 13

Adrian, E.D., and Matthews, B.H.C., "The Berger Rhythm: Potential Changes from Occipital Lobe in Man," *Brain* 57 (1934):355-385.

Andreassi, J.L., *Psychophysiology: Human Behavior and Physiological Response* (New York: Oxford University Press, 1980).

Appel, V.; Weinstein, S.; and Weinstein, C., "Brain Activity and Recall of TV Advertising," *Journal of Advertising Research* 19 (1979):7-15.

Borkovec, T.D., "Physiological and Cognitive Process in the Regulation of Anxiety," in *Consciousness and Self-Regulation*, vol. 1, eds. G.E. Schwartz and D. Shapiro (New York: Plenum, 1976).

Broadbent, D.E., "The Hidden Preattentive Process," *American Psychologist* 32 (1977):109-118.

Brown, C.C., *Methods in Psychophysiology* (Baltimore: Williams and Wilkins, 1967).

Cacioppo, J., and Petty, R., eds., *Social Psychophysiology: A Sourcebook* (New York: Guilford Press, 1983).

Cooper, R.; Osselton, J.W.; and Shaw, J.C., *EEG Technology*, 2nd ed. (London: Butterworths, 1974).

Diamond, S.J., and Beaumont, J.G., "Differences in Vigilance Performance of the Right and Left Hemispheres," *Cortex* 9 (1973): 259-265.

Donchin, E., "Event-Related Brain Potentials: A Tool in the Study of Human Information Processing," in *Evoked Brain Potential and Behavior,* ed. H. Begleiter (New York: Plenum, 1979).

Donchin, E.; Kutas, M.; and McCarthy, G., "Electrocortical Indices of Hemispheric Utilization," in *Lateralization in the Nervous System,* eds. S. Harnad et al. (New York: Academic Press, 1977).

Doyle, J.C.; Ornstein, R.; and Galin, D., "Lateralization of Cognitive Mode: II. EEG Frequency Analysis," *Psychophysiology* 11 (1974):567-578.

Duffy, E., *Activation and Behavior* (New York: Wiley, 1962).

Duncan, R., and Weston-Smith, M., *The Encyclopaedia of Ignorance* (New York: Pergamon Press, 1977).

———, ,*The Encyclopaedia of Delusions* (New York: Pergamon Press, 1977).

Galin, D., and Ornstein, R., "Lateralization of Cognitive Mode: An EEG Study," *Psychophysiology* 9 (1972):412-418.

Harnad, S.; Doty, R.; Goldstein, L.; Jaynew, J.; and Kruthamer, G., eds, *Lateralization in the Nervous System* (New York: Academic Press, 1977).

Hansen, F., "Hemispherical Lateralization: Implications for Understanding Consumer Behavior," *Journal of Consumer Research* 8 (1981):23-27.

Hecker, S., "A Brain Hemisphere Orientation toward Concept Testing,"

Journal of Advertising Research 21 (1981):55-60.

James, W.J., *The Principles of Psychology,* vol. 1 (Cambridge: Mass.: Harvard University Press, 1981).

Kinsbourne, M., ed., *Asymmetrical Function of the Brain* (Cambridge: Cambridge University Press, 1978).

Krugman, H.E., "The Impact of Television Advertising: Learning without Involvement," *Public Opinion Quarterly* 29 (1965):349-356.

_____ , "Brain Wave Measures of Media Involvement," *Journal of Advertising Research* 19 (1971):15-26.

_____ , "Why Three Exposures May Be Enough," *Journal of Advertising Research* 12 (1972):11-14.

_____ , "Memory without Recall, Exposure without Perception," *Journal of Advertising Research* 17 (1977):7-12.

_____ , "Letter to the Editor," *Journal of Advertising Research* 20 (1980):63.

_____ , "The Effective Use of Physiological Measurement in Advertising Research" (Paper presented at the Twelfth Annual Attitude Research Conference, American Marketing Association, Hot Springs, Virginia, 1981).

Lacey, J.I., "Psychophysiological approaches to the evaluation of psychotherapeutic process and outcome," in *Research in Psychotherapy,* eds. E.A. Rubinstein and M.B. Parloff (Washington, D.C.: National Publishing Co., 1959).

Levy, J., "Cerebral Asymmetry and the Psychology of Man," in *The Brain and Psychology,* ed. M.C. Wittrock (New York: Academic Press, 1980).

Lynn, R., *Attention, Arousal, and the Orientation Reaction* (Oxford: Pergamon, 1966).

Martin, I., and Venables, P.H., eds., *Techniques in Psychophysiology* (New York: Wiley and Sons, 1980).

McGuiness, D., and Pribram, K., "The Neuropsychology of Attention: Emotional and Motivational Controls," in *The Brain and Psychology,* ed. M.C. Wittrock (New York: Academic Press, 1980).

Mesulam, M.M., and Perry, J., "The Diagnosis of Love Sickness: Experimental Psychophysiology without the Polygraph," *Psychophysiology* 9 (1972):546-551.

Posner, M.I., *Chronometric Explorations of Mind* (Hillsdale, N.J.: Lawrence Erlbaum Associates 1978).

Ray, W.J.; Cole, H.W.; and Raczynski, J.M., "Psychophysiological Assessment," in *The Clinical Psychology Handbook,* eds. M. Hersen, A. Kadzin, and A. Bellack (New York: Pergamon Press, 1983).

Rossiter, J.R., "Point of View: Brain Hemisphere Activity," *Journal of Advertising Research* ed. (1980):75-76.

Semmes, J., "Hemispheric Specialization: A Possible Clue to Mechanisms," *Neuropsychologia* 6 (1968):11-26.

Sharpless, S., and Jasper, H., "Habituation of the Arousal Reaction," *Brain* 79 (1956):655-680.

Sperry, R.W., "Lateral Specialization in the Surgically Separated Hemispheres," in *The Neurosciences Third Study Program,* eds. F.O. Schmitt and F.G. Woden (Cambridge, Mass.: MIT Press, 1974).

Stern, R.M., and Ray, W.J., "Methods in Sociophysiology," in *Sociophysiology,* ed. W.M. Waid (New York: Springer-Verlag, 1983).

Stern, R.M.; Ray, W.J.; and David, C.M., *Psychophysiological Recording* (New York: Oxford University Press, 1980).

Stewart, D.W., and Furse, D.H., "Applying Psychophysiological Measures to Marketing and Advertising Research Problems," in *Current Issues and Research in Advertising,* vol. 5, eds. C. Martin and J. Leigh (Ann Arbor, Michigan: University of Michigan, 1982), pp. 87-96.

Taylor, J., ed., *Selected Writings of John Hughlings Jackson* (New York: Basic Books, 1958).

Thompson, R.F., and Patterson, M.M., *Bioelectrical Recording Technique: Part B. EEG and Human Brain Potentials* (New York: Academic Press, 1974).

Tucker, D.M., "Lateral Brain Function, Emotion, and Conceptualization," *Psychological Bulletin* 89 (1981):19-46.

Vanderwolf, C.H., and Robinson, T.E., "Reticulo-Cortical Activity and Behavior: A Critique of the Arousal Theory and a New Synthesis," *The Behavioral and Brain Sciences* 4 (1981):459-514.

Van Toller, C., *The Nervous Body* (New York: Wiley and Sons, 1979).

Walters, C., "Clinical and Experimental Relationships of EEG to Psychomotor and Personality Measures," *Journal of Clinical Psychology* 20 (1964):81.

Watson, P.J., and Gatchel, R.J., "Autonomic Measures of Advertising," *Journal of Advertising Research* 19 (1979):15-26.

Weinstein, S., "Brain Wave Analysis in Attitude Research: Past, Present, and Future," in *Attitude Research Enters the 80's,* ed. R.W. Olshavsky (Chicago: American Marketing Association, 1980).

Weinstein, S.; Appel, V.; and Weinstein, C., "Brain Activity Responses to Magazine and Television Advertising," *Journal of Advertising Research* 20 (1980):57-63.

Chapter 14

Kintsch, W., and Van Dijk, T.A., "Toward a Model of Text Comprehension and Production," *Psychological Review* 85 (1978):363-394.

Krugman, Herbert E., "The Measurement of Advertising Involvement," *Public Opinion Quarterly* 30 (1967):583-596.

Leavitt, C., Waddell, C., and Wells, W., "Improving Day-After Recall Techniques," *Journal of Advertising Research* 10 (1970):13-17.

Schlinger, M.J., "A Profile of Response to Commercials," *Journal of Advertising Research* 19 (April 1979):37-48.

Schlinger, M.J.R.; Alwitt, L.F.; McCarthy, K.E.; and Green, L., "Effects of Time Compression on Attitudes and Information Processing," *Journal of Marketing,* in press.

Chapter 15

Anderson, J.R., and Bower, G.H., "Recognition and Retrieval Processes in Free Recall," *Psychological Review* 79 (1972):97-123.

Berger, D., "A Retrospective: FCB Recall Study," *Advertising Age*, October 26, 1981.

Bettman, J.R., "Memory Factors in Consumer Choice: A Review," *Journal of Marketing* 43 (1979):37-53.

Bower, G.H.; Black, J.B.; Turner, T.J., "Scripts in Memory for Text," *Cognitive Psychology* 11 (1979):177-220.

Brown, J., "An Analysis of Recognition and Recall and of Problems in Their Comparison," in *Recall and Recognition*, ed. J. Brown (New York: Wiley and Sons, 1976).

Craik, F.I.M., and Tulving, E., "Depth of Processing and the Retention of Words in Episodic Memory," *Journal of Experimental Psychology: General* 104 (1975):268-294.

Hogan, R.M., and Kintsch, W., "Differential Effects of Study and Test Trials on Long-Term Recognition and Recall," *Journal of Verbal Learning and Verbal Behavior* 10 (1971):562-567.

Kintsch, W., "Models for Free Recall and Recognition," in *Models of Human Memory*, ed. D.A. Norman (New York: Academic Press, 1970).

_____ , *The Representation of Meaning in Memory* (Hillsdale, N.J.: Lawrence Erlbaum Assoc., 1974).

_____ , *Memory and Cognition* (New York: Wiley and Sons, 1977).

Kintsch, W., and van Dijk, T.A., "Toward a Model of Text Comprehension and Production," *Psychological Review* 85 (1978):363-394.

Klatzky, R.L., *Human Memory* (San Francisco: W.H. Freeman, 1980).

Krugman, H., "Why Three Exposures May Be Enough," *Journal of Advertising Research* 12 (1972):11-14.

Langbein, L.I., and Lichtman, A.J., *Ecological Inference* (Beverly Hills: Sage Publications, 1978).

Martin, E., and Noreen, D.L., "Serial Learning: Identification of Subjective Subsequences," *Cognitive Psychology* 6 (1974):421-435.

McCormack, P.D., "Recognition Memory: How Complex a Retrieval System?," *Canadian Journal of Psychology* 26 (1972):19-41.

Rumelhart, D.E., "Notes on a Schema for Stories," in *Representation and Understanding*, eds. D.G. Bobrow and A. Collins (New York: Academic Press, 1975).

Seamon, J.G., *Memory & Cognition* (New York: Oxford University Press, 1980).

Singh, S.N., and Rothschild, M.L., "Recognition as a Measure of Learning from Television Commercials" (Manuscript, University of Wisconsin-Madison, 1982).

Thorson, E., and Snyder, R., "Viewer Recall of Television Commercials: Prediction from the Propositional Structure of Commercial Scripts" (Manuscript, University of Wisconsin-Madison, 1981).

Tulving, E., "Subjective Organization in Free Recall of Unrelated Words," *Psychological Review* 69 (1962):344-354.

Vipond, D., "Micro- and Macroprocesses in Text Comprehension," *Journal of Verbal Learning and Verbal Behavior* 19 (1980):276-296.

Woodward, A.E., Jr.; Bjork, R.A.; and Jongeward, R.H., Jr., "Recall and Recognition as a Function of Primary Rehearsal," *Journal of Verbal Learning and Verbal Behavior* 12 (1973):608-617.

Chapter 16

Clogg, C.C., "Some Latent Structure Models for the Analysis of Likert-Type Data," *Social Science Research* 8 (1979):287-301.

Colley, R.H., "Defining Advertising Goals for Measured Advertising Results" (New York: Association of National Advertisers, 1961).

Goodman, L.A., "The Analysis of Systems of Qualitative Variables When Some of the Variables Are Unobservable. Part I: A Modified Latent Structure Approach," *American Journal of Sociology* 79 (1974):1179-1259.

Lavidge, R.J., and Steiner, G.A., "A Model for Predictive Measurements of Advertising Effectiveness," *Journal of Marketing* 24 (1969):59-62.

Lazarsfeld, P.F., and Henry, N.W., *Latent Structure Analysis* (Boston: Houghton Mifflin, 1968).

Madden, T.J., "Humor in Advertising: Application of a Hierarchy-of-Effects Paradigm" Ph.D. dissertation, University of Massachusetts, Amherst, 1982).

McGuire, W., "Attitudes and Opinions," in *Review of Psychology* 17, ed. P.R. Farnsworth (Washington, D.C.: American Psychological Association, 1966):475-514.

_____ , "An Information-Processing Model of Advertising Effectiveness," in *Behavioral and Management Sciences in Marketing*, eds. H.L. Davis and A.J. Silk (New York: Ronald Press, 1978).

MacKensie, S., and Lutz, R.J., "Monitoring Advertising Effectiveness: A Structural Equation Analysis of the Mediating Role of Attitude toward the Ad," Working paper no. 117 (Los Angeles: University of California, Center for Marketing Studies, January 1982).

Mitchell, A.A., and Olson, J.C., "Are Product Attribute Beliefs the Only Mediator of Advertising Effects on Brand Attitude?," *Journal of Marketing Research* 18 (1981):318-332.

Petty, R.E.; Ostrom, T.M.; and Brock, T.C., "Historical Foundations of the Cognitive Response Approach to Attitude and Persuasion," in *Cognitive Responses in Persuasion*, eds. Petty, Ostrom, and Brock (Hillsdale, N.J.: Lawrence Erlbaum Associates, 1981).

Shimp, T.A., "Attitude toward the Ad as a Mediator of Consumer Brand Choice," *Journal of Advertising* 10 (1981):9-15.

Wilkie, William L., and E.A. Pessemier, "Issues in Marketing's Use of Multi-Attribute Attitude Models," *Journal of Marketing Research* 10 (November 1973):428-441.

Chapter 17

Aaker, D., and Myers, J., *Advertising Management* (Englewood Cliffs, N.J.: Prentice-Hall, 1975).

Cuba, F., "Where Is Television Copy Testing Headed?" (Paper presented at the Annual Conference of the American Academy of Advertising, New York, April 1978).

Fletcher, A., and Bowers, T., *Fundamentals of Advertising Research* (Columbus, Ohio: Grid Publishing Inc., 1979).

Holbert, N., "More Key Articles in Advertising Research," *Journal of Advertising Research* 17 (1977):33-42.

Mitchell, A., "The Use of an Information Processing Approach to Understand Advertising Effects," in *Advances in Consumer Research*, vol. 7, ed. J. Olson (Ann Arbor: Association for Consumer Research, 1980), pp. 171-177.

Oliver, R., "Effect of Expectation and Disconfirmation on Postexposure Product Evaluations: An Alternative Interpretation," *Journal of Applied Psychology* 62 (1977):480-492.

_____ , "A Cognitive Model of the Antecedents and Consequences of Satisfaction Decisions," *Journal of Marketing Research* (1980):460-469.

Watson, P., and Gatchel, R., "Automic Measures of Advertising," *Journal of Advertising Research* 19 (1979):15-26.

Westbrook, R., "A Rating Scale for Measuring Product/Service Satisfaction," *Journal of Marketing Research* 18 (1980):68-72.

Wright, P., "The Cognitive Processes Mediating Acceptance of Advertising," *Journal of Marketing Research* 10 (1973):53-62.

Chapter 18

Headen, R.S.; Klompmaker, J.E.; and Teel, J.E., "An Empirical Examination of Spot TV Audience Exposure Patterns," *Journal of Advertising Research* 16 (1976):49-52.

————, "Predicting Audience Exposure to Spot TV Advertising Schedules," *Journal of Marketing Research* 14 (1977):1-9.

Krugman, H.E., "Why Three Exposures May Be Enough," *Journal of Advertising Research* 12 (1972):11-14.

————, "What Makes Advertising Effective?," *Harvard Business Review* 53 (1975):96-103.

Lastovicka, J.L., "The Extension of Component Analysis to Four-Mode Matrices," *Psychometrika* 46 (1981):47-57.

Leo Burnett Company, *Manual for the Leo Burnett Storyboard Test-System* (Chicago, 1977).

Levin, J., "Three-Mode Factor Analysis," *Psychological Bulletin* 64 (1965): 442-452.

Ray, M.L., and Sawyer, A.G., "Repetition in Media Models: A Laboratory Technique," *Journal of Marketing Research* 8 (1971):20-29.

Schlinger, M.J., "A Profile of Responses to Commercials," *Journal of Advertising Research* 19 (1979):37-46.

Schultz, D.E., "Media Research Users Want," *Journal of Advertising Research* 19 (1979):13-17.

Sissors, J.Z., and Petray, E.R., *Advertising Media Planning* (Chicago: Crain Books, 1976).

Vavra, T.B., "A Three-Mode Factor Analytic Investigation into the Effectiveness of Advertising" (Ph.D. dissertation, University of Illinois, Urbana, 1973).

Author Index

Subject Index

List of Contributors

Linda Alwitt, Leo Burnett Company
Timothy C. Brock, The Ohio State University
John T. Cacioppo, University of Iowa
James D. Culley, University of Delaware
K. Jeffrey Dean, Ralston Purina Company
Leon B. Kaplan, Princeton Research and Consulting Center, Inc.
James R. Krum, University of Delaware
John Lastovicka, University of Kansas
Martin R. Lautman, ARBOR, Inc.
Thomas J. Madden, University of Massachusetts — Amherst
Andrew A. Mitchell, Carnegie-Mellon University
Franco M. Nicosia, University of California at Berkeley
Jerry C. Olson, The Pennsylvania State University
Richard E. Petty, University of Missouri — Columbia
Charles H. Ptacek, Kansas State University
William J. Ray, The Pennsylvania State University
Thomas J. Reynolds, University of Texas at Dallas
John R. Rossiter, New South Wales Institute of Technology
Michael L. Rothschild, University of Wisconsin — Madison
Joel Saegert, The University of Texas at San Antonio
Sharon Shavitt, The Ohio State University
James Shanteau, Kansas State University
Esther Thorson, University of Wisconsin — Madison
David K. Tse, University of California — Berkeley
Peter C. Wilton, University of California — Berkeley
Robert K. Young, The University of Texas at Austin

About the Editors

Larry Percy has been vice-president and corporate research director of CREAMER INC since 1978. Previously he spent more than fourteen years with three other advertising agencies: Gardner Advertising Company in St. Louis; Ketchum, MacLeod and Grove in Pittsburgh; and Young and Rubicam in New York.

Mr. Percy has frequently participated at business and academic seminars and has regularly contributed papers to meetings and conferences of the Association for Consumer Research, American Psychological Association, and American Marketing Association. He is the principal author of an advanced-level textbook, *Advertising Strategy: A Communication Theory Approach* (1980) and is coauthor of *Advertising and Promotion Management* (forthcoming), a general-level textbook. His other publications include contributed chapters in several marketing and communication textbooks, as well as numerous articles in professional journals such as the *Journal of Advertising, Journal of Advertising Research*, and the *Journal of Marketing Research*. He has addressed many graduate school seminars and executive M.B.A. programs on the subjects of communications, advertising strategy, and market research. He currently teaches promotion and advertising at the Graduate School of Business, University of Pittsburgh.

Mr. Percy is on the editorial board of the *Journal of Marketing Research* and *Current Issues and Research in Advertising* and on the editorial board for buyer behavior of the *Journal of Business Research*.

Arch G. Woodside received the Ph.D. from The Pennsylvania State University in 1968 and is now professor of marketing and foundation fellow of the University of South Carolina Business Partnership Foundation. He is also the editor of the *Journal of Business Research*.

Professor Woodside has published extensively in the *Journal of Applied Psychology, Journal of Health and Social Behavior, Journal of Advertising Research, Journal of Social Psychology, Journal of Psychology*, and *Journal of Business*. He is coeditor of *Consumer and Industrial Buying Behavior* and coauthor of *Marketing Channels: Systems and Strategies* (1977) and *Marketing Management: Strategies and Cases* (1978).

Professor Woodside was a senior Fulbright lecturer at the University of Osijek in Yugoslavia in the spring of 1978. He held an appointment as a senior Fulbright lecturer at the Helsinki and Swedish Schools of Economics in Helsinki in 1974. He is the president of Division 23, Consumer Psychology, of the American Psychological Association.